Horizontal Inequalities and Post-Conflict Development

Conflict, Inequality and Ethnicity

Series Editor: Frances Stewart, Emeritus Professor of Development Economics and Director, CRISE, University of Oxford, UK

The series focuses on the relationships between inequality, human security and ethnicity emanating from the work of The Centre for Research on Inequality, Human Security and Ethnicity (CRISE), UK. Some books cover general issues such as mobilization, affirmative action, the role and management of natural resources, and post conflict policies; others are rooted in the experience of different regions, for example South East Asia, West Africa, and Latin America.

The series is unique since it is united by interest in an unusual perspective – that of exploring these issues in relation to horizontal inequalities or inequalities among groups. While each book stands alone, they also have unity of approach and share some basic ideas. The publications from the *Conflict, Inequality and Ethnicity* series will be highly relevant to students, academics and policy-makers working on questions of contemporary conflict.

Titles include:

Yvan Guichaoua (*editor*)
UNDERSTANDING COLLECTIVE POLITICAL VIOLENCE

Arnim Langer, Frances Stewart and Rajesh Venugopal (*editors*)
HORIZONTAL INEQUALITIES AND POST-CONFLICT DEVELOPMENT

Frances Stewart (*editor*)
HORIZONTAL INEQUALITIES AND CONFLICT
Understanding Group Violence in Multiethnic Societies

Rosemary Thorp and Maritza Paredes
ETHNICITY AND THE PERSISTENCE OF INEQUALITY
The Case of Peru

Forthcoming:

Graham K. Brown
THE POLITICAL ECONOMY OF SECESSION
Ethnicity, Inequality and the State

Graham K. Brown, Arnim Langer and Frances Stewart (*editors*)
DEBATING AFFIRMATIVE ACTION
International and Interdisciplinary Perspectives

Conflict, Inequality and Ethnicity
Series Standing Order ISBN 978–0–230–24608–9 (hardback) and 978–0–230–24708–6 (paperback)
(*outside North America only*)

You can receive future titles in this series as they are published by placing a standing order. Please contact your bookseller or, in case of difficulty, write to us at the address below with your name and address, the title of the series and the ISBN quoted above.

Customer Services Department, Macmillan Distribution Ltd, Houndmills, Basingstoke, Hampshire RG21 6XS, England

---

Horizontal Inequalities and Post-Conflict Development

Edited by

Arnim Langer

University Lecturer of International Relations and Director, Centre for Research on Peace and Development (CRPD), University of Leuven, Belgium

Frances Stewart

Emeritus Professor of Development Economics and Director, Centre for Research on Inequality, Human Security and Ethnicity (CRISE), University of Oxford, UK

and

Rajesh Venugopal

Lecturer of Development Studies, London School of Economics (LSE), UK

palgrave
macmillan

First published 2012 by
PALGRAVE MACMILLAN

Palgrave Macmillan in the UK is an imprint of Macmillan Publishers Limited, registered in England, company number 785998, of Houndmills, Basingstoke, Hampshire RG21 6XS.

Palgrave Macmillan in the US is a division of St Martin's Press LLC, 175 Fifth Avenue, New York, NY 10010.

Palgrave Macmillan is the global academic imprint of the above companies and has companies and representatives throughout the world.

Palgrave® and Macmillan® are registered trademarks in the United States, the United Kingdom, Europe and other countries.

ISBN 978–0–230–25184–7

This book is printed on paper suitable for recycling and made from fully managed and sustained forest sources. Logging, pulping and manufacturing processes are expected to conform to the environmental regulations of the country of origin.

A catalogue record for this book is available from the British Library.

A catalog record for this book is available from the Library of Congress.

10 9 8 7 6 5 4 3 2 1
21 20 19 18 17 16 15 14 13 12

Printed and bound in the United States of America

Contents

List of Tables

List of Figures

Foreword

Despite increased international awareness of the terrible consequences of violent conflicts, including loss of lives and livelihoods, shattered families and forced migration and a breakdown of social relations, ethnic and religious violence continues to wreak havoc in a substantial number of countries around the world. The majority of these conflicts take place in developing countries, further slowing down their development process and making life for most people even harder. Yet more developed countries are not immune to violent conflict, as illustrated by the disintegration of former Yugoslavia, the Maoist rebellion in Northeastern India, the Catholic–Protestant conflict in Northern Ireland, Russia and the Chechnya conflict and the Chiapas' uprising in Mexico.

In the last two decades, fortunately, a significant number of conflicts have come to an end, and countries have moved into a post-conflict phase. But this, as we know only too well in West Africa, can be quite fragile and in many cases lasts only a few years before conflict again erupts. It is critically important, then, that we use the post-conflict phase well and introduce policies that will help avoid such a relapse into violence.

While ethnicity and religion are often exploited to mobilize people in violent conflicts, it is not 'cultural' or communal differences, as such, that usually cause the violence to erupt. Indeed, there are plenty of multiethnic countries, including my own, Ghana, which show that people with different ethno-cultural and religious backgrounds can live together in peace and harmony. However, where there are large inequalities between different cultural groups in a society, there is a significant risk of conflict. Regardless of a country's level of development or its location in the world, the underlying causes of many intra state conflicts are the result of an unequal and unfair distribution of economic wealth and political power between different groups in society. In this book, these group inequalities are termed 'HIs'. While the economic inequalities between different ethnic groups or regions in many developing countries often find their origins in colonial times, political inequalities and exclusion are usually the result of irresponsible political elites who are unwilling to share political power.

As President of Ghana, twice chair of the Economic Community of West African States and also once chair of the African Union, I have been involved in a wide range of initiatives to restore peace and stability to conflict-ridden countries on the continent. On the basis of these first-hand experiences, I know that getting conflict parties to stop fighting is a difficult thing to do; yet it pales in comparison with the difficulty of restoring a durable peace. It is therefore not surprising that a large number of conflict countries relapse into conflict after the signing of a ceasefire or peace agreement. An important reason for the high rate of conflict recurrence is the failure to address the underlying causes of the conflict.

This book makes an extremely important contribution to this issue. It analyses to what extent HIs, arguably the main cause of intra-state conflict in today's world, are taken into account in post-conflict reconstruction processes. The book explores these issues by means of a range of fascinating case studies as well as by several thematic chapters. The picture that emerges is alarming. While in most cases the role of HIs is recognized publicly, very little is usually done actually to tackle them and to create a more inclusive and equal societies, both in terms of the distribution of economic wealth and opportunities and in terms of political participation and power. This puts a time bomb under the long-term efforts to establish a durable peace.

The book provides important policy recommendations, which should be carefully examined by both politicians in post-conflict countries and international donor agencies. While tackling HIs is a difficult process, for the sake of the people living in post-conflict situations, we should hope that policy makers involved in post-conflict reconstruction take the lessons learnt from this book to heart.

John Kufuor, former President of Ghana

Preface

This book is the result of a global team effort, investigating post-conflict policies towards HIs. It is a follow-up to the main work of the Centre for Research on Inequality, Human Security and Ethnicity (CRISE) at the University of Oxford, which established that the presence of high HIs increases the risk of conflict. The Centre was financed by the Department for International Development (DFID). We are grateful to DFID for this support, which also supported the work contained in this book. Papers for this volume were discussed at the Economic Policy Research Centre (EPRC) in Kampala, Uganda. We would like to thank the EPRC Director Dr Sarah Ssewanyana and John Mary Matovu (EPRC principal Research Fellow) for their help, and also Emmanuel Mutebile-Tumisiime for his insightful comments. We would also like to thank Patricia Espinoza and Jo Boyce for their assistance.

Arnim Langer, Frances Stewart and Rajesh Venugopal

Acknowledgements

Figure 1.1 uses data from the Uppsala Conflict Data Program. Data are freely available at http://www.pcr.uu.se/research/UCDP/.

Table 1.3 is derived, with permission, from Stewart, F., Brown, G., and Langer, A. (2008) 'Policies towards Horizontal Inequalities', in Stewart F. (ed.) *Horizontal Inequalities and Conflict: Understanding Group Violence in Multiethnic Societies*, Basingstoke: Palgrave Macmillan.

Table 2.5 is derived from Okidi, J. A., Ssewanyana, S., Battegeka, L., and Muhunmuza, F. (2005) *Distributional and Poverty Impacts of Uganda's Growth: 1992 to 2003*, Research Series, Kampala: Economic Policy Research Centre (ECPR).

Tables 7.1, 7.2 and 7.4 are drawn, with permission, from Torres-Rivas, E. (2005) *Guatemala: Estado, heterogeneidad estructural y ciudadanía*, Paper presented in the Workshop Pueblos indígenas de América Latina, Barcelona, 27 and 28 April.

Figures 8.1 and 8.2 are derived from CVR, Comision de la Verdad y Reconciliacion (2003) *Informe Final*, Lima: CVR. Data are freely available at http://www.cverdad.org.pe/.

Notes on Contributors

Graham K. Brown is Senior Lecturer of international development and Director of the Centre for Development Studies at the University of Bath. His research is concerned with the nexus of inequality, identity and development, with a regional focus on Southeast Asia. In the past five years, he has published 13 articles in peer-reviewed journals, including in premier development studies journals *World Development* and *Oxford Development Studies*. He is also one of the editors of *Oxford Development Studies*. He will shortly publish two monographs on the political economy of secession and (co-authored) a comparative study of affirmative action in India and Malaysia.

Corinne Caumartin is a research fellow at the "Compromise After Conflict" project at the University of Aberdeen. She was formerly a research officer at the CRISE at the University of Oxford where she focused on the civil war and its aftermath in Guatemala. Her research interests and activities have revolved around peace and conflict studies, transitional justice/politics and human rights with gender and social justice as key transversal themes.

Christian Dennys has worked on Afghanistan for seven years in a number of roles, including as an advisor to the Afghan government and for several national and international NGOs. He has published a number of reports regarding local conflicts, the ongoing insurgencies, security sector reform, state-formation and local political economy. His area of specialization is the nature of insurgencies, conflict and instability and is currently engaged with fieldwork for his PhD at Cranfield University on stability and intervention in Afghanistan and Nepal. He has a degree in Arabic and Persian and a Masters in Violence Conflict and Development, both from the School of Oriental and African Studies (SOAS) at the University of London.

Sakiko Fukuda-Parr is Professor of international affairs at the New School University in New York. She is a development economist specializing in capabilities and human development, and currently working on human rights and development policy, poverty-conflict nexus and global technology. She has taught at Columbia University, and was a research fellow at the Kennedy School of Government, Harvard University. From 1995 to 2004, she was the lead author and director of the UNDP Human Development Reports. Her other recent publications include *The Gene Revolution: GM Crops and Unequal Development; Readings in Human Development; Capacity for Development: Old Problems, New Solutions*; and numerous papers and book chapters. She founded and is co-editor of the *Journal of Human Development*. She is a member of the UN ECOSOC Committee on Development Policy, and the Human Rights Council High Level Task Force on the Right to Development. She is a board member of the Center for Economic and Social Rights, and Board Chair of Knowledge Ecology International, NGOs that advocate human rights and technology for development. She is a graduate of Cambridge University (UK), the Fletcher School of Law and Diplomacy (USA) and the University of Sussex (UK).

Jonathan Goodhand is Reader of conflict and development studies at the SOAS at the University of London. He worked for some years managing humanitarian and development programmes in conflict situations in Afghanistan/Pakistan and Sri Lanka, and has extensive experience as a researcher and advisor in South and Central Asia for a range of NGOs and aid agencies, including DFID, SDC, ILO and UNDP. His research interests include the political economy of aid and conflict, NGOs and peace-building and post-conflict reconstruction.

Arnim Langer is University Lecturer of international relations and Director of the Centre for Research on Peace and Development (CRPD) at the University of Leuven in Belgium. He is also a visiting research fellow at the Centre for Development Studies at the University of Bath and a research associate at the Department of International Development at the University of Oxford. He has published extensively on the relationship between HIs and violent conflict, ethnic group formation and mobilization, the persistence of group inequalities and issues of post-conflict reconstruction.

David Mansfield is widely recognized as the preeminent expert on opium production in Afghanistan. He has been conducting fieldwork in rural Afghanistan since June 1997 and has worked for a variety of different organizations in Afghanistan including the Afghan Research and Evaluation Unit, the Aga Khan Development Network and the

United Kingdom's Afghan Drugs Inter Departmental Unit and Department for International Development. He has also supported the World Bank, Asia Development Bank and the European Commission in integrating the drugs issue into their rural development programmes in Afghanistan, including their support to National Priority Programmes. Prior to his work in Afghanistan, David worked in overseas development, working in each of the major drug producing regions of the South and South East Asia and Latin America. His published work has sought to contextualize drugs as a development issue.

Janvier D. Nkurunziza is a macroeconomic policy advisor at UNDP, New York. Prior to this, he worked at UNCTAD and UNECA where he co-authored flagship publications on African economies. He also worked at Harvard University where he coordinated a discussion group on African politics; the University of Yaoundé, Cameroon, where he taught advanced econometrics; the University of Burundi where he taught micro and macroeconomics; the IMF as a visiting scholar. He worked as a consultant for the World Bank, Yale University, University of Oxford and the government of Burundi, and holds a doctorate in economics from the University of Oxford where he is affiliated with CSAE. He is a fellow of Africa House, NYU; a resource person with AERC; a member of GDN; and an NBER Africa project contributor. His recent research has focused on economic growth, financial systems in Africa, economics of civil wars and applied industrial organization.

José Carlos Orihuela is a visiting fellow in international studies at the Watson Institute, Brown University. He has a PhD from Columbia University, for a dissertation titled 'Journeys toward Sustainable Development: Policy Entrepreneurs and the Rise of the Green State in Chile and Peru.' He has written on development policy making, institutional change and the political economy of mineral abundance. His current research deals with the environmental governance of the Amazon basin within a comparative political economy framework.

Diego Sánchez-Ancochea is University Lecturer of the political economy of Latin America at the University of Oxford and Governing Body Fellow of St Antony's. His research concentrates on income inequality, social policy and the political economy of development with particular attention to small Latin American countries. Recent publications include the co-edited volumes *The Political Economy of the Budget in the Americas* (2009, with Iwan Morgan) and *Transnational Corporations and*

Development Policy (2009, with Eric Rugraff and Andrew Sumner) as well as a special issue on Latin America's model of capitalism in *Economy and Society*.

Sebastian Silva Leander is currently working as a strategic planning advisor for the UN Mission in DR Congo. He has worked for the UN on post-conflict recovery and reconstruction planning in several conflict and post-conflict countries, including Afghanistan, Rwanda, Burundi and Côte d'Ivoire. In this capacity, he has contributed to several regional and global thematic reports, as well as the Rwandan Human Development Report. Sebastian holds a DPhil in Economics from Oxford University. His research has focused mostly on governance and conflict issues in low-income countries, as well as poverty measurement and inequality. He has been associated as a post-doctoral research fellow at the Global Equity Initiative, Harvard, and as a visiting scholar at Queen Elizabeth House, Oxford.

Frances Stewart is Emeritus Professor of Development Economics and Director of the CRISE at the University of Oxford. Books include *Technology and Underdevelopment* (1976); *Planning to Meet Basic Needs* (1985); UNICEF's influential study *Adjustment with a Human Face* (co-author, 1987); *War and Underdevelopment* (co-author, 2001); *HIs and Conflict: Understanding Group Violence in Multiethnic Societies* (editor, 2008). Her research has focused on appropriate technology; basic needs; adjustment and poverty; development during conflict; group behaviour; HIs; and human development.

Rajesh Venugopal is Lecturer of development studies at the London School of Economics (LSE). He is researching on ethnic conflict, nationalism, post-conflict reconstruction and the politics of development, particularly with reference to Sri Lanka.

Susan L. Woodward is Professor of Political Science at The Graduate Center of the City University of New York. A specialist on the Balkans, her current research focuses on transitions from war to peace, international security and state failure and post-war state-building. She is a member of the United Nations Committee of Experts on Public Administration, 2010–2014, was a senior fellow at The Brookings Institution in Washington, DC, 1990–1999 and at the Centre for Defence Studies, King's College, London, 1999–2000, head of the Analysis and Assessment Unit for UNPROFOR in 1994 and a professor of political science at Yale University, 1982–1989, Williams College, 1978–1982 and Northwestern University, 1972–1977. Her many writings include *Balkan Tragedy: Chaos and Dissolution after the Cold War* (1995) and *Socialist Unemployment: The Political Economy of Yugoslavia, 1945–1990* (1995).

1

Horizontal Inequalities and Post-Conflict Development: Laying the Foundations for Durable Peace

Arnim Langer, Frances Stewart, and Rajesh Venugopal

1.1 Introduction

The global incidence of violent conflict, which increased during the early 1990s, was on the wane from 1993 (although it rose again somewhat from 2003) (see Figure 1.1), with a large number of war-torn countries such as Angola, Liberia, Guatemala, and Sri Lanka having entered a fragile and extended process of transition from war to peace. This in turn has spurred a shift in the policy agenda from 'conflict' to post-conflict and an evolution in the development research agenda from the economic costs and causes of conflict towards the economics of post-conflict recovery and peace-building.

Research has shown that an important underlying cause of violent conflict is the presence of horizontal inequalities (HIs), or group-based inequalities in access to political power and economic resources. Severe HIs can provoke feelings of frustration and discontent, which may cause violent group mobilization and conflict along ethnic, religious, or regional lines (Stewart 2000, 2002). Support for this view has been provided by numerous case studies that document the importance of socio-economic and political HIs in provoking violent conflicts (see, e.g., Cobham 2005; Langer 2005; Ndikumana 2005) and the ways in which these differences were used to mobilize people for conflict. In addition, several quantitative cross-country and within-country studies have also found a significant association between the presence of severe socio-economic HIs and the emergence of violent conflicts (see, e.g.,

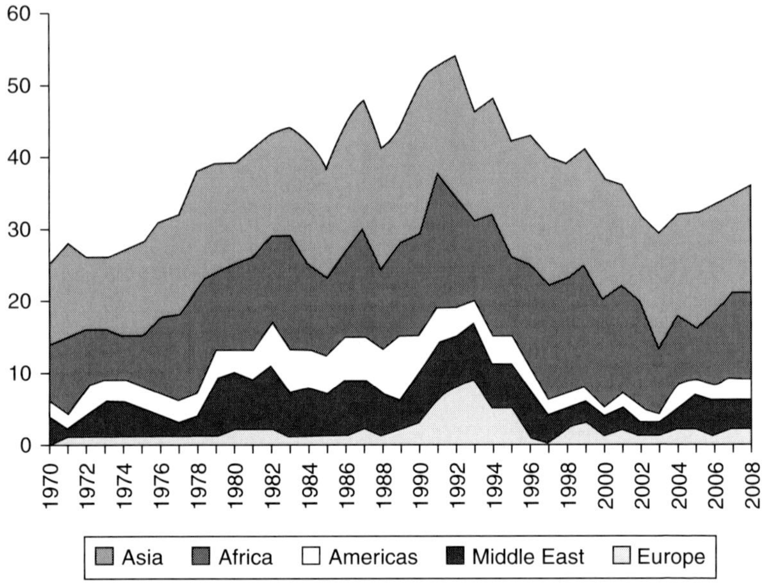

Figure 1.1 Number of conflicts by region and world total
Source: Stockholm International Peace Research Institute.

Cederman et al. 2010; Mancini 2005; Murshed and Gates 2005; Østby 2006).

Despite the widespread recognition of the importance of HIs in causing a range of political disturbances, surprisingly little research has focused on the question of whether and how HIs are being addressed in post-conflict situations and what impact this has had. This book aims to fill this void. It sets out to evaluate the extent to which post-conflict reconstruction has addressed problems of HIs by looking at the experiences of eight post-conflict countries – Burundi, Rwanda, Nepal, Peru, Guatemala, Bosnia and Herzegovina, Afghanistan, and Uganda – and by exploring four cross-cutting themes – on macro-economic policies, privatization, Poverty Reduction Strategy Papers (PRSPs), and employment generation. These thematic chapters include general considerations and draw on empirical studies that extend the empirical and geographical scope of this book to Sierra Leone, Kosovo, Liberia, Haiti, Mozambique, and Cambodia. The book thus represents a natural progression in the research agenda on HIs from the pre-conflict to the post-conflict phase. The findings from these chapters are important because they reveal important gaps in addressing what are often deeply entrenched forms of group-based discrimination and deprivation and marginalization, each of which has distinct implications for policy and for further research.

Post-conflict policies generally include policies aimed at reconstruction, macro-economic stabilization and growth, and the reintegration of ex-combatants. But it is also crucial to include policies that address the root causes of conflict, so as to reduce the likelihood of recurrence. Such policies will vary according to the nature and causes of the war. However, they include a focus on reducing HIs where these have been a major source of conflict, as is frequently the case.

Before looking more closely at the concept of HIs and at its linkages to conflict, it is appropriate to reflect briefly on what constitutes a 'post-conflict' situation. Defining a post-conflict situation is not as easy as it sounds, since conflict and conflict conditions do not generally end abruptly and totally with a peace agreement. Rather than picking one or other condition to define the beginning and end of post-conflict, a more productive approach to conceptualizing a post-conflict situation is to see it as a process that involves the achievement of a number of peace milestones, including: (1) cessation of hostilities and violence; (2) signing of political/peace agreements; (3) demobilization, disarmament, and reintegration; (4) refugee repatriation; (5) establishing a functioning state; (6) economic recovery; (7) and making significant progress towards reconciliation and societal integration (Brown et al. 2008). Taking a process-oriented approach means that post-conflict countries should be seen as lying along a transition continuum (in which they quite often move backwards), rather than being placed in more or less arbitrary boxes labelled 'in conflict' or 'at peace' (Brown et al. 2008).

Further, while post-conflict countries are typically very fragile in the short-to-medium term, with a high risk of return to conflict[1] or of its transformation into other forms of social violence (such as crime or domestic violence), there are also important differences among countries that are at a post-conflict stage of development with respect to their economic state and potential, their political system, their bureaucratic capacities, and the state of security in the country itself (among other things). All these variations are relevant to the appropriate design of post-conflict policies. Both national and international policy makers in situations following conflict are therefore confronted with a range of situations and should not take it that a one-size-fits-all approach would work. A typology based on the three differentiating criteria presented below is helpful in simplifying the complex and diverse environments in which post-conflict policy making needs to be conducted (Brown et al. 2008).

1. *Countries with poverty and lack of opportunity – economies with very low incomes, which are differentiated from middle- or upper-income economies.* Along with poverty there generally goes a particular economic structure (heavily based on primary production), weak human capacities, and a lack of good employment opportunities. Such countries also often have high levels of debt. Appropriate policies for this category of countries are likely to differ from those that are appropriate for middle- or upper-income countries.
2. *Countries with considerable high-value natural resources (oil and minerals).* These countries generally face a very different and more favourable situation with respect to resource constraints, but less favourable conditions in relation to the possibility of conflict recurrence. Post-conflict policies need to be designed so as to take these differences into account.
3. *Countries with high HIs.* Given the relationship of HIs to conflict, high HI countries need to take this factor into account in developing post-conflict policies.

Table 1.1 categorizes the countries for which there are detailed case studies in this volume roughly according to these criteria.

Figure 1.2 demonstrates the extent of the prevailing socio-economic HIs in five out of our eight case studies: Peru, Guatemala, Rwanda,

Table 1.1 Categorization of countries

Country	**Income p. head**	**High value natural resource availability**	**HIs**
Burundi	Low	Low	High
Rwanda	Low	Low	High
Nepal	Low	Low	Medium
Peru	Middle	Medium	High
Guatemala	Middle	Low	High
Bosnia	Upper middle	Low	Medium
Afghanistan	Low	Low	Medium
Uganda	Low	Low at present (but new oil resources developing)	High

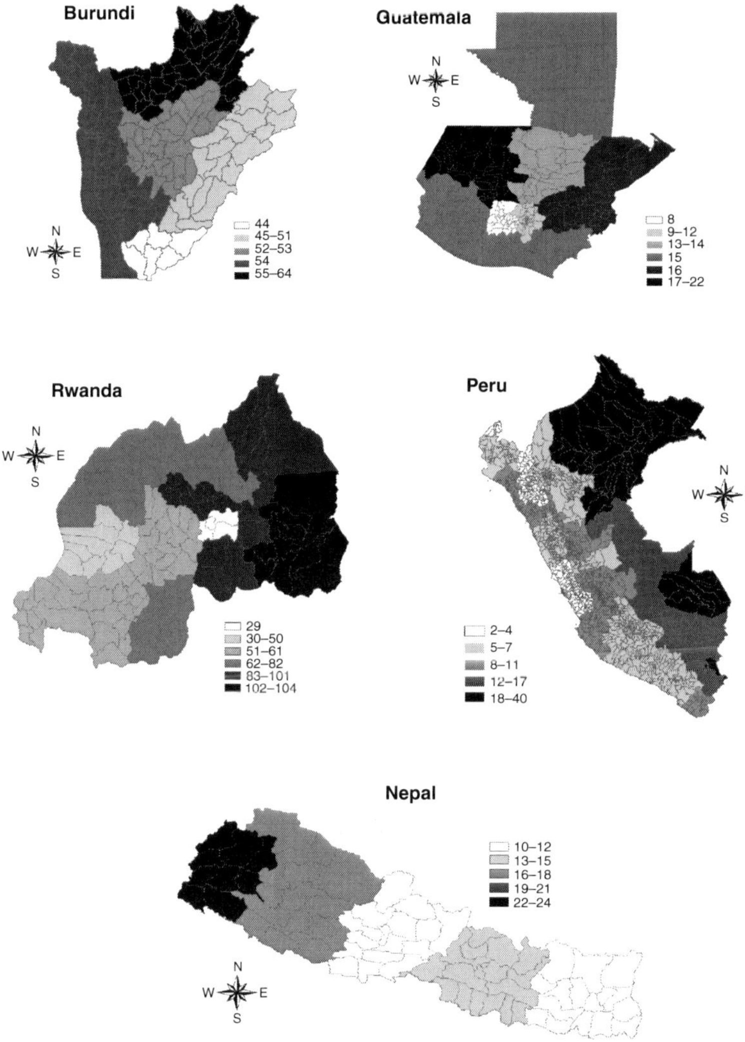

Figure 1.2 Socio-economic inequalities in Peru, Guatemala, Rwanda, Burundi, and Nepal

Source: Authors' calculations on the basis of data from the Demographic and Health Surveys (DHS). For more information on the DHS surveys, visit: Http://www.measuredhs.com.

Burundi, and Nepal. The figure shows the geographical disparities in child mortality rates in these countries. It is clear that there are serious disparities across these countries with respect to this particular socio-economic indicator.

1.2 Horizontal inequalities and violent conflict

The concept of HI refers to inequality among groups[2] and differs from the 'normal' definition of 'inequality' (which we term 'vertical inequality'), because the latter type lines up individuals or households vertically and measures inequality over the range of individuals rather than groups. HIs are conceived of as inherently multidimensional and encompass economic, social, political and cultural status dimensions.[3]

- *Economic HIs* include inequalities in access to and ownership of assets – financial, human, natural resource-based, and social. In addition, they comprise inequalities in income levels and employment opportunities, which depend on such assets and the general conditions of the economy.
- *Social HIs* include inequalities in access to a range of services such as education, health care, and housing, as well as inequalities in educational and health status.
- *Political HIs* include inequalities in the distribution of political opportunities and power among groups, including control over the presidency, the cabinet, parliamentary assemblies, the bureaucracy, local and regional governments, the army, and the police. They also encompass inequalities in people's capabilities to participate politically and to express their needs.
- *Cultural status HIs* include disparities in the recognition and standing of different groups' languages, customs, norms, and practices.[4]

Any study that adopts an HI approach clearly needs to start with a careful analysis of the relevant groups and of the way they have emerged historically. People have multiple identities, including, for example, gender, religion, ethnicity, race, region nationality, and they can thus be grouped in many ways. The relevant groups for an analysis of political mobilization and conflict are those that have such a meaning for people (both those with the particular identity and others) that they can readily be used for political mobilization, among those sharing the identity and/or among others who might potentially attack them. While identities are multiple and socially constructed, some with clear political salience are often evident – especially in post-conflict countries, where they may have been the factor differentiating the conflict parties. Nonetheless, salience of identities can change over time and identities themselves may change with changing circumstances, including evolving political institutions and inequalities. So, while we pick out particular identities as being of clear political salience in the studies, we do not intend to suggest that these are set in stone even in the medium term.

In the countries covered in this volume, we find that the relevant and often overlapping identities that form the basis of politically relevant HIs are as follows:

- ethnicity and region (Rwanda, Burundi)
- ethnicity and region (Uganda)
- ethnicity and class (Peru and Guatemala)
- religion/ethnicity[5] and region (Bosnia-Herzegovina)
- ethnicity, region, and clan (Afghanistan)
- ethnicity, region, and caste (Nepal)

Research into the relationship between HIs and conflict has demonstrated that violent conflict is most likely to arise in areas where economic, social, political, and cultural status inequalities occur simultaneously and where some groups are deprived across every dimension (see Langer 2005, 2008, 2009; Stewart 2008; Ukiwo 2008). In these situations, group leaders, who face political exclusion, and their political followers, who see themselves as experiencing unequal treatment with respect to assets, jobs, and social services, are likely to be inspired to mobilize and possibly engage in violence. The existence of such inequalities and/or the fear of future inequalities appear to have been a critical element in each of the cases studied in this volume.

Recognition of the need to take group and regional inequalities into account in peace-building is perhaps most widespread and sophisticated in the design of political institutions, where consociationalism and power-sharing have gained broad acceptance. Since the end of the Cold War, several new institutional arrangements and constitutional forms were fashioned to distribute power across communal groups from Lebanon's Ta'if Accords (1989), Bosnia-Herzegovina's Dayton Agreement (1995), and Northern Ireland's Good Friday Agreement (1998). Since then, the new constitutions of Afghanistan (2004) and Iraq (2005) have similarly made serious attempts to distribute calibrated amounts of representation and executive power to elites of all major ethnic/religious groups in order to reduce violence and resolve conflicts through institutionalized elite inclusion.[6]

While this growing consciousness of the relevance of political power-sharing represents an important advance, there is no commensurate attention to the equally important issue of economic power-sharing. For example, in a review of 38 peace agreements from 1948 to 1998, Hartzell and Hoddie (2003) find that an explicit commitment to economic redistribution was the least common form of power-sharing, compared to the more commonly addressed issues of sharing central powers, regional devolution, and military integration.[7]

The lack of appropriate attention to economic factors in peace processes and agreements is primarily due to four factors. Firstly, conflict resolution is still considered to be a largely political issue, separate from the economic content of reconstruction and recovery, which is left to technocratic experts preoccupied largely with the standard tools and goals of stabilization and growth (see Langer and Stewart, this volume). While it is now widely accepted that the politics of peace must be supported by a substantial economic agenda of reconstruction, there is a need for broader recognition that the quantity of economic growth must be matched by its quality.

Secondly, there is a firmly entrenched view about what the appropriate macro- and trade policies are – that is, broadly pro-market, *laissez-faire* policies in what has come to be known as the 'Washington consensus' view. Concerns for poverty reduction, for (vertical) inequality, or for environmental sustainability have not dented this view. Yet a conventional approach to post-conflict economic policy that is blind to distributional issues may not only be inappropriate for engendering sustainable indigenous drivers of growth,[8] but may destabilize the peace in the short run or may embed patterns of unequal and distorted development that sow the seeds for conflict in future generations.

Thirdly, there is an assumption that political power-sharing will lead to positive economic consequences and address group-based economic deprivation. This is indeed the case up to a point, particularly where there is substantial institutional reform incorporating enabling measures such as decentralization accompanied by redistributive fiscal transfers, which can be a very important way of overcoming historical forms of discrimination and structural barriers. However, political power-sharing is, by design, predominantly concerned with the empowerment of ethnic elites and can create and enshrine systems of ethnocratic patrimonialism that can limit the distribution of the peace dividend to a very thin privileged layer.

Finally, the redress of historically deep-rooted group HIs requires a sustained and committed medium-to-long-term policy effort that extends well beyond a single electoral cycle, and thus must contend with the endemic short-termism that such a cycle tends to engender. Moreover, much of the international policy agenda for post-conflict peacebuilding focuses on shorter-term measures of stabilization, security, and demobilization, while the time horizon for most aid programmes is also – often – too short to deal with the challenge of addressing structurally ingrained forms of deprivation, which requires longer-term commitment.

1.3 Horizontal inequalities in post-conflict situations: A framework of analysis

With these concerns in mind, this book sets out to investigate the extent to which post-conflict economic policies have addressed socio-economic HIs. The central questions that we seek to draw out are whether HIs have been reduced in the post-conflict period and, if so, through what mechanisms such reductions have been achieved. For the most part, the analytical focus remains fixed on the state and donor agencies as the key actors whose actions and inactions are of critical relevance. We evaluate their role in terms of three cascading parameters relating HIs to post-conflict economic policies.

1. *Recognition*: Have post-conflict countries and donor agencies recognized the role of HIs in conflict, and have they made any commitments to tackling them?
2. *Implementation*: Has the rhetoric of recognition been translated into the reality of policy design, and have these policies been adequately funded, implemented, and mainstreamed into policy?
3. *Effectiveness*: Once recognized and implemented, have these policies actually been effective in addressing HIs, and has this, in turn, had an impact on violence and conflict?

But, besides the more straightforward and intuitive analysis based on the above three parameters, which review the conscious and targeted role of the state and donors in addressing HIs, it is also important to recognize two additional analytical problems of relevance.

Firstly, group dynamics and economic well-being are affected not just by consciously designed policies to reduce HIs, but indirectly by a range of other ancillary economic, social, and military policies, as well as by demographic changes, refugee return, regional and global economic integration, and incentives that are not directly under the control of either states or donors. As such, the evolution of post-conflict HIs occurs in a fluid and changing environment in which the role of conscious state policies is moderated and limited by factors such as the indirect effects of other state policies – for example, counter-narcotics operations – as well as through variables entirely outside the reach of the state.

Secondly, the socio-economic factors and group identities of significance in the formation of a long drawn-out conflict may no longer be as relevant in a contemporary post-conflict scenario. Economic and social change over the course of a conflict can change ground realities, so that there may be new dimensions of group inequalities and fragilities that need to be theorized and addressed anew.

1.4 Chapter summaries

Chapters 2–4 analyse important policy processes that arise in post-conflict settings and how they relate to HIs. These processes include macro-economic policies, privatization, employment policies, and the PRSP process.

In Chapter 2, Langer and Stewart analyse how macro-economic policies affect HIs and explore how they might be designed to improve HIs. The normal objectives of macro-economic policy in post-conflict societies are to facilitate economic recovery and to support sustained growth, while avoiding excessive budget deficits and unacceptably high or accelerating inflation. They do not include any consideration of HIs. The chapter argues that how these policies actually affect HIs depends very much on their specific design, as well as on how different groups are inserted into the economy. For example, more expansionary policies and ones that rely on raising taxation rather than reducing expenditure for stabilization are likely to help poorer groups more. Moreover, complementary policies to assist members of deprived groups to participate in export activities will also make macro-policies more equalizing. Nonetheless, despite considerable complexity in estimating the impact of macro-policies, the chapter argues that, on balance, they are more likely to contribute to worsening rather than improving HIs, especially if they are successful in producing acceleration in market-led growth – because such growth tends to benefit richer areas and people with more skills and capital most. These conclusions are illustrated by experience gained in Uganda, where North–South HIs have widened during the successful post-conflict growth over the past two decades. Of course, continued conflict in the North – partly a result of the HIs – has also been a significant factor. Consequently, strong policies are needed to promote growth in deprived regions and to encourage participation in employment and income earning activities by members of low-income groups in all regions.

In Chapter 3, Frances Stewart explores the issue of employment in post-conflict societies. Employment is a critical issue in most post-conflict states, not only because of its potential impact on HIs, but also because lack of employment among youth is widely regarded as making conflict more likely. Thus post-conflict policies need to give high priority to expansion of employment *and* to its fair distribution across groups. Ex-combatants point to employment as their most important need; and surveys of perceptions show that people are particularly sensitive to discrimination and unfairness in public sector job allocation. This chapter reviews actual employment policies in a range of post-conflict countries and concludes that, while mainstream policies increasingly acknowledge the importance of generating employment, the policies adopted focus excessively on issues related to the supply of labour (training and so on) and not nearly enough on increasing the demand for labour. Partly as a consequence, these policies have had very limited effects in relation to the size of the problem, while they mostly entirely neglect the HI issue. Reviewing the way employment is dealt with in donors' post-conflict discourse in general and in actual donor policies adopted in five cases – Sierra Leone, Uganda, Kosovo, Nepal, and Bosnia-Herzegovina – reinforces these conclusions. Only in Nepal have there been explicit policies to correct HIs. The chapter identifies six areas where policies could contribute to correcting employment HIs: firstly, by modifying macro-policies so as to make them be more employment-friendly and so as to reduce inequalities between groups; secondly, by ensuring that the regional distribution of public expenditure programmes contributes to reducing HIs; thirdly, by ensuring that the emergency employment schemes, which should form an important part of the post-conflict employment programmes, incorporate all major groups and, as far as possible, the opportunities generated are distributed disproportionately to the deprived groups, as has been the policy in Nepal; fourthly, by careful monitoring of the group distribution of employment promoting schemes and of training, apprenticeships, provision of start-up finance, and micro-finance; fifthly, by paying special attention to group distribution of public sector employment, because of its political visibility and salience, while this is also particularly important for monitoring and policy; and, sixthly, policies promoting balanced and non-discriminatory employment in the private sector can also be an important element in post-conflict policy, as illustrated by the experience of Northern Ireland (Cormack and Osborne 1983; McCrudden et al. 2004). Special incentives may be needed to support the private sector in promoting labour-intensive industries in deprived regions.

In Chapter 4, Sakiko Fukuda-Parr reviews the Poverty Reduction Strategy Papers (PRSPs) as a policy vehicle for reducing HIs, examining the cases of Haiti, Liberia, and Nepal – countries characterized by significant levels of HI that have experienced protracted conflict in recent decades. She briefly reviews policies that would contribute to reducing the four major dimensions of HIs – political, economic, social, and cultural status – before investigating the three cases. She argues that integrating HIs into the PRSP process would entail accepting the objective of reducing HIs and of incorporating them into the analysis, into data collection, into policy priorities, and into financing. She finds that, while each of the PRSPs examined includes some reference to reducing vertical inequality (VI) as an *objective*, only Nepal's interim plan explicitly includes the need to reduce HIs. In analysis of the causes of conflict, Liberia's PRSP also makes reference to exclusion. In relation to *data* and *monitoring*, each has some (generally limited) data on VI, but again Nepal's interim plan is the only one that includes HI data. And, on *policy*, there are modest policy efforts towards VI in Liberia, but nothing in Haiti, while Nepal's interim plan, again, has extensive policies towards VI and HI. It is to be noted that, in contrast, the PRSP carried out during the Nepalese conflict was similar to the ones in Haiti and Liberia in ignoring these issues.

Fukuda-Parr's analysis highlights the need to go beyond recognizing HI as a problem, both for including HI reduction as an objective in post-conflict situations and for introducing specific HI correcting policies. She argues that the absence of disaggregated data is a fundamental constraint on introducing HI into post-conflict strategy. She also reveals a misalignment of external resources with priorities in the PRSPs, with a notable underfunding of economic infrastructure, which thus constrains the possibilities of inclusive growth. Given the importance of aid for most post-conflict countries, one priority is to get donor recognition of HIs as an important cause of conflict; another priority is for donor support for data collection and monitoring. It is notable that, in the one case where HIs were recognized as a source of conflict – Nepal's interim plan – they were also incorporated into data collection, analysis, and policy.

Chapters 5–12 analyse particular countries' post-conflict experiences.

Rajesh Venugopal's chapter argues that privatization and private sector development are critical to understanding the trajectory of post-conflict reconstruction. He examines four case studies of post-conflict privatization and private sector development (Sri Lanka, Mozambique, Cambodia, and Bosnia-Herzegovina) to develop a typology of the implications of these processes for stability and for ethnic and regional inequalities. His conclusions are as follows: (1) privatization is an intensely controversial and politicized agenda, and the fear that it may result in a redistribution of ethnic ownership and employment patterns can be destabilizing; (2) privatization can, with appropriate regulation and institutional support, be used to broaden the ethnic structure of the private sector and prevent its domination by particular ethnic groups or by foreign investors; (3) private sector development is blind to HIs, and often contributes to the creation and exacerbation of regional and urban/rural imbalances in development and income levels; (4) private sector development and privatization can become embedded within illicit and ethnically divisive war economies. They can become the vehicle for perpetuating corrupt ethnocrats and for locking the benefits of transitory political power into permanent economic gain.

Discussing the Bosnian experience, Susan Woodward describes the growing economic divergence among the constituent groups, Croats being reported to be the most affluent, followed by Bosniaks and Serbs. She suggests that the internationally imposed political structure in Bosnia – and, even more so, the economic policies required and implemented there – created the conditions for widening inequalities, favouring areas with positive initial endowments – that is, Croat areas closer to Western Europe. Together, the politics of ethnic exclusion in localities, growing social closure in reaction to international pressures for the reversal of war-time segregation, and post-war social and religious conservatism, in return, have inhibited political action in favour of alternative policies. Yet such policies are needed to counter or ameliorate the distributive effects of the power-sharing institutions and the consequences of internationally determined neoliberal reforms and stabilization, including jobless growth, cuts in public employment and welfare transfers, and inequalities related to foreign trade. Woodward notes that regional inequalities contributed to the break-up of Yugoslavia in 1991, and they remain a source of tension in present-day Bosnia.

Guatemalan post-conflict developments are explored by Corinne Caumartin and Diego Sánchez-Ancochea. They describe a contradictory experience in HI reduction. New policies in education have increased the enrolment of indigenous peoples and have slowly modified their position in society. New local and regional governance initiatives have made decision making more broad-based. Yet they note that there are important constraints to this process – the state suffers from weak institutional capacity and is dominated by traditional elites, who are typically resistant to reform. Technocratic solutions to inequality have yielded gains in the short term, but important political and economic reforms of a structural nature, for example meaningful decentralization, land reform, and measures designed to increase revenue, are called for. Moreover, the changing economic circumstances under globalization have had important consequences for HIs in the case of Guatemala, as they have benefited a small group of non-indigenous business groups and have shifted the labour market structure towards the informal sector. Thus, while there have been reductions in some HIs (notably, social and political), economic HIs appear to be widening.

Analysing Peru, Jose Carlos Orihuela's chapter explains that HIs were a key element of the Shining Path insurgency. The rebels were drawn overwhelmingly from indigenous communities from deprived regions, who in turn suffered most from the violence and its repercussions. State action in the past two decades has reduced inter-group gaps in access to publicly provided goods and services, although the gaps remained substantial and the convergence has been patchy. Economic growth in the past two decades has been based largely on the export sectors of mining, hydrocarbons, and coffee, located mostly in the coastal regions – whereas the Andean people depends upon economic activities (agriculture) with the lowest level of dynamism. As a result, the effect of economic growth on group inequalities has been contradictory: on the one hand, the gaps in group access to the basic infrastructure provided by the state have been reduced, while on the other hand the differences in opportunities for economic activities, including employment, have widened.

Janvier Nkurunziza's chapter on Burundi describes how the country's endemic political turmoil since independence in 1962 is based on deep-rooted grievances resulting from a divisive governance system that used ethnicity as a tool for political mobilization. For decades, political and economic powers were controlled by Tutsis from the southern province of Bururi, who directed to themselves a highly disproportionate share of state resources. A successful peace settlement and elections in 2005 brought to power a new leadership – mostly Hutus from traditionally underprivileged segments of society. During the period that followed, HIs in security institutions were addressed adequately. In other sectors, an analysis of programmes and budget allocations shows that a more balanced distribution of expenditure is likely to be reducing inequalities in access to health and education, although the impact thus far has been limited due to resource constraints and poor implementation. Generally speaking, though, apart from some social sector expansion, the benefits of this new political and economic order have not reached the general population, so economic HIs have not changed substantially.

Sebastian Silva Leander's chapter describes how, in Rwanda, there has been a sharp increase in vertical inequality since the mid-1980s, which has been aggravated by the war and by population displacement. He notes that, while there are no data on ethnic inequalities, there has been a large increase in land inequality and a steady increase in the urban/rural poverty gap, which is now among the largest in the world. Since the rural/urban divide has tended to run along ethnic lines, Hutus being more concentrated in rural areas and Tutsis in urban ones, this gap may reflect growing inter-ethnic inequalities – or it could be interpreted in this way by the population. Interestingly, Silva Leander finds that the increase in inequality is explained partly by the capture of resources in the D.R. Congo by Rwandan state elites. He concludes that, in order to break this cycle of structural violence, donors should pay more attention to unresolved political and regional dimensions of the conflict, while supporting economic policies that foster broad-based economic growth.

Jonathan Goodhand, Christian Dennys, and David Mansfield's chapter examines the political economy of post-conflict peace-building in Afghanistan. In the context of a fragile and contested war-to-peace transition, it focuses on the effects of the opium economy and counter-narcotics policies on HIs. The authors argue that the years of war contributed to a rebalancing of power relationships by empowering borderland regions and groups. The illicit economy, whilst frequently seen as predatory and anti-developmental, played an important social protection role and had positive developmental outcomes. Conversely, 'peace', brought in in the wake of the US invasion, has been characterized by new power asymmetries and intensified inequalities. Externally promoted development and counter-narcotics policies may have inadvertently contributed to this state of affairs. The chapter also provides a case study of Nangarhar, which is designed to explore core–periphery dynamics and the emerging nexus of links between drugs, borderlands, and central state actors.

The study of Nepal's experience presented in Graham K. Brown's chapter surveys the political history preceding the outbreak of the Maoist insurgency in 2001 and its major causes. The chapter reviews evidence of long-standing political, socio-economic, and cultural HIs in Nepal, along lines of caste, ethnicity, region, and geography. A number of econometric investigations support the conclusion that these inequalities were a major source of the insurgency. Development programmes before and during the insurgency ignored HIs, echoing policies elsewhere. In strong contrast, HIs were explicitly recognized and taken into account both by the national government and by international donors when the conflict ended. While the peace settlement itself contained provisions to reduce political and cultural HIs, socio-economic inequalities were dealt with through a series of national and international programmes, which provided for community projects and employment schemes in the poorest and war-affected districts. Preliminary evaluation shows that these programmes were probably fairly effective in raising the incomes of poor groups. Yet, as Brown shows, despite the provisions of the Peace Settlement, political HIs remain high, while some members of deprived groups (notably the *janajats*) who live outside the targeted areas have not been reached by the economic policies.

1.5 Key comparative findings

This section starts with a review of the comparative experiences of HIs in post-conflict countries, and then reviews the mechanisms at work.

Allowing for the variability in data availability and quality (issues that we will return to in the Conclusions) and for the difficulties in drawing conclusions and comparable inferences across the case studies, the record on ameliorating HIs in post-conflict countries is very mixed. Out of the eight case studies presented here, there is evidence that the HIs actually decreased somewhat only for three – Guatemala, Peru, and Burundi. Of clear concern is the evidence that HIs have increased in four of the most high-profile post-conflict countries – Afghanistan, Rwanda, Uganda, and Bosnia – all of which have received very high amounts of foreign aid. Although Chapter 12 demonstrates the existence of most explicit and extensive policies towards reducing HIs, it is still too early to draw firm conclusions about their effectiveness. Chapter 5 suggests that the ethnic composition of business owners in Mozambique and Cambodia has broadened in the post-conflict period.

What emerges from these chapters is that, even in cases where HIs have been reduced, this has happened in a somewhat haphazard and inconsistent manner, through patchy implementation, with gaps in coverage, and with strong doubts as to the sustainability of this improvement. In addition, there is a clear pattern of evidence which suggests that improvements in some metrics of HIs are being offset or rendered ineffective by new forms of group inequalities, particularly those linked to neoliberal reforms and global economic integration. On both counts, it is crucial not just to understand what happened to HIs, but to unravel and differentiate the mechanisms by which this has occurred.

Recognition

An important finding of this book is that recognition that HIs contribute to the emergence of conflicts and that they need to be addressed in post-conflict situations is increasing, as shown by the rhetoric of governments in some post-conflict countries and by some of the policy and programming documents of donor agencies. In Guatemala, for example, this finding is illustrated by an increased awareness of indigenous rights and of accords/provisions on socio-economic issues and indigenous rights. Similarly, in Burundi, Nepal, and Peru, the need to reduce group-based deprivation has been widely recognized; it is also increasingly present in the international policy discourse of PRSPs in post-conflict situations. This is not to say that the recognition is universal or balanced – Frances Stewart's chapter on employment policies describes how 'very little attention has been paid to the issue of HIs'. Nevertheless, it is important to note that there is growing attention – implicitly, if not explicitly – to the issue of HIs in conflict prevention. To the extent that such recognition has occurred, it represents a significant step forward for three reasons:

Firstly, from the perspective of the societies themselves, given that many post-conflict states were clearly discriminatory in their practices and in their rhetoric and went through decades of rhetorical denial, recognition is an important and historic step forward.

Secondly, from the perspective of the international policy/academic community, which has been dominated by instrumentalist and individualistic interpretations of conflict motivation and by security/terrorism compulsions, this recognition is a welcome shift in attention, towards the socio-economic roots of conflict.

Thirdly, this recognition represents the first step towards the design and adoption of policies to address HIs, and it is shifting the debate, beyond the issue of recognition, towards implementation and effectiveness. This in turn requires engagement and research on the ways in which contentious HI-reducing policies have been negotiated, sequenced, and prioritized in post-conflict political institutions. As the case studies in this book demonstrate, introducing effective policies has proved to be an extremely challenging task, in which the circumstances are rarely supportive.

However, analysis of the discourse both of governments in post-conflict countries and of international actors shows that the recognition is by no means universal.

Implementation

Some post-conflict states have made progress in translating the recognition of HIs into policy design, but there remain important gaps in translating the discourse of recognition into reality. This is clearly illustrated by the country studies (see Table 1.2), which show that, in almost every case where policies have been introduced, implementation has been partial or weak, and frequently offset by the unequalizing effects of market forces. Moreover, two of the three post-conflict PRSPs reviewed by Sakiko Fukuda-Parr did not address HIs despite having given some measure of recognition to their existence and role.

One of the most important variables in understanding the political economy of implementation relates to the nature of conflict termination. In Burundi and Nepal, after negotiated conclusions to the conflicts, the rebel leaders gained power, and this resulted in explicit policies aimed at reversing some of the ethnic and regional imbalances. In Peru and Rwanda, however, where the conflicts ended in victory for one side, explicit recognition of HIs as a cause and commitment to reducing HIs have been weaker. This is not to say that HIs have been ignored in such countries but that, where they have been taken into account, the process by which they were addressed has followed unusual and sometimes unintended pathways, being influenced by elite interests, ethnocratic patrimonialism, illicit crops, and the aftermath of the economies of war.

In Peru, for example, the extension of public works and services such as roads, health, and education to historically disadvantaged indigenous areas occurred not so much as part of a post-conflict strategy, but as part of a post-hyperinflation 'pacification' strategy embedded within an extremely violent campaign of counter-insurgency. Indeed, Peru is a curious case where there was implementation, but not much explicit recognition of HIs. Similarly, in Afghanistan, Goodhand, Dennys, and Mansfield describe how HIs were reduced during the war and by the drug economy, while state-building and counter-narcotics strategies have paradoxically restored older imbalances.

Table 1.2 Summary of parameters in countries studied

Country	What happened to HIs	Recognition	Implementation	Effectiveness	HI dynamics
Afghanistan	Probably worse	Unclear	Inadvertently worsened HIs	Inadvertently worsened HIs	War and drugs reduced HIs. State-building and counter-narcotics worsen it
Nepal	Worsened during conflict; too early to tell post-conflict	Yes	Yes	Early signs of effectiveness	
Rwanda	Probably worsened	No. No explicit use of ethnic categories permitted	N.a.	Ineffective	New inequalities from war economy
Burundi	Some improvements in social sectors and public sector jobs, not economy	Yes	In part	Partial; inadequate resources	Improvement in public sector job allocation, as required in the political agreement that brought an end to the war
Peru	Social HIs improved; economic worsened	A decade later	In part, in social sectors	Yes, but gaps remain	New market-based group inequalities
Guatemala	Social HIs improved; economic worsened	Yes by donors, less so by the state	In social sectors	Yes, but gaps remain	New market-based group inequalities
Bosnia	Getting worse	For political HIs but not economic	No	Inadvertently worsened HIs	New within region in equalities as well as in market-based group inequalities
Uganda	Worsened	Somewhat	Weak	Weak	War in the North and market dynamics worsened HIs

Indeed, the real-world trajectories of post-conflict reconstruction are inevitably fragile, inconsistent, uneven, and violence-prone, rarely resembling the idealized discourse and linear transitions implicit in much academic and donor discourse.

Effectiveness

How effective have state policies been in addressing HIs, and how has this come about? In Guatemala, Peru, and Burundi the case studies reveal that the post-conflict period has given rise to explicit policies towards regional and ethnic disparities. In all three cases there was an explicit commitment to reform, but the extent of the impact and its effectiveness have been limited by factors such as the extent of commitment by elites in actuality, state capacity, resource constraints, and the limited attention to measures designed to facilitate group economic empowerment.

In Guatemala, significant improvements in access to education came about largely as a result of a commitment to the objective of extending basic education to all, as agreed in the peace accords, while the failure to achieve more broad-based improvements in economic welfare is attributed in part to an inability to deal with important issues such as land redistribution. In Burundi, the effectiveness of ambitious programmes intended to improve access to education and health is being limited by resource constraints and inadequate planning. In Peru, improved access to public services came at the cost of political and civil freedoms, while no attention was paid to improving economic inequalities. As Orihuela notes, 'the political consensus was that Peru had to sacrifice freedoms in order to achieve progress'. Privatization policies in certain limited cases have resulted in an effective broadening of the ethnic base of entrepreneurship and business ownership – but the efficacy of these policies requires strong transparent and development-oriented institutions of the kind that are, almost by definition, rarely available in post-conflict situations.

Thus effective outcomes required strong recognition and commitment to HIs, adequate funding, the presence of reasonably strong institutions, and sustained policy attention to a comprehensive range of ancillary social–political interventions.

In contrast, weak outcomes or worsening HIs occurred in post-conflict Afghanistan, Bosnia-Herzegovina, and Rwanda. Employment policies also suffered from poor design and effectiveness, partly because of their mostly exclusive focus on supply-side measures such as training and improved labour market information, and not on the demand-side, in the form of the creation of jobs; and also because they have been accompanied by employment-destroying adjustment and demobilization policies. Susan Woodward describes how the imposition of neoliberal reforms by the international community, combined with the obstacles – social, cultural, and political as well as institutional – to political action in support of alternative policies not only created the conditions for growing inequalities, but also made it difficult for state intervention to address this situation. In Rwanda, which is often depicted as a post-conflict economic success story, the apparent worsening of HIs has taken place in the context of a market-centred model of development and of the enrichment of a largely Tutsi-dominated ruling elite partly through illicit plunder of resources from the DRC.[9] In Afghanistan, the authors argue that the centralization of power implicit in the process of donor-funded state-building and in the imposition of a counter-narcotics strategy has inadvertently contributed to an intensification of inequalities.

In sum, then, the major causes of the negative outcomes were inadequate recognition of, and commitment to, HIs by the states and international actors, the presence of countervailing policies, weaknesses in institutional design and state capacity, and the growth of sources of economic prosperity that directly or indirectly benefited some (usually richer) parts of society disproportionately.

1.6 Policies towards horizontal inequalities

Countries can take different approaches to dealing with HIs[10]. At one extreme, countries can target HIs directly, through group-based affirmative action policies. At the other extreme, countries can ignore them altogether in their development programmes. Many countries fall somewhere in between these two approaches. In this section, we introduce a typology of policy approaches and discuss the merits and demerits of each approach across the four dimensions of HI – political, economic, social, and cultural status. Ultimately the policies are aimed at eliminating, or substantially reducing, group inequality in economic well-being, political participation, and cultural recognition. In practice, however, the policies have to be directed at processes affecting these outcomes rather than at the outcomes themselves. We will also explore which of these policies have been used by our case study countries.

Policies across all four dimensions can take either a direct or an indirect approach towards correcting group inequality (Stewart et al. 2008).

Direct approaches involve targeting groups directly, positively (for the deprived) and negatively (for the privileged). Indirect approaches aim to achieve the same HI-reducing impact indirectly, via general policies affecting everyone in society; but, because of their design in relation to the circumstances of the various identity groups in society, they reduce HIs. Ethnic quotas for education or ethnic electoral rolls fall in the first category, while regional expenditure policies or decentralization of power across the country fall in the second. The first type of policy unavoidably increases the salience of identity difference, while the second is broadly neutral in this respect, and may indeed contribute to greater integration over time. Given the objectives of increasing people's adherence to national identity and of reducing the salience of subnational identities that can form the basis of conflict, it is desirable for the first type of policy to be time-limited. A third type of policy is explicitly directed at reducing the salience of group boundaries by increasing integration (and less concerned with HI reduction). Examples are incentives for shared social, economic, or political activities across groups (see Table 1.3).

It is helpful to differentiate policies intended to correct regional inequalities (which often subsume some ethnic ones, because of the geographic concentration of ethnic groups) and policies designed to correct ethnic inequalities directly, both within and between regions. Depending on the ethnic and religious demography of a country, this might require two different approaches: a 'regional' channel, which aims to reduce HIs by stimulating and creating economic activities in relatively deprived regions; and an 'ethnic'[11] channel, which would aim to improve relatively deprived groups' human capital and employment situation and their 'marketability', wherever they are located. The regional channel could include a range of measures such as research and development on agricultural cash crops suitable for poorer regions, selective subsidies for production in such regions (as applied in Europe, for e.g.), credit schemes to support economic activities, and increased public investment in economic infrastructure. Within the ethnic channel, a number of policy options are available, ranging from anti-discrimination laws, improved information about jobs for deprived groups, and monitoring of employment procedures and outcomes to affirmative action programmes. These policies are similar to those adopted by many countries in dealing with gender inequalities, which are gradually improving the position of women.

It should be stressed here that there are many considerations to be taken into account in designing development policies, particularly in

Table 1.3 Examples of approaches to reducing HIs

		Policy approach		
		Direct HI-reducing	**Indirect HI-reducing**	**Integrationist**
Dimension	Political	Group quotas; seat reservations; consociational constitution; list proportional representation	Design of voting system to require power-sharing across groups (for example, two-thirds voting requirements in assembly); design of boundaries and seat numbers to ensure adequate representation of all groups; human rights legislation and enforcement	Geographical voting spread requirements; ban on ethnic/religious political parties (national party stipulations)
	Economic	Quotas for employment; special investment or credit programmes for particular groups	Anti-discrimination legislation; progressive taxation; regional development programmes; sectoral support programmes (for example, Stabex)	Incentives for cross-group economic activities
	Social	Quotas for access to public education; for scholarships; subsidies for school meals for particular groups	Comprehensive access to services; regional programmes of support for social infrastructure and services	Requirement that schools are multicultural; promotion of multicultural civic institutions
	Cultural status	Minority language recognition and education; symbolic recognition (for example, public holidays, attendance at state functions)	Freedom of religious observance; no state religion	Civic citizenship education; promotion of an overarching national identity

Source: Stewart et al. (2008).

a post-conflict environment, in addition to those directed at HIs. Thus political policies usually aim to introduce democracy and the rule of law and to protect human rights generally; economic policies aim to achieve macro-economic stability, promote efficiency and growth, and reduce poverty; and in post-conflict societies policies also aim to reintegrate combatants, to reconstruct basic infrastructure, and to address other important causes of conflict, such as unemployment and opportunities for rent-seeking. Policies towards HIs should not displace these other policy objectives or the relevant instruments to achieve them, although sometimes they may involve some trade-offs in policy objectives and some modifications in instruments. Moreover, the exact nature of policies is clearly context-specific, and what is appropriate in one country may not be appropriate in another.

1.7 Conclusions

The major conclusions of this chapter are summarized below:

- HIs need to be taken into account in post-conflict policies in order to reduce the risk of recurrence of conflict, as well as to build just and inclusive societies;
- The evidence in this volume is that, in many cases of post-conflict polices, but by no means in all, HIs *are* recognized as being one of the important root causes of the conflict.
- Yet policy towards addressing HIs in the cases studied has been very limited, usually confined to actions towards the social sectors and a few development projects in poorer regions, but with almost nothing done towards improving employment and the economic activities of deprived groups more generally. However, one important exception is Nepal.
- International donors sometimes acknowledge HIs as being of importance, but they do not give priority to HI considerations in actual policy recommendations, privileging instead more conventional (macro- and other) policies, which can actually lead to a worsening of HIs, as shown in the macro chapter.
- In the event, HIs appear to have worsened in more than half of the cases analysed in this volume.
- When we investigated why, it turned out that part of the explanation was weak implementation and budgetary constraints, as well as the fact that policies were partial or ineffective.

- However, the main reason was that inequalities were accentuated by the operation of market forces, which generally favoured groups and regions that were already relatively rich.
- However, the state itself played a role in some cases, notably in Afghanistan.
- HI data availability is notably problematic and systematic monitoring is very rare. In most countries there are no ethnically or even regionally differentiated data for investment flows, public expenditure, income, or human development indicators. This clearly complicates policy making in major ways. The lack of HI data availability both reflects the limited concern with the issue and encourages neglect of the issue. Political motivations and concerns with the sensitive nature of this kind of data often underlie the failure to collect such data or to make them publicly available.

Our major policy recommendations are as follows:

- HI considerations should be taken more seriously both by national governments and by the international donor community;
- The first essential step in devising policy to correct HIs is to gain a thorough understanding of the current status and dynamics of HIs in the country. Even in the absence of systematic data, much can be done to gain an understanding of prevailing HIs in a country through investigating existing sources of data thoroughly and through conducting small surveys.
- In general, much more systematic data collection on regional and ethnic inequalities is a high priority.
- We identified three types of policy towards HIs: direct, indirect, and integrationist. In a post-conflict context all three can play a role, but indirect policies and integrationist ones are particularly appropriate, as direct policies can arouse severe tensions, while it is especially important to encourage inter-group reconciliation and cooperation.
- The nature of policies towards public expenditure aimed at reducing HIs are fairly well-known – in particular extending social and economic infrastructure to the whole country and ensuring equality of access to basic services.
- But our finding is that, while this is essential, the big problem for improving HIs arises from unequalizing market operations.
- Ideally, the 'market' should be restructured in such a way that it may contribute to the reduction of inequalities, or at the least it may not exacerbate them. Policies need to be aimed at reducing both regional

and ethnic inequalities in market opportunities. Appropriate policies vary according to the ethnic and religious demography of a country.

- In principle, two different approaches might be needed, one directed at regional inequalities and the other at ethnic inequalities within and across regions. The latter includes anti-discrimination legislation affirmative action policies and policies to improve the power of deprived groups.
- Policies are needed to strengthen the ability of deprived groups/regions to participate in market opportunities.
- In practice, once the need to reduce HIs is widely acknowledged by national governments as well as by international actors, policies to achieve this objective should evolve according to the circumstances of the country, as they have in the many multiethnic nations whose governments work to support good relations within their territories. The policy suggestions in this book are derived from such experience.[12] There has been less experience in post-conflict nations to date, and consequently policies are likely to evolve to reflect the special circumstances of such societies.
- However, in implementing policies to reduce HIs several caveats are in order. Firstly, there is no one-size-fits-all approach to HIs. Understanding the nature and extent of HIs is essential to the design of appropriate and effective policies and requires the gathering and analysis of data. In addition, some aspects of HIs and their consequences are context-specific, and thus the policies that seek to address them should reflect this specificity: what is appropriate in one setting may not be so in a neighbouring country. Secondly, the policy environment of countries coming out of conflict is clearly not easy, and there are likely to be problems of limited capacity to formulate and implement policies, as well as political tensions surrounding the introduction of these redistributive policies. Thirdly, obviously these are not the only policies needed. Policies to correct HIs should, wherever possible, complement other development policies towards reconstruction, growth, employment, and poverty reduction; sometimes there may be trade-offs, and then priorities will need to be determined. Finally, it is important that policy makers be conscious of, and sensitive to, the tensions and controversies that might arise from the implementation of policies aimed at redistributing resources across groups. The policies can arouse resentment and opposition among losing groups, and targeting specific groups may entrench perceived differences. Both these effects can potentially increase the propensity to mobilize along group lines. Policies can be designed to

reduce these risks, for example by putting more emphasis on indirect policies and less on direct. In general, policies need to be introduced cautiously and sensitively.
- Despite these cautions, doing nothing and permitting HIs to escalate is a dangerous policy in post-conflict societies.

Notes

1. Collier and Hoeffler (1999) found that, in 53 per cent of the cases included in their study, conflict parties returned to war within five years. However, Collier et al. (2006) found a much lower recurrence rate, conflict countries having on average a 23 per cent risk of returning to war within four years.
2. See Stewart (2000, 2002) for an elaboration of the concept of 'HIs'.
3. See Stewart (2008) for an extensive conceptual discussion and for empirical findings on the relationship between HIs and conflict.
4. See Langer and Brown (2008).
5. In Bosnia ethnicity and religion coincide.
6. On consociationalism, see Lijphardt (2008).
7. Hartzell and Hoddie (2003).
8. See UNDP (2008).
9. Data collection by ethnicity is not permitted in Rwanda – hence our interpretation is based on indirect evidence.
10. This section draws heavily on Stewart et al. (2008).
11. Into 'ethnicity' here we include a range of identity differences – religious, racial, and so on.
12. Some of these policies are briefly surveyed in Stewart et al. (2008); and see also Brown et al. (2012).

2
Macro-Economic Policies in Post-Conflict Countries

Arnim Langer and Frances Stewart

2.1 Introduction

What happens to the macro-economy is very important – not only for the level and growth of output and for employment but also for the evolution of horizontal inequalities (HIs). In many contexts it is the macro-policies and macro-consequences of these policies that determine opportunities across regions and sectors, and this in turn is the major determinant of HIs. Specific policies may be introduced at meso-level and micro-level to correct HIs, but, generally speaking, it is macro-developments that are most important; they can easily offset the effects of any specific policies.

The objectives of macro-policies in a post-conflict setting, of course, go well beyond the issue of HIs. Important objectives are to facilitate economic recovery and support sustained growth, and to avoid unacceptably high or accelerating inflation. In order to achieve these objectives, the policies also need to support external balance and, in particular, growth of exports, which contributes not only to external balance but also to growth of incomes. Here we accept the importance of these objectives, but add to them the consideration of how the policies affect HIs, in particular whether and how the conventional objectives can be achieved without worsening and, if possible, by improving HIs in countries where the HIs are severe. There has been considerable attention devoted to appropriate macro-policies in post-conflict environments for recovery, and our focus here is therefore primarily on the issue of HIs.

In this chapter we will first consider, through general analysis, how macro-policies are likely to affect HIs, and we will come to some broad conclusions on the consequences of macro-policies for HIs and on how this differs across types of economy. We will then present some evidence on some policies and outcomes in selected post-conflict countries, differentiating between countries that experienced a strong recovery and countries that experienced weak recovery. Thirdly, we will review actual policies and present evidence on macro-economic outcomes and on the evolution of HIs for post-conflict Uganda since 1986. The final section draws some conclusions with respect to the impact of macro-policies on a country's HIs.

2.2 What macro-policies?

Post-conflict macro-policies have to be designed in the context of the severe negative heritage of war. As summarized by the UNDP: 'A shrunken economic base, moderate to high inflation, chronic fiscal deficits, high levels of external and domestic debt and low domestic government revenues are among the most prominent features of these economies' (UNDP 2008: 107–108).

The major elements of post-conflict macro-policies are as follows:

1. fiscal policies
2. monetary policies
3. aid flows, including debt relief
4. policies towards the exchange rate, import tariffs and quantitative restrictions (QRs) on imports
5. policies towards the capital account.

Fiscal policies include policies towards the aggregate level of taxation and expenditure. Often, at the end of a conflict, both taxation and expenditure are low, and there is a fiscal deficit.[1] Consequently post-conflict policies often include efforts to raise both taxation and expenditure. Generally the aim is to raise tax revenue more than expenditure, so as to reduce the fiscal deficit – which tends, if large, to lead to inflation and excessive debt and to adverse external balances.

There is a critical need for public expenditure in a post-conflict context to finance reconstruction and essential infrastructure, as well as to extend services to the population generally, which can be important in preventing conflict recurrence. Expenditure is normally supported by inflows of aid as well as by local revenue, but, if aid flows are large, they may potentially create 'Dutch disease', sustaining the exchange rate and thereby providing a disincentive for exports. The most appropriate level and phasing of aid in post-conflict situations continues to be a topic of considerable debate. In addition, an important issue for international policy makers is how far to write off or relieve war-incurred debts.

As far as monetary policy is concerned, the main issue is whether to adopt a relaxed low interest policy or a tight monetary policy involving high formal interest rates and stringent controls over the money supply and bank credit. Monetary policy in a post-conflict environment is confronted with two conflicting requirements: on the one hand, a fairly loose monetary policy may be desirable, so as to ensure low interest rates and encourage investment; on the other hand, there is a danger that such a policy may generate inflation. Monetary policy is, of course, inextricably connected to fiscal policy, especially in developing countries with limited bond markets. Large fiscal imbalances tend to be associated with lax monetary policies, and conversely.

Post-conflict countries often face severe external imbalances, as exports tend to perform poorly during conflict due to disruptions in supply and in transport and communications and to labour migration and embargos, while imports are often relatively sustained, in order to finance arms and essential goods. Moreover, countries in conflict usually accumulate large international debts, and debt servicing contributes to external imbalances (Stewart, Fitzgerald and Associates 2001). Consequently one general desideratum is to improve the current account balance. Policies adopted include moving towards market exchange rates, generally including devaluation of the exchange rate. Often, too, conflict has been a time of heavy import restrictions (quantitative and through tariffs), and there is strong pressure from the international community to liberalize imports, abolish QRs and reduce tariffs.

Finally, during conflict, there is normally considerable capital flight (Davies 2007); and an important issue is how to attract this capital back after the conflict ends.

2.3 How would one expect these policies to affect horizontal inequalities?

The likely distributional impact of these policies depends on two factors. The first concerns precisely how the policies are designed – and this includes both the aggregates and their components. For example, in the case of revenue, this is a matter both of the total level of government revenue and of the type of taxes adopted to produce this revenue; and, for expenditure, similarly, it is both a question of the total level of expenditure and of its distribution across sectors, regions and income groups. When it comes to policies aimed at improving the external balance, the distributional effects will depend partly on the choice of instrument – devaluation, tariff reform, export incentives and so on.[2] The second factor determining the distributional consequences of particular policies concerns how the different salient groups are positioned in the economy.

Fiscal policies

Suppose there are just two groups – a richer group, R and a poorer group P – and HIs are measured in summary by the ratio of average per capita incomes of the two, y^r/y^p.[3] The two groups will then differ on average as to their consumption and income levels; so, if the additional taxation is progressive (bears more heavily on the rich), it will reduce incomes of R more than incomes of P, and consequently it will reduce HIs; but if it is regressive, the reverse will occur. The two groups are also likely to differ in how they benefit from public expenditure. Social expenditure tends to be distributed progressively and the rest of public expenditure more regressively, while the overall distributional impact of public expenditure varies across societies; on balance, it seems to be mildly progressive – that is, slightly favouring the poor (Chu et al. 2000; Cornia 2004; Van de Walle and Nead 1995). Then public expenditure that is disproportionately concentrated on the social sectors will help P relatively to R, and conversely if it is concentrated on other sectors.

This assumes that the only way the two groups differ is with respect to income levels; but salient groups should not be defined only by their incomes, but also by some cultural characteristics that may affect the distributional impact of taxation and expenditure. For example, some groups save more than others, so they will be less affected by consumption taxes as against income taxes; some groups consume less alcohol, so they will be less affected by alcohol tax rises; groups differ in the use they make of public services (for example, some groups may be more likely to attend school for cultural reasons, others less likely, while some may withdraw from public sector schools to attend religious schools), and thus they will be differentially affected by different types of expenditure. Moreover, groups are often concentrated in particular regions – for example Muslims in the North of Nigeria; indigenous people in the highlands of Peru. Consequently, any tax or expenditure increases that are not regionally neutral will have implications for group distribution.

In general, a typical aspect of a society with severe HIs is that the distribution of the benefits of public expenditure is unequal across the groups – in other words $p^p < p^r$, where p^p represents public expenditure benefits per head of group P, and p^r represents public expenditure benefits per head of group R. While 'neutral' increases in expenditure (that is, increases affecting everyone proportionately to their initial benefits) would leave HIs unchanged (ignoring the distributional impact of taxes raised to finance such expenditure), such neutrality cannot be assumed, as it is likely that group R will control the budget and may ensure that they benefit more than proportionately.

We have so far considered the two groups as consumers of public goods, but they are also producers. As producers, some groups may gain more than others, for example in terms of contracts for government expenditure, employment on the construction of the facilities and employment in their operation, because of the groups' specialization in particular activities because they have different levels of education and because contacts with the government vary between groups. For the most part, it can be expected that R will gain more than P. However, the gaining groups may be different for some types of expenditure – such as labour-intensive infrastructural expenditure located in poor regions, where P might gain most.

If taxes rise in order to finance rises in expenditure, poor groups may gain more than rich ones, because in general expenditure is progressive (poorer groups receive more benefits in relation to their original income, even if not in absolute terms), while taxation is often neutral (proportionate to income).

Hence a careful analysis of the characteristics of the different groups and of the design of tax and expenditure increases is necessary in order to identify the impact on HIs of macro-policies. It is therefore difficult to make any a priori generalizations, though one can make the following points fairly confidently : (a) a larger public sector, with higher taxation and public expenditure, is likely to be more beneficial for poor groups than a smaller one; (b) progressive taxes are more beneficial than regressive ones for poorer groups; (c) expenditure focused on social sectors is generally likely to improve HIs relative to expenditure on other items, though in some contexts particular marginalized groups receive very little benefit from any kind of government expenditure; and (d) public sector employment often benefits R more than P, and this is where anti-discrimination policies and efforts to correct HIs in employment are particularly important (see employment chapter).

From the perspective of recovery and growth, the critical requirement of fiscal policies is that they support rising infrastructure investment, while market expansion is sufficient to encourage private production and investment. What is important here is that there be sufficient government investment, which can be supported by tax revenue, aid and/or deficit financing. Stringent requirements for the deficit (of zero or very low) can therefore be extremely harmful to recovery, although much depends on the level of aid inflows and on how aid is dealt with – whether or not it is included as 'revenue', in estimating the budget deficit.

Aid policies

As far as aid is concerned, considerations similar to those found in relation to public expenditure more generally apply here too, in relation to how it affects HIs. In general HIs are not an explicit consideration in any of the main aid modalities – project aid, budget support or the PRSPs (Brown and Stewart 2006). Indeed aid is often allocated in such a way that it worsens HIs, and this needs to be avoided by making the impact on HIs an explicit consideration and then by careful monitoring the allocation of aid across groups.

One important type of aid is debt relief. According to the established rules, post-conflict countries cannot qualify for generous debt relief, as they have not yet completed the required PRSPs and established a 'good policy' history. Yet the case for immediate debt relief is very strong – since the debt was generally incurred not for development but for war expenditure – quite often by political actors who are no longer in power. Moreover, debt servicing can be a millstone that diverts resources away from productive expenditure. Debt relief as such has no obvious impact on HIs, but the resources it releases can be used to reduce such inequalities.

Monetary policies

As far as the immediate impact on HIs are concerned, monetary policies probably have only minor effects. In the first decades of countries' independence most countries kept interest rates low, monetary policy was relatively passive and credit was rationed. But then it was argued that this led to inefficiency of resource allocation and discouraged savings, and interest rates were raised to something approaching a competitive level. There's not much evidence that the change in policy affected either savings or investment much (see e.g. Gelb 1989; Gupta 1987), but it may have been favourable to HIs. Low interest rates in the formal sector (accompanied by very high rates in the informal sector) would generally help more privileged groups relatively to less privileged ones. In regional terms, most of the formal sector private investment is located in the richer parts of developing countries, so a low interest rate policy probably tends to worsen HIs. But the aggregate effect is unlikely to be large. More important for post-conflict countries is whether a high interest rate policy discourages recovery – which seems plausible. The post-conflict context may therefore be a time when a more relaxed policy is appropriate.

The other big issue for monetary policies is how they affect inflation. For this, one needs to consider monetary policies along with fiscal ones. If there is a big fiscal deficit financed by monetary policy (basically by printing money), inflation is likely. If rapid, and especially if variable, this process can discourage investment and impede recovery. There is also the question of how inflation affects HIs. Poorer groups may be relatively insulated from inflation, as they are more in the non-monetary economy and are not likely to own many monetary assets that are devalued by inflation. On the other hand, they can suffer from inflation in food prices and from policy reactions to excessive inflation, often involving severe expenditure cuts.

Trade and exchange rate policies

Turning to exchange rate and tariff policies – which we will define as 'switching policies', since they are intended to switch resources into tradeables in order to improve the external balance – we again need to differentiate the impact on groups as producers and on groups as consumers. The outcome on groups as producers depends largely on the group's specialization in production. This is often quite marked, as a result of colonial policy, and its aftermath, and of geographic disadvantage. Thus colonial policy involved a sharp racial division of labour in Malaysia, the Chinese forming the trading and entrepreneurial class, while the Indians were imported to work on plantations and the Malays were subsistence farmers (Brown 1997). Similarly, in many African economies, particular groups were picked out by colonialists for privileged education and for specialization in cash crops – often a specialization associated with advantages of geography, so that Southern groups were favoured for education and cash crops in both West and East African countries (see, for example, Songsore 2003 for Ghana; and Ghai and Court 1974 for Kenya). In other economies, settlers took all the best land and the top jobs in the civil service, and where settlers remained in the country after independence, as in Latin America and in South and Central Africa, this became a major source of HIs (Figueroa et al. 1996). In some economies colonial powers imported indentured or slave labour to work on plantations (for example, Brazil and Guyana) and to build roads or railways (for example, Kenya). Consequently, for these and other reasons, R and P tend to be differently inserted into the economy.

Exchange rate devaluation favours some sectors (tradeables) and hurts others (non-tradeables). Hence the impact on HIs depends on whether the ethnic division of labour follows this tradeable/non-tradeable distinction. For some economies it is clear that there is such an overlap, P being more specialized in non-tradeables (subsistence) and R more specialized in tradeables. This broadly seems to be the case with respect to cash crops in many African economies. Examples of post-conflict countries with these characteristics are Côte d'Ivoire and Uganda.

However, elsewhere the impact is somewhat different. In economies with plantations and very poorly paid plantation labour, the workers (typically members of a particular group) are often the poorest segment of society, with incomes below those of the peasant food producers; for example the Indian plantation workers in Malaysia or Guyana or the Afro-Brazilians in Brazil. For these economies, switching policies may favour plantations and hurt the somewhat richer peasant farmers. However, these gains are not necessarily passed on to the workers, but may go largely to the plantation owners, who belong to the R group. None of the current post-conflict countries has this type of economy, although examples from the 1980s are central American economies such as El Salvador and Guatemala.

A third type of economy is one where there are incipient labour-intensive manufacturing industries and switching favours this sector. The HI implications depend on the group the new labourers come from. In Malaysia, the poorest group, the *bumiputera*, supplied much of this new labour – being assisted by supportive education and employment policies (see Faaland et al. 2003). Cambodia and Vietnam are post-conflict countries in which labour-intensive manufactures were encouraged by switching policies. But in these cases the richer (majority) groups were primarily employed in the labour-intensive sectors.

A fourth type of economy is one in which comparative advantage lies with skill or capital-intensive products (like software services and call centres in India, or airplanes in Brazil). The more developed post-conflict countries, like Bosnia-Herzegovina and Croatia, fall into this category. In these cases switching policies will favour producers of these items, who are generally likely to be in group R. However, in the case of skill-intensive products, this also depends on complementary education and training policies that might be designed to improve capacities and job access of P.

There can also be regional and HI consequences from growth, where one region of a country benefits much more than others, creating regional and, quite often, ethnic HIs. Nepal is an example. Thailand is another. Although Thailand has seen rapid growth and labour-intensive industrialization over the past 25 years, the three mainly Malay–Muslim provinces have remained at levels well below the national average. While two of three Muslim–Malay provinces – Yala and Narathiwat – experienced a significant decline in their relative economic standing, each falling by around 20 per cent of relative GDP (gross domestic product) per capita, the third one, Pattani, did better, but remained nonetheless significantly below the national average (Brown 2008).

A fifth type of economy is one that specializes on minerals – for example, oil. In such economies the revenue from the resources tends to be disproportionately received by R, either directly or indirectly, via government redistributionary policies. Where this is the case, any across-the-board depreciation would increase such revenue and tend to worsen HIs. But multiple exchange rates might prevent this effect and could be designed to help particular groups. Angola provides an example of a mineral rich country in the post-conflict category.

A further complication is that non-tradeables extend beyond subsistence agriculture to import-substituting activity behind heavy protection. Often it is R rather than P that is concentrated in this sector. If this protection is withdrawn as part of the switching policies, then undoubtedly some R will lose. This may apply in any of the five types of economy differentiated above.

Turning to the impact of exchange rate changes and tariff reforms on groups as consumers, the outcome depends on the design of the policies. It appears that tariff and quota reductions tend to favour richer groups, as import tariffs often bear most heavily on luxury consumption; but such reductions may not be universal (although they normally are), but could be retained on the products consumed by the rich, thereby altering the distributional impact.

On the basis of this discussion, it is possible to come to some general conclusions about the likely impact of switching policies on groups as producers. First, in economies where there is crop specialization by group and crops constitute the main tradeables, switching policies are likely to increase HIs; secondly, in plantation economies, they may somewhat improve them; and, thirdly, in economies in which the policies promote labour-intensive industrialization, those with basic education are likely to gain (see Wood and Ridau-Cano 1996), which in the normal case would tend to favour the richer and better educated group(s), although this can be offset by education and employment policies that favour the poorer groups; fourthly, with respect to regional distribution, effective switching policies that promote rapid industrialization are likely to lead to regional concentration of industry and consequently to regional imbalances, accentuating or creating regional HIs; fifthly, where the policies dismantle the protection of privileged import-substitution, it is possible that they improve HIs. Finally, like tax and expenditure policies (but to a lesser extent), switching policies can be designed to help or hurt particular groups.

Capital market policies

One thrust of many post-conflict policy packages is to try and attract the war associated capital flight back into the country. This requires stability of the economy, and particularly of the banking sector; and monetary incentives can be provided. The only caution here is to avoid generous incentives favouring the richer groups, which obviously would worsen HIs.

2.4 Some characteristics of macro-policies and outcomes in post-conflict countries

As a result of reviewing 36 countries where conflict ended after 1989, recent post-conflict recoveries can be classified into three broad groups, following Mcleod's methodology: first, those countries that experienced sustained income growth per person for a significant period of time after conflict – which we term 'strong growth recovery' (SGR); the second group consists of countries that had not recovered their levels of growth by 2007 (these are termed 'weak growth recovery' – WGR); the third group is characterized by countries in which conflict is either localized to one region, and so economic activity was not significantly disrupted, or by countries in which conflict was ongoing. Our analysis focuses on the first two groups.[4] Tables 2.1 and 2.2 list the countries in each group. The SGR group meet three criteria:

1. Per capita GDP growth averages 2 per cent or more for at least six years;
2. Post-conflict growth rates are on average higher than pre-conflict growth, indicating a break with the past, turnaround or transition to a new higher growth path;
3. Conflict must have interrupted growth, so that the notion of recovery discussed in (1) and (2) applies.

The second group includes those countries which failed to meet these three criteria.

Table 2.1 Strong Growth Recovery Countries (SGR)

Country	Years of conflict	Average annual pre-conflict GDP pc growth	Average annual in-conflict GDP pc growth	Years after conflict	Average annual post-conflict GDP pc growth
Afghanistan	1978–2001	–0.4%	–2.9%	6	18.5%
Angola	1975–2002	2.1%	–1.1%	5	11.7%
Azerbaijan	1991–1994	–	–17.8%	13	10.8%
Bosnia and Herzegovina	1992–1995	–6.4%	9.9%	12	9.9%
Cambodia	1970–1991	–	–2.1%	16	5.6%
Chad	1965–1990	–	–0.6%	17	3.3%
Congo, Dem. Rep. of the	1996–2001	–4.1%	–5.8%	6	2.4%
Croatia	1991–1993	–	–12.9%	14	4.9%
Ethiopia	1974–1991	0.8%	–1.1%	16	4.7%
Georgia	1991–1994	2.2%	–25.2%	13	8.2%
Liberia	1989–2003	–1.5%	–4.0%	4	2.8%
Mozambique	1976–1992	2.6%	–1.3%	15	4.9%
Rwanda	1990–1994	0.5%	–7.1%	13	5.4%
Solomon Islands	1998–2003	1.3%	–5.6%	4	3.8%
Sierra Leone	1991–2001	0.3%	–6.1%	6	6.1%
Tajikistan	1992–1997	–9.1%	–17.0%	10	6.6%
Uganda	1979–1991	–3.0%	–0.9%	16	3.2%
Average		**–1.1%**	**–6.0%**	**10.9**	**6.6%**

Source: Authors' calculations based on data drawn from the World Bank – World Development Indicators (WDI) – and United Nations Statistics Division (National Accounts Main Aggregates Database http://unstats.un.org/unsd/snaama/dnlList.asp).

During conflict, the average per capita growth of SGR countries was significantly lower than that of WGR countries (–0.6 and –2.5 per cent, respectively). But average per capita growth rebounded more sharply and remained higher for the SGR group after conflict ended. Part of the explanation of this bounce-back effect is in the sharper collapse in growth that SRC experienced the year conflict ended (see Figure 2.1).

The average post-conflict growth rate for SGR countries is 6.6 per cent, in sharp contrast to the 0.7 per cent achieved by the WGR countries in the same period (Table 2.1 and 2.2). However, during the pre-conflict period, WGR countries had a better performance in terms of growth than SGR countries (1.4 per cent compared to a –0.7 per cent, respectively).

Table 2.2 Weak Growth Recovery Countries (WGR)

Country	Years of conflict	Average annual pre-conflict GDP pc growth	Average annual in-conflict GDP pc growth	Years after conflict	Average annual post-conflict GDP pc growth
Burundi	1991–2002	1.0%	−2.5%	5	−0.9%
Congo, Rep. of	1993–1999	2.2%	−2.4%	8	1.8%
Côte d'Ivoire	2002–2003	−0.2%	−1.7%	4	−1.3%
El Salvador	1979–1991	2.8%	−1.7%	16	2.1%
Eritrea	1974–1991	0.8%	−1.1%	16	1.6%
Guatemala	1965–1995	–	1.0%	12	1.4%
Guinea Bissau	1998–1999	0.7%	−12.6%	8	−1.2%
Lebanon	1975–1990	4.7%	−0.7%	17	3.4%
Haiti	1991–1995	0.3%	−5.7%	12	−0.6%
Namibia	1973–1989	0.6%	−0.3%	18	1.9%
Nicaragua	1978–1990	2.4%	−5.6%	17	1.6%
Papua New Guinea	1989–1996	3.3%	3.1%	11	−1.0%
Average		**1.7%**	**−2.5%**	**12.0**	**0.7%**

Source: Authors' calculations based on data drawn from the World Bank – World Development Indicators (WDI) – and United Nations Statistics Division (National Accounts Main Aggregates Database http://unstats.un.org/unsd/snaama/dnlList.asp).

Figures 2.2–2.5 show some important macro-policies and outcomes, namely aid flows, public sector deficits, changes in exchange rates and inflation rates.

We see from these figures that a major difference between the SGR and WGR is that aid ballooned in the SGR in the five years following the end of conflict, amounting at one point to as much as 30 per cent of gross national income (GNI), and then it fell back to the level pre-conflict and to the level of the WGR countries. The latter saw no expansion of aid. From this data one can detect no negative impact of aid, either on growth or on the exchange rate. The exchange rate performance of the two groups was similar, with a post-conflict depreciation. Both sets of countries also showed similar performance on public sector deficits (at more than 4 per cent of GNI for the first four years after conflict), but the SGR countries then reduced their deficits rapidly

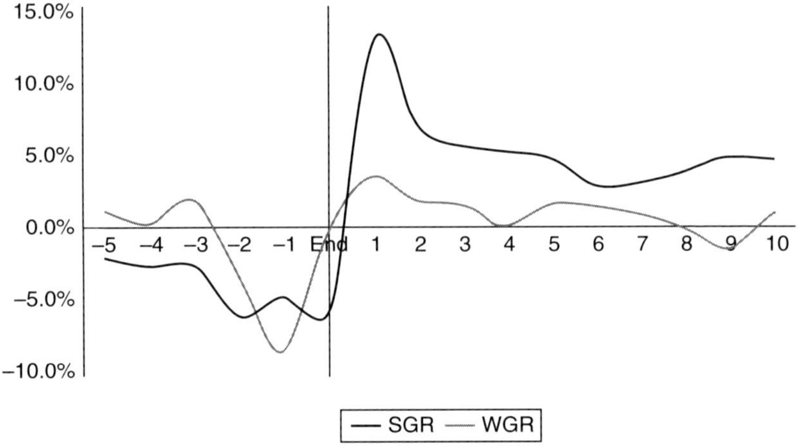

Figure 2.1 Average GDP per capita growth: Strong vs. weak recovery countries
Source: Authors' calculations based on data drawn from the World Bank – World Development Indicators (WDI) – and United Nations Statistics Division (National Accounts Main Aggregates Database http://unstats.un.org/unsd/snaama/dnlList.asp).

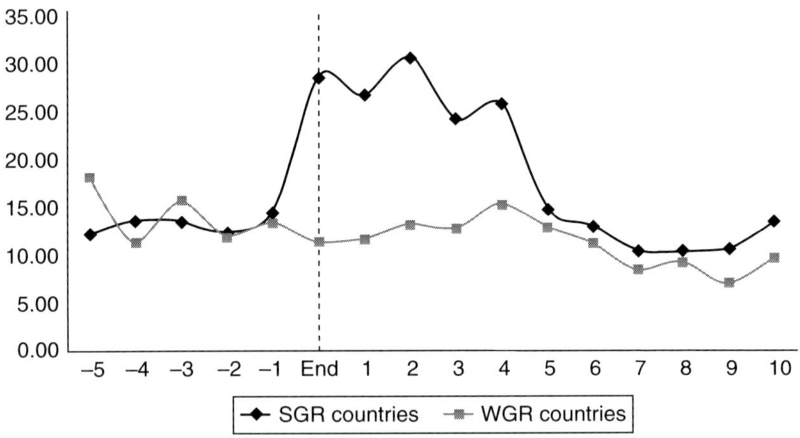

Figure 2.2 Aid flows: SGR vs. WGR countries (% of GNI)
Source: Authors' calculations based on data drawn from the World Bank – World Development Indicators (WDI).

while the WGR countries deficits widened. This evidence thus suggests that improved deficits are the consequence, rather than the cause, of good recovery. As far as inflation is concerned, both sets of countries succeeded in reducing their rate of inflation from very high rates during

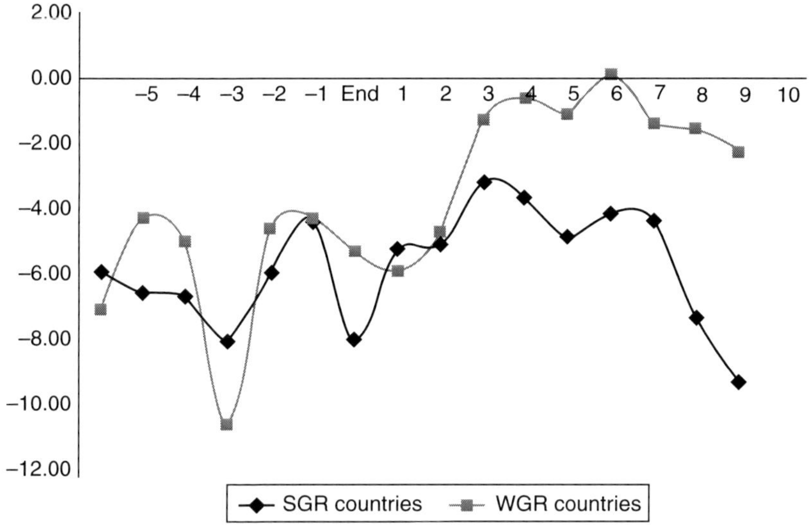

Figure 2.3 Public sector deficits (% of GDP)
Source: Authors' calculations based on data drawn from the UNDP Crisis Prevention and Recovery Report 2008. Appendix M.

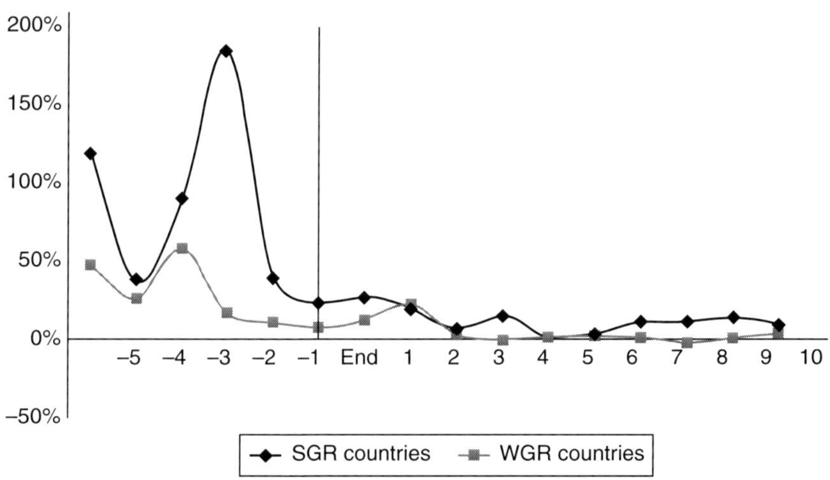

Figure 2.4 Annual changes in the official exchange rate
Source: Authors' calculations based on data drawn from the World Bank – World Development Indicators (WDI).

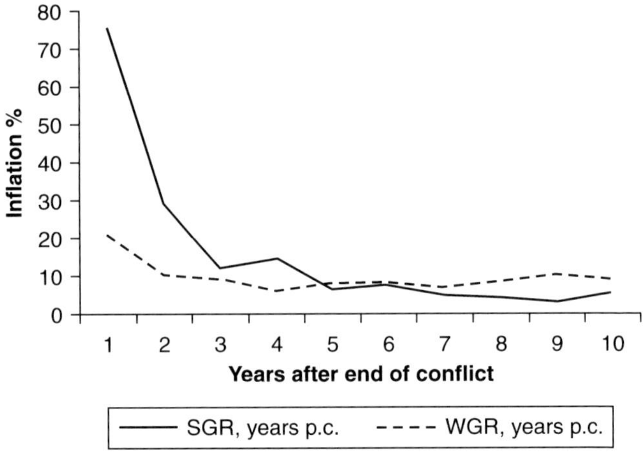

Figure 2.5 Inflation rate in post-conflict years
Source: Authors' calculations based on data drawn from the International Monetary Fund (IMF) – World Economic Outlook Dataset.

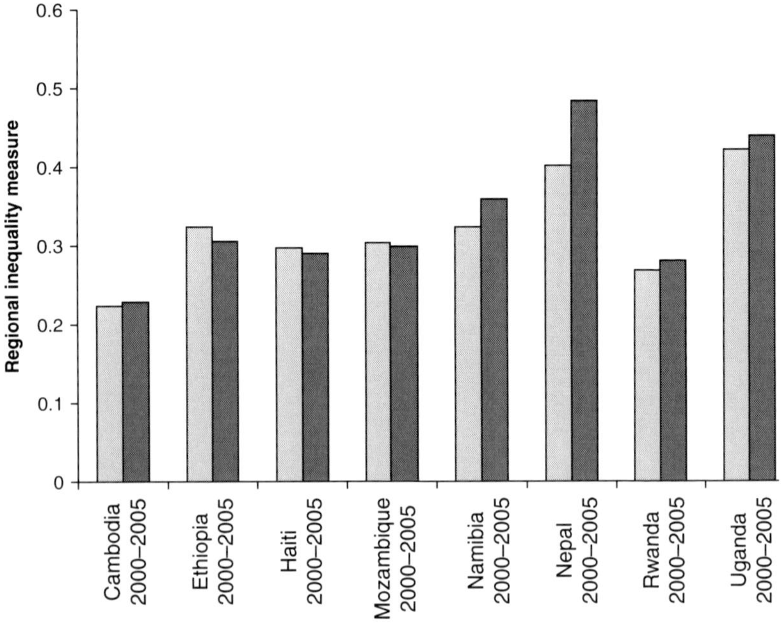

Figure 2.6 Changes in HIs in the post-conflict era
Source: Authors' calculations based on data drawn from the Demographic and Health Surveys (DHS) (available at: http://www.measuredhs.com/).

conflict to 10 per cent or less, although the SGR group was less successful in the very short run; but then it reduced its rates to around 5 per cent on average, while the WGR countries remained at around 10 per cent. During conflict both groups had very high rates of inflation, although with large differences among countries.[5]

We are constrained by limited data in our assessment of changes in HIs over time associated with different patterns of macro-recovery. However, Figure 2.6 shows a measure of regional HIs based on DHS 'wealth' data for some post-conflict countries. There are data for only two 'weak' recovery countries (Haiti and Namibia). It shows no particular relationship between inequality or change in inequality and success in recovery. In most cases there are only small changes over time, apart from Nepal, which shows a sharp deterioration over the conflict years.

2.5 Macro-economic policies and horizontal inequalities in post-1986 Uganda

To explore how macro-policies affected HIs in a particular post-conflict country, we discuss the case of Uganda.

Although at independence in 1962, Uganda had promising economic potential and relatively good health and education services, the first two-and-a-half decades after independence were characterized by political instability, violent rebellions, widespread violence against civilians and a dramatic economic decline. Most observers agree that a fundamental cause of Uganda's political conflicts and instability in this period was competition for power and resources between rival ethnic and religious groups (Kasozi 1999; Klugman et al. 1999a, 1999b; Robinson 2005). Throughout Uganda's post-colonial history, different ethnic groups and regions were victimized, prosecuted and excluded (both politically and economically), depending on the group in control of the state.

However, after the violent removal from power of President Milton Obote, in January 1986, by the National Resistance Army (NRA) led by Yoweri Museveni, Uganda's fortunes changed dramatically for the better. When Museveni and his National Resistance Movement (NRM) assumed power in 1986, Uganda's economy was in dire straits: there was negative economic growth, high inflation, a collapse of tax revenues, heavy debts, a highly overvalued exchange rate, serious shortages of foreign reserves and severe balance of payments problems. The Museveni/NRM regime was not only able to restore peace and stability in many parts of the country, but also achieved an impressive economic turnaround, as demonstrated in Table 2.3.

Uganda's macro-policies after 1987 can be divided into three phases: macro-economic stabilization (1987–1991); deepening of reforms and increased government ownership (1992–1998); and reform consolidation under a poverty reduction umbrella (1999–present) (see Bigsten and Kayizzi-Mugerwa 1999; Robinson 2005). The priorities of the initial programme – called the Economic Recovery Programme (ERP) – were the restoration of macro-economic stability and the promotion of long-term economic growth. In order to achieve these objectives, the ERP introduced strict monetary and fiscal policies, attempted to increase investment in physical assets and infrastructure, sharply devalued the Ugandan shilling and implemented measures to move towards a more market-determined exchange rate (see Bigsten and Kayizzi-Mugerwa 1999; Golooba-Mutebi 2008; Reinikka and Collier 2001; Sharer et al. 1995).

By 1989 Uganda's economy started showing signs of improvement, marked by a sharply reduced inflation rate, a return of positive economic growth and an improved balance of payments (see Table 2.3). However, the improved macro-economic situation and the restoration of economic growth depended to a large extent on the large amounts of foreign aid that Uganda received from international donors. Illustratively, excluding grants, Uganda's current account deficit actually worsened dramatically from 1.8 per cent in 1986/1987 to more than 19 per cent in 1990/1991 (Sharer et al. 1995).

The year 1992 marked the beginning of a new phase in the reform process, which was characterized by increased local ownership and a widening and deepening of the reform programme (Bigsten and Kayizzi-Mugerwa 1999; Kayizzi-Mugerwa 1999; Kreimer et al. 2000; Reinikka and Collier 2001; Robinson 2005). In the second phase (1992–1998), Uganda continued to pursue strict fiscal and monetary policies and completed a number of reforms started in the first phase, including the liberalization of the trade system, the coffee sector and the exchange rate system. Other structural reforms introduced in the second phase included the creation of a semi-autonomous tax body – the Uganda Revenue Authority (URA) – the privatization of a large number of state enterprises, the liberalization of interest rates and the establishment of a Treasury Bill market. The government also started a civil service reform programme. Due to the improved security situation in early 1990s, the government also proceeded with a programme of military demobilization in 1993/1994 (see Colletta et al. 1996).

Table 2.3 Uganda's macro-economic performance (1987–2004)

	1987	1988	1989	1990	1991	1992	1993	1994	1995	1996	1997	1998	1999	2000	2001	2002	2003	2004
Gross domestic product (% change)[1]	4.0	8.3	6.4	6.5	1.8	2.8	8.2	6.4	11.3	9.1	5.5	3.8	8.2	5.4	5.2	8.6	6.6	6.8
GDP per capita (% change)[1]	0.2	4.3	2.5	2.8	−1.7	−0.6	4.8	3.1	7.9	5.9	2.4	0.8	4.9	2.2	1.8	5.0	3.0	3.2
Inflation (%)[1]	215.4	166.7	130.8	45.4	20.8	42.2	30.0	5.9	6.8	7.5	7.7	5.8	0.2	5.8	4.5	−2.0	5.7	5.0
Gross capital formation (% of GDP)[2]	9.7	10.8	11.1	12.7	15.2	15.9	15.2	14.7	12.4	20.2	18.2	16.4	19.5	20.0	18.6	19.3	20.5	22.3
Exports (% of GDP)[2]	8.2	7.6	8.0	7.2	7.5	8.8	7.1	8.7	11.8	12.0	13.4	9.6	12.3	11.2	12.1	11.9	12.4	13.7
Imports (% of GDP)[2]	18.0	17.8	18.1	19.4	21.9	24.3	21.2	19.1	20.8	23.4	20.8	20.4	24.3	23.0	24.3	26.6	26.6	27.6
Current account balance (% of GDP)[1]	−0.9	−1.4	−2.6	−5.9	−11.2	−5.1	−8.7	−0.4	−1.6	−7.0	−4.1	−7.5	−9.4	−6.7	−3.7	−4.6	−5.5	−3.0
Total debt service (% of exports of goods, services and income)[2]	47.9	75.7	67.6	81.4	74.8	59.7	51.5	27.5	19.8	18.2	20.2	20.8	13.8	7.8	4.7	6.1	7.2	7.0
Tax revenue and grants as % GDP[3]											15.8	16.6	17.6	19.1	19.1	19.1	22.2	
Government expenditure and lending % GDP[3]											16.9	19.3	26.7	21.8	24.4	23.4	23.9	

Source: Data drawn from: (1) IMF World Economic Outlook Database and (2) World Bank World Development Indicators (3) IMF 2005.

In the period 1992–1998, Uganda made substantial progress towards macro-economic stability and economic recovery, as illustrated by the relatively low inflation rates, high economic growth rates, smaller current account deficits and higher investment rates (Table 2.3). The reforms also began to have positive supply-side effects, especially in the agricultural sector. According to Dijkstra and Van Donge (2001), the increased export of coffee and cotton was a direct consequence of the liberalization of Uganda's agricultural pricing and marketing systems, as well as of the increase in world coffee prices from 1993/1994.

In the third phase (1999–present), reform consolidation and poverty reduction became the main objectives of Uganda's economic policies (see Robinson 2005; Golooba-Mutebi 2008). The issue of poverty reduction had not been a central feature of the first two phases of adjustment and economic recovery. However, from the mid-1990s on, NGOs and donors increasingly voiced their concerns about the impact of the reforms on the poor and vulnerable groups (Robinson 2005). In recognition of the relatively high levels of poverty and of the domestic and international calls to focus more on vulnerable groups, the government introduced the Poverty Eradication Action Plan (PEAP) in the second half of the 1990s. It is not surprising, in view of the active involvement of the multilateral donor agencies in the design and formulation of the PEAP, that its priorities are consistent with Uganda's reform programme, with an emphasis on cultivating a supply-side response from poor farmers, on improving public services and on promoting investment and economic growth as a means of providing employment (Robinson 2005).

While Uganda's post-1986 economic success is widely recognized, the impact of the country's macro-economic policies and reforms on the prevailing HIs has received much less attention. Before analysing the actual evolution of Uganda's HIs (as approximated by the country's regional inequalities) since 1986, we consider how the main macro-economic policies and structural reforms are likely to have affected Uganda's four regions (Central, Eastern, Western and Northern). Development in these four regions was historically uneven, partly due to differing agro-climatic conditions, partly to colonial policy, and partly to almost continual violent conflict in the North over the past 30 years. The Central region (which includes the capital, Kampala) produces the most lucrative cash crops, such as coffee, and has the most extensive road network and the highest urbanization rate. The Northern region is definitely the least developed in terms of socio-economic indicators, partly due to persistent conflict and partly due to climate, which is primarily suitable for pastoralism and for the cultivation of sorghum. The

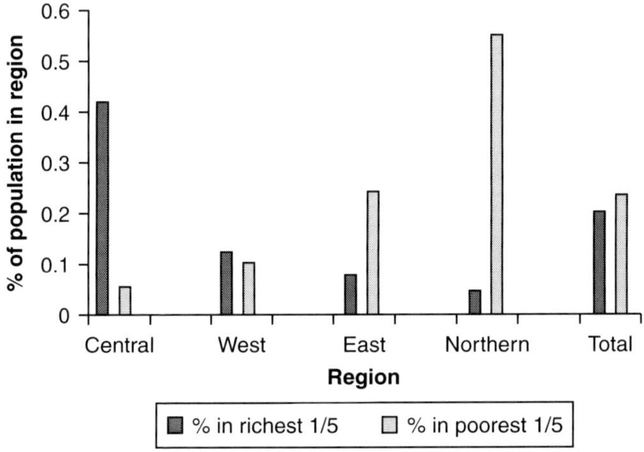

Figure 2.7 Uganda, % of population in richest and poorest quintiles by region (2006)

urbanization rate is very low and the road network is underdeveloped. Most indicators suggest that the Eastern region is poorer than the Western but richer than the Northern region.[6] These differences are illustrated in Figure 2.7, which uses DHS wealth data.

Monetary policy. The main objectives of Uganda's post-1986 monetary policy were to reduce and subsequently contain inflation below 5 per cent and to maintain stability in foreign exchange markets (Bigsten and Kayizzi-Mugerwa 1999; Sharer et al. 1995). Together with stricter fiscal policies, Uganda's monetary policy successfully reduced inflation to about 6 per cent in 1994, and since then inflation has generally been kept below the 5 per cent target. Determining the main beneficiaries of the reduction in inflation is difficult, because the result depends simultaneously on what happens to money incomes as well as to consumer prices. Another complicating factor is that one also needs to take into account the costs of the anti-inflationary measures and their distribution. According to the World Bank, 'inflation essentially taxes all those who participate in the market as buyers of goods and services, and generally distributes the benefits in favour of government' (World Bank 1993: 53). Usually the World Bank further argues that the poor are more negatively affected by inflation than the rich (because they are less able to protect themselves), but there is little evidence that supports this view. Indeed, redistribution in favour of the government as a result of inflation might actually benefit the poor, depending on the policies and priorities of the government. Moreover, those mostly outside the monetary sector – in the subsistence sector – are less affected by inflation, and these people are generally among the poorest.

Bringing inflation down from very high levels (as in Ugandan in the 1980s) to more moderate levels can generally be expected to be beneficial to most people in society (both rich and poor), but it is especially beneficial for fixed income earners in the formal sector. In the Ugandan case, the reduction of inflation after 1986, and especially after 1994, is likely to have had a positive impact on all regions and ethnic groups, because it seems to have facilitated general recovery and growth. The Central region, however, which is where the capital is located, may have benefitted somewhat more because of the positive effects on those on fixed government pensions, and also because this was the centre of economic recovery.

Financial sector reforms. Financial sector reforms were an important aspect of Uganda's structural adjustment programmes. Arguably, the most important reform undertaken was the liberalization of interest rates. Until 1992, all formal financial sector interest rates were set by the Bank of Uganda, after approval by the Ministry of Finance and Economic Planning. By June 1994 most interest rates were market-determined and rose sharply to much higher levels than before (Nachega 2001). Other financial sector reforms aimed at increasing the efficiency of the banking sector and at promoting financial market development included the removal of restrictions on commercial banks' operations and asset holdings, higher capital requirements and the elimination of entry barriers into the banking industry (Nachega 2001).

The impact of the financial sector reforms on the vast majority of Ugandans is likely to have been very limited, since they do not use the banking system. However, for companies and relatively rich individuals who want to invest or save money respectively, a well-functioning financial sector, with positive real interest rates and a sufficient number of solvent and, more importantly, well-performing financial institutions, is helpful. Together with other policies and reforms, such as the introduction of a new Investment Code in 1991, exchange rate liberalization and a strict monetary policy, the financial sector reforms conducted in the 1990s appear to have had a positive impact on local and foreign investment. Most of this investment appears to have gone to Kampala in the Central region. The expansion of the number of financial institutions has also mainly benefitted Kampala.

Exchange rate liberalization. In the period 1987–1994, Uganda introduced a flexible foreign exchange regime. This process started with a sharp devaluation of the Ugandan Shilling of 77 per cent in 1987 and was followed by a series of mini-devaluations through October 1989 (Sharer et al. 1995). By early 1994, the foreign exchange rate was fully market-determined and the government expressed its commitment (as part of IMF's Articles of Agreement) to an open and free payments and exchange system (Sharer et al. 1995).

The distributional impact of a devaluation and/or exchange rate liberalization on different regions and ethnic groups in society depends on different groups' positioning in the economy as well as on a whole range of other economic policies. In Uganda the exchange rate liberalization was complemented by price, market and trade liberalizations, and the country's export sector – both of traditional (coffee, cotton and tea) and non-traditional (flowers, fresh and frozen fish, fresh fruit and vegetables) goods – received a major boost. The regions most actively engaged in the production of these export products – the Central region, the Western region and to a lesser extent the Eastern region – are likely to have benefitted most from these economic reforms.

Trade liberalization. Trade liberalization was one of the most important structural reforms to be initiated after 1987. The nontariff barriers were gradually removed, and in 1995 only a short negative list remained, which was finally lifted in 1999 (Collier and Reinikka 2001). Further, in the early 1990s the structure of trade taxes switched from export taxation to import taxation (Collier and Reinikka 2001). Together with the liberalization of the exchange rate, trade liberalization provided strong incentives for the export-oriented sectors, which are located in the Western, Eastern and especially Central regions. The abolition of QRs permitted the import of luxury consumer goods, which had previously been restricted, and this benefited the richer groups most.

Coffee liberalization. The coffee sector is Uganda's most important export sector. When the NRM regime assumed power in 1986, the coffee sector was dominated by a government-controlled marketing and pricing system. With the support of the World Bank, the coffee sector was drastically reformed in 1991/1992: the Coffee Marketing Board (CMB) lost its export monopoly and was converted into a publicly owned corporation; the Uganda Coffee Development Authority was established and became responsible for regulation and quality issues; commercial banks took over crop financing from the Bank of Uganda (BOU); taxes on coffee exports were abolished and the formation of joint venture companies was made possible (Bigsten and Kayizzi-Mugerwa 1999; Collier and Reinikka 2001).

Coffee producers were hard hit when world coffee prices fell rapidly from 1987. However, at the same time as Uganda liberalized its coffee sector in 1991/1992, world coffee prices started recovering. Due to the increased world coffee prices and to the reform of the coffee sector, the absolute producer price received by Ugandan coffee growers increased sharply after 1992 (Collier and Reinikka 2001). While coffee growers enjoyed good times until the late 1990s, the period 1998–2003 was characterized by relatively low world coffee prices. From 2003 world prices started increasing again. Since the main coffee-growing areas are located in the Central and Western regions and to a lesser extent in the Eastern region, these are the regions that have benefitted most from the recovery of the coffee sector.

Fiscal policies and reforms. On assumption of power, the NRM regime was confronted with a fiscal mess. One estimate suggested that revenue was as low as 2 per cent of GDP in 1991 (Fagernas and Roberts 2004). However, due to significant improvements in the revenue collection system as well as to the economic recovery, from the late 1980s, Uganda's fiscal position improved markedly in the 1990s. The main improvement in revenue collection was the creation of the Uganda Revenue Authority (URA) in 1991, a semi-autonomous body with much better terms of service than the rest of the civil service (Kayizzi-Mugerwa 2002). Revenue as a proportion of GDP rose to 11 per cent in 2001 (Fagernas and Roberts 2004).

There have also been important changes in the sources of government revenue. Arguably, the most significant change was the switch from export to import taxation in the early 1990s. From the mid-1990s import taxation was gradually reduced and a more uniform tariff tax structure was introduced (Collier and Reinikka 2001). Import duties and excise tax on petroleum have been the largest sources of tax revenue since 1991/1992, contributing more than 30 per cent of total revenues (Chen et al. 2001). The second largest source of revenue is sales tax/VAT. In the period 1990–1995, sales tax on goods and services provided about 25 per cent of total revenue. Some goods, which are particularly important for the lowest income earners (such as unprocessed foodstuffs, social services, passenger transport services and fuels), are exempt from VAT. Chen et al. (2001) have shown that Uganda's tax system after the reforms remained progressive in nature, income and import taxes being the two most progressive categories.

The overall impact of the tax reforms on the different regions is difficult to determine, but it appears that: (1) the switch from export to import taxation is likely to have benefitted the three main export regions (Central, Eastern and Western) and was unfavourable to relatively richer people, who are mainly located in Kampala/Central region, and who could afford imported consumer goods; (2) higher income taxes and more diligent collection of these taxes also appear to have mainly affected people in Kampala/Central region, since the vast majority of formal sector workers are based there; (3) the change from sales tax to VAT in 1996 (with a number of exemptions for goods and services that are important to the lowest income earners) slightly benefitted the poor sections of society throughout the country; (4) the reduction of QRs on consumer imports and of import tariffs from the mid-1990s tended to favour the relatively richer people, mainly found in the Central region and (to a lesser extent) in the Western region; and (5) the increase in excise duties, particularly on paraffin, which is heavily consumed by the poor, appears to have had negative impact on most people (especially the poor) throughout the country.

On the expenditure side, it is important to note that a dearth of resources in the late 1980s forced the government to cut its spending drastically in order to reduce the existing budget deficits. From the early 1990s, however, the government's limited domestic revenues were no serious constraint on expenditure, mainly because of the influx of massive amounts of foreign aid (Kayizzi-Mugerwa 1999). But, due to the ongoing security threats in different parts of the country (especially in the north), defence expenditures were given priority over health and education throughout the 1990s (Kayizzi-Mugerwa 1999). It was only after the introduction of PEAP in 1997 that education and health expenditure won the budgetary battle against military expenditure. Although regional expenditure data are not readily available, anecdotal evidence suggest that all regions have benefitted from the spending under the PEAP umbrella. However, due to the difficult implementation environment in the north, this region appears to have benefitted considerably less.

Public sector reforms. Uganda's public sector reforms included a civil service reform programme and an extensive privatization scheme, undertaken in order to improve the government's capacity to deliver public services. The civil service reform programme was aimed at rationalizing and restructuring government ministries, at downsizing the civil service and at moving towards a minimum living wage for civil servants (Robinson 2005). The programme was initiated in 1992 and eliminated 40,000 ghost workers from the government's payroll, reduced the number of temporary employees by 60,000 and laid off another 14,000 civil servants (Sharer et al. 1995). In addition, a voluntary redundancy scheme was introduced. Although a more efficient civil service might have beneficial effects on the delivery of public services in the medium term, in the short term the retrenchment measures are likely to have had a negative impact on most regions, and especially on the Central region, since the main state institutions and most civil servants are based in Kampala.

Another aspect of the public sector reforms was the privatization of parastatal enterprises. In 1992 the government launched a programme of public enterprise reform, which aimed to reduce the financial and administrative burden on public resources of parastatal enterprises by means of divesture and liquidation of specific enterprises (Sharer et al. 1995). By 1999 the government had privatized 62 and liquidated 31 parastatal enterprises in the industrial, commercial, agricultural and hotel sectors (Collier and Reinikka 2001). In most cases privatization is estimated to have had positive effects on the running of the enterprise involved, with increased output and efficiency, higher tax payments, significant new investment and some job creation (Collier and Reinikka 2001). While the privatization and liquidation measures initially appear to have had a negative impact on incomes and benefits – again, especially in the Central region – in the long term the increased efficiency, higher investment and employment creation were quite positive. The distributional impact of privatization also depends on who receives the shares in the privatized industries and at what price. In the case of Uganda it seems likely that people from richer groups and from those groups close to the government (that is, people from the centre and southwest) benefitted most, raising HIs.

Although they are not strictly macro-economic policies, in this section of the chapter, we will also consider policies introduced to offset some of the adverse effects of macro-economic policies as part of the macro-policy package. In Uganda, these policies included the Programme to Alleviate Poverty and the Social Costs of Adjustment (PAPSCA), the PEAP and the Northern rehabilitation programmes.

The Programme to Alleviate Poverty and the Social Costs of Adjustment. The PAPSCA was initiated in the late 1980s, with the support of the World Bank. It was aimed at improving the basic social infrastructure of the most vulnerable groups. However, due to the small scale of the PAPSCA, its positive impact was, at best, rather moderate. The Northern region is likely to have benefited the least because of the ongoing fighting between the government and the northern rebel groups at the time and the fact that it was primarily an urban programme.

The Poverty Eradication Action Plan. The PEAP was introduced in 1997 in order to translate the growth into poverty reduction (Okidi et al. 2003). Key elements included a programme for agricultural modernization, universal primary education and primary health care, improving the road network and private sector promotion (Robinson 2005). By increasing the resources allocated to social and agricultural sectors and by safeguarding them from budget cuts from 1997, the PEAP contributed positively to the socio-economic situation throughout the country. However, due to the precarious security situation in the North, again this region is likely to have benefited considerably less than others from this increase in social spending.

Northern rehabilitation programmes. In 1992 the government initiated the Northern Uganda Reconstruction Project (NURP), with strong support from international donors. The NURP (1992–1997) was a regionally targeted, multi-sectoral project (Kreimer et al. 2000; Republic of Uganda 2003). However, the positive impact of the NURP on the situation in the Northern region is likely to have been rather limited, because the re-escalation of violence from mid-1990s seriously hampered its implementation (Kreimer et al. 2000: 56). In the late 1990s, the NURP was followed up with NURP II. Yet – again – the scale of the NURP II project was too limited to have a major impact on the Northern region as a whole.

International aid and the presence of donors. Uganda has benefitted from generous amounts of foreign aid since it embarked on its ambitious reform programme in 1987. Illustratively, between 1987 and 1991, Official Development Assistance (ODA) increased from 4 per cent to 28 per cent of GDP (Fagernas and Roberts 2004). The share of development expenditure funded from foreign sources increased from 56 per cent in 1987 to 92 per cent in 1993 (Fagernas and Roberts 2004). While during the initial reform period most foreign aid was provided by multilateral donor agencies, in the 1990s bilateral grant aid became the dominant source of external finance (Collier and Reinikka 2001). Foreign aid has been argued to have had an important impact on Uganda's growth performance and thereby to have contributed substantially to the reduction of poverty as well (see Appleton 2001). The presence of a large donor community from the late 1980s is itself likely to have had a positive impact (for example, through increased expenditure and employment creation) on the Central region, especially Kampala. Assessing the impact of international aid flows on the HI situation is extremely difficult, because one cannot differentiate the aid on HIs from that of government expenditure as a whole.

Table 2.4 summarizes the likely impact of the main economic policies and reforms on Uganda's four regions. Considering the multiplicity and interdependence of factors influencing the distributional impact of a particular economic policy and reform, as well as the relatively long period under review, the conclusions clearly remain tentative. Overall it appears that, while the reforms often had some clear negative effects

Table 2.4 Regional impact of the main economic policies and reforms (1986–2004)

Policies and reforms	Central region	Western region	Eastern region	Northern region
Monetary policy				
Reduction of inflation	++	+	+	+
Financial sector reforms				
Liberalization of interest rates	(+)			
Better functioning banking sector	(+)			
Exchange rate and trade liberalization	+	+	+	(+)
Public expenditure (1987–1997)				
Social (education and health)	First (−) then +	First (−) then +	First (−) then +	First (−) then (+)
Infrastructure	++	+	+	(+)
Military (including demobilization)	+	+	(+)	(+) (indirectly)
Changes in tax structure	−/+ (?)	−/+ (?)	−/+ (?)	−/+ (?)
Coffee liberalization	++	++	+	
Price changes:				
Food prices	−/+ (?)	−/+ (?)−	−/+ (?)−	−/+ (?)−
Manufactures	−	(−)	(−)	
Gasoline/paraffin	−	−	−	−
Hospital	−	−	(−)	(−)
Education	−	−	(−)	(−)
Public sector reforms				
Civil service reform	First – then (+) (?)	First (−) then (+) (?)	First (−) then (+) (?)	First (−) then (+) (?)
Privatization	First (−) then (+) (?)	First (−) then (+) (?)	First (−) then (+) (?)	
the creation of URA	(+)			

PEAP/PAF (1997–present)				
Education	+	+	+	(+)
Health	+	+	+	(+)
infrastructure	+	+	+	(+)
Agricultural modernization	(+)	(+)	(+)	
PAPSCA	(+)	(+)	(+)	
Northern rehabilitation programmes (NURP I & II)				(+)
Presence of international donor community	++			

Note: The symbols in this table express the nature of the effects of adjustment as negative and positive. The symbols are doubled where the effects have been relatively strong; they are put within brackets where they have been relatively weak. Blanks indicate that there have been no or negligible effects.

in the short term (for instance, reduced social expenditure and higher prices), in the long run the aggregate national benefits of the economic policies as a whole appeared to have outweighed these initial costs. However, although all four regions appear to have benefitted from the post-1986 economic policies and recovery, the Northern region benefitted by much less; and this was due to a considerable extent to the persistence of the precarious security situation, which greatly hampered the delivery of services and policy implementation. However, this is not the only factor, as the cash crops that the reforms favoured were not in the North. While the people in Kampala/Central region were hardest hit with respect to some policies, they also benefitted from a range of other policies, and from the economic recovery more generally, much more than people in other regions did.

Table 2.5, showing the evolution of poverty across different regions and professional groups, supports the previous conclusion. All four regions showed a decline in the incidence of poverty from 1992/1993 to 2002/2003. However, the Central region, which started with the lowest rate of poverty, benefitted the most, both in terms of absolute percentage reduction in poverty and in terms of proportionate reduction. The Central region was followed by the Western region, the other main coffee-exporting region, while the Eastern region was in third place. While the poverty situation in the Northern region also improved in the 1990s, both in terms of absolute percentage reduction and in relative terms the poverty reduction in the North was much lower than in the other regions. Regional HIs thus increased over this period.

Table 2.5 Regional and sectoral distribution of poverty (1992–2003)

	1992/ 1993	1997	1999/ 2000	2002/ 2003	Change 1992/1993–1999/2000	Change 1992/1993–2002/2003
National	55.7	45.0	33.8	37.7	21.9	18.0
Rural	59.7	49.2	37.4	41.7	22.3	18.0
Urban	27.8	16.7	9.6	12.2	18.2	15.6
Central	45.6	27.9	19.7	22.3	25.9	23.3
Eastern	58.8	54.3	35.0	46.0	23.8	12.8
Northern	72.2	60.9	63.6	63.3	8.6	8.9
Western	53.1	42.8	26.2	31.4	26.9	21.7

Source: Okidi et al. (2005: 5).

2.6 Some conclusions

The main objectives of contemporary macro-policies in post-conflict countries are to facilitate economic recovery, supporting sustained growth while avoiding excessive budget deficits and unacceptably high or accelerating inflation. If successful, and sustained growth ensues, this is also likely to contribute to sustaining peace. But it is also important to consider how these policies affect HIs, since high HIs make any peace potentially fragile, even in a context of economic growth. The aim of this chapter has been therefore to explore how the macro-policies commonly adopted affecrt HIs.

As we can see from Table 2.6, which summarizes the expected impact on group distribution of the most important macro-policies, the effects are ambiguous, depending not so much on the broad policy as on the design of each policy, on the complementary policies adopted, on the nature of the economy and on the ways in which particular groups are inserted into the economy. For example:

- Reducing budget deficits may be achieved by some combination of tax rises and/or expenditure reductions. In general, the higher the reliance is on tax rises and the lower on expenditure reduction, the more likely the package is to reduce HIs.
- But this depends on the nature of the tax rises, which may be progressive or regressive; and, similarly, on the nature of any expenditure cuts, which may be directed at expenditures that do not benefit poor groups much (like military expenditure), or at expenditure

on primary education, from which poorer groups are likely to benefit.

- Greater emphasis on switching policies (for instance, exchange rate changes) and less on deflationary policies to achieve improvements in the balance of trade is likely to have a more positive impact on employment, and probably on poorer groups, than a policy that puts the main emphasis on deflationary policies. The amount of external resources available, usually primarily aid, influence the extent of deflation required. It is notable that the brief review of macro-policies comparing strong and weak recovery countries showed that the big difference between strong recovery countries and weak ones was a large inflow of aid in the four or five years immediately following the end of conflict.
- The impact, on HIs, of switching policies must also be considered. For economies reliant on manufactured exports, switching policies are likely to favour more skilled workers; however, this effect might be offset by special training schemes for poorer groups and by affirmative action. For economies that are reliant on cash crop exports, devaluation is likely to favour richer groups, which are mostly responsible for the bulk of cash crop exports, as in Uganda – unless new cash crop opportunities can be identified (like cut flowers) that can be produced in poorer regions. In economies that export minerals, the distributional benefits of additional income to the sector depend largely on how the government decides to use the revenues received. Moreover, differential exchange rates may be used to help particular groups. And dismantling of import protection together with tariff reform can be designed in ways that impose the greatest burden on richer groups. However, this is generally not a consideration, and reduced tariffs often permit imports of luxury goods at low prices.
- Complementary policies can help improve the macro-policies contribution to reducing HIs. In particular, education and training of the poorer groups will enable them to exploit the opportunities offered by a more open trading regime. Similarly, anti-discriminatory employment policies will make it easier for people from poorer groups to participate in the gains from international trade. Moreover, compensatory policies can be introduced in order to offset some adverse effects. Again, such complementary or compensatory policies do not normally form part of the adjustment policy packages. Indeed, in the efficiency promoting part of the reform package, formal direct affirmative action can come under attack.

Table 2.6 Expected impact of macro-policy changes on HIs

Type of exports of economy	**Primary product agricultural products**	**Labour-intensive industrial products**	**Capital or skill intensive industrial products**	**Minerals (for example oil)**
Switching policies	Worsen HIs	Depends on labour force skills, complementary policies; may worsen regional HIs	Probably worsen HIs	Worsen HIs
Reduced import-substituting protection	Improve HIs			
Tax rises	Improve HIs, but depends on design			
Expenditure rises	Depends on design			
Aid inflows	Depends on design			
Monetary policies	Low interest rates likely to worsen HIs (mildly) Inflation may improve HIs.			
Capital market	Generous incentives to attract back capital flight may worsen HIs			

However, despite the possibility of designing macro-policies together with complementary policies in a way that improves HIs, there are five reasons why we find that they are mostly likely to favour richer groups in relation to the poor, and consequently to widen HIs:

- First, improved prices for, and expansion of, exports favour the groups most involved in exports; and these tend to be the richer groups.
- Secondly, as production expands for domestic consumption as well as exports, groups who already have more education and market experience are likely to benefit most. There tend to be cumulative cycles of economic growth, often geographically located, which essentially means that better of regions/groups are favoured relative to poorer ones.

- Thirdly, in many cases, these cumulative forces are further supported by the distribution of public expenditure (and often aid), partly because disbursements are controlled by the dominant (and usually richer) group.
- Fourthly, national targets, like the MDGs, can encourage a focus on richer areas/groups because it is often easier to reach people in these groups (say, people near to the capital city instead of those in remote and poorer areas).
- Finally, the continued economic and social stagnation of poorer areas/groups relative to richer areas/groups on account of these factors may lead either to violent conflict against the government or to internal disputes, and these in turn make the situation of the deprived areas even worse, in a vicious cycle.

We saw each of these factors operating in the case of Uganda, where expansion of the economy generally and of exports in particular favoured the (richest) Central region, while the (poorest) Northern region did worst. Conflict against the central government occurred in the North and continued, in a low-level sporadic way, for decades, further harming the Northern economy and its ability to attract private investment, and also constraining the implementation of public programmes.

The tendency for HIs to worsen rather than improve as a result of post-conflict macro-policies should not be taken as inevitable and unavoidable, however, but rather as a reason for vigorous efforts to correct this tendency, through the distribution of aid and public expenditure research, by identifying alternative economic activities for poorer regions and groups, focussing on education and training for such regions/groups and elements of affirmative action.

Notes

1. The evidence for many of these statements about the economic situation of countries coming out of conflict is in Stewart et al. (2001), Collier (2004), Abadie and Gardeazabal (2001), and Boyce (2007).
2. Stewart et al. (2009) elaborate on the distributional consequences of fiscal policies.
3. This is a simplified way of measuring HIs; we might use a measure that also incorporates some weighting for different parts of the income distribution of the two groups (see, Mancini et al. 2008).
4. This section of the chapter owes a lot to the ideas and methodology of Darryl McLeod, which were developed for UNDP (2008).

5. The average rate of inflation among the SGR countries in the six years before and including the year when the conflict ended was 183 per cent; among the WGR it was 510 per cent, but in the former case very high rates in Congo and Tajikstan were largely responsible, while in the latter it was hyperinflation in Nicaragua.
6. Descriptions of regions are based on Appleton (2001); Fan et al. (2004); and World Bank (1993).

3

Employment Policies and Horizontal Inequalities in Post-Conflict Situations

Frances Stewart

3.1 Introduction

Most accounts of the underlying socio-economic causes of conflict concur that a deficiency of employment opportunities, especially for young men, raises the risk of conflict (e.g. Keen 1998; Urdal 2006).[1] Consequently a deficiency in employment opportunities represents a risk factor in post-conflict situations. However, it is not just a question of the total *level* of employment, but also of how it is *distributed across groups* (or of *employment horizontal inequalities*) which may affect the likelihood of conflict recurrence, since employment, and in particular public sector employment, is a particularly visible indicator of HIs. This chapter, therefore, considers what sort of employment policies should be adopted in a post-conflict setting with the aim of reducing the likelihood of conflict recurrence, taking into account both total employment in relation to the size of the labour force and the way it is distributed across groups.

The chapter reviews actual employment policies in a range of post-conflict countries and concludes that, while mainstream policies increasingly acknowledge the importance of generating employment, the policies adopted are too focussed on improving the conditions in the labour market (often known as 'supply-side conditions'), for example through training, and insufficiently focussed on increasing the 'demand side' by increasing the demand for labour directly, via public employment schemes, or indirectly, through the expansion of monetary demand in the economy (with consequent increase in demand for labour). The supply-side measures have had very limited effects on total employment in relation to the size of the problem. Moreover, the issue of HI in employment has been mostly ignored.

The chapter is organized as follows: Section 3.2 considers what theories of conflict causation have to say on employment as a fundamental cause. This is followed by a brief discussion of what sort of employment is likely to meet the requirements suggested by these theories, and by some data on the nature of employment prevalent in some post-conflict economies (Section 3.3). We then explore how the employment issue is dealt with in the donors' post-conflict literature generally and in the actual policies adopted in five cases – Sierra Leone, Uganda, Kosovo, Nepal and Bosnia-Herzegovina (Section 3.4). Section 3.5 makes some recommendations about employment policies in post-conflict settings. Conclusions are presented in Section 3.6.

3.2 The root causes of conflict: The role of employment

Three prominent explanations that have dominated recent analysis of the underlying causes of conflict point to the employment situation as one important element: these explanations include, first, theories pointing to group motives and group inequalities as a source of conflict, where the distribution of employment among groups becomes relevant; secondly, theories that focus on individual gains from conflict, where the lack of alternative employment opportunities makes the economic gains from fighting appear relatively attractive; and, thirdly, accounts of conflict pointing to the 'youth bulge' as the fundamental cause of conflict, where it is not just the bulge itself but, again, the lack of opportunities for the young that is important.

Group motivation

Significant differences in access to economic or political resources across groups provide both leaders and followers with a strong motive to fight, and consequently increase the potential ethnic or religious mobilization. Such differences have been defined as 'horizontal inequalities' – HIs (Stewart 2001, 2008).

The relevant HIs are those that matter to people, and this varies across societies. But in many countries inequality in access to formal sector (and especially public sector) jobs forms an important HI. Thus surveys conducted by the Centre for Research on Human Security, Inequality and Ethnicity (CRISE) across seven countries found that access to public sector employment was regarded as the most pervasive source of ethnic inequality in seven out of eight countries; it was also regarded as an important factor in private sector employment in most countries, but less so than in public sector employment (Figure 3.1).

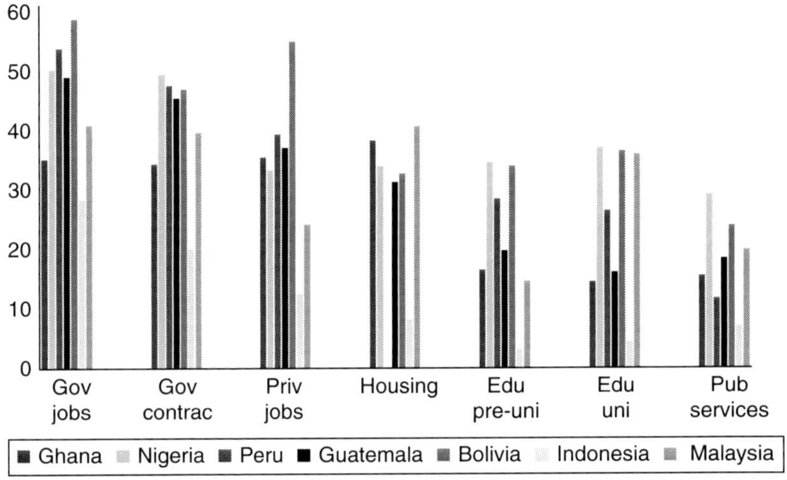

Figure 3.1 Where ethnicity counts
Source: CRISE surveys.

Private motivation

People who fight are, of course, individuals with their own personal motivation, as well as being members of a group. Political sociologists, such as Keen (1998) and Duffield (1994), and economists, such as Collier and Hoeffler (2004), have emphasized individual motivation as the fundamental cause of conflict.

Alternative opportunities for employment and enrichment are among the many ways that war can confer individual benefit on particular categories of people (Keen 1998): it permits uneducated young men to gain employment as soldiers; it offers opportunities to loot, to profiteer from shortages and from aid; to trade arms; and to carry out illicit production and trade. Where alternative opportunities are few because of low incomes and poor employment, and the possibilities of enrichment by war considerable, wars are likely to be more numerous and longer. Indeed, the young from whom the rebels in Niger are drawn actually call themselves the 'ishumar' (a word derived from the French word for unemployment).[2]

The 'youth bulge'

Some have argued that conflict incidence is higher, the higher the proportion of young people (15–24) in the population (Goldstone 1991). According to (Urdal 2006), 'in countries where youth make up

35 per cent of the total adult population, the risk of conflict, with all other factors being equal, increases by 150 per cent compared to countries where youth make up only 17 per cent of the adult population' (Urdal 2006: 617). However, it is not having a lot of young people as such, but having a lot of young people with little to do, that raises the risk of violence. Once again, the quantity and quality of employment becomes a critical issue. A United States Agency for International Development (USAID) document concludes:

> Although a large pool of young people is not inherently destabilizing, there is a strong correlation between large youth cohorts and political violence. When young people – particularly young men – are uprooted, jobless, intolerant, alienated, and have few positive opportunities for positive engagement, they represent a ready pool of recruits for groups seeming to mobilize violence. (USAID 2005)

Two strong conclusions emerge for employment policies in a post-conflict situation. First, such policies need to take into account, and where necessary address, HIs in the distribution of employment opportunities, especially public sector employment. Second, a deficiency in income earning opportunities for young people creates a high-risk situation, so that there must be concern with the total amount of employment as well as with its distribution. Employment opportunities are likely to be particular deficient after a conflict because, in most cases, war reduces the size of the formal sector and of income-earning opportunities generally, while demobilization and returned refugees add to the supply of labour (Stewart 2001).

3.3 The type of employment

So far the concept of 'employment' has been taken as unproblematic. In fact there are many types of employment and, as Sen has pointed out, three different types of benefit arise from employment: providing incomes for those employed; providing recognition for those employed; and generating production for society (Sen 1975). All three are important in a post-conflict setting: the first two – incomes and recognition – contribute to conflict prevention; and the third – production – contributes to economic recovery. However, employment does not always deliver on these three aspects: thus, very low paid work may offer little in the way of incomes; certain occupations attract disrespect rather than recognition (as some lower caste activities in India do); and it is perfectly possible to be employed but not to produce anything.

In the post-conflict context, then, it is thus not a matter of *any* employment, but of employment that offers adequate incomes and recognition. The ILO has defined the sort of work needed as 'decent work': 'defined as being productive work for women and men in conditions of freedom, equity, security and human dignity' (ILO Key Indicators of the Labour Market: Chapter 1, p. 1).

Some types of employment contribute to the objective of creating decent work, while others do not. At one end of the spectrum, full-time formal sector employment generally offers both recognition and adequate incomes. Yet, for most post-conflict countries, the size of the formal sector is very small in relation to the total labour force. The openly unemployed and seeking work form another category – typically not a very big one in situations where there is no unemployment insurance and people have to rely on savings or family to support them while job-seeking. The rest of the labour force is generally involved in informal sector activities of various kinds, both in agriculture and in non-agriculture, consisting of both self-employment and employment for varying hours per week. Within the informal sector, where the vast mass of any labour force is normally located in low-income economies, there are large variations in incomes and recognition.

Given the need to provide adequate recognition and incomes in post-conflict situations, relevant employment encompasses jobs in the formal sector and in the 'modernising'[3] part of the informal sector, that is, opportunities *offering adequate incomes* (broadly defined as 'income above the poverty line'[4]).

Before reviewing actual policies, it is helpful to review the starting position of post-conflict countries. On the one hand, it can be assumed that all post-conflict countries face a problem of deficient employment opportunities, especially for the young, particularly in view of the additions to the labour force formed by the demobilized and the returnees; and it is also likely that there are HIs in employment. On the other hand, there is considerable variation in the composition of existing employment (Table 3.1). The limited data show that agriculture is of overwhelming importance in the low-income countries. There are large variations in the unemployment rate, with very low rates in the poorest countries (Uganda, Nepal and Cambodia), where most people can't afford to be unemployed, and a very high rate (almost half the labour force) in Kosovo. Clearly, the initial employment situation conditions what policies are appropriate.

Table 3.1 Composition of employment in some post-conflict countries, % of total employment

Country	Year	Regular wage employment	Agriculture	Open u/e 2003, as % of active labour force
El Salvador	2003	29.9	19	6.9
Guatemala	2002	–	39	2.7
Nicaragua	2002	16.8	31	10.3
Cambodia	2001	–	70	1.8 (2001)
Ethiopia	1999	–	93	–
Kosovo	2004	–	–	39.7
Namibia	2000	–	31	30.8 (2001)
Nepal	2003	–	79	1.2 (1999)
Rwanda	1996	–	90	–
Sri Lanka	2003	11.7	34	8.8
Uganda	2003	–	69	0.9

Source: Ghose et al. (2008); UNDP (2010), Kosovo Human Development Report (2010).

3.4 Post-conflict employment policies

The discourse

Analysis of the statements international documents make about employment shows that the need to create employment in post-conflict situations is widely accepted; but there is little attention to the question of HIs in employment.

According to an ILO Report, as early as the 1919 Treaty of Versailles, 'it was acknowledged that employment creation was critical for building sustainable peace' (ILO 1999: 15, quoted in Date-Bah 2003: 2). This view is echoed in recent UN reports. For example: 'In a post-crisis situation, employment is vital to short-term stability, reintegration, economic growth and sustainable peace' (UN-System-wide Paper 2009, para 1).

However, employment does not feature in the World Bank's 2003 Comprehensive Development Framework for Conflict-Affected Countries (World Bank 2003a), nor in many other World Bank documents. Nonetheless, as the case studies below endorse, it is fair to say that there is general acceptance that employment should be promoted in a post-conflict context.

In contrast, very little attention has been paid to the issue of HIs. For the most part this question is ignored altogether, although occasionally there is mention of the need to be inclusive: for example, Date-Bah (2003) notes: 'In the post-conflict context, the labour market should function to maximise not only labour absorption but also reintegration and social inclusion' (p. 19). And the UN System-wide Paper points to the need to 'provide resource allocation and employment opportunities without discrimination' (para. 13), noting that '[e]thnic, religious and regional tensions can be aggravated if UN programs appear to favour one group or region' (para. 17).

While these comments are in the direction of support for correcting HIs, they are insufficient for several reasons: first, because countering overt discrimination is a necessary, but not sufficient condition for correcting HIs in employment; secondly, making sure that UN programmes don't aggravate inequalities is likewise probably necessary, but certainly not sufficient if there are severe employment HIs system-wide; thirdly, promoting opportunities for previously excluded ethnic groups is clearly desirable and would reduce HIs, but it is undefined in terms of quantity and quality of the opportunities in question.

Post-conflict employment policies in practice

To assess policies adopted in practice, we review five post-conflict cases from the perspective of employment – Sierra Leone, Kosovo, Uganda, Nepal and Bosnia-Herzegovina – covering a spectrum of cases, geographically and regionally, in terms of the level of development and of the nature of the conflicts experienced.

Sierra Leone

Sierra Leone suffered a bitter conflict from 1991 to 2002; around 50–70,000 people were killed and 2 million people displaced. Among many factors believed to account for the conflict, lack of employment and security among young males has been argued to be a major element (Keen 2005; PAC 2000; Reno 2000; Riddell 2005). Significant HIs between the North and Mende in the South, and the local population and the returned liberated slaves (crio) may also have played a role.

Deficient employment opportunities are widely regarded as a major threat to stability in the post-conflict period. For example, an International Crisis Group report noted that 'an ever-growing army of unemployed, socially alienated youth is a perennial threat to security' (ICG 2008), while the All People's Congress (APC) election manifesto called youth unemployment a 'time bomb' (ICG 2008: 5). In 2006, the government developed a National Action Plan for Youth, with the aim of providing employment opportunities in both the short and the medium terms (UNOWA 2007).

About 35 per cent of the population is aged between 15 and 35. Although the national unemployment rate is not very high, the urban unemployment rate is 17 per cent among the 15–19-year-olds; and many more are not in the labour force, being discouraged by low employment rates. For example, for the age-group 20–24, one in three urban youth are not in the labour force. In general, opportunities for young people are worse than for older workers, in terms of employment, wages and so on (Peeters et al. 2009).

The World Bank (WB) country assistance strategy has supported employment promotion through a general improvement in the investment climate and in access to finance for the private sector, and has increased infrastructural investment and growth in the agriculture and mining sectors; while successive Poverty Reduction Strategy Papers (PRSPs) have put increasing emphasis on employment (World Bank 2007b). Policies recommended to achieve employment growth are primarily 'continued implementation of sound economic policies to attain macro-economic stability and for private sector development' (World Bank 2007b: 75).

> Specific strategies for youth development will include the following: a) setting up a framework for effective youth development and employment policy formulation and implementation involving all stakeholders and the youth themselves at district and national levels; b) capacity-building and training for unskilled or semi-skilled and unemployed youth, including former demobilised combatants, in the informal sector system and linking them to job opportunities in the private and public sectors in urban and rural areas, c) promoting the structures for effective social integration of young men and women into mainstream society and d) sports development for social cohesion, cultural solidarity, healthy living and above all, as a source of employment and livelihood. (World Bank 2007b: para 370, p. 103).

The few systematic evaluations of employment-promoting schemes show that the policies have had only limited impact (Peeters et al. 2009: 97–98). A number of studies have questioned the success of the

Demobilization, Development and Reconstruction (DDR) scheme (reintegrating ex-combatants). For example, a follow-up survey of the Youth Reintegration Training and Education for Peace Program, which provided 55,000 young people with advice and training, found that many failed to find jobs and their skills soon evaporated, while there was lack of financial support for entrepreneurial initiatives (Hansen et al. 2002). Another study found that employment of ex-combatants was frequently not sustained (Simon 2003). Nonetheless, the schemes do seem to have been successful in securing demobilization. Similarly, '[a] recent survey suggests that many of the basic education and vocational training programs implemented by donors and international agencies resulted in few direct and visible impacts on employment of young people' (Peeters et al. 2009: 99, drawn from UNOWA 2007b).

The most common weaknesses identified were the supply-driven nature of most schemes, the variable quality of training and the poor targeting of participants (Peeters et al. 2009: 100). Focus group discussions 'confirmed that in many communities, young people cannot use their recently acquired skills as a result of limited demand' (Peeters et al. 2009: 100). The most promising projects schemes evaluated were public works and public service employment (Peeters et al. 2009: 101).

In summary, while there is widespread recognition of the importance of the issue, actual policies have been largely limited to supply-side interventions, most of them promoting training. As a review notes:

> Many programs designed to promote the employment and skill development of young people suffer from a mismatch between the skills these programs develop and the demands of the labor market. The result is limited success in easing the transition to the labor market and saturation in a few skill-specific markets. (Peeters et al. 2009: 57)

The need to include considerations of HIs in the generation of employment has not been acknowledged.

Uganda

Since its independence in 1962, Uganda has had a turbulent political history, with a series of violent insurgencies and conflicts. From 1986, however, most of the country has been at peace following the victory of the National Resistance Army, led by Yoheri Museveni in 1986, after five years of civil war. But violence continued in the northern part of the country with the rebellion of the Lord's Resistance Army (LRA).

Immediately after Museveni took power, the economy was in complete disarray (Matovu and Stewart 2001). Among other things, 'unemployment is so high that it is not even counted and many factories are closed' (Warnock and Conway 1999: 1). The employment challenge was made more acute by the rapid growth in population, and consequently in the size of the labour force. The current population growth rate is 3.3 per cent per annum (one of the highest in the world), and on average 300,000 young people enter the labour market each year.

Yet none of the recovery programmes of the 1980s or early 1990s specifically mentioned employment (World Bank 1987, 1990, 1991). Nonetheless, although Uganda's economic recovery programme did not include specific employment-creation schemes, the employment situation was helped by the programme's focus on the rehabilitation of the agricultural sector, which employs the largest number of people (about 80 per cent in 1990). Moreover, there was strong recovery in economic growth – with GDP and GDP per capita growing on average by respectively 7 per cent and 3.5 per cent per year between 1988 and 1995. This is likely to have generated a resurgence in productive work, though there is a lack of data on employment trends (Sharer et al. 1995).

In the short term, following the ending of the Obote/Museveni war, employment was sustained by the maintenance of a very large army (opposed by the international donors), which incorporated elements from opposing forces.[5] One reason why substantial demobilization was delayed until 1993 was 'fears that soldiers would be more of a problem once demobilized than while on the payroll' (Kreimer et al. 2000: 59). A similar logic was behind the reabsorption of elements from opposing armies into the new national army (Mudoola 1991). The National Resistance Army (NRA) was further expanded by general recruitment throughout the country, from all regions and ethnic groups.

Significant demobilization began in 1993, with the active support of the World Bank, USAID and DFID, as the general security situation improved. Programmes were adopted to 'assist demobilised soldiers to re-settle and become economically productive members of their communities' (USAID 1994: 4). Projects included agricultural credit and training. The demobilized soldiers are believed to have been successfully reintegrated into smallholder farming activities and kin-group support systems (Kreimer et al. 2000).

From 1992, there was also a significant negative impact on employment through the downsizing of the civil service as part of a public sector reform programme. The programme, supported by the World Bank, eliminated 40,000 'ghost' workers from the government's payroll, reduced the number of temporary employees by 60,000 and laid off another 14,000 civil servants (Sharer et al. 1995). In addition, a voluntary redundancy scheme was introduced. By March 1995, the civil service had been reduced to less than 150,000, which constituted a 50 per cent reduction compared with 1992 levels (Bigsten and Kayizzi-Mugerwa 1999). It is noteworthy that this programme was not introduced immediately after the war of the 1980s ended, but six years later.

More attention to employment began with the PRSP of 2000 (Uganda Ministry of Finance Planning and Economic Development 2000), which recognized that '[e]conomic growth and employment-generation are necessary conditions for poverty eradication' (Uganda Ministry of Finance Planning and Economic Development 2000: 14). The main focus was on agriculture, but the Report noted that 'employment outside agriculture can be promoted by microfinance, advisory services, and vocational training' (Ibid.: 16). However, subsequent progress reports (of 2003, 2005 and 2007) do not mention employment explicitly.

While overall unemployment is relatively low (at about 3.2 per cent in 2003), youth employment remains high – at 22.3 per cent in 2003, and higher in the capital (32.2 per cent).[6] President Museveni has said that Uganda needs to create 6 million jobs from 2007–2011 to absorb all the youth seeking work. In a country with a history of violent rebellion and a number of salient ethnic identities that often overlap with socio-economic and political exclusion and inequalities (i.e., with HIs), the high level of youth unemployment clearly constitutes a dangerous situation.

The Ugandan situation points to the importance of macro-economic trends for productive work opportunities. It also indicates that public sector downsizing and military demobilization can be a potent source of employment reduction. Therefore the adopting and timing of such polices need to be treated cautiously in a post-conflict situation.

Kosovo

The Kosovan conflict started in 1998, with the armed resistance of Kosovar Albanians, who wanted to leave the Federal Republic of Yugoslavia (Hayden 1999: 36). NATO bombing followed the attempted forceful repression by Serbia, and this resulted in Serbian withdrawal and effective rule by the United Nations. High HIs, the Kosvars being disadvantaged in almost every way, both within the province and *vis-à-vis* the rest of Serbia, was a major factor behind the separatist movement.

Unemployment among youth is an important issue. The 'YVG Kosovo [Youth Voices in Kosova] considers the problems of quality of education and employment as biggest problems that the young population of Kosovo is facing today' (YVG Kosovo, World Bank 2007a: 3). In 2002, the overall unemployment rate was 47.2 per cent, with 15–19-year-olds at 79.4 per cent and 20–24-year-olds at 69 per cent. By 2006, the overall unemployment rate had come down to 44.6 per cent, but youth unemployment was no lower, at 76 per cent (15–24), while the employment rate was only 11 per cent and labour force participation was 46 per cent. Moreover, four out of ten unemployed youth had been unemployed for more than a year (data from World Bank 2008a).

The problem of unemployment, and of unemployed youth in particular, has been widely acknowledged as important both in itself and as a source of poverty (World Bank 2004a, 2005a, 2008a; USAID 2006a). However, little mention is made of ethnic imbalances in official reports. In fact, there are considerable regional imbalances within Kosovo, and a much higher proportion of youth is considered to be 'in jeopardy' in Mitrovica and Ferizaj than in the rest of the country (World Bank 2008a: 32). Mitrovica contains a concentration of Serbs and has been subject to violent protests. The focus groups and interviews of minorities in the Ferizaj region concluded that none of the government services offered them any help, while only two out of fourteen minority group members had been offered jobs in a UNDP project. The minorities in question were Roma, Ashkali and Egyptians. Women from these groups were especially disadvantaged.

The World Bank has focussed on training, employment services and the promotion of small private enterprises in most employment-oriented interventions. It has introduced a 'business environment and rural enterprise project', which included 'strengthening access to finance and the financial sector more broadly; policy engagement as appropriate on privatisation issues; fostering the competitiveness of the SME sector; and continued support for the agriculture sector which provides the bulk of employment in Kosovo' (World Bank 2004). DFID's 2004 strategy, however, makes no mention of employment, concentrating on building central government capacity, security and justice, and economic growth and strengthening social protection (DFID 2004a).

The Kosovo Youth Employment Action Plan (KYEAP), prepared with ILO assistance, has been described as the 'flagship' employment project (World Bank 2008). It is a comprehensive government strategy aiming to promote employment among young people; to increase decent work opportunities for young people; and to prevent social exclusion of youth through targeted labour market measures. But implementation has been weak (World Bank 2008a). One problem is the lack of staff in the implementing agencies, and most young people do not register with the institution responsible for providing services. Despite an annual expenditure of Euro 7 million, programme coverage is low: only 10,000 youth were covered in 2007, or 6.3 per cent of the unemployed of this age group (World Bank 2008a: ix). Operating costs are also high at an estimated €700 per beneficiary.

Most expenditure in this scheme has been on vocational education and training. Yet these programmes have received mixed evaluations. A major problem with training programmes is lack of demand for labour: 'While investments in training can provide young labour market entrants with skills, which can increase their employability, training programs are not successful if labour demand is weak' (World Bank 2008a: x).

Programmes financing start-ups were more successful, with 80 per cent of these enterprises still in existence after 2–3 years. But they had 'very high costs per beneficiary and very limited coverage' (World Bank 2008a: 42). In contrast, public works had the highest coverage, providing 3,160 people with short-term employment and 2,200 with longer term employment each year; and these programmes had the lowest cost per beneficiary.

Thus in Kosovo, despite full acknowledgement of the acute problem of youth unemployment and active policies, the policies have been broadly ineffective. The effectiveness of supply-side policies (notably training) has been constrained by weak growth of employment opportunities, associated with slow growth in the economy as a whole. Thus it is not surprising that public works policies have been more effective, as they create jobs directly. While the issue of social exclusion is acknowledged, the exclusion referred to concerns youth as a whole, and not particular minorities. There is evidence that the situation of youth in minority populations is even worse than that of youth in general. Consequently, the employment situation poses a potential threat to peace.

Bosnia and Herzegovina

When the 1991–1995 conflict in Bosnia came to an end, 'the economy of the country lay shattered' (Black 2001: 176). Economic damage was estimated at US$50–60b, GDP had fallen about one-quarter of prewar levels and over half the population had been displaced (Black 2001; UNDP 2007). There were subsequently massive post-conflict aid inflows – $3.5 b were invested in infrastructure from 1996 to 1999 (UNDP 2002).

The need to create employment was immediately recognized by the World Bank: 'the most important challenge for the economy recovery program will be to create employment opportunities for returning refugees, displaced persons and demobilised soldiers' (World Bank 1996a: 11). Unemployment at the time was estimated at 64 per cent, and the threat this represented to peace was recognized: 'Such high unemployment levels could threaten peace and economic recovery unless ways are found to create jobs rapidly' (World Bank 1996a: 1).

In the short term a three-fold strategy was recommended: micro-credit and entrepreneurship support; public works; and housing construction. The WB instituted an Emergency Public Works and Employment Project in 1996, intended to be labour-intensive and to rehabilitate public infrastructure (World Bank 1996b). Again in 1997, the WB noted that 'serious measures are needed to expand employment as quickly as possible' (World Bank 1997: 67); however, by then, just two years after the end of the war, the emphasis was no longer on public works but on lowering payroll taxes, on reducing wage rigidities and on improving job search mechanisms and training and education. Moreover, privatization was advocated (associated with employment reduction in the short-term). The initial Emergency Project was expected to provide for 100,000 man months – or about 8,300 jobs, which is very small in relation to the size of the problem. After the Dayton Agreement, about 450,000 people were demobilized.

Despite the explicit focus on employment, youth unemployment rates remained extremely high, although data differ according to the source. On the basis of Living Standards Measurement Survey data, unemployment for the 15–24 age group was around 40 per cent for the period 2001–2004, while rates among older age groups were much lower (Fares and Tiongson 2007). UNDP estimates for 2006 are that 57 per cent of the 'labour-capable population is inactive in the formal labour market' (UNDP 2007: 31).

One reason for the poor employment performance was the slow recovery in economic activity: GDP per capita remained at less than half of the pre-war levels in 2000 and showed fairly slow growth in the 2000s. In addition, there has been a massive informalization of the economy. The stagnation of formal employment in the context of (moderate) growth was almost certainly due to labour shedding – not only from the military and militia (in 2000 one-third of the unemployed were estimated to be demobilized soldiers), but also as a result of privatization and of closures following increased competition from foreign direct investment.

Employment HIs in post-conflict Bosnia and Herzegovina operate at two levels: across regions, since the war and ethnic cleansing led to ethnic segregation by region and there are quite significant regional inequalities, in particular with the Serb Republic having substantially less income (and worse employment) than Bosnia or Herzegovina; and in terms of inequalities among ethnic groups within regions, the minorities in any region generally being worse off than the majority. The WB public works projects do not refer explicitly to group allocation at all, although the criteria, which include size of the population, number of refugees, war damage and numbers of unemployed, are likely to have led to a fair balance across territories, though probably not contributing significantly to correcting the quite severe regional HIs that pertained. Within each region, the projects were administered by the municipalities and the cantons. Here the pervasive discrimination against minorities in *each* territory is likely to have implied no correction in local HIs in employment. Amnesty International reports that 'minority returnees are widely discriminated against both in private and public sector employment', which resulted in a situation where virtually no minority returnees are reported to be employed in the private sector and, in most municipalities, public administrations and state-owned companies reportedly tend to employ 'only members of the majority ethnic group or persons affiliated with the ethnically based political party in power' (Amnesty International 2006: 6).

To summarize a complex story, in the post-conflict era in Bosnia-Herzegovina, the World Bank (the lead donor) recognized the critical need to generate employment; but, despite a number of projects, formal employment stagnated and unemployment, especially among youth, remained high. This was probably due to the combination of a sluggish economy and considerable labour shedding through demobilization, privatization and competition. There was no overt recognition of the need to reduce HIs in employment; in practice it is likely that employment projects were distributed across regions in a balanced way (i.e., in relation to population and needs), but not in a way that did much to correct regional employment inequalities; however, the continued discrimination among municipalities meant that, within area employment, distribution is likely to have favoured the majorities in each region.

Nepal

Nepal had a fierce civil war that lasted about a decade; it was led by members of the Communist Party, who wanted a constitutional reform leading to a republic. Deaths as a result of the war are estimated at around 10,000. The war ended in 2006 and was shortly followed by elections. The newly elected parliament (in which the Communists formed the largest single party) voted in favour of ending the monarchy and establishing a republic.

Both academics and officials have recognized that HIs were among the fundamental roots of the conflict. For example, Do and Iyer (2005) and Murshed and Gates (2005) both provide econometric evidence that spatial inequalities are one element explaining the outbreak of conflict. This view has been accepted by various official donors. A report of a DFID conference states: 'Group inequality based on caste, gender, ethnicity and geography has been a critical factor in Nepal's conflict.' The document goes on to highlight the role of HIs in government employment:

> Lack of access to the benefits of state employment – in the civil service and the security forces – is a key grievance for many groups. The civil service and security forces are overwhelmingly dominated by high caste groups, and recruitment from the lowland plains (terai) – where 50 per cent of the population lives – is negligible (DFID 2007)

Moreover, a World Bank document noted: 'Without taking adequate steps to ensure that Nepal is becoming more inclusive socially, politically and economically, the underlying tensions will not be resolved' (IDA 2007: para 5). The note argues that the inclusion agenda must contain 'an affirmative action in the civil service' (IDA 2007: 21).

There has also been general agreement that creating employment is important in order to combat poverty and exclusion. The newly constituted government introduced a public employment programme entitled 'One household, one earner', offering 100 days of guaranteed employment per household in 5 districts 'severely impacted by the conflict and which currently suffer from a serious problem of isolation, unemployment and poverty' (World Bank 2007b: 1). But, for financial reasons, the programme did not extend to anywhere near all the districts in need, and it was underfunded even in relation to the districts it did cover. Subsequently the scheme was extended by a World Bank programme which recognized that 'employment creation is the most viable mean of providing poverty relief and to achieve social inclusion and assuring a peace dividend' (World Bank 2007b: 1). The objective of the World Bank Emergency Employment project was declared to be 'to provide quick cash infusion through temporary employment creation into the poorest areas of Nepal so that people perceive a *peace dividend*' (World Bank 2007b: 2). This extended the government programme to 24 mountain districts, the mountainous districts being the poorest ones in Nepal and those where conflict was concentrated. The two objectives of the programme were to generate quick employment for targeted communities and to provide useful economic infrastructure for the communities that might 'kickstart' development in the area. The project also provided funds to cover the financial shortfall in the government scheme. The enhanced scheme might cover as many as one-quarter of a million households – or 1.5 million people, on the assumption of 6 people per household. This amounts to 5 per cent of Nepal's population: still only a fraction of the poor, who are estimated to account for over 30 per cent of the population.

A second major World Bank project was aimed at providing support for small-scale village and community infrastructure, for income-generating projects, by providing matching grants to self-selected groups of poor and excluded people, 'based on objective criteria including ethnicity, caste, gender and poverty levels' (World Bank 2007a: 6), for particular innovatory schemes and for a variety of capacity-building efforts. Employment was expected to be generated through participation in the infrastructural projects and by longer term employment that this scheme stimulated, as well as through the income-generating projects. It was estimated that one million households would be included.

USAID, too, recognized the need to reduce social exclusion and to generate employment, and proposed a project to 'reduce Nepal's sources of fragility – lack of economic opportunities, inequitable growth, social exclusion, and government ineffectiveness. Upon completion of the project, an estimated 2.5 million rural Nepalese will have earned income from employment on labour intensive construction projects' (USAID 2006b: 1).

The situation of Nepal thus stands out from the other experiences described, for several reasons: firstly, because socio-economic HIs are acknowledged as a fundamental source of the conflict by observers and donors; secondly, because employment creation is regarded by both government and donors as critically important in the immediate post-conflict situation and large emergency employment schemes were put into effect; and, thirdly, because in these schemes, and in other policies, a conscious effort was made to address HIs. Unfortunately the schemes have not yet been evaluated.

3.5 Employment policies – what have we learned

Putting together the findings of this chapter, a clear mismatch emerges between what is desirable for post-conflict employment policies and most practice. While there is increasing recognition of the importance of giving priority to employment generation, in practice most policies focus on the supply side (training, information and so on) and offer only limited additional demand for labour, via public works. Moreover, other policies simultaneously adopted – notably demobilization, privatization and increased competition – lead to labour shedding, at least in the short term. In contrast to the general recognition of the need to raise the level of total employment, most official discourse ignores the need to correct employment HIs. However, Nepal represents an important exception, both with respect to the way employment has been tackled – with much greater emphasis on demand-side policies; and with respect to the acknowledgement of the need to reduce HIs and the incorporation of this objective into policy.

Overall employment levels and growth

Employment creation is one of the most important peace-supporting measures. Indeed, the majority of former Sierra Leonean combatants interviewed by Humphreys and Weinstein stated that what they wanted was more help in finding jobs (cited by Mcleod and Davalos 2008: 53). Yet in most post-conflict countries, despite acknowledgement of the importance of employment for stability and a series of interventions to support employment creation, employment growth has been slow and youth unemployment remains high. There seem to be several reasons for this.

Firstly, the impact of the employment policies themselves has been small because of the prime focus on supply-side interventions, such as training or improved information, or improving the climate for private investment, with too little attention to creating employment through public works. Yet supply-side interventions tend to be rather ineffective unless the macro-economy is providing job opportunities. As the World Bank notes with respect to Kosovo, '... employment services and training programs are of limited use in a labour market as slack as Kosovo's currently,' (although they then argue they will be of use once labour demand picks up) (World Bank, 2009: viii). General evaluations of training schemes have endorsed this view. An overview of evaluations of training programmes in the OECD countries, for example, showed very few positive impacts of training programmes with some even having negative effects (Kluve 2007).

Secondly, where public works have been introduced, they have tended to be small in relation to the size of the problem and short-lived, as in Bosnia-Herzegovina. Yet public works can be extensive and do create employment. For example, in Cambodia, from 1992 to 2002, the Labour-based Rehabilitation Project provided over 3 million work-days which contributed to the reconstruction of roads, bridges and irrigation schemes (Shone 2003). In Mozambique a feeder road programme, begun even before the conflict ended, 'provided 8 million worker-days for 40,000 people, and rebuilt roads vital to the recovery of the country's agricultural economy' (UNDP 2008: 75), this was not thought to be sufficient to offset the 'large job losses' associated with the structural adjustment programme (Date-Bah 2003: 41). Reconstruction needs in post-conflict countries provide plentiful opportunities for such employment, while it has been estimated that using labour-intensive methods can increase direct employment three-fold compared with capital-intensive and a further one and a half jobs are created via multiplier effects (Krishnamurty 2003: 65). Yet frequently, as in East Timor, capital-intensive methods are adopted (Krishnamurty 2003: 66).

Thirdly, the adjustment policies generally advocated by international donors tend to reduce employment in the short-run. These include import liberalization and enhanced competition, privatization and public sector reform. In the Bosnia case, privatization together with enhanced competition had a negative impact on formal sector employment. In the case of Uganda, the public sector reforms greatly reduced public sector employment, involving a 50 per cent reduction in civil service employment. Similar reductions in public sector employment occurred in Mozambique. In poor countries, with small industrial sectors, the public sector often provides a considerable proportion of formal employment, which makes cuts particularly serious. For example in 1985, public sector employment accounted for almost a third of the non-agricultural employment in four Sub-Saharan African countries; 18.4 per cent in five Asian countries; and 20 per cent in ten Latin American countries according to data provided by Marinakis; the data of (Kraay and Van Rijckeghem 1995) are similar. Consequently, a cut in public sector employment can have a substantial impact on the formal labour market. Yet, as Marinakis notes, while adjustment policies in the 1980s were primarily focussed on wage cuts in the public sector from the 1990s the focus was on employment cuts (Marinakis 1994: 50). Adjustment policies that are likely to reduce employment in the short to medium term should be delayed until peace is well established (as indeed did happen in Uganda).

Fourthly, demobilization can release hundreds of thousands of young men onto the labour market. In Bosnia and Herzegovina, one-third of the unemployed consisted of former combatants. From the point of view of stability, it is advisable to adopt a policy of employing all former combatants in the national army, or elsewhere, in the short term, at least until there are effective demobilization programmes and peace is well established, again as was the policy in Uganda.

Fifthly, in the majority of contemporary post-conflict countries, the starting point is one where the vast mass of the population are self-employed (or employed by small informal sector enterprises), so that it is neither realistic nor desirable to aim to provide formal sector 'jobs' for the majority of the population. While formal sector jobs are important – especially for the educated or partially educated who are likely to lead violent mobilization – it is also important to focus on improving productivity in agriculture and small non-agricultural enterprises. This, of course, is difficult to do comprehensively and effectively and the slow impact is not likely to affect peace-propensity much in the short term. But the Nepal case suggests that a focussed approach, targeted at ex-combatants and at deprived groups and areas, may be more effective from this perspective.

Employment policies and Horizontal inequalities

In addition to policies towards the total *level* of employment, the distribution of employment among salient groups is important for conflict-prevention, where HIs have been a significant cause of conflict. As we have seen, this is rarely acknowledged in donor analysis.

Policies which influence HIs in terms of the distribution of adequate work opportunities include

1. Macro-policies that influence the sectoral and regional distribution of opportunities, and, consequently, the group distribution of opportunities in so far as there is group regional or sectoral (or both) concentration. Such a concentration is often the case, partly as a product of colonial policy – with effects that last to the present day. For example, in both West and East Africa, colonial policy promoted the development of the Southern parts of the countries, benefitting Southern groups, though social and economic infrastructural development, the promotion of particular crops favourable to these regions and subsequently through the development of industries in the South. This tendency, undoubtedly encouraged and accentuated by climatic differences, has led to severe North-South HIs (Azam et al. 1999; Klugman 2000; Stewart 2008). The net result is that current reform policies, such as trade liberalization and exchange rate changes, favouring particular sectors (generally the cash crop agricultural sector) tend to reinforce many existing HIs. Careful monitoring

of these effects is required, together with policies to attempt to reduce or offset any adverse effects.

2. Public expenditure programmes often have regional distributional implications, in turn influencing group opportunities for employment in creating such public infrastructure as well as other income earning opportunities. Unless there is careful oversight of the HI implications of these programmes, they frequently worsen rather than reduce existing HIs.
3. This also applies to the emergency employment schemes that should form an important part of the post-conflict employment programmes – these need to be monitored to be sure that they are well distributed across groups, and that the benefits are, if possible, distributed disproportionately, to the deprived groups, as has been the policy in Nepal. There geographic targeting has directed the employment benefits to deprived regions and districts and there is some additional targeting towards poorer groups within districts.
4. The need to monitor the group distribution of benefits also applies to the many employment-promoting schemes adopted in post-conflict situations, such as training, apprenticeships, provision of start-up finance and micro-finance. Again the Nepal situation provides an example, where matching grants for income-generating projects are provided mainly to people from deprived groups.
5. The group distribution of public sector employment itself is a particularly important area for monitoring and policy. As noted, not only does this often form a large proportion of total formal sector employment, but it also appears to be an area where unfairness is most visible and resented. Very often a particular group is found to dominate higher echelons of the public sector, reflecting the composition of those in power and historic educational advantages of particular groups. Correcting such inequalities should be an important element in post-conflict policy as the experience of Northern Ireland indicates (Cormack and Osborne 1983; McCrudden et al. 2004).
6. A further important issue is that of formal *private* sector employment. This may be of lesser importance in many poor countries since it forms a smaller proportion of total employment. Nonetheless, it can be important as a source of inequality and a location of discrimination, as seems to be the case, for example, in Bosnia-Herzegovina. Strong anti-discriminatory policies can make a difference here, as indicated by the experience of Northern Ireland, where these were backed up by government contracting arrangements, where government contracts were only offered to private firms where the firm

could prove they had not been discriminatory (McCrudden et al. 2004). Special efforts may be needed to support the private sector in promoting labour-intensive industries in deprived regions.

3.6 Conclusions

This chapter has presented an overview of employment policies in post-conflict situations, looking both at the total level and the distribution of employment. Our review of mainstream discourse and policies shows that the question of the level of employment, especially for the young, in post-conflict contexts, is increasingly at the forefront of analysis and policy. But, in most countries reviewed, the actual policies adopted have achieved little, partly because they are focussed on the supply side, and not the demand side; and partly because they have been accompanied by employment-destroying adjustment and demobilization policies. Public works are the most effective way of generating employment and need to be introduced on a large scale; and employment-destroying policies need to be postponed, and then introduced only gradually, when peace is well established and the economy has picked up and is generating new employment opportunities.

HIs in employment can be a significant source of grievance; consequently it is important to avoid or correct them in post-conflict settings. Yet the issue of HIs in employment is much less widely recognized, though it has been acknowledged and incorporated into policy in the case of Nepal. This chapter identified six areas in which policy would need to change if the issue of HIs in employment were taken seriously. These include policies towards the macro-economy, public expenditure programmes, emergency and other employment schemes and public and private sector employment. Considerations of policies to support improved HIs also need to be incorporated into the deployment of aid funds, which are often on a generous scale in post-conflict years.

Finally, we found that data were grossly inadequate, both on levels and quality of employment and on HIs. Monitoring the employment situation carefully, both as to levels and as to HIs, is essential for the formulation of good policy.

Notes

1. I am grateful to Carmen Osorio for very helpful research assistance, to Arnim Langer for material on Uganda, to Graham K. Brown for allowing me to draw on some joint work on the causes of conflict in Section 3.1 and to Diego

Sanchez, Arnim Langer and Rajesh Venugopal for helpful comments on an earlier draft.

2. I am grateful to Yvan Guichaoua for pointing this out to me.
3. Ranis and Stewart (1999) distinguish between the 'modernizing' part of the sector, which offers reasonable incomes and productivity, and the traditional part, which allows people to scrape a living with very limited equipment and weak markets.
4. This is actually quite arbitrary; see Ruggeri-Laderchi, Saith and Stewart (2002).
5. According to Museveni, in a speech given to the Combined Arms Center at Fort Leavenworth, Kansas, 'Strategy of the Protracted Peoples' War', the post-1986 army included more than 100,000 people.
6. World Bank, 'Uganda Grapples with Youth Unemployment as WDR 2007 is Launched', available at: http://web.worldbank.org/WBSITE/EXTERNAL/COUNTRIES/AFRICAEXT/UGANDAEXTN/0,,contentMDK:21245160~menuPK:374871~pagePK:2865066~piPK:2865079~theSitePK:374864,00.html.

4
Correcting Horizontal Inequality as a Development Priority: Poverty Reduction Strategy Papers in Haiti, Liberia and Nepal

Sakiko Fukuda-Parr

4.1 Introduction

If horizontal inequalities (HIs) are a source of conflict (Stewart 2008), what should be the policy response? In this chapter I argue that the risks of conflict can be reduced by addressing and reducing HIs through appropriate economic, social and governance policies.[1] The chapter reviews the Poverty Reduction Strategy Papers (PRSPs) as a policy vehicle that could achieve these objectives and examines the cases of Haiti, Liberia and Nepal, countries characterized by high levels of HI that have also experienced protracted conflict in recent decades. The next section outlines relevant development policies for correcting HIs. Section 4.3 presents the three country cases. Section 4.4 contrasts the ways in which HIs have been addressed in post-conflict PRSPs, and identifies some key constraints. The final section draws lessons from these country cases to identify some key policy issues concerning PRSPs as a policy vehicle that involves not only national governments, but also donors and civil society, as stakeholders in a coordinated development strategy.

4.2 Development strategies to reduce risks of violent conflict

One of the strongest findings of the research on the relationships between violent conflict and economic development is the inverse relationship between risks of violent conflict and the level of per capita income.[2] One might conclude from this finding that economic growth would be an important condition for reducing conflict risks. However, this would not necessarily imply that growth is sufficient. Moreover, in the absence of strategies specifically aimed at reducing HI, growth might reinforce disparities even further. In societies marked by HI, unequal structures of economic assets and social opportunities are likely to be embedded so that development may well reproduce or exacerbate existing inequalities, unless explicit measures are taken to correct them. Post-conflict reconstruction and development programmes such as public investments in basic social services and productive infrastructure are far from distributionally neutral. In such contexts, HI reducing economic and social development policies would be instrumental to the peace-building process.

HIs are wide-ranging and extend to disparities in political participation and power, economic and social opportunities, and recognition of cultural identities and practices. Correcting HI needs to address all of these dimensions apply policies with the following broad elements (Langer and Stewart 2008; Stewart 2005; Stewart et al. 2008; Stewart et al. 2009):

Political: policies to build greater political inclusiveness include structural reforms aimed at power-sharing among groups in key institutions such as the legislature, the armed forces, the judiciary, the police, local to national level administration, the cabinet and the executive. Examples include federalism in the organization of the state and decentralization in governance when identity groups are territorially concentrated. Governance processes are also important – for instance institutional reforms designed to remove discrimination and to equalize protection under the law, to equalize participation and voice in decision-making and to strengthen accountability of government. Institutional reforms for economic governance aimed at more efficient economic markets also contribute to removing discrimination and unequal access. One root of exclusion is non-democratic governance, where excluded groups are without a voice to influence public decisions and authorities are unaccountable to people (World Bank 2000; UNDP 2002). For example, reforms and a strengthening of judicial institutions are necessary in order to implement land rights, and civil society audits of budgets are effective in ensuring that local authorities have transparent budgets and are held accountable. However, democratic institutions as such are not sufficient to ensure political inclusion of all major groups and specific policies may be needed, for example, reserving representation for particular groups;

Economic: policies to enhance opportunities include measures to address inequalities in assets, employment and incomes. Measures to redistribute assets, such as land reform and responding to claims of indigenous groups over natural resources, are likely to be most difficult to pursue politically. On the other hand, redirecting public investments so as to benefit the excluded is likely to be more politically feasible. Such investments would include investments in environmental protection of ecological resources, expansion of physical infrastructure, support to smallholder agriculture, and access to employment. Economic growth is also important for correcting HIs, since redistribution alone is not likely to be a feasible means of improving the incomes of the disadvantaged groups. Growth that generates employment for the unskilled, especially for youth, is particularly important in post-conflict contexts, where high unemployment is a destabilizing factor in a volatile political situation. Core policies for HI reduction in a post-war development agenda are measures to promote growth designed to favour the regions where excluded groups are concentrated. Without affirmative action policies, reversing entrenched discrimination may be overwhelmingly difficult. Affirmative action policies have been used effectively, for example in India to open opportunities for the Dalits, in South Africa for black Africans and in Malaysia for Bumiputras;

Social: policies for equalizing social opportunities include expanding access to education, health services, safe water, housing and social safety nets for excluded groups. These policies are important not only because they improve basic well-being, but also because they increase opportunities for employment, enhance productivity and increase income-earning capacity. HIs in outcomes such as literacy and educational attainment are often the result of a sustained bias in government spending. A core policy for HI reduction involves redirecting social investment resources to benefit groups that have been disadvantaged;

Cultural: policies of multiculturalism, for instance in matters of language and religion, allow for greater access to opportunities and power in political, economic and social life. For example, language can be an important barrier in access to justice or education. Two kinds of exclusion and discrimination affect subaltern cultural groups.[3] The first is 'participation exclusion', where access to important opportunities such as education, employment, health services or political office are biased or restricted. The second is 'living mode exclusion', such as restrictions on the use of language or the practice of religion (Kymlicka 2003; Langer and Brown 2008; UNDP 2004).[4]

4.3 Integrating horizontal inequalities correction objectives in Poverty Reduction Strategy Papers

Integrating HI correction polices in post-conflict PRSPs would entail several aspects of the formulation process including:

i. *objectives* – HI reduction would be an explicit objective of the strategy, either as an end in itself, because inequality is intrinsically objectionable and discrimination is a violation of human rights, or because it is an obstacle to preventing the recurrence of violent conflict;
ii. *analysis* – key features of HI and their causes would need to be analysed as part of the development constraints and challenges, and as a factor in the history of violent conflict in the country;
iii. *data collection* – data on socio-economic and political participation are often not disaggregated by identity groups. Such data are essential for analysis of HI as a development factor, for designing corrective policies and for monitoring policy impact. In cases where identity groups map well onto administrative units, disaggregated administrative data (to provincial and, further, to local levels) could be substitutes.
iv. *policy priorities* – policy priorities would need to include economic, social, cultural and governance reform measures that aim to reverse HI, which is likely to be a result of discrimination based on race, language, ethnicity or religion or of bias in the allocation of development resources.
v. *financing implementation* – while the PRSP is a broad strategy paper, implementation depends on financing. In most post-conflict countries, this depends in turn not only on government budget allocations, but also on donor allocations of aid budgets, over which recipient governments do not have full control.

How effectively are the HI correcting policies included in PRSPs? The next section considers the cases of Liberia, Haiti and Nepal.

4.4 Country cases

All three countries have emerged from protracted violence associated – in different ways and to varying degrees – with a history of elite rule and exclusion of groups. Each is marked by high degrees of vertical and HIs. The countries are also similar in that the international community played a major role in political stabilization, in ending armed conflict and in financing reconstruction and post-conflict development. However, the countries are diverse in geographic location and historical background, as well as in development characteristics such as level of income and human development, and in the degree of aid dependence (Table 4.1).

Haiti

Political instability has marked the history of Haiti over the centuries, but it has been particularly acute since the 1986 overthrow of Jean-Claude Duvalier – a period interspersed with the violent overthrow of regimes.[5] Although there has not been a full-scale civil war, the protracted instability and violence have necessitated the intervention of UN missions from 1993 to 2000, then again from 2004 after a period

Table 4.1 Development planning context

	Haiti	**Liberia**	**Nepal**
Documents analysed	PRSP	PRSP	Interim plan
GNI per capita (Atlas method) (2007, US$)	520	140	350
Poverty headcount ratio at $1.25/day PPP (2007) (% population)	55 (2005)	84	NA
Prevalence of undernourishment (% population)	58	40	15
HIPC country	Yes	Yes	Yes but no application
Aid per capita (2007) (US$)	73	187	21
Aid as % GNP (2007)	11	124	6
Tax revenue as % GDP (2007)	–	–	10

Figures have been rounded to significant digits.
Source: World Development Indicators, http://ddp-ext.worldbank.org/ext/DDPQQ/report.do?method=showReport except as noted.

of escalating armed conflict. The destructive impacts of this violent conflict are not clear-cut but are arguably among the critical factors in the economic and social stagnation of the country, whose gross domestic product (GDP) per capita contracted by an average of 0.7 per cent per year over the last four decades. Recurrent natural disasters and poorly managed economic liberalization are often cited as sources of this decline, while it is also acknowledged that the comprehensive economic sanctions imposed by the international community from 1992 to 1996 effectively destroyed the Haitian economy and institutions (Rosenthal 2005). Today Haiti is a low-income country with a per capita income of $520 in 2007, and is highly dependent upon aid. In 2007, aid flows totalled $73 per capita or 11 per cent of the GDP, one of the highest percentages in the world (see Table 4.1). Most of this aid comes from a small number of donors, namely the US, EU, the Inter-American Development Bank, the World Bank and the UN system.

High levels of HI have historically been a feature of the country. Race and language have identified socio-economic and political divides; lighter skinned mixed-race and bilingual (French and Créole speaking) bourgeoisie make up a social elite distinguished from the black majority, who do not speak French. However, while Papa Doc espoused *noirisme* (Nicholls 1985), race has not always been, nor is currently, a major factor in politics. While grievances against the ruling class propelled the overthrow of the Duvalier regime in 1986 and have been a factor in Haitian politics ever since, racial identity has not been a factor in political mobilization for violence.[6] Nor is racial identity recognized as a relevant policy issue, and data are not available on racial demographics and socio-economic characteristics.

Poverty is widespread, and is particularly concentrated in rural areas where very few of the elite live. The disparity between the metropolitan region and rural areas is sharp, whether it is in incomes, health and education outcomes or in access to infrastructure.[7] The PRSP data for 2007 show the incidence of extreme poverty in rural areas at 67 per cent, compared with 57 per cent in urban areas and with 23 per cent in the Metropolitan region. Vertical income distribution is one of the most unequal in the world, the *gini* coefficient among households registering 0.65 (République d'Haiti 2007).[8] The top 20 per cent of the income group accounts for 69.6 per cent of the national income, and the bottom 20 per cent for a mere 1.4 per cent; the top 10 per cent has 47.7 per cent of national income, and the bottom 10 per cent only 0.7 per cent.

The broad aspirational vision of Haiti's PRSP 2008–2010 is to make 'a qualitative leap' in growth and poverty reduction. The strategy is built around three pillars: growth vectors; human development (basic services); and democratic governance (justice and security). The PRSP is underpinned by a macroeconomic framework, agreed upon with the International Monetary Fund (IMF) under the Poverty Reduction and Growth Facility financing, which aims to create a stable macroeconomic environment and to introduce reforms to improve budgetary and other economic management processes.

Inequality and exclusion are key issues identified in the analysis of poverty, and reversing them is a major objective stated in the PRSP. However, there is no reference at all to HI in the document. The analysis concludes that, 'in Haiti, poverty is essentially linked to a historical process where political power is constructed and the economy organized around the interests of a minority' (p. 41). Yet the document does not identify who the 'minority' are. Moreover, unequal distribution and access to opportunities are at the root of poverty, as well as weaknesses in policy that have not adequately considered the distributional impacts of liberalization and deregulation reforms. It is also curious that the PRSP makes no reference to the history of violent conflict as a factor behind poverty and stagnation; nor does it include an agenda for preventing the recurrence of violence.

The policy agenda is stated in general and aggregate terms, which make it difficult to see how explicit measures to address inequality and exclusion could be put in place. The monitoring and evaluation indicators refer only to aggregate national data and do not contain any that would reveal the distribution of benefits. The growth strategy emphasizes the role of agriculture, including the small-scale farm sector, and the role of infrastructure. This could be a strategy of pro-poor growth, but a direct link is not made between the importance of investments in agriculture and infrastructure in pro-poor growth.

Implementation of the 2008–2010 PRSP is estimated to cost \$3.86 billion (Gdes 154.6 billion) over three years and depends largely on external financing. Domestic revenue amounts to about \$580 million (or about 10 per cent of GDP) and covers mostly personnel and other fixed recurrent costs of the administration. Haiti receives about \$500 million in development aid, which finances most of the public investments. The requirements of the PRSP would involve a significant increase in financing, especially from donors.

A key constraint to implementation is that donor financing is not fully aligned with the PRSP priorities, and leaves pillar 1 (growth) seriously underfunded. According to the Minister of Planning and International Cooperation, the economic growth pillar is the least funded (about a fifth of requirements) of the three PRSP pillars, while by early 2009 the social pillar had received nearly half the requirements.[9] Data on donor allocation of resources are difficult to track down, as there is no single consolidated data set on donor flows that is structured by type of aid and by sectoral/regional/ministerial allocation. Using the Organization for Economic Cooperation and Development (OECD) database, Table 4.2 shows the sectoral allocation of official aid flows (including OECD member donors and multilaterals, but not Venezuela and other non-OECD members). Data for 2007 disbursements show that only 9 per cent of total aid went to productive sectors and 9 per cent to productive sectors and economic infrastructure, while the bulk remained focused on social infrastructure and services (52 per cent). As Haiti only receives 9 per cent of aid in the form of budget support, the national budget has little available for investment in productive sectors and in economic infrastructure in general.

It is true that the population is in dire need of basic services in health, education, water and sanitation. Moreover, these are investments in their productivity. Yet the allocation of resources appears to be

Table 4.2 Haiti: Allocation of donor resources to PRSP pillars

Pillars	**PRSP allocations (Gdes millions)**	**PRSP allocations (%)**	**DAC donor disbursements 2007 (%)**
Pillar 1: Growth vectors; DAC: economic infrastructure, production	78.3	51	9
Pillar 2: Basic services; DAC: social infrastructure, humanitarian	33	21	52
Pillar 3: Democratic governance	12.3	8	
Cross-cutting and specific policies	31	20	6
DAC: budget support			9
Food aid, humanitarian aid			15
Debt relief			9
Total	154.5	100	100

Source: columns 2 and 3 – République d'Haiti 2007; column 4 – OECD Stats Extract Aid Activities Dataset <http://webnet.oecd.org/wbos/index.aspx> Retrieved 23 March, 2009.

unbalanced and seriously undermines the short-term growth objectives of the strategy. Together with food aid (8 per cent), and humanitarian aid (7 per cent), 71 per cent of all aid disbursements in 2007 from OECD member donors and multilaterals went to meeting basic needs (see Table 4.2). This is extremely high; for example, it is nearly four times the 20 per cent of social expenditures that UNICEF and others had advocated under the 20:20 initiative launched after the 1995 World Social Summit. The severe underfunding of the growth pillar reflects a chronic pattern of neglecting the agricultural sector and rural development, and, more broadly, investments in the productive capacity of the poor and marginalized. This is amply documented by the World Bank (2008) in its Public Expenditure and Management Review Report.[10] To illustrate, the Ministry of Agriculture and Rural Development accounted for only 3.3 per cent of the recurrent budget over 2002–2004 and 4.4 per cent over 2005–2007, and only some 4 per cent of the investment budget. This was less than 10 per cent of what the Ministry had requested. OECD data show donor commitments to agriculture averaged around 7 per cent of the total from 1995 to 2006 but declined to 2 per cent in 2007. These are very small allocations for a sector that is the source of livelihood for more than half of the population of the country, and for a large proportion of the poor.

The growth pillar of the PRSP is essential for improving household incomes of the poor. From 2004 to 2009, the Haitian economy made an important recovery, reversing the years of economic contraction and achieving positive growth. Stronger macroeconomic management – maintaining stable balances and reducing inflation to single digit figures – was an important achievement of these five years. However, this has not translated into a perceptible improvement in reducing income poverty or in expanding employment. Given the high levels of inequality in Haiti, growth is likely to trickle down to the poor only slowly, if at all, and more proactive measures are needed to improve the incomes of the poor directly.

Liberia

Liberia suffered a 14-year civil war that ended with the 2003 Comprehensive Peace Agreement. The war caused extensive damage to the country's infrastructure, schools and health facilities, and disrupted government administration. Over this period, the GDP fell by 87 per cent, from $1269 in 1980 (2005 prices) to $163 in 2005. Liberia is a highly aid-dependent country, with external assistance amounting to a whopping 124 per cent of GDP (see Table 4.1). Even before the war, it had a poor record of human development despite its rich natural resource endowments. The pre-war development model of Liberia epitomizes 'growth without development'.

High levels of HI are evident in the multiple disparities, but most notably in the divide between the Americo-Liberians and the Native Liberians, between the coast where the Americo-Liberian populations are concentrated and the rural hinterland, and amongst the ethnic groups of the Native Liberian population. The Americo-Liberians are descendants of some 300 families who founded Liberia after being freed from slavery in the US and the Caribbean in the nineteenth century. Historically, economic and political power has been concentrated in this group, which accounts for about 5 per cent of the population (Guannu 2009). The overthrow of the Americo-Liberian regime by Doe brought rule dominated by his own ethnic group – the Krahns, a small minority group. Grievance against successive elite governments and corrupt misrule, which came with them, is commonly identified as an important source of the armed conflict, though not the only one. While several authors have offered competing explanations for the civil war,[11] reviews of this literature by Omeje (2009) and Humphreys and Richards (2005) both conclude that multiple factors were at play.

Liberia's first PRSP was prepared in 2008 and reflects a strong commitment to correcting HI as an over-arching social goal. The introductory chapter states: 'The new Liberia aims to acknowledge and begin to move beyond the divisions, marginalization, and exclusion of the past and to create circumstances where differences are discussed, not fought over' (Republic of Liberia 2008a: 20). This objective is evident throughout the document.

HI is not only widely acknowledged as an issue, but also specifically identified by the government as a root cause of the civil war. Unlike many other post-conflict countries, the PRSP preparation process included a systematic reflection on the role of socio-economic factors in the civil war. Group-based exclusion and discrimination, along with corruption and misrule were identified as underlying causes that needed to be a major focus of the development strategy (Fukuda-Parr and McCandless 2009). According to the PRSP (Government of Liberia 2008: 20),

> [t]he origins of the conflict can be traced to two broad factors. First, significant portions of society were systematically excluded and marginalised from institutions of political governance and access to key economic assets. The founding constitution was designed

> for the needs of the settler population, with less consideration and involvement of the indigenous people. In the early days, land and property rights of the majority of Liberians were severely limited. Later, marginalisation was perpetuated by the urban-biased policies of successive administrations. Political power was concentrated in Monrovia and primarily at the level of the presidency. Most infrastructure and basic services were concentrated in Monrovia and a few other cities. [...] The consequence was a high level of resentment toward the ruling elite, which in part led to the bloody military coup of 1980 and its initial support among the people. [...] Second, economic collapse helped propel the crisis.

The PRSP is built around four pillars: consolidating peace and security; revitalizing the economy; strengthening governance and the rule of law; and rehabilitating infrastructure and delivering basic services. It includes a core institutional reform agenda designed to make government more accountable, while the economic strategy emphasizes infrastructure, social services and regenerating agriculture, mining and logging. Equity and inclusion are clearly reflected among the objectives in each of these pillars. The PRSP also identifies six key issues, all related to HI and conflict risks, that need to be addressed in order to reduce risks of conflict resurgence: land conflicts, youth employment, political polarization, mismanagement of natural resources, the relationship between the state and citizens and the judicial system.

However, the PRSP falls short of addressing HI in several important ways. First, the document interestingly does not refer to cultural identity groups in addressing exclusion and inequalities. The document singles out the need for special attention to children and youth, ex-combatants, women and the 'vulnerable' – rather than to the historically marginalized non-Americo-Liberians, certain ethnic groups or the rural hinterland.

Second, the operational programmes are defined in highly aggregated terms and do not target particular beneficiary groups. For example, agricultural investments could significantly correct HI if they were directed towards increasing support for small-scale farmers. This could serve as an important starting point for building food security, reversing the neglect of rural, African indigenous populations and stimulating pro-poor growth. Conversely, if these investments were to go to the plantations sector, which is predominantly owned by Liberian elites and multinational companies, current HI would be further reinforced. The PRSP neglects to break down resource allocations between types of activities. A key obstacle for both better programming and monitoring of HI reducing interventions is the lack of disaggregated social and economic data. The Bank/Fund staff review also comments on these data gaps. However, the issue has not been pursued further in these and other Bank/Fund reports. Finally, the PRSP does not raise the issue of the distributional impact of growth by identity group. The strategy aims to stimulate growth and allocates 62 per cent of the resources to economic and social infrastructure, mostly to roads and bridges, which addresses a critical bottleneck for all economic activity. But the PRSP contains no indication of where these investments would be directed, and whether the policy is to target their allocation to achieve an equalizing impact. While objectives such as employment creation and support to small-scale farmers are emphasized, costing is not disaggregated beyond broad sectors. There is a risk that the growth model would rely on the traditional engines of growth – plantations, mining and logging – rather than pursue more broad-based development. The pattern of 'growth without development', with high levels of HI in pre-war Liberia, could be replicated. A major issue is support to smallholder agriculture, a concern voiced in the donor community, notably by the UN's human rights section and by the World Bank/IMF staff review of the PRSP.[12]

Implementation of the PRSP depends on financing that is not entirely in the government's control. The costing of the PRSP over three years is estimated at $1.6 billion (averaging $533 million), of which government finance would cover only 32 per cent, even on the most optimistic assumptions about growth and domestic revenue raising, which anticipate a rise in total government revenue to 27 per cent of GDP. The rest, or approximately $360 million a year, would need to come from external resources. This is beyond what donors are likely to finance, since the 2007 aid flow was estimated at $230 million (Government of Liberia 2008). Considering the constraints of macroeconomic expenditure ceilings set in the agreement with the IMF for financing under the Poverty Reduction and Growth Facility, and bearing in mind that Liberia operates on a cash-budget basis, implementation would require a significant increase in external financing in the form of grant aid.

Development aid has not only been inadequate quantitatively, but also is not aligned with PRSP's priorities. While economic infrastructure is at the core of the PRSP economic and social recovery strategy, the donor allocations as a whole prioritize social infrastructure (education, health, water and sanitation). The 2008/2009 government budget shows 15 per cent of donor project disbursements being allocated to roads and bridges, energy, telecommunications and transport, while the PRSP allocation for this sector was 34 per cent. Education and health receives 26 per cent of donor funds, when the PRSP allocation was 17 per cent.

Table 4.3 Liberia: Allocation of resources to PRSP pillars

Pillars	**PRSP allocations 2008/2011 (US$ millions)**	**PRSP allocations (%)**	**Aid allocations in national budget 2009/2010 (%)**
Pillar I – Peace and security	252	16	14
Pillar II – Economic revitalization	141	9	27
Pillar III – Governance and the rule of law	224	14	13
Pillar IV – Infrastructure and basic services			
Econ infrastructure: Roads and bridges, energy, posts and telecom, transport	554	34	15
Education and health	376	17	26
Water and sanitation	143	9	4
Total	1,612	100	100

Source: Columns – Republic of Liberia budget (2007).

Economic revitalization receives 27 per cent, rather than the allocated 9 per cent (Table 4.3).

Tracking donor allocations and disbursements is difficult in Liberia, as elsewhere, since these resources are 'off budget' with the exception of budget support and debt relief funds. They are not included in the national budget and are not managed by national authorities. Moreover, donors do not report these to national authorities in a timely fashion and in temporal and sectoral categories that are in line with national budgets. Liberia has taken an important step in redressing this situation by creating shadow budgets; annexes to the annual budget from 2008/2009 list aid projects and pooled funds with projected disbursements (Republic of Liberia 2008). Because these lists may not be complete, another, more complete data source is the OECD Development Assistance Committee (DAC) reporting system. The 2007 disbursements for project aid reported there indicate only 8 per cent going to economic infrastructure, 2% to the productive sectors, and 22 per cent to social infrastructure (OECD 2009).

Nepal

Nepal has experienced over 10 years of violent conflict, which started in 1996, when the Communist Party of Nepal (CPN Maoist) launched its 'people's war' against the elite exclusionary rule that had resulted in extreme poverty and the exclusion of lower castes and ethnic groups from political power and benefits of development. The insurgency started in, and was initially confined to, the remote western and mid-western regions, but the conflict escalated across the country after 2001. A Comprehensive Peace Accord was signed by the government and the CPN Maoist in November 2006 bringing an end to the conflict (which claimed at least 13,000 lives). Since then, the country has lived through outbreaks of violence and has experienced a political evolution, while a UN political mission has been in place since 2007 to support the peace process.

The issue of social exclusion and discrimination against ethnic and caste groups – Dalits and other low castes, indigenous ethnic groups and the Madhesis in the Terai region – is widely recognized as a key factor behind the armed conflict. The concentration of power in the hands of the high caste hill Hindu (predominantly Brahmin, Chetri and Newar) groups had been entrenched over the centuries. The issue is at the centre of the current political dynamics and of the peace process as the country prepares the constitution and consolidates its democratic institutions and processes. Academic studies have also identified HI as an important causal factor in the conflict (Brown 2007; Gates and Murshed 2005). In his review of the evidence, Brown (2007: 1) concludes that

> there is very strong evidence of a link between processes of social exclusion, ethnic and caste-based HIs and the emergence and intensity of the Maoist rebellion, but that this relationship is very complex. While the Maoist movement sought to mobilize – and legitimize – its insurgency by evoking caste discrimination, the empirical evidence suggests that the main *socio-economic* determinant of its mobilizational success was the extent of *regional* inequality between different provinces and districts combined with *political* discontents framed along ethnic rather than caste lines. This is not to say the caste discrimination or inequalities are normatively or objectively unimportant in Nepalese society, but rather that they were less important in the mobilization of the Maoist insurgency than regional and ethnic divisions.

It is not surprising that correcting HI is one of the key commitments of the Comprehensive Peace Agreement (Government of Nepal 2006). Section 3 of the agreement, 'Political–Economic–Social Transformation and Conflict Management', specifically commits the parties to 'end discrimination based on class, ethnicity, language, gender, culture, religion and region and to address the problems of women, Dalit, indigenous people, ethnic minorities (Janajatis), Terai communities (Madhesis), oppressed, neglected and minority communities and the backward areas' (p. 4). The commitments include specific measures to restructure the state to address political exclusion. However, on economic and social exclusion, the commitments include broad measures for social justice and equal rights to education, health, shelter, employment and food security. They do not include specific measures to restructure economic and social opportunities such as affirmative action measures.

Correcting economic and social HIs is also a key priority of government, donor agencies and NGOs. This requires reversal of past policies, since development priorities benefited those in political power for decades. Development aid had done little to challenge the undemocratic concentration of power and to question the overt discrimination that has existed against Dalits, women, and some indigenous groups, or feudal practices in violation of human rights, such as bonded labour. In fact patterns of development aid reinforced existing hierarchies and structures, and donor activities may have effectively reproduced dominant hierarchy in the distribution of their resources among development priorities, as well as in their hiring practices, as the majority of their national employees were from high caste 'hill people'. In Nepal, in contrast to Haiti and Liberia, there exists a great deal of data and analysis of HI, thanks to numerous studies undertaken by government, donor, civil society and academics.[13]

The Nepal PRSP is also the country's Tenth Plan, covering the decade 2002–2007. There has been no follow-up PRSP, but an Interim Five-Year Plan was adopted in December 2007 for the period 2008–2010. The Interim Plan is squarely situated in the post-conflict context and sets out a strategy for reconstruction and development that is inclusive and seeks to redress the exclusions of the past. It includes an extensive analysis of disparities, including detailed data disaggregated by region, gender and rural/urban divides. Thus, correcting inequalities and exclusion of all forms, including HI, is explicitly set out as an overriding objective of the plan. The plan includes specific and multifaceted programmes to implement these objectives.

Reducing inequality and exclusion is also an explicit objective of each of the sectoral and programme priorities, from agriculture, to education, to decentralization. The plan seeks to achieve 'pro-poor growth' and includes programmes and measures for this purpose. The Interim Plan includes a special chapter (6) on 'Social Justice and Inclusion', which gives a detailed assessment of the HI reflected in higher levels of poverty and lagging social indicators for Dalits, Janjatis, women and rural populations. It addresses discrimination as a problem framed within human rights principles – implying that removal of discrimination is an objective that is intrinsically, not just instrumentally, important – and sets out a rights-based policy agenda. The plan sets out explicit HI-correcting policies, targeted particularly at marginalized groups including Dalits, Adibasi Janjatis and Madhesis, as well as women, disabled and the displaced. These policies include measures such as scholarships, proportional representation in village committees that would decide on agricultural development interventions, human rights education and capacity development, and, in particular, important support for employment programmes (see the chapter by Stewart in this volume) and for small-scale agriculture, which is the principal source of income for 79 per cent of the poor.

The new policy thrust of the Interim Plan (2008–2010) contrasts with the previous Tenth Plan (2002–2007)/PRSP in its treatment of HI. Prepared while the insurgency was escalating, neither the Tenth Plan/PRSP, nor its progress reports up to 2006 or its Bank/Fund reviews of 2006 and 2003 address issue of HI and of other forms of exclusion and marginalization. None of these government and Fund/Bank documents included disaggregated data on incomes, employment, health and education status for the different groups, which are systematically included in the chapters of the Interim Plan document.

4.5 Comparing approaches to horizontal inequality in the Poverty Reduction Strategy Papers of Haiti, Liberia and Nepal

Horizontal inequality in Poverty Reduction Strategy Papers

The PRSPs of all three countries recognize inequality as a source of political violence, but they vary significantly in the degree to which this is reflected in the design of policies, analysis and resource allocation. The comparison is summarized below (Table 4.4).

Only Nepal has integrated HI correction as an important objective in its development agenda and has included explicit policies in its plan document. In contrast, the development policy frameworks of Haiti and Liberia do not explicitly refer to culturally defined group

Table 4.4 Vertical inequality (VI) and horizontal inequality (HI) in Poverty Reduction Strategy Papers (PSRPs)?

	Haiti PRSP	**Liberia PRSP**	**Nepal PRSP**	**Nepal interim plan**
Objective – VI, HI	VI	VI	VI	VI, HI
Analysis – VI, HI and poverty	Weak	VI	VI	VI, HI
Analysis – VI, HI and conflict	None	VI, HI	None	VI, HI
Data – VI, HI	VI Weak	VI Weak	VI	VI, HI
Policy choices – VI, HI				
growth	None	Weak	None	Yes
social services	None	Weak	None	Yes
governance	None	Yes	None	Yes
cultural recognition	None	None	None	Yes
affirmative action	None	None	None	Some
Implementation financing, key constraints	Weak, inadequate donor support to pro-poor growth	Weak, inadequate donor support to pro-poor growth	None	NA

inequality, but define the objective as reducing inequality and exclusion generally – in other words, as reducing primarily vertical rather than HI.

Nepal's Three-Year Interim Plan 2008–2010 identifies exclusion and discrimination against culturally defined groups in social, economic, political and cultural spheres as a major issue, and specifically as a human rights issue. It also identifies HI as a source of conflict, one that is intrinsically problematic for national life. The plan includes analysis of HI as well as of other forms of exclusion, as it relates to the poverty situation and to armed conflict in particular. It includes disaggregated data by cultural group. Most importantly, the plan includes explicit policies designed to end group-based discrimination and to promote the inclusion of excluded and marginalized groups. Dalits, Jayanatis, Madhesis and indigenous groups are singled out along with women and people displaced by conflict. How effectively the plan will be implemented is still an open question. However, it is worth noting that Nepal's PRSP is also the national plan, and is more institutionalized through the national administrative implementation process than other PRSPs. Moreover, the majority of funding is from domestic resources (72 per cent), while the external resource requirements are in line with historical levels of foreign aid received.

In the other two countries, there is a strong commitment to greater inclusion of all groups into the development process as an objective. This is particularly strong in Liberia, but its PRSP stops short of fully articulating exclusion as a result of discrimination or as a human rights issue. The Liberia PRSP is particularly focused on inequality and exclusion as part of the problem of misrule and as a source of the civil war.

However, it should be noted that, apart from an initial reference to the history of Americo-Liberian domination, the issue raised is not explicitly about group-based inequality, especially among culturally defined groups, but rather about exclusion and marginalization in general. The issue is reduced to a general problem of vertical rather than HI, although, given that groups in Liberia are basically 'ranked' hierarchically according to the Horowitz (1985) categorization, effective policies towards vertical inequality would also improve HI. There are no data disaggregated by ethnicity or race, nor are particularly disadvantaged culturally defined groups identified. Perhaps this reflects a hesitation to express the issue of inequality as being identity-based, because of the risk that this might deepen rather than heal political divides and tensions. In the case of Nepal, cultural identities are not only socially but also politically salient and have become the main dynamic behind current politics of the peace process. Reducing HI has become a major purpose objective of restructuring political power. In contrast, the country's previous plan and PRSPs ignored HI and HI-linked armed conflict, even though they were prepared at a time when the fighting was escalating throughout the country.

In Liberia's and Haiti's PRSPs, the stated commitment to inclusive development is not translated into explicit policy priorities and programme design. With respect to social policies, these documents do not contain targeted policies to redirect expenditures to disadvantaged groups in order to equalize access, nor to monitor distributional impacts. A major obstacle is the lack of disaggregated data; but there are also no proposals to develop disaggregated data, planning and monitoring systems.

With respect to economic policies, the Nepal and Liberia PRSPs include important elements of pro-poor growth, especially in support of small-scale agriculture and rural areas, where most of the poor and excluded groups are concentrated. But in the case of Liberia, as well as in that of Haiti, these activities receive little donor support, and without this financing they are unlikely to be implemented. The growth model in all three countries is market-oriented, and in the absence of compensating measures it would be likely to entrench rather than reverse existing inequalities.

With respect to political exclusion, Nepal is undertaking a serious effort at rewriting the constitution, which, if accepted will reduce political HIs. The Liberia PRSP is generally aimed at more accountable and participative, democratic governance rather than at HI specifically. Yet improving political HIs is an important basic condition for correction of socio-economic and cultural HIs. With respect to cultural exclusion, this is a major issue in Nepal and one area representing a major gap in its interim plan. The document does not contain significant provisions for multicultural policies such as in the areas of language. In Haiti, the political agenda is to stabilize democratic institutions in a context where HI remains an issue but is not recognized as such (Hallward 2007).

4.6 Key constraints

Several common themes emerge from these experiences that point to some key constraints for integrating HI in post-conflict development strategies.

Lack of data and analysis: The absence of disaggregated data is a major obstacle to recognizing and addressing HI. In Nepal, the availability of detailed socio-economic data disaggregated by culturally defined groups and studies of HIs by donors have provided an important basis for policy response by government and donors. Such data and studies are strikingly absent in Haiti and Liberia.

Domestic resources and political economy of taxation: Whatever the government policy might be with respect to HI, implementation depends on finance, which is constrained by donor priorities in aid-dependent countries and by domestic financing possibilities. In all three countries, limitations on domestic revenues are a fundamental constraint. How these constraints could be addressed is a question that requires further exploration. Technocratic measures can improve revenue collection, but political economy constraints are likely to be paramount. The experience of Guatemala's 1996 Peace Accords is of particular relevance here. Guatemala's peace accords involved a commitment to 'overcome the poverty, extreme poverty, discrimination and social and political marginalisation which have impeded and distorted the country's social, economic, cultural and political development and have represented a source of conflict and instability', and the accord specifically committed the state to increasing the education expenditures by 50 per cent between 1995 and 2000 and to targeting the most marginalized populations. Yet despite increases in spending, the total level remains low; for example, spending on health, which totalled only 1.3 per cent of GDP for the 2006 budget, is still one of the lowest in Central America. The basic constraint has been an inability to raise tax revenues, which amounted to only 12 per cent of GDP in 2005 – one of the lowest ratios in Latin America.[14]

External resources: Aid-dependent countries may agree with the donor community on priority objectives and policies. But implementation could be blocked or distorted if the level and allocation of external resources do not follow. In the case of Liberia and Haiti, the financing requirements of PRSPs hugely exceed not only domestic resource capacity, but also historic aid receipts. Because donor financing decisions are made by donors separately rather than collectively and coordination is weak, it is difficult for government to direct or redirect social spending and economic infrastructure support to correct for unbalanced development. Even if the Liberian and Haitian governments intended to do so, they have neither the control over decision-making nor the information to programme and monitor the distribution along spatial or beneficiary group lines.

PRSPs are a policy vehicle created not only for the purposes of guiding the different bodies of the government with priorities, but they are also a basis for agreement with the donor community on priorities for financing. A key issue that emerges from these cases is that the external aid allocations are not aligned with the government priorities reflected in the PRSPs. Another related issue concerns the gaps in mechanisms for aid management and coordination, which require not only national government processes but actions by donors to provide information and to coordinate with one another.

Recent trends in global aid allocation show high priority given to basic services in the social sectors, namely education, health, water and sanitation, and low priority given to economic infrastructure and productive sectors (see Table 4.3). Looking only at post-conflict countries, it would appear that humanitarian aid declines after the signing of peace agreements, and support to social infrastructure and services increases. But support to productive sectors, budget support and debt relief does not increase. In other words, donor financing does not give priority to supporting economic recovery overall, without which it is difficult to generate employment and other income-earning opportunities for the disadvantaged populations. The assumption behind this trend is not only that investing in basic social services is a priority for poverty reduction, but also that growth would be generated by private sector investment once a stable macroeconomic environment and political peace are maintained. This assumption neglects the fact that the impact of growth on reducing poverty – let alone reducing inequality – is slow and uneven in the presence of structural inequalities.

4.7 Concluding remarks: Poverty Reduction Strategy Papers and aid

This chapter has reviewed PRSPs as a policy vehicle for reducing risks of violent conflict by adopting appropriate economic, social and governance policies to reduce HIs. The analysis highlights the need for going beyond recognizing HI as a problem and including HI reduction as an objective, to introducing specific HI correcting policies.

The chapter also reveals the absence of disaggregated data as a fundamental constraint to introducing HI into the post-conflict strategy. Without collecting disaggregated data, analysis of HI is not possible, resource allocations cannot be guided and disparities in socio-economic outcomes cannot be monitored. Data availability is a major problem in Liberia and Haiti and is a general problem in low-income countries, and especially in post-conflict settings. But, just as efforts are made to restore data collection and estimations for macroeconomic variables, priority should be given to the rapid collection of socio-economic indicators and to their disaggregation. There is a surprising absence of systematic analysis of HI, and, for that matter, of vertical inequality, in both Liberia and Haiti. The lack of data only partially explains the general lack of attention to the issue. Giving priority to inequality analysis and to collecting the necessary data requires support from the donor community, as with any activity that requires external financing for its implementation.

Another major issue that the present chapter has revealed is the misalignment between external resource allocation and PRSP priorities, notably the underfinancing of productive sectors. In both countries, the underlying economic strategy behind the PRSPs is to put in place a stable macroeconomic environment as the first objective to lay the conditions for private sector investments. In Liberia, the core strategy is to restore the traditional engines of growth, which require foreign investment in the extractive sectors.[15] In Haiti, a new strategy is to rely on the export promotion zones.[16] Much less emphasis is placed on the role of economic infrastructure and government services necessary to stimulate and support small- and medium-sized operators, including small-scale service and manufacturing, smallholder agriculture and the informal sector. But these are precisely the economic development programmes that are important for improving the employment, productivity and incomes of excluded groups, and thus for correcting HI. Relying on the macroeconomic environment to stimulate investments may well lead to a pattern of growth that does not do much for the poorer and excluded segments of the population. 'Pro-poor' growth strategies require direct investment and efforts to support productivity of the poor.

The misalignment of external resources with PRSP priorities also reveals a process gap in aid coordination. In both Haiti and Liberia, as elsewhere in aid-dependent countries, governments and donor communities have been struggling with the challenge of coordinating diverse aid sources into a unified framework. The PRSP is intended to serve as the strategic framework. But, without mechanisms for integrating inputs into a single programming and budgeting process, coordination is theoretical. The Liberian government has introduced a shadow budget as an important step forward. Nepal has made the Interim Plan the PRSP. But gaps remain that show the need for a more coherent set of processes to align donor inputs with PRSP priorities.

Although PRSPs are national documents and are intended to promote national ownership of the development process, it is unrealistic to neglect the role of donors. National governments do not have full control over the financial resources needed to implement the PRSPs. Donor support to HI correcting policies is thus essential to their integration into the development strategy – as has happened in the case of Nepal.

Both donors and government officials need to recognize the importance of HI as a risk factor. A consensus on this point cannot be achieved without evidence-based research specific to the country itself. As the World Bank 'stocktaking' note on PRSPs in post-conflict settings points out, analysis of the specific context of the country and assessment of causal factors and of the poverty impact of conflict are essential starting points. A World Bank retrospective study of nine countries (World Bank 2005) concludes that, while poverty diagnostic included consideration of the impact of conflict on poverty, it stopped short of examining systemic conflict factors. The assessment also concluded that countries were subjected to political constraints faced by their government in addressing poverty–conflict linkages. Further research and analysis of HI and of the structural factors that contribute to the outbreak of political violence must be conducted by scholars, NGOs, governments and donor agencies alike. This work will prove essential in bringing about greater consensus concerning the importance of economic and social policies in reducing conflict risks.

Notes

1. This chapter is based on a paper prepared for the CRISE workshop on HIs and Post-Conflict Reconstruction, held at the Makerere University, Kampala, Uganda, 16–18 April, 2009. This chapter is based on realities in Haiti, Liberia and Nepal as of that date and does not reflect important evolutions that occurred since then. The chapter has benefited from comments from the workshop, notably from Frances Stewart and Arnim Langer, as well as from the research assistance of Tanushree Dutta Isaacman and Patrick Guyer. The author is responsible for any errors or omissions.
2. See Murshed (2007) for a review of literature on conflict–poverty links.
3. See UNDP (2004) for a full exploration of concepts and for evidence of cultural exclusion.
4. Also referred to as 'cultural status' exclusion in Brown and Langer (2006).
5. Since this text was completed, the country experienced a major earthquake in January 2010, with unprecedented consequences, and prospects for development are dramatically changed. This analysis was completed in September 2009 and does not take account of these new circumstances.
6. See Hallward (2007) for a detailed account of the political history of Haiti.
7. In addition to the PRSP, inequality data are to be found in Dorte Verner (2008) and in ONPES (2009).
8. DSNCRP, p. 35, table 2.
9. Interview with SFP March 2009.
10. World Bank, March 2008, Republic of Haiti: Public Expenditure Management and Financial Accountability Review (PEMFAR).
11. See Omeje (2009) and Humphreys and Richards (2005) for reviews of studies on the causes of the civil war. Both sources are sceptical of single explanations for the conflict and critique the role of poverty and youth unemployment, and 'greed' for natural resource rents. Humphrey and Richards (2005) identify a 'cluster of factors including weak state capacity, poor regulation of natural resource industries, ingrained corruption, alienation of population from governmental processes, and rural disaffection, particularly among youths, arising from poor education and employment opportunities' (p. 10). Omeje (2009) concludes that, 'beyond the explanations proffered by various schools of thought, there is a great measure of consensus among leading African scholars that the Liberian civil war as is the case with many of the contemporaneous civil wars in Africa and elsewhere [...] comes under the rubric of what the UN in the 1990s described as Complex Political Emergencies (CPEs) [...] characterised by multi-causality, and requiring multi-dimensional international responses, including a combination of military

intervention, peace support operations, humanitarian relief programs, high level political intervention and diplomacy' (p. 10).

12. See report for the UN Office for High Commissioner for Human Rights (Fukuda-Parr and others 2007) and IMF (2008).
13. See particularly the extensive World Bank study led by Lynn Bennett (2006).
14. Several efforts to raise taxation in Guatemala met with strong opposition in the recent past. See Fukuda-Parr et al. (2007); and Caumartin and Sanchez in this volume.
15. See Fukuda-Parr (2008).
16. See Fukuda-Parr (2009).

5

Privatization, Private-Sector Development and Horizontal Inequalities in Post-Conflict Countries

Rajesh Venugopal

5.1 Introduction

One of the most important strands of contemporary writing on liberal peace-building and post-conflict reconstruction has been a critique of the donor emphasis on rapid post-conflict market reforms.[1] Even in non-conflict countries, privatization is one of the most politically controversial and technically problematic components of the market reform agenda, because (1) it is very difficult to reverse; (2) it often results in the loss of scarce formal sector jobs; and (3) the process is often accompanied by a lack of transparency and corruption (Adam et al. 1992; Campell-White and Bhatia 1998; Commander and Killick 1988). Such problems and their repercussions are compounded in post-conflict countries that are struggling to deepen institutions, preserve socio-political stability and overcome a legacy of conflict in fragile, deeply divided societies.

There has been a vast literature on privatization over the past 30 years, but very little that is specific to the post-conflict environment as such, and no study (that we are aware of) that attempts to look at this issue from a comparative perspective. There is a substantial literature on the role of the private sector in conflict zones and in peace-building, often within the rubric of corporate social responsibility (CSR), but that is largely relevant to foreign direct investment and multinational corporations.[2] The dominant themes in the privatization literature have largely to do with efficacy; that is, they revolve around issues of process, mode, sequencing and transparency. The debates within this topic relate to the comparative benefits of voucher-based mass privatization, which is politically more palatable, versus alternatives such as management buy-outs or sales to foreign investors (which have the advantage of bringing in technical and managerial expertise and fresh investment). As such, there are two important characteristics of this literature to note. Firstly, it views privatization as a largely technocratic exercise. As Feigenbaum and Henig (1994: 186) describe it:

> Privatisation is an intensely political phenomenon and ought to be analyzed as such. Yet much of the literature deemphasizes its consequences for political ideas and political institutions and instead presents it as a pragmatic adaptation of well-tested administrative techniques or as a necessary exercise in economic adjustment to structural constraints.

Secondly, the dependent variable in these studies is typically a measure of the economic success of privatization, for instance the dollar value of privatization receipts, increases in firm-level output or productivity.[3]

In contrast, there is a small alternative literature that inverts the relationship under investigation to place the social effects of privatization as the dependent variable.[4] For example, one recent study estimates that mass privatization resulted in a 12.8 per cent increase in adult male mortality rates in post-communist countries over 1989–2002 (Stuckler et al. 2009). One of the key methodological problems facing any such study, however, is the difficulty in isolating the impact of privatization alone, because it is not a bounded policy choice whose effects can be studied in isolation from other contemporaneous policies and non-policy effects.[5]

Similarly, although it is possible to identify similar dynamics unleashed as a result of the privatization process in many post-conflict countries, the overall political, economic and social results that are ultimately manifest vary significantly from one case to another, being based largely on the strength and design of state institutions, the actions and inactions of donors and the differential evolution of state–capital relations in the pre-war, war and post-war periods. It is, as a result, complicated to undertake any comparative study on the effects of privatization and to arrive at broadly applicable abstract policy conclusions on how post-conflict privatization should be approached.

This chapter uses four case studies of post-conflict privatization and post-conflict private-sector development to advance a typology of the implications for post-conflict stability and for ethnic and regional inequalities. Privatization, foreign investment and private-sector development are critical elements in the revitalization of post-conflict economies, and they are priority items on the agenda of donors and post-conflict governments. Under the urgent imperatives of generating employment, creating economic growth and bringing new investment in war-ravaged societies, the reliance on the private sector is critical and unavoidable. In effect, the success or failure of post-conflict reconstruction often depends on the disaggregated micro-level investment decisions of thousands of small, middle-sized and large private-sector entrepreneurs, both domestic and foreign, whose actions and inactions are modulated through their social identities, and on the way in which this process relates to the politics of the conflict and post-conflict dispensation.

Given the extent of economic destruction and capital flight that frequently transpires during violent conflict, the creation and expansion of new private-sector investment in post-conflict countries have important historical parallels in the earlier periods, of transition to capitalism, parallels that must be taken into account – particularly in terms of the socio-political repercussions that they generate. The uneven transition of pre-capitalist agrarian economies to mercantile or industrial capitalism under colonial rule or in ethnically segmented societies resulted in two major problems that had significant social, economic and political repercussions over the course of the twentieth century.

Firstly, this transition resulted in the rise of ethnicized capitalisms, such that access to business opportunity and occupation were frequently stratified by bounded ascriptive categories. In countries like India or Nigeria, commercially oriented ethnic or caste groups such as Marwaris or Igbos grew to dominate trade, finance and industry during the colonial period. In East Africa and Southeast Asia there was a clear economic trifurcation of the population with respect to the economy: the apex of banking, international commerce and plantation agriculture was in European hands; rural commerce and small enterprises were largely in the hands of immigrant groups of Indian or Chinese 'barefoot capitalists'. Meanwhile, the indigenous populations, who comprised the large majority, were largely restricted, sometimes through legislation and coercion, to peasant agriculture.[6]

The dominance of certain ethnic groups in business ownership during the colonial period, and the systematic under-representation of many groups, including large indigenous majorities, and their exclusion from participation in avenues for prosperity and upward mobility often contributed to the creation of very sharp forms of rigidly bounded ethnicized inequalities. By the mid-twentieth century these became the roots of substantial economic grievances, which triggered mass support for anti-colonial uprisings and for populist ethnic and 'bhumi-putra'-type political movements that have animated ethnic politics and the dynamics of political violence in post-colonial states.

Secondly, the colonial experience resulted in very widespread geographic differences in development, often mapping onto unequal levels of welfare and income for specific ethnic groups. Due to the impact of factors such as proximity to sea-routes, the location of natural resource investment and the differential impact and forms of direct versus indirect colonial rule within the same territories, the spread of private enterprise, of commercial relations and of the formal and informal institutions of capitalism has been very uneven. This unevenness has in turn helped to define and re-define differences in identity between particular regions and populations, often becoming the basis for lasting ethnic inequalities that have persisted for decades, well into the post-colonial period.

Both of these factors – the ethnic dominance of business and the uneven geographic patterns of private-sector development – remain critical issues of concern in post-conflict economies, although for the most part there is little explicit attention to this matter in the discourse and practice of post-conflict reconstruction. Indeed, in what appears to be a generational reversion into the past, the World Bank's 2009 World Development Report explicitly makes a spatial version of the Kuznets curve argument against efforts at ameliorating regional inequalities:

> Economic growth is seldom balanced. Efforts to spread it prematurely will jeopardize progress. Two centuries of economic growth show that spatial disparities in income and production are inevitable. (WDR 2009: 5–6)

Numerous post-conflict reconstruction programmes, particularly in the early to mid-1990s, featured a heavy emphasis on early, rapid privatization, with very little (if any) attention to the social and regional distortions that might result. From the perspective of the donor agencies, the rationale was three-fold:

1. Firstly, this emphasis on rapid privatization and private-sector development reflected a standard application of orthodox development theory to post-conflict countries. State-owned enterprises (SOEs) were identified as inefficient and as a drain on government finances

(Bayliss and Cramer 2001). Privatization would lead to better incentives and increased firm output and would contribute to private-sector-led economic growth, creating the developmental basis for post-conflict stability and success. To the extent that this idea was grounded in any sensitivity to the specificities of a post-conflict environment, it was based on a very linear conception of the development–conflict nexus – the idea that conflict is the flip-side of development and that rapid development can help to overcome the legacy of conflict and to promote peace.[7]

2. Secondly, privatization was explicitly identified as a desirable goal, which was possible and achievable in the post-conflict *terra nullius* situation. In some post-conflict countries, donor policy documents argued that politically difficult reforms could be achieved in the immediate post-conflict moment, before networks of anti-reform activism and influence could coalesce against it. The most recent and concise statement of this position (Collier 2009) explicitly states that 'the political context for reform is more favourable' in post-conflict situations. Similarly, Bray (2009) contends that 'it is harder to implement reforms later on because delays make it easier for those with post-conflict vested interests to entrench their position'.
3. Thirdly, and somewhat related to the above point, there was the conscious idea that early, rapid privatization was actually a valuable conflict-mitigating strategy, as it would remove patronage-able assets from the state, preventing ethnically imbalanced post-conflict governments from distributing patronage in ways that could exacerbate socio-political inequalities and risk, re-igniting the conflict.

Despite the substantial differences in the analytical understanding of the conflict–development linkages that underpin these three approaches, they all share a common policy conclusion that emphasizes the positive aspects of privatization at the cost of ignoring its negative consequences. Furthermore, in the relatively few cases where post-conflict reconstruction has been sensitized – at least in discourse, if not in practice – to issues of ethnic/regional inequalities, the method of evaluation and intervention often concentrates on state-led and aid-led policy levers, in which average incomes, poverty rates or political participation are the relevant indicators, rather than private-sector participation.

This chapter suggests instead that it is relevant to pay greater attention to the actions of business leaders, to their social composition and to their investment decisions. Importantly, the chapter starts out with an analytical frame that explores the implications these factors bear for ethnic and regional inequalities. Through a stylized description of the privatization experiences in four post-conflict countries, it outlines the great complexities and the highly contingent outcomes that result from the application of very similar policies in very different societies. The findings do not result in the isolation of critical variables on the basis of comparative analysis, but in the clustering and detailing of four broad typologies of problems that emerge through a privatization process:

1. Privatization is an extremely controversial policy agenda item, which can involve distinct changes in welfare for specific groups and can be conflict-inducing. Opposition to privatization, particularly where it is imposed through external pressure, can strengthen the hand of extremist and nationalist groups, who seek to institute ethnic/party dominance or a return to conflict. In deeply divided societies, the fear that privatization can result in a redistribution of ethnic ownership and employment patterns can influence the form and process of privatization.
2. Private-sector development can result in the dominance of the business elite in its formative stage by small, commercially oriented ethnic groups or by foreign investors. It can contribute to the early creation of the basis for lasting post-conflict ethnic inequalities. In such situations, the privatization process might, with appropriate regulation and institutional support, be used in order to ensure the broadening of the ethnic structure of the private sector.
3. Private-sector development can contribute to the creation or exacerbation of regional and urban/rural imbalances in development and income levels, which can subsequently become the basis for social instability.
4. Private-sector development and privatization can blend into a continuation of illicit and ethnically divisive war-economies. Far from ending patrimonial and predatory forms of ethnically biased politics, privatization can be the vehicle for the perpetuation of corrupt elites and for locking the benefits of transitory political power into permanent economic gains for certain groups.

The four country cases that are used to illustrate these points are (1) Sri Lanka; (2) Mozambique; (3) Bosnia and Herzegovina and (4) Cambodia. In summary, the case of Sri Lanka in the 2001–2004 period is an example of the ways in which the popular backlash (particularly from the majority community) to an ambitious post-conflict privatization and market reform agenda helped to destabilize a fragile peace process.

In Mozambique, which is frequently cited as a success story of post-conflict reconstruction, post-conflict development has sharpened existing regional inequalities between the south, the centre and the north. In Bosnia, post-conflict privatization and private-sector development have taken place in the shadow of a highly ethnicized and fragmented state authority and have contributed in certain ways to the consolidation of a weak state and divided population. In Cambodia, the emergence of a new private sector, based on close links to predatory state elites and to their capture of public assets such as land, has become overshadowed by a rapid industrial transformation, controlled almost entirely by ethnic Chinese entrepreneurs from neighbouring countries.

5.2 Sri Lanka

The Sri Lankan civil war, which started in 1983, is the product of an underlying political conflict between the island's majority Sinhalese community and the minority Tamils, who had by the mid-1970s developed a demand for self-determination and for the independence of the Tamil-dominated north and east of the island. In the context of several failed peace negotiations and of war continuing for almost two decades, the cease-fire agreement of February 2002 between the Sri Lankan government and the Liberation Tigers of Tamil Eelam (LTTE) gave rise to the most promising possibility for peace to date.

Nevertheless, just over two years later, in April 2004, the government that signed the cease-fire lost power in mid-term elections and was replaced by a new government, far more hostile to the peace agenda. From that point onwards there was no more progress on the peace process; there was instead a slow slide towards war over the next two years. The reasons for the collapse of the peace process and for the resumption of civil war in mid-2006 are complex, and blame must be apportioned to several parties, including the international community.

One of the most noteworthy features of the Sri Lankan peace process was the extent to which it was accompanied by a well-articulated post-conflict economic strategy which enjoyed the strong 'ownership' of the government and the support of the donors. In the years prior to the initiation of the peace process, the Sri Lankan economy had entered a period of crisis and contraction, due in part to the effects of the war and aggravated by political instability. In early 2001, Sri Lanka was forced to seek an International Monetary Fund (IMF) bailout that set stringent conditions for fiscal austerity, particularly with respect to a number of politically sensitive issues, such as the fertilizer subsidy. The crisis spurred both donors and influential business groups to lobby heavily for the emerging post-conflict economic policy agenda to have a strong market reform component, including the privatization of a significant number of SOE, such as the banking sector.

The promotion of this agenda alongside the evolving peace process by the government, donor agencies and leading domestic corporate groups was explicitly based on a two-fold, interlocking rationale: faster economic reforms and privatization would spur a rapid post-conflict economic bounce-back; the cease-fire and peace process, in turn, would lift the economic burden of war that was weighing on the economy. Together, these two factors would be mutually synergistic and lead into a second stage, where economic growth would provide the peace dividend necessary to consolidate and expand public support for further progress in the peace process.[8]

On the part of the aid donors, particularly the World Bank, this kind of strategization of the conflict–development relationship paradoxically emerged as part of the transformation in attitudes and practices towards a more conflict-sensitive approach. As with the business community, many donors felt that they could no longer work around the conflict and pretend it did not exist; they would have to address it more directly, through their programmes, through policy dialogue with the government and perhaps even through conditionality (Frerks and Klem 2006; Goodhand 2001). The World Bank's 2001 internal evaluation audit on Sri Lanka remarked, self-critically, that the bank's activities needed to be far more directly conflict-sensitive. But in the same breath the document asserts, without any apparent contradiction, the need for such conflict-sensitivity to go hand in hand with market reforms:

> Completion of the structural reform agenda and a resolution of the conflict in the North and the East are the key missing elements for Sri Lanka to accelerate growth and achieve further poverty reduction. Bank assistance should help overcome both these constraints.[9]

In reality, many of the assumptions in this model proved to be flawed. The reform agenda generated deep anxiety among an increasing number of social groups, for whom privatization proposals involved vital decisions relating to their livelihoods. The government's cutbacks on social expenditures, rural infrastructure, fertilizer subsidies and public sector employment meant that there was very little in the way of a peace dividend to distribute.

As direct political negotiations with the LTTE opened in late-2002, the government's break-neck pace of reform, the domestic effects of the fiscal compression, and the spreading concerns that the government was about to announce a wave of privatization began to cause a wave of public unease. Over the course of the government's second year in power, by mid-2003, an increasingly vigorous opposition to the reforms emerged from trade unions, farmers groups and welfare recipients. Although there was no explicit ethnic element to this new mobilization, SOEs had typically employed the majority Sinhalese community to a disproportionate extent. Largely as a result of this factor, the Sinhala nationalist opposition to the peace process was able to capitalize on the unease that many Sinhalese felt at the compression of state employment through privatization.

The peace process and the brief pause in conflict that ensued between 2002 and 2006 certainly did have positive economic consequences and led to a brief spurt of economic growth. But the material benefits – apart from the immediate relief that it briefly afforded to the population of the war-torn northeast – accrued in a direction that aggravated the existing axes of economic maldistribution, favouring the richer, more globally connected, Colombo-based segments of society at the expense of poorer, fixed-income groups of the Sinhalese majority, who lived in the rural hinterland and urban periphery.

Not only did government policy not correct, mitigate and compensate for these extant tendencies, which were largely the result of a spontaneous private-sector-led bounce-back; but, in the wake of a fiscal austerity programme implemented as a condition of an IMF rescue package, it actually worsened the problem. Furthermore, the government's ambitious plans to reform labour law, rationalize poverty alleviation schemes and privatize large segments of the public sector extended the sense of insecurity to larger segments of the population. In essence, the theorization of 'development' as an abstract antidote to conflict proved to be near-sighted and counter-productive. There was indeed a surge of post-conflict development in Sri Lanka during the brief peace process, but it was clearly a case where the benefits for the few appeared to come at the expense of the growing insecurity of the many. As a result, development gave rise, not to a reversal of conflict, but to a reversion to conflict.

5.3 Mozambique

After three decades of violent conflict, Mozambique emerged into post-conflict status in 1992 as the poorest country in the world, with the lowest level of gross domestic product (GDP) per capita and very low levels of infrastructure and productive economic assets, both human and physical. Yet within a decade Mozambique had been transformed into one of the more successful cases of peace-building and post-conflict reconstruction. The two main parties to the civil war, Frelimo and Renamo, had undergone a successful transition from violent rivalry to peaceful political competition under a devolved, liberal democratic framework.[10]

Mozambique's post-conflict economy also grew at high rates, with GDP growth at levels of 8 per cent per annum over the period 1994–2007, buoyed by high levels of foreign aid and private foreign investment. As Castel Branco et al. (2001) describe: 'Privatisation, together with liberalisation and deregulation, constituted the core of economic demobilisation' (p. 1). Around 1,400 companies were privatized in Mozambique, mostly during the decade of the 1990s, in what constituted the largest privatization programme in Africa (Cramer 2001).

Prior to the outbreak of war and independence from Portugal, Mozambique's economy was characterized by very high disparities in regional development, a racialized segmentation of the economy and very low levels of income and public expenditure for the vast majority of the indigenous African population. The relatively small formal private sector was entirely dominated by entrepreneurs of European and Asian/Indian ethnicity, with a heavy concentration in urban enclaves – particularly in the far south, around the capital Maputo, due to its proximity to South Africa. Following independence in 1975, a significant part of the formal private sector effectively collapsed when most Europeans and Asians, who comprised the majority of the country's business owners, as well as the managerial and technical elite, left the country. Formal sector private enterprises were further heavily constrained during the socialist period of 1977–1983, when many were nationalized or subject to heavy government regulation and intervention.

It is in this context – of colonial-era ethnic/regional imbalances, post-colonial socialist policies and destruction due to the war – that Mozambique offers a case study in understanding how privatization and post-conflict reconstruction affect the composition and geography of a newly re-created private sector. It is important, however, to bear in mind that market reforms were initiated in Mozambique in 1987, five years before the end of the war and seven years before the first post-conflict elections in 1994. Furthermore, the continuation of the ruling Frelimo party, in power during the war and the post-war periods, has meant that the impact of the end of the war did not signify a change in policy direction or leadership as much as an increase in the level of aid and private investment.

Privatization was a key item on the donor agenda in the post-1987 period, but there was also considerable internal pressure for privatization from domestic investors. As Hanlon (2002), Pitcher (2002) and Castel Branco et al. (2001) describe, domestic investors wanted a faster pace of privatization to occur prior to the conclusion of peace negotiations, which would give them an opportunity to acquire control of state enterprises before the arrival of larger and better financed foreign investors. Between 1990 and 2000, the government authorized the sale of nearly 1,000 SOEs, the large majority of which were small- to medium-sized companies located in Maputo Province (Pitcher 2002). Until 1996, 90 per cent of the buyers of SOE's were domestic Mozambican buyers, who were given very generous and extended payment terms (Castel Branco 2001).[11] Many of these new entrepreneurs were closely linked to the Frelimo-controlled state and included former or current government officials, ruling party members, military personnel and state enterprise managers (Castel Branco 2001; Hanlon 2002; Pitcher 2002). Cramer (2006) reports how the Frelimo government reserved some public-sector companies to retired officers outside of the normal bidding process in order to reintegrate them into civilian life and to appease them politically. Overall, this process resulted in the significant expansion of business ownership and in affluence for new strata of black Mozambicans. As Cramer describes:

> Even where state enterprises were sold to foreign investors, there were Mozambicans who either formed joint ventures with these investors or took up seats on the boards of enterprises that retained a state stake. To a large extent the state took control of assets during nationalisation and then influenced their allocation through privatisation: it created and managed the allocation of rent.[12]

Under the overlapping circumstances of post-conflict and post-socialist transformation, the state became an important vehicle for the accumulation and re-allocation of assets. This created the possibility for expanding business ownership on the one hand, but this process went together with a manifold expansion of opportunities for corruption, rent-seeking and the establishment of predatory and counter-developmental forms of state–business relations.

Data from the World Bank's Regional Program for Enterprise Development (RPED) enterprise survey conducted in 2002 in Mozambique show that almost half of the sampled manufacturing enterprises were privatized companies. The data (see Table 5.1) also demonstrate the clear ethnic segmentation of the business community and provide information that suggests the predominance of Asian and European owners in larger enterprises, and of African owners in smaller companies and in privatized companies. Due to data limitations, it is not possible to evaluate the regional and ethnic composition of the African ownership category any further, but the clear dominance of non-Africans among owners suggests that these are relevant categories for understanding the composition of business ownership. Furthermore, there are comparable patterns of ethnic ownership in the other southern/eastern African countries (Kenya, Tanzania, Zambia and Zimbabwe), which have comparable RPED data.

The data show that black Mozambicans control and manage less than half of all manufacturing enterprises and that their participation is greatest in smaller sized firms, and decreases steadily with size. This relationship of size to ethnic ownership structure is replicated in Kenya, Zambia, Zimbabwe and Tanzania, although the situation in Mozambique compares favourably to some extent with that of Kenya, where as much as 96 per cent of all the large firms sampled were owned by Asian/Indians, who comprise just 1 per cent of the population.[13] Importantly, the proportion of black Mozambican owners of small and medium enterprises corresponds closely to the proportion of the enterprises that were privatized (in the sample surveyed). This suggests (but greater confirmation is required) that, although black Mozambicans have extraordinarily low representation in business ownership compared to their 99.6 per cent share in the population, the structure of the privatization programme in its early phases may have had a critical impact on enabling the creation

Table 5.1 Ownership of Mozambican manufacturing enterprises by ethnicity and size. Comparative data by ethnicity provided for Kenya, Zimbabwe, Zambia and Tanzania

	Small (%)	**Medium** (%)	**Large** (%)	**Moz.** (%)	**Kenya** (%)	**Zimbabwe** (%)	**Zambia** (%)	**Tanzania** (%)
African	53	45	29	38	47	41	61	74
European	20	29	42	37	0.5	40	11	0
Asian/Indian	25	24	29	21	52	16	26	24
% privatized	44	52	53	48				

Source: RPED survey data, drawn from Nasir et al. (2003), Mozambique Industrial Performance and Investment Climate 2003. RPED/CPI/CTA. Data for other African countries drawn from Ramachandran. V. and M.K. Shah (1999), 'Minority Entrepreneurs and Firm Performance in Sub-Saharan Africa', *Journal of Development Studies* 36(2): 71–87.

and support of black Mozambican entrepreneurs in a situation where very few, if any, existed previously.

It remains, however, critical to decompose further the African ownership category, largely because of the close association of privatization with the ruling Frelimo, and because Frelimo leadership was dominated by the southern Shangana-Ronga and northern Makonde groups. Although Mozambique was not a case of ethnic conflict as such, and although Frelimo has since its inception explicitly promoted a supra-ethnic, pan-Mozambican identity, it remained the case that networks of mobilization, support and territorial control during the war followed the contours of ethnic and regional identities. Although there is no datum to evaluate the ethnic composition of black privatization recipients or enterprise owners, the regional concentration of existing enterprises and new foreign investment proposals does provide important insights and sources of concern.

In the colonial period industry, commerce and finance were concentrated largely in the far south of Mozambique, due to the location of the capital Maputo there, and also because of its proximity to South Africa. These pre-existing regional disparities have continued; and they have exacerbated since the early 1990s, for three main reasons. Firstly, Maputo has experienced greater economic growth in general because it is the capital city and has a large portion of government salaries and population concentration.[14] Secondly, regional disparities have been exacerbated along rural/urban lines, the largest cities and ports, Maputo and Beira, receiving a larger portion of government expenditures and private investment.[15] Thirdly, regional disparities have occurred largely in the context of greater economic integration from South Africa and along the 'Maputo Corridor' – the 50 km stretch of road that links the capital to the South African border, and on towards Johannesburg (Nuno 2004).

Table 5.2 shows the scale of regional concentration of private-sector investment in Mozambique: Maputo city and province, which contain about 15 per cent of the population, received 73 per cent of the total investment over the 1996–2000 period. A significant portion of this investment came in the form of a single 'mega-project' investment in the Mozal aluminium complex near Maputo, which alone accounted for 27 per cent of the total investment in the country over this period. But, even excluding Mozal, there remains a sharp imbalance towards Maputo, at 63 per cent of the total investment.

Such imbalances in development continue to feed into perceptions that the central regions in particular, where Renamo has its strongest

Table 5.2 Mozambique: Regional distribution of foreign and total investment (1996–2000)

	Foreign (US$ 000's)	% of Foreign	Total (US$ 000's)	% of Total
Cabo-Delgado	15,338	1.30	71,268	1.40
Niassa	628	0.10	36,603	0.70
Nampula	124,670	10.30	364,365	7.30
Zambezia	33,329	2.80	223,232	4.50
Tete	2,471	0.20	98,829	2.00
Manica	23,230	1.90	100,868	2.00
Sofala	60,647	5.00	259,284	5.20
Inhambane	16,550	1.40	67,343	1.30
Gaza	18,192	1.50	55,830	1.10
Maputo	893,390	73.90	3,639,004	72.80
(of which Mozal)	(500,000)	(41.40)	(1,340,000)	(26.80)
Multi-province	20,250	1.70	75,875	1.50
	1,208,695		4,992,501	

Source: Drawn from Nasir et al. (2003), Mozambique Industrial Performance and Investment Climate 2003. RPED/CPI/CTA, drawn from Mozambican Investment Promotion Centre. Total investment equals foreign investment plus domestic equity investments and commercial bank loans.

support, are deliberately being neglected.[16] This perception is likely to be enhanced if regional elites linked to Renamo are conspicuously under-represented in private-sector participation. As Vaux et al. (2006) identify in Mozambique's Strategic Conflict Assessment (SCA) report, regional differences, particularly between the centre and the south or between the capital and the rest of the country, are a major threat, which might underlie future fragility and conflict.

5.4 Bosnia

Bosnia-Herzegovina suffered a devastating conflict between 1992 and 1995, in the context of its declaration of independence from Yugoslavia and of the competing claims and contradictory aspirations of statehood held by its three constituent ethnic groups: (Muslim) Bosniaks, Croats and Serbs. In the course of an exceptionally violent war, in which between 100,000 and 200,000 people were killed and up to half the population was displaced, the formal sector almost completely collapsed, both because of the massive war-time dislocations within Bosnia and because the Bosnian economy, which was one of the poorest components of Yugoslavia, became unhinged from the economic geography it had long been a part of.

As a result, Bosnia took twice as long as most formerly socialist economies to recover from the early shock of transition. While income levels in most Eastern European countries had by 2000 returned to 1990 levels, it will take Bosnia until 2011, or two full decades, to return to its 1991 level of income. Ten years after the Dayton peace accords – a period referred to as the 'lost decade' of development – the World Bank's review of Bosnia's post-conflict reconstruction experience was stark and pessimistic:

> Time lost during the war, combined with subsequent difficulties in coping with the double challenge of post-conflict reconstruction and the transition to a market economy have left BH far behind the most successful countries of central and eastern Europe (CEE). While post-conflict reconstruction has been successful, mainly because of large aid flows, the analysis in the report shows that BH lags on many of the structural reforms that have accompanied economic transition in the region. These include strategic privatization, product and labor market liberalization and enterprise restructuring. (World Bank 2005: ii)

After more than four decades of worker-managed market socialism, on the eve of the war in 1991, Bosnia-Herzegovina had low levels of income inequality, high levels of unemployment, few legal avenues for private enterprise and private accumulation and no sizeable class of domestic entrepreneurs (Woodward 1995). This changed almost overnight during the 1992–1995 war, when nationalist militias funded their political and military activities by controlling the movement of arms, fuel, tobacco, alcohol and foodstuff (Pugh 2002). New entrepreneurs, who used their links to the ethnic militias, and powerful nationalist politicians came into being through the misappropriation of aid, violent dispossession, illegal trade and other such forms of what Marx describes as 'primitive accumulation'.[17]

In a short period of time, these entrepreneurs became the richest people in the region and consolidated their war-time accumulation and the political links forged in that period into post-conflict networks of informal, semi-legal and illegal economic activities, which thrived on the weak post-war Bosnian state and on the tight links with nationalist political parties, which gained control of the post-war state. As Donais (2005) describes, 'a new post-war symbiosis emerged between those at the top of Bosnia's largely criminalized political economy and the country's political elites' (p. 69). As a result, the privatization process was much more complicated and problematic in Bosnia than in most post-conflict or post-socialist states.

The most important factor in this process was the institutional structure of the Dayton Accord, which created a thin shell of a central Bosnian state, in which real power rested within two constituent ethnocratic statelets: the Bosnian Serb-controlled Republika Srpska (RS) and the Croat–Muslim Federation of Bosnia-Herzegovina (the Federation). The Croat–Muslim Federation, in turn, had many powers devolved to the level of cantons – smaller geographical entities, many of which were also designed as mini-ethnocracies. As a result, the nationalist parties that led the conflict remained in power for years after the civil war, presiding over a devastated formal sector economy that operated at perhaps 20 per cent of the pre-war level, and over a vast array of crumbling and often completely non-functioning state enterprises.

Under these circumstances, the privatization process in Bosnia became a contentious agenda item, promoted overwhelmingly by the international community, the donors and the Office of the High Representative (OHR), and vigorously resisted by local political leaders (Donais 2005). In a situation where there were extremely high levels of unemployment among all three ethnic groups and inadequate efforts at employment-creation on the part of the international community (Woodward 2000), the ethnic control of state assets and of state employment opportunities was a critical source of influence and power exercised by the nationalist parties that came to power in both the entities. Under the terms of the Dayton Accord, privatization was effectively devolved down to the constituent ethnocratic political units, with separate and parallel privatization agencies and processes underway in the RS, in the Federation and to some extent in the constituent cantons of the Federation. What this meant was that the micro-politics of privatization in Bosnia has revolved around two closely related factors: (1) the neo-patrimonial interests of ethnically divided state elites seeking to control sources of patronage; and (2) the compulsions of preserving ethnic control over enterprises, and particularly ethnic employment patterns.

As a result, the pace of privatization was very slow in the first five years after Dayton, as mono-ethnic parties empowered in the statelets preferred to retain tight control of their assets. However, following heavy pressure from the donor community for greater speed and transparency in the privatization process, domestic state elites sought to find new ways in which their interests for patronage accumulation and ethnic control might still be served through privatization. This was, as Michael Pugh describes, a process of 'ethnic privatisation':

> 'ethnic privatisation' was a compromise that emerged after a phase of resistance until about 1998, when nationalist elites sought to control the process, management, and ownership so that they could take advantage of development funds that were conditional on measures toward privatisation.[18]

Between 2001 and 2004, the large majority of smaller and medium-sized SOEs in both entities were privatized through a voucher system. The state privatization entities handed out vouchers, technically to all residents, who then reinvested those vouchers with designated fund management companies (Bayliss 2005; Donais 2005). Voucher privatization provided an easy way out for state elites to respond to pressure from above (donors who demanded more privatization), from below (electorates who resisted privatization), and from within (state elites who wanted to retain patronage and ethnic control of enterprises). There would be privatization, but this would be done in a non-threatening manner, and so that the state still retained a substantial degree of control over enterprises. In this process, voucher-privatization not only did nothing to address the stagnation, low-growth and absence of employment-creation that had characterized the pre-privatization period (due to continued under-capitalization and outdated equipment), but the absence of investment and employment generation in the new SOEs perpetuated the *status quo* of high levels of unemployment, and hence the exacerbation of ethnic tensions over scarce jobs.

Following the voucherization of small- and medium-scale enterprises, there has been a separate process whereby larger and strategically more valuable companies have been reserved for outright sale and have attracted buyers from Austria, Switzerland, Russia and the former Yugoslav republics. Many of these privatizations have been largely transparent and fair, and have resulted in commitments to protect employment and to increase investment and technological capability.

But a significant number of high-profile privatizations during 2007–2008 have come under scrutiny, both for the non-transparent and potentially corrupt nature of these transactions, and for the clear ethnic/political implications they bear.

For example, the Bosanski Brod oil refinery, which was sold to the Russian state refiner and to three Russian private investors, has been the subject of significant controversy, both for its below-market valuation and for the fact that it was sold by the RS to Russia, a friendly pro-Serbian country. Similar concerns were raised in 2007, when the state telecom monopoly of the RS, Telekom Srpska, was sold to the Telecom monopoly of Serbia, Telekom Srbija, for 650 million Euros, in the largest privatization and foreign investment in Bosnia to date. The concerns raised by Muslim and Croat Bosnians were that these massive deals were manipulated to engineer the sale of Bosnian assets to Serbian companies, and were thus part of a quiet economic re-integration of the RS into Serbia.

Indeed, despite the fact that accession to the EU and integration within the larger European economy remains one of the most important policy goals for Bosnia, there are distinct signs of an economic regional integration of pieces of Bosnia back into parts of the former Yugoslavia, with companies from the much larger economies of Serbia and Croatia using their links with the RS and Croatian-controlled cantons of the Federation to buy Bosnian economic assets. In Croat majority areas of Herzegovina, the ruling nationalist party encouraged co-capitalization from companies in Croatia; but the process of economic disarticulation goes beyond the active role of state entities. Although Austria is currently the single biggest foreign investor in Bosnia, with a cumulative foreign direct investment (FDI) of $1.3bn, Serbia and Croatia are the second and third largest investors, respectively, who together surpass Austrian investment at $1.4bn.

The fact that many Serbian investments are directed at the RS and that many Croatian companies invest in the Croat cantons of the Federation suggests that privatization is becoming a factor in the disarticulation of a nascent pan-Bosnian economy. As Donais argues, 'overall, the way the privatisation process has unfolded [...] has done more to entrench the economic positions of the country's nationalists and to reduce the prospects of ethnic reintegration' (Donais 2005: 119).

5.5 Cambodia

After two decades of violent conflict, and after the extremely traumatic Khmer Rouge period, during which 1 million out of a total population of 8 million died, Cambodia emerged into post-conflict status with the Paris Peace Agreements of 1991. As in Mozambique, the colonial economy in Cambodia was structured along strictly ethnic lines, such that a tiny minority of European and Chinese entrepreneurs controlled an overwhelming number of business enterprises,[19] while the vast majority of ethnic Khmers were tied to the peasant economy. This structure was almost entirely dismantled during the war, and particularly during the genocidal Khmer Rouge period, so that the post-conflict period was also a period when private enterprise and entrepreneurs were created anew.[20]

Under the circumstances of heavy militarization and weak institutional development, the slow emergence of capitalism in Cambodia since the late-1980s has resulted in a massive expansion of illicit forms of 'primitive accumulation', with members of the Cambodian People's Party (CPP)-governed state using their positions of state power and military control systematically to 'privatize' land, natural resources and a vast array of state and collective property (Global Witness 2007; Le Billon 2002). This process began in the prelude to the Paris peace accords, when the anticipation of a diminution of party–state links and of executive arbitrariness as a result of power-sharing and a UN peacekeeping mission caused a speeding up of the privatization process.

The scope of the privatization process *per se* was smaller in Cambodia than in Mozambique or Bosnia, because of the smaller size of the public sector as a whole. But what is remarkable in comparison to these other countries is the extent of secrecy and the almost complete lack of information available about the number of companies and the identities of the buyers. The sparse available information suggests that there were about 30 companies privatized between 1991 and 2004, all to Cambodian nationals, for fairly low amounts of around $100,000 per transaction. There were, in addition, 139 SOEs that were leased out to private investors in the early 1990s and about which few further data exist.[21]

In a country which, at the time of the Paris peace accords, was overwhelmingly dominated by one single ethnic group (Khmers or ethnic Cambodians), the main issues that arose from the nature of the privatization of SOEs and the broader 'privatization' of state assets such as land and natural resources related less to the ethnic composition of the private sector as such than to the extent to which the process was clearly corrupt and at times extremely predatory, even violent. As a result, the composition of Cambodia's newly emerging business elite in the early 1990s in effect came to resemble that of the ruling political elite very closely, including many ethnic Khmers where there were previously very few.

Since then, the ethnic composition of post-conflict Cambodia's business community has undergone considerable change. Following the end of the conflict and the growth of private-sector economy in 1991, many Cambodian-Chinese, including those who were in exile during the war, were able, often in close association with the CPP government, to return and re-establish their traditional pre-eminent position in commerce and industry.[22] This resumption of ethnic Chinese domination over business ownership has undergone a significant transformation with the influx of new waves of ethnic Chinese entrepreneurs from Mainland China and Southeast Asia in the context of regional economic integration.

In response to the granting of Most Favoured Nation status under the Generalized System of Preferences (MFN/GSP) by the US and EU, Cambodia's garment export grew explosively in the decade between 1996 and 2006, causing a significant transformation of the Cambodian economy in the process. By 2006, the garment sector amounted to 14 per cent of GDP, with $2.5 billion in exports – or 80 per cent of all Cambodian exports. The sector employed 330,000 people, which represented 10 per cent of the whole labour force, and 45 per cent of the manufacturing workforce (World Bank 2007c), supporting 1.7 million people – that is, around 12 per cent of the total population.

An analysis of garment investors based on membership data of the Garment Manufacturers Association of Cambodia (GMAC), the leading industry lobby group, reveals that the sector is dominated by investors from East Asia. With company size estimated by number of employees, it appears that 85 per cent of garment factories in Cambodia are owned by ethnic Chinese investors (from Hong Kong, Taiwan, Malaysia, Singapore and China in addition to the Cambodian-Chinese ones), and another 9 per cent by investors from South Korea. Moreover, these data do not include the significant numbers of mainland Chinese entrepreneurs, who have established a presence in various parts of the Cambodian economy.

Relations between ethnic Khmers and Chinese minorities have historically been cordial and marked by high rates of inter-marriage, integration and the cross-fertilization of cultural and religious practices. In contrast to many other Southeast Asian countries, which have experienced anti-Chinese sentiments and even violence, this has not been the case in Cambodia, where it is the ethnic Vietnamese minority that has traditionally been the subject of hostility. Nevertheless, in conditions of increasing inequality (World Bank 2007c), and with the widespread appropriation of logging and natural resource wealth by individuals closely linked to the Hun Sen government (Global Witness 2007), it is not inconceivable that dissatisfaction with the political dispensation becomes articulated in ethnic terms, particularly given that there are large number of high-profile ethnic Chinese in positions of authority.

5.6 Conclusions

This chapter has explored some of the diverse social and economic effects that privatization and private-sector development have had upon post-conflict countries, particularly in relation to ethnic and regional divisions. Indeed, the effects that are manifest are so varied and context-dependent that it they are not conducive to generating abstract, generalized policy conclusions on how post-conflict privatization policies might be improved. Nevertheless, there are important similarities and common threads that are visible across the four cases, and that can be taken into consideration in understanding and re-evaluating the role and consequences of privatization in post-conflict societies.

Firstly, business ownership is an important dimension of horizontal inequalities (HIs), one that deserves greater attention in its own right, and also for the extent to which ethnic dominance of business perpetuates population-wide economic HIs. This is a subject that requires greater empirical research, particularly with regards to questions such as the ethnicity of the privatization recipients in post-conflict countries.

Secondly, regardless of how technocratically they have been conceived and how impartially they have been executed, the effects of privatization policies are widely perceived, evaluated and acted upon in terms of their impact on inter-group inequalities. This is particularly so in cases of ethnic conflict, such as Sri Lanka or Bosnia, where ethnic politics are closely tied with opposition to privatization and to perceived changes in the ethnic control of state employment ratios.

Thirdly, privatization is not necessarily a useful vehicle to remove patronageable assets from ethnically biased states. In Bosnia, ethnically oriented state elites used privatization as a way to lock in ethnic ownership in ways that perpetuate divisions and are counter-productive to peace-building. Similarly, the widespread allegations of corruption that have accompanied the privatizations of SOEs in Mozambique and Cambodia suggest that these processes can worsen problems of governance and corruption, creating and strengthening clientelist and predatory behaviour on the part of both state elites and business owners.

Fourthly, post-conflict private-sector development is blind to concerns of HIs, and can supersede the impact of horizontal inequality-sensitive policies implemented by donors and governments. It can, within a relatively short period of time, lead to the overwhelming domination of business ownership by small ethnic groups and to highly unequal geographical patterns of development.

Fifthly, to conclude, the possibilities of using targeted policy action and an ethnicity-sensitive approach to address inequalities in private-sector composition make such action and policy often extremely complicated to conceive, administer and control; and, even where they are successful, they are likely to have only limited, transitory and even counter-productive effects. In Mozambique they had some effect in altering the composition of business ownership towards black Mozambicans, but they could not significantly transform the overwhelming dominance of middle- and larger-sized enterprises by non-blacks, who account for less than 1 per cent of the population. More problematic is the case of Bosnia, where an ethnically conscious approach to privatization has served only to preserve and consolidate ethnic divisions. But the most serious problem with any activist approach to engineering private-sector ownership ratios along the ethnic lines is the distinct possibility that the process will become intensely controversial and corrupt and will serve as the basis on which predatory rather than developmentalist forms of state–business links are forged (Evans 1989). While this can be addressed through more indirect mechanisms or through greater transparency and competitive procedures (Gomez 2005), it is also important to be conscious of the great difficulty in implementing and monitoring such mechanisms in the post-conflict context.

Privatization and private-sector development, as such, remain at the heart of understanding the success or failure of post-conflict reconstruction. As this chapter has sought to argue, the problems are many; the solutions are as yet few; and there are important gaps that require further research and fresh empirical work.

Notes

1. See Benedicte et al. (2006); Paris (2004); Woodward (2002).
2. See, for example, Berdal and Mousavizadeh (2010); Bray (2009).
3. See, for example, Netter and Megginson (2001); Brune et al. (2004); Feigenbaum and Henig (1994).
4. See also Birdsall and Nellis (2003); Cook and Kirkpatrick (1995); Bayliss and Cramer (2001).

5. As Cramer (2001) argues, 'it is missing the point to isolate privatisation and to make sweeping claims for its success or failure as a discrete policy tool'.
6. For example, with respect to Kenya, see Vandenberg (2006).
7. See Collier et al. (2003) for a clear statement of this idea, and Cramer (2006) for a critique.
8. For more details, see Venugopal (2009).
9. See World Bank (2001), p. 14.
10. On war and peace, see Nordstrom (1997) and Manning (2002).
11. Although, as Cramer et al. (2001) note, '[g]iven the country's history, if there was any intent to sell state-owned enterprises to people with experience and knowledge and some money, this would necessarily translate into beneficiaries being largely Frelimo members, but it does not translate into a complete conspiracy of the nomenklatura to take all such assets into their own private hands. Indeed, the majority of assets did not go to party "bosses" '.
12. Cramer (2006), p. 271.
13. Drawn from V. Ramachandran and M. K. Shah (1999), 'Minority Entrepreneurs and Firm Performance in Sub-Saharan Africa', *Journal of Development Studies* 36(2): 71–87. On the Asian/Indian dominance over business enterprises in Kenya, see Vandenberg, P. (2003), 'Ethnic-Sectoral Cleavages and Economic Development: Reflections on the Second Kenya Debate', *The Journal of Modern African Studies*, 41(3): 437–455.
14. Hodges and Tibana (2004) demonstrate that there are large regional differences in budgetary allocation, such that the capital Maputo City receives twice the per capita amounts allocated to Zambezia and Nampula.
15. See Bowen (2000). Especially part 3 describes how socialist and post-socialist development in Mozambique has been biased in favour of urban areas and urban elites at the expense of the rural majority.
16. Morgan, G. (1990), 'Violence in Mozambique: Towards an Understanding of Renamo', *The Journal of Modern African Studies*, 28(4): 603–619.
17. See Divjac and Pugh (2008); Pugh (2006).
18. Pugh (2002).
19. P. Edwards (1996), 'Ethnic Chinese in Cambodia', in *Interdisciplinary Research on Ethnic Groups in Cambodia*. Centre for Advanced Study, Pnomh Penn; W. E. Willmott (1967), *The Chinese in Cambodia*. University of British Columbia: Vancouver, BC.
20. See World Bank (1992); Irvin (1993).
21. These data are obtained from the IMF Statistical Appendix to Cambodia over 1997–2004.
22. See Crispin (2007); Fulbook (2004).

6
The Bosnian Paradox: On the Causes of Post-War Inequality and Barriers to Its Recognition and Reduction

Susan L. Woodward

6.1 Introduction

The Bosnian case is particularly intriguing for a theory of conflict based on the risks inherent in horizontal inequalities (HIs) – whether as a motive for civil war or as a threat to post-war stability. Bosnia's pre-war government, as a federal unit of socialist Yugoslavia, guaranteed political equality among its ethno-national groups, including quotas for all public sector employment. Socialist principles of social and economic equality protected women and subsidized the welfare and development budgets of poorer towns and regions. Its post-war government, designed by outsiders as a solution to ethnic conflict, guarantees political equality among its three ethno-national groups on the basis of even more extensive, ethnically defined institutions, group rights, and power-sharing rules.[1] The first system did not prevent war. The second has not prevented rising post-war inequality, ethnic exclusion, and group discrimination. According to a large research literature and many significant foreign and Bosnian political actors, the externally imposed 'Dayton constitution' has made post-war Bosnia-Herzegovina more unstable by institutionalizing group differences, ethnicizing social relations, and building ethnic conflict into government decision-making. If so, this chapter will argue, that instability will not be a result of inequality.

The argument has three components. First, the data available show that most post-war inequality is not among ethnically defined groups. Second, the governmental structure creates multiple barriers against the politicization of non-ethnic differences, and also against doing anything about inequality. Third, the conviction, on all sides of the ongoing constitutional conflict, that the source of all post-war Bosnian problems is the constitution prevents all but a few economists and sociologists from paying attention to the real causes of post-war inequality: the choices made, almost entirely by outsiders, on economic policy, and a domestic politics driven by the identities, values, and political behaviour of a society emerging from war. After a brief background to the conflict, the chapter will set out each of these three components. The lessons of the Bosnian case point to policies chosen by external actors – diplomatic, economic, administrative, and humanitarian – and to their disregard for local values and local consequences.

6.2 Pre-war system and history of the conflict

Like all civil wars, the Bosnian War of 1992–1995 was about the state, and, because the externally imposed outcome was an independent country in which all three warring parties had to coexist and share power, the conflicts that led to war did not end with the cessation of violence but still continue, 17 years later, in disagreements about the causes of the war and about a correspondingly legitimate post-war state.

The occasion for war was not, however, a Bosnian quarrel. That was the quarrel over economic policy and constitutional reform, during the 1980s, between and among the federal government and the three wealthier northern republics of the Socialist Federal Republic of Yugoslavia and the decision taken by two, Slovenia and Croatia, to secede in June 1991. Even then, the breakup of the country as a result of European Union (EU) recognition of Slovene and Croatian independence, *de facto* in October 1991 and *de jure* that December, would not have provoked war in Bosnia had the EU not hastily invited the other four republics to request independence, ignoring full warnings about the consequences for Bosnia without a prior negotiated agreement among members of its governing coalition.

The federal units of Yugoslavia were defined by the Leninist (and thus Austro-Marxist) approach to the 'national question',[2] recognizing constitutionally the rights to national self-determination of the five 'founding' nations (Croats, Macedonians, Montenegrins, Serbs, and Slovenes) within a community of equal peoples and a socialist, one-party system. Bosnia-Herzegovina was an exception. Its formation recognized its historical and cultural identity, not a national one. Because national equality applied to individuals regardless of the republic in which they lived, for example with an expansive rule of proportional representation in all positions of authority (called the national 'key'), the Bosnian communities of Croats and Serbs had 'constituent nation' status individually in the republic; during the 1960s, first at the republic level and later in federal constitutional amendments, Muslims also acquired constitutional status as a nation. The many other ethnic and religious minorities, together, had representation as 'others'. Because of this mixed population and its crucial role in the communist parties' national liberation struggle in World War II, the greatest supporters of the party's principle of 'brotherhood and unity' among nations were in Bosnia – but so, too, was the greatest sensitivity to ethnic difference and to its political dangers.

The 1980s quarrel that led eventually to the country's demise was over its socialist principles, however. These principles of solidarity and redistribution, although within a highly decentralized and open economy, were profoundly disturbed by the 1979–1981 debt crisis and the International Monetary Fund (IMF) programs of macroeconomic stabilization and structural adjustment in 1982 and 1985. Because federal decision-making was based on consensus among equal representatives of the nationally identified republics (and of two autonomous provinces within Serbia), and because the IMF program called for a restoration of federal authority over jurisdictions necessary to macroeconomic stability after a long period (beginning in 1952, but especially in the 1960s) of ever greater devolution to the republics, it was easy for opponents to charge violation of their republican, and thus 'national', rights to 'sovereignty' over economic resources and policy. As the deep recession and stabilization program led to ever higher unemployment (concentrated among youth after 1972), to a freeze on all consumption-related imports, and to cuts in public expenditures that had subsidized the welfare budgets of localities whose gross domestic product (GDP), and thus local revenue, was below the country average, the effect on individual living standards (which had been the envy of all of eastern Europe) also provoked accusations of 'exploitation' (in the Marxist sense) by one national group against another. No national group saw any need to provide evidence, and it was not easy to contest these claims because of a long-standing political taboo on publishing economic data on ethnonational patterns of inequality, unemployment, and social welfare (and the mixed nature of residential patterns, marriages over generations and even identities would have made such claims contestable in any case). The *coup de grâce* came when US and European support for the

Slovene and Croatian leaderships ignorantly accepted their justification for secession, that their 'national' rights and freedoms were being denied in Yugoslavia. The interpretive framework for international policies was set, and the fate of multinational/multiethnic Bosnia totally unclear.

At the time of the EU decisions that dismantled Yugoslavia between June and December 1991, Bosnia was governed by a coalition of ethnonationalist political parties that had defeated civic (primarily liberal and social democratic) parties the previous November, in the first multiparty elections in socialist Yugoslavia, as part of the ongoing constitutional reform that was gradually ending the socialist system politically and economically and that cascaded through the republics, starting with Slovenia and ending with Serbia and Montenegro.[3] The government was a collective presidency on the Yugoslav model, with two representatives for each of the three Bosnian 'constituent nations' and one representing 'others' with the decision-making rule of consensus. Differences on independence emerged immediately, when the European Community (EC)[4] declared Yugoslavia in 'a process of dissolution' in October 1991. After the sitting chair of the collective presidency (an annually rotating position) accepted the December EC (EU) offer to request independence (unfortunately, without consulting the other members), the EU required Bosnia, on the advice of an advisory commission of jurists, to hold a referendum on independence, and then initiated tripartite negotiations with the three 'national' groups on the shape of an independent state. The negotiations failed, it is generally agreed due to US interference, and the Serb parties boycotted the referendum. Nonetheless, the EU and the US recognized Bosnian independence a month later (on 6 and 7 April 1992), and the localized hostilities since the previous September exploded into full-scale war.

The war had two components: a war of independence and the borders of that new state, and a civil war about who would rule and how in the resulting borders. Although the internal debate from October 1991 to February 1992 had coalesced into three national positions (Croat, Muslim, and Serb), the dynamic of the war reflected multiple shifts in positions, temporary coalitions, much international involvement, and a nearly total lack of influence of political parties and civil-society groups which chose not to take up arms but to lobby internationally for a separate, civic outcome. The speed of events outside the control of any Bosnian group also prevents any assessment of what Bosnian citizens would have chosen had there been time for public deliberation or popular participation (aside from the self-defensive arming that did occur within local communities). Even the extent of electoral support for the nationalist parties/armies with whom international mediators chose to negotiate Bosnian fate was never tested by a second election.

In brief, the Bosnian Croat and Bosnian Serb political parties/armies preferred a change in borders that would allow them to live in the new, post-Yugoslav states that were their homelands, Croatia and Serbia. These governments supported their cause militarily and, some argue, were themselves driving the war, with the goal of creating a Greater Croatia and a Greater Serbia. But many Bosnian Croats and Serbs, such as central Bosnian Croats or Sarajevo Serbs, did not live in areas contiguous to Croatia or Serbia and, for historical and cultural reasons as well, they preferred, together with a large urban professional class, an independent but pluralistic, multiethnic or non-ethnic Bosnia-Herzegovina within its Yugoslav federal borders.

The second option for Bosnian Croats and Bosnian Serbs was an independent, but ethnically cantonized and decentralized Bosnia. As numerical minorities – in the 1991 census,[5] Bosnian Croats were around 17 per cent and Bosnian Serbs around 34 per cent – they both claimed a fear of subordination to a centralized Muslim state. Their common war strategy was to gain bargaining leverage in future negotiations about the state and in any future referendum or election by securing military and political control over territory that they claimed, largely through population displacement (whether forced migration or anticipatory flight). Although used successfully also by the Croatian government in 1991 and 1995, the label of 'ethnic cleansing' is indelibly associated with the Bosnian War, and especially with Bosnian Serbs.

The third warring party, the Bosnian Muslims (after August 1993, Bosniacs[6]), was also a minority within Bosnia – 44 per cent in 1991 – and, in addition, had no homeland state in Yugoslavia. An independent Bosnia was considered necessary to their survival as a nation, but also justified historically. The war was not a civil war, but a case of territorial aggression from neighbours; but their pre-war parliamentary alliance with Bosnian Croats made it necessary to downplay Croatian claims to Bosnian territory and to focus international attention entirely on Serbian aggression. Although one proportion of Bosnian Muslims, just like the Croats and Serbs, preferred a secular identity as political liberals or social democrats and an independent Bosnia in its pre-war borders but under a pluralistic, civic constitution, the leadership's strategy to gain international support by calling on international obligations to prevent territorial aggression and genocide consisted in ethno-national appeals.

International involvement in the Bosnian War was extensive, from the decisions on early recognition, which provoked war in 1992, to a massive humanitarian intervention protected by the largest ever United Nations troop deployment at the time, continuous EU- and UN-led negotiations among the three ethno-national parties (excluding unarmed parties and groups), increasing NATO involvement such as in the form of a sea blockade, no-fly zone, bombing against Serbs to protect safe areas in Muslim-held territory, a US covert violation of the arms embargo, overt arrangement, with Germany, of a Bosniac–Croatian political–military alliance against the Serbs (the Washington Agreement of March 1994) that included a Bosniac–Croat federation, and, in November 1995, negotiations of a peace accord and post-war constitution at Dayton, Ohio.

The American solution was to require Bosnian Serbs and Bosnian Croats to accept an independent Bosnia-Herzegovina within its pre-war federal borders, thus reconfirming EU and US decisions from September 1991 to April 1992, but within a highly decentralized, federal, power-sharing ('consociational') constitution that recognized the right of national self-determination of the three armed parties in a two-entity state acknowledging wartime political structures – a Serb Republic (RS) and the 1994 Bosniac–Croat Federation (FBiH) joining the Croats' Herzeg–Bosna and the Bosnian government in Sarajevo. The negotiators compensated the Croats by subdividing the Federation into ten cantons (four Bosnian Croat, four Bosniac, and two mixed) and used a 49–51 formula and a complex, computerized program to draw an 'inter-entity boundary line'.[7] A 60,000, NATO-led Implementation Force (IFOR) replaced the wartime UN Protection Force (UNPROFOR) and a committee of more than 60 interested states and international organizations, a Peace Implementation Council (PIC), was established to oversee implementation, including authorization and deputation of an international administration set up in Sarajevo: the Office of the High Representative (OHR), which has ruled Bosnia over the subsequent 15 years as a *de facto* protectorate.

6.3 Post-war inequality

Social and economic indicators for the first decade of post-war Bosnia-Herzegovina (1996–2006) display 'paradoxical results', writes Christine McNab, United Nations Development Programme (UNDP) Resident Representative in Sarajevo, in her foreword to its *National Human Development Report 2007* (UNDP (NHDR) 2007b: 9). On the one hand, they measure 'ongoing improvement' in education and health and in reasonable economic growth, averaging 4.8 per cent annually from 2000 to 2007 (UNDP (EWSR) 2006: 71).[8] By 2006, the country crossed the threshold of 0.800 to the highest global rank on the human development index (HDI), rising steadily from 0.718 in 2000 to 0.802 in 2006 and from 99th of 166 to 62nd of 177 (UNDP (BiH) 2002; IMF (PRSP) 2004; UNDP 2007c). On the other hand, this HDI score is higher than the country's GDP would predict, because two of the three components (life expectancy and education) are due to socialist-era policies, and these scores will fall unless post-war policy changes (UNDP 2007b). The HDI and access to social rights also vary substantially across regions in the country (UNDP (BiH) 2002; UNDP (NHDR) 2005). Per capita income in 2000 was 65 per cent lower, and in 2005 60 per cent lower, than in 1990, even after a decade of deindustrialization, recession, and high unemployment (UNDP 2007c; UNDP (NHDR) 2005). Inequalities in income, education, employment, and health have grown continuously since the war.

Although such references to growing inequality since the end of the socialist period in 1990, and even to greater inequality since the end of the war in 1995, are so widespread as to amount to conventional wisdom, data are very difficult to find or to trust, and for three reasons. First, there has been no post-war population census (and the pre-war baseline, the 1991 census, is highly contested). Second, no official data include the 'grey' (informal) economy, which the most reliable sources estimate at 25 to 30 per cent of GDP. Third, there is a lingering political taboo from the socialist period, justified for some by the war itself, against research and data on ethnic relations, for fear that evidence might provoke conflict. This Yugoslav-era sensitivity was greatest in Bosnia, but the hefty political reaction against the UNDP for publishing socio-economic data by ethno-national groups, followed by the decision of UNDP staff not to repeat such analysis in subsequent years,[9] suggests the sensitivity continues. By contrast, data on income, employment, and welfare measures are regularly provided by age, gender, and the governmental unit responsible for collecting the particular numbers, which suggests that such group differences are expected and acceptable.

The UNDP's National Human Development Report (NHDR) for 2007, however, focused directly on social inclusion. In three separate indexes that it developed, it found 50.32 per cent of the Bosnian population to be 'socially excluded in some way' (p. 9); 22 per cent faced 'extreme' exclusion; and 47 per cent were 'at risk of long-term social exclusion' (p. 11). Although by global standards a poverty level of 19.1 per cent in

World Bank calculation is not high, an additional third of the population, the 'relatively poor', were so close to the margin that they would succumb with any slightest worsening in economic conditions (as began in 2008). Opinion surveys by the UNDP Early Warning Surveys (EWSR), moreover, suggest the numbers are much higher. Only 12.5 per cent of members of the Bosnian population say they can live comfortably on their income, whereas 44 per cent live in 'difficult' or 'very difficult' conditions because of their income (UNDP (NHDR) 2007b). A UNDP effort in 2005 to capture all sources of households' income (including non-cash and informal economy sources) and to measure their ability to purchase a basic consumption basket of 500 Konvertible Marks (KM) monthly found two-thirds of the population (58.7 per cent) living on less; one-third, in fact, had less than 300 KM monthly income; and only five per cent 'reported sufficient income to meet all their needs' (UNDP (EWSR) 2006b: 92).

Despite low inflation and respectable economic growth between 2001 and 2005, moreover, a decline in the average monthly income from 556 KM in 2001 to 466 KM in September 2005 suggests a rise in inequality (UNDP (EWSR) 2006). Equally important as the numbers, as the Bosnian authors remark, is the sense of loss, that 'poverty of this sort was unknown in pre-war BiH' (p. 10). Data from social welfare institutions reinforce this perception, showing a more than three-fold decline from 2002 to 2007 in subventions for rent, heating, and funerals and in humanitarian assistance to the poorest, even though the numbers needing aid were rising at a faster rate (Bosna i Hercegovina 2008).

The greatest cause of socio-economic inequality in Bosnia is unemployment. Although it has been declining from 43 per cent in the first post-war years to 31.1 by 2006 and to 29.0 in 2007 in the official Labour Force Survey, which is based on the approach of the International Labour Organization (ILO) (Labour Force Survey 2008),[10] the size of the 'labour-capable population' classified as 'inactive or discouraged' was very high – in 2006, 57 per cent (UNDP (NHDR) 2007b). Only in 2007 did the proportion of the population registered as employed (29.7 in 2006, 31.2 in 2007) overtake the percentage unemployed.

In ferreting out information about HI, one can detect an important distinction between patterns of economic activity that affect groups differently and direct discrimination. Both are subject to policy, but their causes differ. According to the NHDR on social inclusion/exclusion, individual measures on income, unemployment, and access to social services and to structures of political power and decision-making form a pattern of disadvantage along generational, gender, and, in some aspects, urban/rural lines, to such an extent that the authors refer to the marginalization of the elderly, children and youth, and most women, regardless of ethnic identity. Young people, children under 15 – households with more than two children are the poorest in Bosnia, with life-long effects on their children – youth aged 15–25, and the elderly (over 65 years, and especially elderly women) are disadvantaged on all criteria, including the dramatic decline in humanitarian assistance and social benefits mentioned earlier.

Women have improved their formal political representation (UN measures of 'gender empowerment') over the post-war years due to internationally imposed quotas, and they still benefit from the pre-war legacy of egalitarian educational and health policies. But the Gender Development Index (GDI) is consistently lower for the entire country, and the inequity is much larger in the Federation than in the RS, with substantial inter-cantonal variation and much weaker empowerment scores (UNDP (NHDR) 2005) (Table 6.1).

The primary component of gender inequality is employment discrimination. Rates of activity and of employment differ significantly between men and women, as do pay rates. For example, in 2000, women's average income in purchasing-power-parity US dollars was $1,793 as against $4,135 for men (UNDP (BiH) 2002); in 2003, the contrast was $3,771 to $8,958, and in 2004 $4,744 to $10,520 (UNDP (NHDR) 2007b). In 2005, the female economic activity rate was 58.3 per cent, as opposed to 86 per cent for men (UNDP 2007c) (Table 6.2).

Table 6.1 Gender inequality: Gender development index

	2000	2001	2002	2003
GDI	0.707	0.731	0.744	0.782
HDI	0.718	0.744	0.784	0.793

Source: UNDP (NHDR) (2007b); HDR (2007/2008).

Table 6.2 Gender inequality: Income

	Average income		Income differentials					
			2003			2004		
	2003	2004	BiH	Federation	RS	BiH	Federation	RS
Women	$3,771	$4,744	0.315	0.297	0.352	0.333	0.306	0.361
Men	$8,958	$10,520	0.685	0.703	0.648	0.667	0.694	0.639

Source: UNDP 2007: 78; 173.

Table 6.3 Gender inequality: Employment

	Federation						RS					
	Male			Female			Male			Female		
	2006	**2007**	**2008**	**2006**	**2007**	**2008**	**2006**	**2007**	**2008**	**2006**	**2007**	**2008**
Activity rate	57.2	56.9	56.4	30	28.8	29.4	54.8	59.6	58.7	32.4	35	35.8
Employment	40.3	40.9	43.3	18.8	18.3	21.1	39.6	45.4	48	22.7	25.4	27.2
Unemployment	29.5	28.2	23.1	37.5	36.4	28.3	27.6	23.8	18.2	30	27.5	24.1

Source: Anketa o Radnoj Snazi (2008); Labour Force Survey (2008: 24–25).

The looser definition of activity and employment in the official data looks better overall, but not their differential. Gender inequalities were growing so sharply on all measures, however, that the Bosnian authors of the 2007 UNDP report refer to a 'historically-reversed situation' reflecting a 'return of the patriarchal society, rooted in wartime activities and the explosion of radical nationalism' (p. 23) (Table 6.3).

Explicit discrimination, by contrast, is recorded for three groups: (1) utterly shocking data on the condition of Roma, whose social deprivation and exclusion are extreme on all measured indicators, explode from the pages of the UNDP report (UNDP (NHRD) 2007b), and, while discrimination against Roma was not unknown in pre-war Bosnia, it was carefully limited and, in some republics, even reversed; (2) a post-war phenomenon, disabled persons (including war invalids) and socially stigmatized groups such as those with HIV/AIDs, sexual minorities (gays and lesbians), and current or former drug users; and (3) residential minorities, those who have constitutionally guaranteed equal rights as members of one of the three constituent peoples, but who do not reside in the territory where their group is numerically and politically dominant.

Equally or more consequential in terms of the effects of economic policy is the second type of inequality, 'the growing disparities between and within the two entities' that point not to ethnic difference but to 'a pattern of inequity rooted in other dynamics, including economic and specific locational factors (such as inadequate infrastructure, remoteness, sparsity and lack of natural resource endowments)' (UNDP (NHDR) 2005: 39). Differences between the two entities can be stark, in favour of the Federation, such as the difference in adjusted incomes of 34 per cent (UNDP (NHDR) 2005: 36); of 82 per cent in official employment figures in December 1999, which is 21 per cent higher than the difference (61 per cent) in population (UNDP (BiH) 2002); and in consumption standards (Table 6.4):

The greatest regional differences, however, are to be found in the growing disparity between wealthy western Herzegovina and greater Sarajevo (where international actors concentrate) and the rest of the country (UNDP (NHDR) 2005).[11] Some data according to ethnic groups rather than regions can be found, but these must be treated with some caution. For example (Table 6.5):

According to the World Bank, 'Croats are less likely of all to be at risk of falling into poverty', whereas the risk 'is greatest for the Serb population in the RS' (Kostic 2002: 22). Perceptions of discrimination,

Table 6.4 Regional inequality

	Federation	Serb Republic
Below the LSMS poverty line	15.6%	24.8%
% below 500 KM/mo.	36.0%	72.0%
Self-assessment as poor	21.0%	29.6%
Difficulty covering food needs	9.4%	21.8%
Able to eat but not buy clothing	39.7%	49.1%
Able to buy food, clothing, and 'save a bit'	40.8%	25.9%
Can afford expensive things	9.5%	2.8%
Human Poverty Index (HPI) 2006	12.5%	15.6%
HPI capability-poverty	14.0%	17.8%
HDI 2006	0.819	0.784

Source: 2001 LSMS/2002 EWSR.

Table 6.5 Ethnonational inequality

Average 2001–2005	Croats	Bosniacs	Serbs
Income pc 2001–2005	800 KM	493 KM	429 KM
Median income	716 KM	375 KM	333 KM
Percentage below 500 KM/mo.	36%	n.a.	72%
Report being employed 2004	40%	30%	32%

Source: EWSR (2000–2006: 74).

by contrast, show no pattern over time in the opinion surveys done by the reputable polling firm PRISM for the UNDP EWSR, but if one takes a recent snapshot, in January–March 2006 'levels of concern over discrimination on ethnic or religious grounds' were, quite in contrast to the facts, greatest in Croat areas, where the majority complained most of discrimination (up from 15 per cent to 34 per cent over the previous year), whereas such perceptions were 'stable in Bosniak majority areas' and had 'improved considerably in Serb ones' (UNDP (EWSR) 2006b: 9) – even though Serbs continued to perceive themselves as significantly more impoverished than the rest of the country (UNDP (NHDR) 2005). The most likely explanation, in fact, is that inequalities were growing within these three communities.

6.4 Explanations

Most analysts and most Bosnians explain these data institutionally, as a consequence of the internationally imposed constitutional structure created by the Dayton peace accord (though its goal, ostensibly, was to end ethnic conflict). This governmental structure can only explain some of the post-war economic policy, however. The preferences of international political and economic actors on economic policy are equally important, or more, in explaining the outcomes for inequality and, secondly the limits, domestically – in political identities, values, and collective action – to doing anything about it.

Political institutions

The Dayton constitution defines political rights ethno-nationally, with members of both entity and state-level assemblies elected to represent their 'constituent nation' proportionally. This principle extends to parity in a power-sharing executive branch composed of a council of ministers, a collective, tripartite presidency, and consensual decision-making rules. Further protection for each is provided in their constitutional right to halt legislation perceived to be against their 'vital national interests'. Although some political parties are not ethnically defined, for instance the social democrats, they are at a distinct disadvantage electorally, because of this ethno-national basis of representation and because wartime and immediate post-war displacements created overwhelmingly homogeneous territories. Local governments are largely single-party dominant (UNDP (NHDR) 2005), despite an electoral system of proportional representation. Any residential minority (whether a Bosniac, Croat, or Serb living outside the area now dominated by their nation or by any of the 17 ethnic minorities recognized in the 2003 legislation and granted cultural rights[12]) has thus no political representation as such.

The ease with which ethnic discrimination can occur, and even be considered constitutional and legitimate at the local level in this system, can explain some inequalities, such as the economic disadvantage of residential minorities in access to jobs and welfare benefits; but ethnic discrimination appears to explain a very small part of post-war

Bosnian inequality, with the appalling exception of Roma. The institutional causes of inequality must be sought in Dayton's distribution of jurisdictional competencies among governmental levels.

The powers of the central state were minimally defined at Dayton with no jurisdiction over taxation, defence, labour, or social policy (including education, health care, and social welfare). International pressure did reunify economic activity in stages, from uniform automobile registration plates (in 1998) to currency (in 2001), which reduced substantial differences in retail prices and gains from speculation among the three areas of wartime administration, and after extreme pressure by the IMF, a central value-added-tax (in 2005). But the central government has few tools for economic policy. It has no control over monetary policy, because negotiators at Dayton imposed a Currency Board with a foreign, IMF-appointed director, initially for seven years but with no end in sight. Tax authority lies with the entities, cantons, and municipalities, limiting central fiscal policy. There is no authority centrally even to set minimum, country-wide standards, such as for the labour market; to harmonize cross-entity and cross-cantonal differences on tax rates, social welfare, or education standards (UNDP (BiH) 2002), or even to address poverty at the country level until after 2001, when the process to design an international financial institution (IFI)-required Poverty Reduction Strategy Paper (PRSP) began (UNDP (BiH) 2002). Under persistent international pressure, a core curriculum for elementary and secondary education was finally introduced in 2004, but schooling remains under local jurisdiction. Thus, under ethno-national control, curricula and schools are segregated (even when children attend parallel classes in the same building).[13]

The level of decentralization is greater in the Federation, where cantons are responsible for education, health care, and social welfare (the latter shared with municipalities), and per capita municipal expenditures vary by a factor of 5 to 1 (UNDP (NHDR) 2005).[14] The RS is more centralized, to positive effect on equality, because standards can be imposed on municipalities and it has a mildly redistributive tax-sharing scheme based on a four-fold developmental criterion (though in practice subject to political manipulation). Greater centralization also creates the conditions for more effective citizen protest, as evidenced by the RS authorities' response in 2003–2005 to pensioners demanding that they be paid their pensions in full (EWSR 2006).[15]

One clear consequence for inequality of the ethnicized aspect of the Dayton constitution is its vulnerability to central stalemate – either through the use by parliamentarians of the vital interest clause or through the need for tripartite consensus within the presidency – and resulting difficulty in creating country-wide policy. Peter Klincov illustrates this difficulty with the failure to have any policy toward the petroleum industry in the mid-2000s, even though it would be a 'key engine of development for the country as a whole' and it would increase entities' revenues by one-third:

> Myopia and the entity governments' desire to control resources rendered unacceptable the idea of pooling manufacturing and distribution capacity under centralised ownership for sale at a decent price to a major international company. Instead, the Bosanski Brod refinery, the most modern in the region, lies idle and the public fill their tanks and send their money abroad. The native oil distributors are disappearing. (EWSR 2006)

Yet ethnic differences have not prevented Bosnian leaders from changing the Dayton constitution under international pressure (primarily from the High Representative), with an increasing transfer of competencies from the entities to the state – such as defence, intelligence, a state border service, and a statistics bureau. The state's difficulty in accessing its portion of the customs revenues collected by the entities (particularly repeated refusal by Croat authorities on the wealthy Herzegovina border) was substantially reduced by an EU fraud and auditing inspectorate and by a UN-created uniform and professional border service after 2000. The EU Commission reports impressive progress on financial sector reform, while legislation and its implementation on external economic relations with countries in the region and with the EU demonstrate a capacity for central economic policy decisions. When stalemate or delay occurs, the High Representative has simply made decisions for them, but the question then becomes, why these decisions and not others?

The extent of decentralization in economic policy was also decided at Dayton by outsiders, not on an ethnic power-sharing model to end the war but to replace the Yugoslav system with a market economy, on the mistaken assumption that the Yugoslav economy, as socialist, had been too centralized. The model of a minimalist state and of extensive decentralization has parallels in many post-conflict countries, independently of any ethnic factor, where the neoliberal economic philosophy of the IFIs and of some bilateral donors (such as the US) held sway. As for social policy, Stubbs (2001) shows that the 'fragmented and localised, residualised, category-based rather than needs-based, and depoliticised' (p. 101) post-war 'welfare regime', what he calls a 'new feudalism' (p. 100), was a consequence of the ways that humanitarian aid was provided by international NGOs (INGOs) during the war. The Dayton agreement made matters worse by 'not seeing social policy, in any sense, as a priority' and then by creating an institutional contradiction between entity-based rights and the variation in 'size, resources, and revenue-raising abilities' of the cantons and municipalities, which built 'fundamental inequities' into the realization of those rights. By recycling themselves from relief agencies to 'conduits for later development assistance' after the war, these private INGOs then created a 'complete separation between human rights and solidarity-based approaches' (p. 103). They marginalized the pre-war social welfare agencies by recruiting their most innovative staff and denying them resources, leaving them by default 'to become vehicles for social exclusion and discrimination' of local authorities. Most donors, including the World Bank, ignored social policy, but those who did not reinforced the pattern by creating parallel local agencies run by local or international NGOs for those excluded – the minorities, the refugees, and the internally displaced persons (IDPs) (p. 104).

Economic policy

Bosnian economic outcomes, in sum, are not a direct result of the ethnicized and decentralized constitution written at Dayton, and the dominant role of international actors has continued well beyond the peacemaking phase. As a knowledgeable Bosnian official, surprised at my questions, replied: 'but we have no economic policy'. An easy second explanation of post-war inequality, therefore, is that choices on economic policy have been made by outsiders, not by Bosnians. Distributional effects have been largely indirect, through monetary and trade policy, but the more direct effects of fiscal and social policy, too, have been driven by outsiders' resources and choices.

Post-war macroeconomic policy governed by a Currency Board and IMF programs has, predictably, been consistently restrictive with 'jobless growth', the primary cause of inequality since the war, and with such impressive price stability, low budget deficits, and public debt-to-exports ratios that, by the end of 2005, Bosnia had met the formal convergence criteria for European Monetary Union (EMU), even though the EU would not yet sign an association agreement with Bosnia on political grounds (for instance, internal disputes over an EU requirement of centralized police reform). As the UNDP (NHDR) 2007b authors conclude: 'We believe the current policy framework remains too targeted on stability at the expense of expansion and, moreover, tends to neglect growing inequities' (p. 87).

In theory, Bosnia was in much better straits on fiscal policy than most post-conflict countries, because the normally harsh limits on public expenditures required by the IMF to settle the country's debt arrears so that it be eligible to borrow from the IMF, World Bank, and capital markets – a framework that bilateral donors always accept for their aid as well, but that is widely criticized in the literature on post-conflict peacebuilding – were not imposed, because the Netherlands assumed responsibility for Bosnia's debts temporarily. This advantage was sharply limited by the Dayton constitution's denial of fiscal authority to the central government and by the lack of fiscal harmonization among the cantons and entities. Yet the state was the beneficiary of massive external assistance, beginning with a five-year $5.5 billion Priority Recovery and Reconstruction Program (PRRP) designed by the World Bank while the war was still raging and pledged at subsequent donor conferences beginning in January 2006. The greater problem of fiscal policy was that the Bosnian government had no role in setting its priorities or the additional projects of the many bilateral donors.

The government was not even allowed a representative in the sectoral task forces established within the OHR in 1996 under US initiative to coordinate the aid rushing in. The PRRP took a traditional World-Bank approach to development, emphasizing large infrastructural projects, which have relatively long gestation periods and are capital-intensive, not employment-generating. The same can be said for EU assistance (focusing, for example, on telecommunications and inter-European transportation networks). US assistance was also large but devoted primarily to the creation of a commercial banking system and to related aspects of financial reform; this priority was said to be aimed at the development of small and medium enterprises, yet it did not have that effect, as local access to credit remained the most serious obstacle to domestic investment, even 15 years later. The World Bank assistance also aimed, as did the US, at dismantling the socialist institutions and creating market-friendly reforms alongside the Currency Board – the Washington consensus of macroeconomic stability, liberalization, and privatization. The contentious history of this foreign pressure for privatization is too complex to detail here, but the extent of the delays and the levels of corruption (including of the OHR) did little to help raise productive domestic investment until more than a decade after the war (and then, with far greater success in the RS than the Federation).

This economic philosophy of IFI and major-donor aid thus defined Bosnian development policy: standard emphasis on incentives to foreign direct investment and globally competitive, export-oriented production. The result was an 'open economy' – Bosnian total trade was 95 per cent of GDP by 2007, up from 87 per cent in 2006 (Commission of European Communities 2008: 32) – but the primary economic problem for Bosnia, according to all World Bank, EU, and UNDP documents, has been a persistent trade deficit (at 35 per cent of GDP in 2006 and 37 per cent in 2007: Commission of European Communities 2008: 25; Didik and Gligorov 2007)[16] and thus continuing pressure for further liberalization. As Klincov writes in 2006, the 'authorities have done little to alter the economic environment and promote development or employment' (EWSR 2006: 12).

When the PRRP drew to a close in 2000, international authorities in the PIC and OHR renewed pressure on the Bosnian authorities to do the economic reforms that they said had not been made so as to replace the evaporating aid, and the IFIs instructed the government to begin preparation of a PRSP to get additional IFI financing. At the same time, the Brussels-directed Stability Pact, an international coalition led by the US, EU, and Contact Group countries after the NATO bombing of Serbia in March–June 1999, introduced a range of regional policies aimed at reconciliation among the Yugoslav successor states, including first bilateral trade agreements and then in 2003 a regional trade pact.

Preparation of the Bosnian PRSP began in April 2002 was completed in March 2004 and updated in 2007, and was the product of a vast consultative process in the country that led Bosnians to believe that finally they had taken lead on economic policy.[17] It differs little, however, from PRSPs in other countries. Officially named the Mid-Term Development Strategy (MTDS), it had as its primary goal to 'restore a partial creditworthiness on the international capital markets, establish functioning market economy and strengthen the capacity of domestic companies to compete in external markets, particularly the EU market', by the end of 2007 (IMF (PRSP) 2004: 10). The second goal was to reduce poverty, but through structural reforms that would 'in the short term [...] cause job losses, and consequently an increase in poverty' while reducing unemployment benefits substantially (IMF (PRSP) 2004: 12–19). The third goal was to 'accelerate EU integration' (IMF (PRSP) 2004: 12–19).[18] These three goals required the following priorities: a consensus on reform, macroeconomic stability, fiscal system reform (further decentralization!), 'faster growth of the export-oriented private sector', public administration reform, reductions in the public debt and in public expenditures (on education, health, social transfers, defence, and police), judicial reform aimed at faster resolution of economic disputes and greater protection of creditors and of private property rights, increasing enterprise competitiveness by cutting taxes, liberalizing labour markets, continuing privatization, reorganizing the 'system of protection' (health insurance, unemployment benefits), sectoral reforms in education and agriculture, liberalization of the electric power market and of posts and telecommunications, a Stabilization and Association Agreement (SAA) with the EU, and full membership in the World Trade Organization (WTO). No change in these three goals occurred in the 2007 update, although a new emphasis, among external actors (especially the OHR, US, EU, and World Bank), on the fiscal burden of the Dayton constitutional structure could be detected in the strategy's new emphasis on cutting public employment.

The effect of this development strategy as trade policy on the Bosnian private sector, according to a survey of the 150 top Bosnian businesses in April–August 2005, when growth was rising, and before the deep recession of 2008–2009, was not encouraging. No more than 19 per cent (11 per cent in the RS in April, 19 per cent in the Federation in May, and 14 per cent in both entities in August) said that implementation of the economic reforms 'had helped their company's operations'; the other 81 per cent said they did not know or had been harmed. In the same survey of these companies on the influence of the free trade agreements, no more than 42 per cent in the RS in June 2004, but down to 15 per cent in the Federation and 25.5 per cent in the RS in August 2005 said they had been helped. Data on the impact of trade liberalization on the trade deficit, which were reported in the Third Semi-Annual Report on the PRSP/MTDS in October 2005, were also negative.

Export-oriented investment policy also explains the pattern of inequality in Bosnia, namely the growing disparities between western Herzegovina and wider Sarajevo, on the one hand, and the rest of the country, on the other, as well as the income advantage of Bosnian Croats against Bosniacs and Serbs.[19] The majority of the major trading companies are based in the Croat areas, in western Herzegovina, because of its border with Croatia and with good trade routes to the west. Bosniac areas, as the wartime Bosniac leader, Alija Izetbegovic, emphasized in all political negotiations, are land-locked. Sarajevo-based firms were among the most successful trade and export firms in all of former Yugoslavia, through their cultural links and entrepreneurship in the Middle East; but those firms have been the unmitigated target of external demands for their privatization, which was preceded by their break-up into separate companies for the sale (they were large conglomerates) and by the resulting delays in post-war revival. Although the Serb Republic has an external border just like the Croat areas of the Federation, few international routes cross it; where trade had flourished before the war, neighbouring Croatia blocked all crossings and trade for more than five years after Dayton. The other neighbour, Serbia, was not a source of trade-based revenues because it was under sanctions for almost a decade (as were the Serb areas in Bosnia) and remained under some until 2009 and because it was still recovering from the massive NATO bombing in 1999 and from continuing political obstacles to economic relations with the EU.

In terms of production profiles, most of pre-war RS had always been poor, agricultural, and exporters of natural resources (hydroelectric power, timber), not of value-added industry. It had long been a region of emigration (primarily to Serbia). Overall, economic activity in the Federation produces more value-added goods: in 2006, production increased mostly in 'electrical machines, devices, and apparatus, followed by metal ore extraction, and thirdly recycling', whereas in the RS the three leading sectors in 2006 were 'other ore extraction and quarrying, coal mining, and base metals' (EWSR 2006: 20). While these regional profiles are sufficient to explain the distinct difference in poverty rates between the RS and the Federation, the low level of processing industries constrains all of the country; as Klincov writes, 'the leading exporters [ten large companies continue to dominate the export market] are offering raw materials or semi-finished goods. We are exporting what nature has given us: electricity, ores, and wood' (UNDP (EWSR) 2006: 12, 22).

Nonetheless, as the NHDR on social inclusion urges, there should be some room for reducing inequality through labour market and social policies. Unfortunately, the institutional obstacles to a 'countrywide strategy for employment' and labour market policy reinforce the limits on social policy of the economic policy of liberalization. Social welfare budgets, especially for pensions and unemployment insurance, are paid by taxes on wages and employers; the lower the employment rate, the lower the revenue. Whereas the ratio of pensioners to employees in 1991, the year before the war began, was 1:3, by the end of the war in 1995, it was 1:1.3 and by 2003, it was 1:1.4. In the RS, where pensions are a third lower than those paid in the Federation, there are even more pensioners than insured employees (a ratio in 2003 of 1.08:1) (IMF (PRSP) 2004). Yet the primary explanation provided in the PRSP and the EU Commission reports for insufficient employment growth is the 'structural rigidities' of the tax on wages and employers. To increase jobs, enterprise and wage taxes must be cut. While EU Commission reports of Bosnian progress on an association agreement repeatedly note 'little progress in the area of economic and social rights' (e.g. Commission of the European Communities 2008: 19), the resource constraint is clear. Local spending in total is a mere 8 per cent of total public spending, barely 5 per cent of GDP in either entity (UNDP (NHDR) 2005). According to the MTDS in 2004, the country 'spends less on social welfare than any other country in the region',[20] and the 'system of social protection in both entities of BiH is in grave difficulty' (IMF (PRSP) 2004: 152).

Here, too, external assistance has had different priorities. Beginning in 1998, all fungible monies and new programs were directed, through the OHR's Reconstruction and Return Task Force, to the international goal of returning refugees and the internally displaced to their pre-war homes, on the assumption that restoration of the pre-war settlement pattern would eliminate the ethno-national politics and policies of post-war Bosnia. In fact such aid increased wartime segregation, because only communities from which people had fled or been expelled received aid, and because the simultaneous aim of international actors to create a real estate market with a property claims commission enabled those who were mobile to return, but only to claim and then sell their property and move back to an area where they were in the majority or to another country. Those without such property, the rural farmsteads (predominantly elderly, illiterate women) and the propertyless, could not benefit, and they suffer, as residential minorities, from systematic discrimination in access to jobs, welfare, and political power (as discussed above).

Political action

The result of international decisions on the institutional structure of politics and policy-making and on economic policy for the first 15 years of post-war Bosnia has been to create conditions strikingly similar to pre-war Yugoslavia. The extent of decentralization, of republican authority over economic policy, and of consensual, power-sharing decision-rules limited central authority so much and led to stalemate so frequently that constitutional reform was seen to be essential (particularly by the IMF) if economic reforms to address the persistent trade deficits and foreign debt were to succeed. Monetary, trade, and development policy prioritizing financial stability and exports favoured those areas of the country where export industries and trade and communication links were most developed and were closest to western markets, and did little or nothing to alter those initial endowments in the economic profile of a region after the defence-oriented industrialization drive of 1948–1949. Ever rising regional inequality under these conditions did not lead to efforts to meliorate those differences but instead, as discussed above, to a tax revolt by the richer (export-earning) republics against the federal budget for defence and development aid to the south, to ever greater resistance to those striving for more effective central policy, and to increasing polarization over economic strategy and philosophy. The ethno-national identities of the republics became the means by which the constitutional conflict led to the multiple wars of 'national' independence and to the country's break up. Could the same pattern of regional inequality, youth unemployment, and economic discrimination against minorities provoke a similar fate for independent Bosnia-Herzegovina?

While Bosnian economists are also polarized over economic philosophy and policy, and while the pressure from external actors and some Bosnian parties for constitutional reform, to strengthen central powers and resources, has repeatedly led to system-threatening crisis (most seriously in 2006–2009), it is highly unlikely that political conflict over inequality will influence the outcome. At the same time, paradoxically, patterns of political participation and post-war political identities and values are additional obstacles to addressing those inequalities.

First, the pattern of regional inequality does not reinforce the lines of ethno-national conflict over constitutional questions. The partial exception – that Croat areas and households are wealthier than others – has declined over time, with increasing inequality among Croat households and among Croat cantons. While the wealth and power of Sarajevo, which provoked much pre-war and wartime conflict in Bosnia, has only increased, the declining differences between most Bosniacs and most Serbs do not reduce their constitutional conflict.

Second, post-war politics has been instead a process of increasing social closure exercised by the three ethno-national groups, each one of which achieves, by social inclusion in ethnic enclaves and by parallel discrimination against minorities, to 'exclude people from other ethnic backgrounds' (Kostic 2007; UNDP (NHDR) 2007b). As studies in pre-war Croatia discovered, the more ethnically homogeneous the community, the lower the level of tolerance in general (and vice versa) (Massey et al. 1999). This social closure extends to voting patterns, particularly at the local level. A contentious constitutional court ruling in 2000, which required the three constituent peoples to have electoral representation throughout the country, not only in their entity, has not influenced the level of governmental jurisdiction over social welfare and employment policy – namely the municipalities, which, as mentioned above, are overwhelmingly single-party systems.

Social closure extends far deeper than the ethno-national group, however. People socialize with families and close friends, and expect others to 'look only to themselves', not to want to help others (3.4 on a scale of 1 to 10, measuring trust in people's fairness in a 2006 study), and to try to take advantage of them, if they could (3.9 on a scale of 1 to 10). The result, according to public opinion surveys, is a striking 'lack of concern over social inclusion and solidarity' (UNDP (NDHR) 2007b: 52 and 203). Aside from voting, Bosnians are not politically active. Only 8.3 per cent in a random survey, made by PRISM, of Bosnians aged 15 or older were members of political organizations, and only 9.3 per cent belonged to non-governmental organizations, cultural associations, or sports clubs. More than 90 per cent (90.7) had never participated in any meetings organized by a political organization (p. 52 and Annex 4). While the NGO sector is relatively large because of donor priorities and financial assistance, civil society organizations operate at the local level, being focused primarily on delivering social services, and have little or no influence on policy. Analyses of their political activities find them limited to criticism of existing policy rather than going for positive advocacy or mobilizing public support and action for change.

While the historical reversal (UNDP (NHDR) 2007b) to patriarchal values, shown in the data on social and economic discrimination against women, can be explained by the shift from socialist to ethno-religious political parties, the remarkably conservative opinions on the role of political action to effect change among the younger generation, according to a survey of values in 2006, may also be a result of war. Although only a snapshot of opinions, the results are worth citing at length:

> 61 per cent of young people consider that 'what matters most for the success of a group is to find an energetic, austere and just leader whom everybody would respect and listen to'. Almost the same percentage is of the opinion that young people, when they come of age, 'need to avoid rebellious ideas and should calm down'. Furthermore, 32.8 per cent of young people consider that when resolving important social problems 'one should keep quiet and wait to see what others think of it', while another 22.3 per cent are 'indecisive'. In addition, over 40 per cent of young people consider that 'one should return to traditional customs and lifestyle, and that one should not be engaged in resolving the complex issues of life'. Almost

> the same percentage of interviewees does not want to accept the duties that would oblige them to 'deal with important social issues'. Almost 50 per cent of interviewees, including the indecisive ones, consider that 'those who let things go are much happier'. (UNDP (NHDR) 2005: 52)

Instead of organizing in order to change their circumstances, most Bosnians, regardless of ethnic difference, want to leave the country (consistently 45–50 per cent of the surveyed population) (EWSR 2006). More than 60 per cent of all youth 'do not see their future' in Bosnia (p. 23). This number was also rising: in the EWR survey of the first quarter of 2006, 71.3 per cent of Bosnians aged 18 to 35 'would leave BiH if they could' (UNDP (EWSR) 2006: 31, 56). One would expect to find this wish to emigrate mostly among those who face discrimination as residential minorities; in fact they are the least inclined, most likely because of a realistic assessment by Roma, elderly rural women, and similar minorities of their opportunities elsewhere.

Finally, the identities according to which people do organize to protest or change governmental policy on inequality have been, as Stubbs argues, deeply shaped by an aid regime that was highly localized, 'project based and focused on client groups: children; people with disabilities; older people', not proceeding on general social rights and 'the broader functioning of the system'. Pensioners in the RS, the women of Srebrenica protesting the diversion of aid funds in Tuzla canton, or veterans protesting the World Bank demand that subsidies and pensions to them be cut are examples, politically influential but limited to public assistance categories and sporadic.[21]

6.5 Lessons to be learned for discussion

The interpretation of the Bosnian War as a quintessentially ethnic war and the focus of international assistance on rewarding multiethnic cooperation and reconciliation as the best road to peace have done little to prevent the rise of social, economic, and political inequality in post-war Bosnia. They have created conditions that make it very difficult to address those inequalities and new forms of post-war discrimination. This is a larger lesson from the Bosnian case as well. Power-sharing solutions to civil wars create decision-making rigidities and institutionalize the lines of wartime conflict, regardless of the type of war and its causes. Economic policy that favours financial stability, foreign investors, and export producers results in jobless growth and regional inequality, which are likely to generate forces for social exclusion – through voluntary ghettoization, through the cultural and economic protection of a local majority against all minorities, and through other forms of discrimination. Insistence on decentralization and cuts in public employment and welfare transfers reinforce this outcome by preventing redistributive and solidaristic policies. If constitutional and policy priorities are set by outsiders because these outsiders have the balance of power and resources in countries emerging from war, it is difficult to see how the conditions for post-war transformation of wartime identities, conflicts, and politics will emerge.

Notes

1. For the diplomatic reasoning on power-sharing, see Sisk (1996); for a good summary of the theoretical reasoning, called consociational democracy, see Andeweg (2000); the critical literature on its effects in peacebuilding is sizeable.
2. For outsiders to the national question in Yugoslavia, confusion among ethnic, national, and religious categories is understandable. The difference among the three peoples of Bosnia-Herzegovina is in religion and its related cultural practices and identities, but their recognition as 'nations', that is, as peoples with political rights to statehood, originates in the Ottoman *millet* system; it gains a Habsburg gloss under the protectorate (then annexation) of 1878–1914; it becomes constitutionally recognized in the Yugoslav federal system after 1945; and it defines the claims for independence that broke up Yugoslavia in 1991, except for Bosnia, which retains the Yugoslav system in its post-war, 'Dayton' constitution.
3. During 1990, as a result of the ongoing constitutional reform that was gradually ending the socialist regime both politically and economically, multiparty elections were held in each republic. In Bosnia, in November, ethno-nationally organized political parties won against civic parties (liberals and social democrats primarily).
4. The European Union changed its name from the European Community at the end of 1991.
5. This census was, and remains, highly disputed, but few dispute the relative proportions.
6. Bosnian Muslim representatives elected in 1990 to the Bosnian parliament decided, in a separate assembly in August 1993, to rename themselves Bosniacs. Reflecting internal debates with a long history, the choice in 1993 was aimed at international support, calculating (probably correctly) that they would benefit by a designation that connoted nation more than religion and western, not eastern, provenance. The resulting elision among external audiences between Bosniac and Bosnian probably also helped, despite the erasure of more than half the Bosnian population from view.
7. The peace agreement did permit small post-Dayton adjustments among villages, mediated by the international military deployment.

8. GDP growth in 1997, due to international reconstruction aid, was 36.6 per cent, but it fell to 9.9 per cent in 1998 (personal communication from S. Mitra, World Bank), and over the 3 years 1998–2001 was only 16.5 per cent (UNDP (BiH) 2002); annual rates vary in 2000–2007, e.g. 3.5 per cent in 2005, 6.7 per cent in 2006, 6.8 per cent in 2007 (Commission of European Communities 2008), but the global recession brought negative growth beginning in 2008.
9. Roland Kostic, personal communication, Stockholm, January 2009.
10. The rate of unemployment depends on one's source. An external Living Standards Measurement Study (LSMS) survey led by the World Bank and reported in May 2002 set unemployment at 16.1; the official rate in 2001 was 28.1 per cent; UNDP provides a table in its Human Development Report for 2007/2008 of the different ways of calculating it, which vary in 2006 from 22.2 to 43.6 per cent (UNDP 2007c).
11. The best measure of increasing regional inequality, researchers from the Sarajevo Economics Institute find, is the variation in value-added-tax revenues by canton and entity; but these remain in-house data (UNDP (NHDR) 2005: note 19, p. 31).
12. Law on the Protection of Rights of Ethnic Minorities (Official Gazette of BiH, No. 12/03). It establishes advisory councils for ethnic minorities for legislative bodies, foresees representation in judicial and executive bodies, and electoral rights at the local level (through an amendment to the election law of 26 April 2004) (UNDP (NHDR) 2007b: 67).
13. See UNDP (NHDR) (2005: 80) for a brief, useful summary on the relation between inequality and education.
14. The UNDP (NHDR) 2005 provides data and legislated rules on the variation in tax-sharing rules between canton and municipality in the Federation.
15. According to the EWSR research team, however, the protests' success is due as much to the 'institutional capacity' of fiscal authorities, which make the RS government more able to collect revenues and reallocate budgetary funds than the Federation (EWSR 2006).
16. The current account deficit as percentage of GDP was 47.8 per cent in 1996, 43.3 per cent in 1997, 31.6 per cent in 1998, 24.3 per cent in 1999, and 24.1 per cent in 2000 (personal communication from Vladimir Gligorov). According to Didik and Gligorov (2007), it grew from 8 per cent to 22 per cent, and the external debt from 57 per cent to 60.5 per cent, during 2000–2005; but see their discussion of serious problems with the official data.
17. For details, see the initial paragraphs, pp. 3–4, of the report on the IMF website.
18. The benefit of EU accession in the short run is actually the large fiscal effect expected from EU structural funds that accompany an association process, though these funds would be targeted at the cantonal level.
19. Anecdotally, however, the boom in western Herzegovina in the first years of the century was due to Bosniac entrepreneurs from the Sandjak area of southern Serbia attracted to its locational advantages, so that one cannot assume that local Croats are direct beneficiaries.
20. The percentage of GDP spent on social and child protection (though not including war veterans, who receive preferential treatment throughout the country in social benefits, and the disabled), was 1.1 per cent in the RS and

0.7 per cent in the Federation; by comparison, Slovenia was 1.1, Bulgaria 1.4, Macedonia 1.6, Croatia 1.9, Latvia 2.4, and Estonia 2.1 (IMF (PRSP) 2004: 144).

21. Social spending in 2004 was around 5 per cent of GDP, of which 66 per cent (49 per cent in the Federation and 17 per cent in the RS) went to disabled war veterans (UNDP (NHDR) 2007b: 125).

7
Explaining a Contradictory Record: The Case of Guatemala

Corinne Caumartin and Diego Sánchez-Ancochea

7.1 Introduction

Guatemala is not only one of the most unequal countries in the world, but one in which indigenous peoples (mostly of Mayan origin) have been historically marginalized. Until the second half of the twentieth century, they lived in semi-slave conditions, in the rural sector, and even today they have little influence on the process of economic and political decision-making. Indigenous peoples also suffered disproportionately from the civil war that afflicted the country for more than three decades; according to some estimates, more than 80 per cent of the victims of violence were indigenous.

The Peace Accords that ended the long civil war created high expectations among civil society organizations and indigenous communities. Despite their vagueness and other limitations, the accords highlighted the need to create a more equitable economic model and to increase the political and economic participation of indigenous groups. Two accords (the 'Agreement on Identity and Rights of Indigenous Peoples' and the 'Agreement on Socio-Economic Issues') stressed the importance of indigenous culture and values and established goals in terms of cultural recognition, social spending, tax revenues and other economic variables.

What has been the impact of the agreements on horizontal inequalities (HIs)? Has their implementation in the context of transition to democracy been successful? Can we regard Guatemala as an example of successful reduction of HIs in a post-conflict setting? This chapter aims to address these questions, paying special attention to the opportunities created by decentralization, particularly in education, and to long-term structural constraints. We argue that Guatemala has achieved some moderate successes in closing the education attainment gap thanks to a process of decentralization and growing awareness of indigenous rights in some areas. Yet a sustained reduction of HIs requires a more serious modification of some structural constraints on development policy, such as the weakness of the state *vis-à-vis* business groups and the limitations of the neoliberal economic model.

Before evaluating the policies and discussing the constraints, it is important to describe the characteristics and sources of HIs (Stewart et al. 2008) and to explain the nature of the conflict – our task in Sections 7.2 and 7.3. Section 7.4 reviews the advances in decentralization, with particular attention to the educational reform. Section 7.5 analyses two long-term constraints on the reduction of HI: the nature of the neoliberal model (including its effect on capital concentration) and the weakness of state institutions. The chapter finishes with some reflections on the importance of considering structural constraints (both economic and political) when thinking about the design and results of policies towards the reduction of HIs.

7.2 The characteristics of horizontal inequalities in Guatemala

In Guatemala, sharp HIs have long been evident between indigenous peoples and the population of mixed or European descent (labelled 'ladinos' in Guatemala).[1] The indigenous population, which descends from pre-Columbian ancestors and accounts for 40 to 60 per cent of the population, has suffered systematically from a lack of recognition of its indigenous culture and from lower levels of income, access to social services and political participation than those of the population as a whole.[2] Over three quarters of the indigenous people live in poverty, compared with 41 per cent of the non-indigenous, and they have little presence in the upper middle class. Table 7.1 presents some striking evidence on the nature of ethnic stratification in Guatemala: 70.9 per cent of the people that had very low income (equivalent to extreme poverty) around 2000 were indigenous, while only 2.7 per cent of the highest income groups were indigenous.

This stratified income structure has its roots in one of the most unequal distributions of land in the world, which has persisted for centuries. In 1979, 2.1 per cent of holdings accounted for 64.5 per cent of the agrarian land, and properties between 0 and 6.9 hectares represented 88 per cent of total holdings, but only 17 per cent of the land. In 2003 things had not changed significantly, as properties between 0 and 6.9

Table 7.1 Ethnic stratification and inequality in Guatemala, circa 2000

Income levels	% Indigenous	% Non-indigenous	Total in absolute numbers
Very low	70.9	29.1	2,153,866
Low	48.5	51.5	5,658,171
Medium low	20.5	79.5	2,577,215
Medium	6.8	93.2	899,176
High	2.7	97.3	165,148

Source: Torres-Rivas (2005).

hectares represented 92 per cent of the holdings but only 22 per cent of the land. Indigenous households have been particularly affected by this pattern of ownership; they represent around half of all Guatemalan producers, but they control (directly or through tenancy agreements) just 24 per cent of the arable land (PNUD 2005).

Given the historical dominance of the agriculture sector in the Guatemalan economy – coffee was for a long time the most dynamic economic sector and the main export – the lack of access to land has severely constrained the economic opportunities of most indigenous actors and has reinforced an economic model based on high stratification along class and ethnic lines. The situation was particularly striking during the late nineteenth century and at the beginning of the twentieth century, when the coffee elite used different coercive methods to secure its labour supply and promoted the expropriation of communal land (Perez-Sainz 2007; Taracena and Ruano 2001). Since the 1950s, Guatemala (like the rest of Central America) developed new non-traditional primary exports like cotton and sugar. Yet these products sharpened even more the division between export and subsistence agriculture (Bulmer-Thomas 1987) and did not contribute to a sustained expansion of full-time high-quality employment.

High HIs are also reflected in many other economic dimensions (Barrón 2008), some of which are highlighted in Table 7.2. Non-indigenous peoples are more educated, are not as dependent on agriculture and have a better position in the labour market. Particularly dramatic is the fact that 69 per cent of indigenous children suffered from malnutrition in 2000, nearly double the percentage of non-indigenous peoples. The distribution of political resources is also highly unequal, thus increasing the likelihood of severe conflicts. In 2007, just

Table 7.2 Various dimensions of HI between indigenous and non-indigenous (2000)

% of the population	Non-indigenous	Indigenous
Employment in agriculture	29	50
Receiving less than minimum wage	32	61
Literacy rate (15+)	84	59
Child malnutrition	36	69

Source: Barrón (2008); Vakis (2003).

9 per cent of deputies in Congress and two ministers/vice-ministers were indigenous.

Finally, disadvantages of ethnicity and gender compound each other disastrously and indigenous women are the most disadvantaged groups in Guatemalan society, notably in terms of education, employment and poverty. In 2000, for example, indigenous women aged 25 or more received 1.3 years of schooling, compared to 2.9 years for indigenous men, 4.6 years for non-indigenous women and 5.5 years for non-indigenous men (Barrón 2008).

7.3 A short chronology of the civil war and the peace accords

Guatemala suffered a bloody civil war for 36 years (1960–1996), with dramatic consequences on economic performance and, more importantly, on human lives. There were more than 200,000 killings (80 per cent of which were indigenous peoples), more than a million people displaced and many communities destroyed (CEH 1999; Sieder 1998).[3]

The first, failed phase of the civil war took place in the ladino rural regions of the east of the country and was triggered by leftist insurgent movements with a class discourse. In the 1970s a group of surviving guerrilla members regrouped in the western Guatemalan highland, where the majority of the indigenous population lives. Two of the main Guerrilla groups, the Organizacion del Pueblo en Armas (ORPA) and the Ejercito Guerillero de los Pobres (EGP), actively sought to enrol the support of indigenous individuals and communities. ORPA paid particular attention to the question of racism and indigenous subordination in its analysis of the Guatemalan context. However, on the whole the guerrillas' discourses of mobilization were articulated along class rather than ethnic lines, encouraging the 'poor' to revolt against the 'rich' rather than the 'indigenous' against whites or 'ladinos. In this sense, HIs played a key role in the unfolding of the Guatemalan civil war from the 1970s onwards, as many indigenous people were part of the mobilized poor; but ethnicity and class were always linked.

The civil war highlighted the structural inequalities and lack of human rights in the country, but the guerrilla was never able to threaten the state itself – something that did happen in El Salvador. Nevertheless, the combination of external pressures from the United States and neighbouring countries and growing internal desire to end the conflict resulted in the transition to formal democracy in 1985 and in the launch of a peace process. Discussions concluded with the signing of the Peace Accords between 1994 and 1996. According to Sieder (1998: 246), the accords represented 'a unique national learning exercise in consultation and pact-making in a country characterised by the historical absence of mediation and negotiation'.

The Peace Accords included 11 different agreements with more than 300 provisions and articles about demilitarization, transitional justice, human rights and many other issues. The importance of reducing HIs, of improving socioeconomic development and of expanding the political, economic, cultural and social rights of indigenous peoples became a central component of the process. As the principal agreement states, 'to achieve social justice and economic growth [...] the state should expand the level of participation of [civil society] and should become stronger to orientate national development [...] This requires an expansion in fiscal revenues and a reorientation of public spending towards social investment'.[4]

From the perspective of correcting HIs, the two most relevant accords were the Agreement on the Socio-Economic Issues and the Agrarian Condition (ASIAC) from1996 and the Agreement on the Identity and Rights of Indigenous Peoples (AIRI) from 1995. The former established a set of relatively ambitious targets in terms of tax collection, social spending and other variables, although it was vaguer about the mechanisms to secure the achievement of the targets. The latter stressed the importance of indigenous cultures and recognized and emphasized the high levels of inequality and discrimination as endemic problems. While the AIRI included chapters on diverse issues like identity, discrimination and cultural and economic rights, particularly important commitments were

1. the recognition of the multi-ethnic, multicultural and multilinguistic nature of Guatemala;
2. the protection of and respect for all languages spoken in Guatemala;

3. a radical reform of the education system to incorporate indigenous culture and values. Decentralization would play a particularly important role in this process (we will come back to this in the next section);
4. the recognition of indigenous forms of justice and the promotion of the participation of indigenous peoples in local governments. Decentralization would also be a central instrument here;
5. the promotion of access to land of indigenous peoples and of their right to decide on the best use of natural resources.

Although evaluating the performance of the Peace Accords in any detail is beyond the objectives of this chapter, three points are particularly important. First, the accords became a significant break with the past and constituted 'an ambitious political agenda with a reformist ethos [...] that gave a chance to confront historical limitations and shortcomings' (III 2005: 15). They were thus a window of opportunity to design new policies to resolve HIs – the focus of this chapter.

Second, the agreements went much further in some of the areas regarding political rights than in the economic components. In particular, there was no serious attempt to introduce a land reform that would significantly transform Guatemala's ownership structure. The market-based approach to land redistribution may have been the easiest one to sell politically, but it created serious constraints on the reduction of HIs in the long run. Third and most importantly, the effective implementation of the Peace Accords has been slow and patchy and has confronted numerous structural obstacles, including insufficient commitment of significant segments of the elite and the weakness of the state (a point discussed below). There are multitude examples of these failures (III 2005): Table 7.3, for example, offers a good summary of Guatemala's inability to meet some basic quantitative goals set for 2000.

Table 7.3 reveals a sharp contrast between successes in achieving budget allocation and social spending targets (reining in military spending whilst increasing that of education) and failures to achieve social targets. Thus, even when spending targets were met, this did not necessarily translate into rapid improvement of outcomes, and none of the social targets listed here had been met by 2000. The health sector indicators are a particular source of concern, but confusion over the data makes it unclear whether maternal mortality worsened or improved somewhat between 1995 and 2005.[5] Yet on the whole, some positive changes have indeed taken place in Guatemala, and the general trend seems to be towards improvement rather than worsening of social outcomes. This is

Table 7.3 Selected peace monitor indicators

Economic and fiscal targets	**Base 1995**	**Target 2000**	**Actual 2000**	**Latest figures available**	
Growth rate (% per year)	6	6	3.3	5.6	(2007)
Tax revenues (% of GDP)	7.6	12	9.6	9.6 11.6	(2005) (2008)
Health spending (% of GDP)	0.9	1.3	1	1.1	(2001)
Education spending (% of GDP)	1.6	2.5	2.5	2.8	(2001)
Judiciary spending (% of GDP)	0.2	0.3	0.5	0.6	(2001)
Military spending (% of GDP)	1	0.7	0.7	0.4	(2006)
Social target	**Base 1995**	**Target 2000**	**Actual 2000**	**Latest figures available**	
Literacy rate	64.2	70	68.9	70.0	(2004)
Infant mortality (death per 1,000 live births)	49	20	39	32	(2005)
Maternal mortality (per 100,000 giving birth)	270	48.5	240	290/138	(2005)

further illustrated and explained in the following section, which focuses on two prominent areas of change: education and decentralization. Yet the issues and concerns with post-conflict reconstruction in Guatemala relate to the pace, depth and sustainability of change, particularly if the deep structural constraints preventing effective tackling of HIs – discussed in Section 7.5 – are not resolved.

7.4 The role of decentralization in combating horizontal inequality: General process and the case of education

The Peace Accords considered decentralization as a fundamental instrument in the reduction of HIs. The economic agreement, for example, argued that 'considering that the citizens of a department or municipality, businessman, workers, cooperativists and *community authorities* can define better the measures that benefit and affect them, we should adopt a set of instruments that institutionalize the decentralisation of decision-making'. In the particular case of education, the AIRI set the government's commitment 'to promote a reform of the education system with the following characteristics [...] (a) [t]o be decentralised and regionalised so that it is better adapted to linguistic and cultural needs and specificities'.

The expansion of the autonomy of departments and municipalities was supposed to increase the efficiency in service provision – a standard argument in the decentralization literature – and to enhance the links between the state and indigenous peoples. If one considers the classification of policies towards HIs that Stewart, Brown and Langer (2008) develop – and other chapters in this volume discuss – decentralization was an indirect approach that in many ways did not promote integration between different groups. It was, in principle, geared towards all citizens, but it created opportunities for specific policies (e.g. community schools) that favour the indigenous population. Decentralization, however, could not accelerate the integration of citizens as a whole into a national identity, since it allowed space for tailoring policy specifically, for different regions and municipalities.[6]

The record of decentralization as a policy tool to reduce HIs, which we review in this section, has been mixed. Decentralization has increased the opportunities that indigenous peoples have to affect socio-economic policies at the local level. More importantly, it may have contributed to the expansion of access to some basic social services, a point that we will illustrate with the discussion of education. Nevertheless, decentralization has taken place slowly and has not opened as many opportunities as initially promised.

The process of decentralization in Guatemala

The initial promotion of decentralization came hand in hand with the transition to civilian rule in 1985 and with the drafting of a new constitution, but it was never fully implemented.[7] A fundamental change brought by the 1985 Constitution was the establishment of a new fiscal regime for municipalities, whereby 8 per cent of the central budget (*'presupuesto ordinario'*) was transferred to municipalities, being increased to 10 per cent of the central budget in 1993 (Rivera 2005: 3).[8] Decentralization was revisited during the peace process (1988–1996) when the guerrilla group Unidad Revolucionaria Nacional Guatemlateca (URNG in the Spanish acronym) and the government agreed on the principle of a decentralization process in Guatemala. Additionally, the provision of key public services (education, health and construction and infrastructure) was also decentralized in the 1990s (Puente and Linares 2004: 237).

The institutional design of decentralization was the subject of lengthy debates and political manoeuvring, which slowed down the adoption of the chief instruments of decentralization until 2002 and included (CPD 2003: 5):

- a general law of decentralization (ley general de descentralización, Decreto No 14-2002)
- a new municipal code (código Municipal, Decreto No 12-2002)
- a new law of urban and rural development councils (Ley de Consejos de Desarrollo Urbano y Rural, Decreto No 11-2002).

The general law of decentralization provided a conceptual and legal framework and was accompanied by the setting up of further institutions designed to implement the decentralization process.[9] The AIRI influenced the drafting of the municipal code, notably with regard to the status and judicial capacity of indigenous communities and their authorities, as well as promoting fair and even-handed distribution of public expenditure amongst indigenous and non-indigenous communities (Puente and Linares 2004: 239).[10] Article 23 of the Development Councils Law (modified by Decree Number 49–88) established criteria for the distribution of transfers to municipalities, which attempts to balance the distribution between the most populated municipalities, those with a greater number of rural communities, in accordance with their capacity to collect revenues autonomously from the central state – in other words to balance between poorer and richer municipalities (for a detail of the formula, see Alcatraz and Linares 2004: 244–245).

The law of urban and rural development councils re-established local development councils (dormant since they were deemed unconstitutional in 1988). The system of development councils was designed to work at national, regional and local level and to encourage participation in the formulation, planning and budgetary implementation of development public policy (Aguilera Peralta 2009). In addition, the councils are also designed to encourage the participation of women and indigenous people in development planning. The councils comprise elected and unelected representatives of the state and of civil society (women, peasant and indigenous organizations, as well as business groups and academics) and operate at five distinct levels:

- national
- regional (comprising a group of departments)
- departmental (CODEDES, Consejo Departamental)
- municipal (COMUDES, Consejo Municipal)
- community (COCODES, Consejo Comunitario).

The setting up of COCODES and COMUDES was initially uneven and problematic; communities were uncertain of the roles and functions of the councils and registration required strong leadership and organizational skills (Aguilera Peralta 2009), which were in short supply following the pervasive repression of community organization in the 1980s and early 1990s. However, from an initially slow start, the number of local councils steadily increased and, by 2008, 75 per cent of the municipalities had established COMUDES (compared to 60 per cent in 2005).[11]

Decentralization contributed towards a renewed dynamism of local committees and municipal development work, and in the context of post-conflict Guatemala, where community organization and development had been brutally curtailed in the 1980s, this is an achievement of sorts. There are some positive experiences regarding local indigenous leadership and effective relations between indigenous mayors and the formal public sector (Piñol 2008), as well as pro-indigenous reforms of the judicial system at the local and regional level. In addition, as was noted above, the allocation of 10 per cent of the national budget to municipalities is far from negligible and compares favourably to other processes of decentralization in the region (Rivera 2005). Significantly, decentralization also facilitated the gradual expansion of social service provision, including the health program Sistema Integrado de Atención de Salud (SIAS) and the reforms of the educational system. In this way, decentralization has partly contributed to the expansion of human capital and to the reduction of HI, a point to which we come to below.[12]

Yet, in spite of these advances, decentralization has also been problematic, with significant shortcomings in terms of inequality and inefficiency. On the one hand, there have been endless issues of misappropriation of funds and corruption at the municipal level, and the relationships between citizens, municipal authorities and development councils have been extremely conflictive in a number of departments (PNUD 2005). In some cases the development councils have acted in a corrupt, abusive and undemocratic manner, approving unnecessary work, without due regard for the views and opinions of the community they were supposedly representing (El Periodico, 29th December 2007).[13] This may have contributed to an inefficient allocation of public resources – which continue to be very limited. Finally, some Mayan organizations point out that, to date, the decentralization process has failed to implement key aspects of the Agreement on Identity and Rights of Indigenous Peoples, chiefly by strengthening formal municipal governments and mayors but failing to recognize or incorporate traditional Mayan and community authorities.

The extension of education

Education has been one of the sectors in which decentralization has achieved some positive results, despite advancing slowly. In 1996 the creation of departmental Education Bureaux, which are in charge of planning, coordinating and implementing education intervention, began (Marques and Bannon 2003). In 1998 the government created a system of school committees in all public schools, to promote participation of parents and communities. In the last few years there has been a decentralization of supporting services like school meals and material and general maintenance. By 2006, there were 4,600 education committees with municipal presence, more than 9,000 school councils, which affected more than 2.2 million children in Guatemala (Ministerio de Educacion 2006).

One of the most important initiatives in the education sector has been the National Community-Managed Program for Educational Development (PRONADE), which was launched in 1992, but which experienced a significant expansion after the Peace Accords. Inspired by a similar initiative in El Salvador called EDUCO, PRONADE aimed to expand primary schools in remote rural areas and to improve their effectiveness through parent involvement. The program created a parallel school system in the rural sector, with community-run schools in which the government paid for teacher salaries and for some other fixed costs (USAID 2007).

PRONADE grew rapidly, going from a small pilot program funded by the United Nations Development Programme (UNDP) and other international institutions in 19 rural communities to a national program that benefited 445,000 children in 4,100 communities (World Bank 2005b). According to some estimations, PRONADE is responsible for at least half of the expansion in primary enrolment (years 7–12) since its creation, and it is particularly important for indigenous peoples (McEwan and Trowbridge 2007: 63). In 2000, 16 per cent of indigenous children went to PRONADE schools, compared to just 4 per cent non-indigenous.

The creation of PRONADE was, in many ways, a typical indirect policy towards the reduction of HIs because of its focus on the rural sector – where a disproportionate number of the indigenous poor live – and because of its accent on community organization. According to the rules of the program, potential construction sites have to be at least three kilometres away from other public schools, and must involve able and interested communities (World Bank 2005b). In this way the PRONADE schools may have enhanced 'the collaboration of parents, organisations and indigenous leaders in the education committees, all of which become participants, for example, in the selection of teachers that know the language, customs and needs of the communities' (Piñol 2008).

PRONADE was accompanied by other initiatives oriented towards the expansion and improvement of primary education, particularly among indigenous peoples. The government introduced a variety of scholarships: in 2007, 190,000 students received fellowships, 2.3 million received free school meals and 12,500 received student financial support. The strengthening and expansion of 'intercultural, bilingual education' resulted in the expansion of teachers and schools that combine Mayan and Spanish in their teaching (PREAL 2008). An additional step in the direction of improving bilingual education was taken in 2005 with the creation of the Strategic Plan for the Revitalization of Intercultural, Bilingual Education in Guatemala. The expansion of bilingual education can make a decisive contribution to the improvement of education for indigenous peoples and the reduction of inequality. A study by Patrinos and Velez (2009: 5) uses data from the early 1990s to show that 'bilingual education increases Spanish language proficiency, which in turn leads to an increase in the average educational attainment of Guatemala's large indigenous population'. However, the implementation of bilingual education programmes is still partial and erratic, being characterized by a general lack of trained bilingual teachers,[14] a general failure to allocate bilingual teachers to relevant linguistic regions and a pervasive lack of readily available education materials.[15] Just as problematic is the fact that, while the benefits of bilingual education are generally recognized amongst education scholars in Guatemala, this recognition and acceptance does not always extend to the general population. Rather, many of parents still regard bilingual education with a degree of suspicion, identifying instead access to education in Spanish as the key priority in their children schooling.[16]

Nonetheless, the new programs were accompanied by an expansion of financial resources at the beginning of the period: according to data from the Ministry of Education of Guatemala, public spending in education increased from 1.9 per cent of gross domestic product (GDP) in 1997 to 2.6 per cent in 2001 but remained stagnant from then on.[17] The increase in enrolment has been more dramatic. Between 1996 and 2005, the number of children in primary education expanded from 1.5 m to 2.3 million and the enrolment rates went from 69 per cent to 94 per cent (Ministerio de Educacion 2006).

The impact of some of these efforts on school attainment has been quite impressive, even if inequality in education is still high and the overall numbers poor. Table 7.4 presents some education statistics comparing indigenous and non-indigenous people and highlights the narrowing down of educational HIs. Between 1989 and 2006 the literacy rates grew so as to be almost four times higher for indigenous than for non-indigenous people, and something similar took place in the matter of average years of education. By 2006, 80 per cent of the indigenous youth between 15 and 25 years of age were able to read and write accurately, compared to only 54 per cent in 1989.

In education, decentralization has certainly achieved some successes, but evaluations of PRONADE vary, some indicating better results in

Table 7.4 Educational attainments for indigenous and non-indigenous people in Guatemala (1989–2006)

	1989	**2000**	**2006**	**% change, 2000–2006**
		Literacy rate 15+		
Non-indigenous	73.8	79.4	83.4	5.04
Indigenous	35.6	50.1	59.6	18.96
		Literacy rate, population 15–25 years old		
Non-indigenous	85.9	89	92.2	3.6
Indigenous	54.2	69.8	80.3	15.04
		Average years of schooling		
Non-indigenous	4.4	5.5	6.1	10.91
Indigenous	1.3	2.4	3.1	29.17

Source: Barrón (2008).

terms of completion and student satisfaction (USAID 2007), whilst others point towards general quality issues and a higher desertion rate (12 per cent desertion in PRONADE to 7.4 per cent standard state school rate in 2004, Edwards 2006: 25). In addition, decentralization has advanced at a slow pace and has been unable to resolve the asymmetries in the quality of provision between regions and between groups.[18] According to PNUD (Programa de Naciones Unidas para el Desarrollo) (2008: 220), 'there are two educational systems in the country defined not only by their source of finance, but also by their geographical location: one has low quality and is located in the central part of the country and the other with worse quality is in the rest of the country' – where a majority of indigenous students live. Decentralization has also involved sharp asymmetries in teacher experience and pay between the different systems (PRONADE vs central government), questioning the sustainability of the system and damaging the opportunities to improve quality provision (Gershberg et al. 2009).

7.5 Facing long-term structural constraints for more sustainable equitable policies

Despite all the shortcomings, the promotion of decentralization and the process of education reform have at least considered the importance of expanding the influence of indigenous peoples and of reducing HIs. Nevertheless, real advances in these areas have been hampered by major shortcomings in the Guatemalan politico-economic system and by the lack of attention to group inequalities at the macroeconomic level.

Guatemala – like many other countries in post-conflict situations – suffers from having a weak state, which is highly dependent on the interests of the (non-indigenous) elite and does not have the financial resources or institutional capacity to promote a better distribution of resources. At the same time, the neoliberal policies adopted under the Washington Consensus have failed to promote sustainable growth, to create more dynamic comparative advantages or significantly to expand the number of well-paying jobs. In this environment it is thus very difficult to envision a rapid reduction in HIs in decades to come, as we demonstrate in the following two sub-sections.

The limitations of the neoliberal policy model

Guatemala, like the rest of Central America, adopted most components of the Washington Consensus from the early 1990s (Segovia 2004). Despite the stated objectives in the Peace Accords, the new policy model did not pay much attention to HIs, and politicians talked about economic growth and poverty reduction more than about inequality. The bases of the new economic model were laid down at the beginning of the 1990s and the Peace Accords did not lead to a significant policy shift. Successive administrations adopted the following measures, which expanded the role of markets and the space for private accumulation[19]:

- Liberalization of the current account. Guatemala entered into the General Agreement on Trade and Tariffs in 1991 and reduced tariffs significantly since then. According to data from the World Bank (2006), average weighted tariffs decreased from more than 20 per cent in 1987 to 8 per cent in 1998 and 6 per cent in 2001. The entry into force of the Central American Free Trade Agreement (CAFTA) with the United States in 2006 triggered a gradual process of further reduction of protection in most sectors of the economy.
- Promotion of non-traditional exports, both in the agricultural and in the manufacturing sectors, through the creation of free trade zones and different tax incentives. The Reagan administration's launch of the Caribbean Basin Initiative (CBI) in 1984 and the rebirth of the Central American Common Market in the 1990s also contributed to the growth of new exports in Guatemala and the rest of Central America.
- Privatization of state-owned enterprises with a particularly ambitious program, between 1996 and 1998, which affected telecommunications, electricity and other sectors.
- Liberalization and deregulation of the financial sector. In 1993 the Central Bank implemented the Financial Modernization Program for Guatemala, which consolidated the liberalization of the financial and banking sector started four years earlier. It was followed by other reforms in 1994, 2001 and 2002, which increased the autonomy of the Central Bank, facilitated access to foreign credit and eliminated most restrictions for private banks.

The new economic model has tended to benefit high-income groups more than any other segment in society, thus consolidating the unequal character of the Guatemalan economy. According to PNUD (2008: 116), 'the evidence [...] tends to suggest that the model of growth between 2000 and 2006 did not favour low income groups but, in relative terms, was more beneficial for the middle and high sectors in society'. Particularly important was the increasing concentration of capital in a small number of national business groups with close ties to transnational corporations – a trend shared with other Central American countries (Robinson 2003; Sánchez-Ancochea 2005; Segovia 2005). In the Guatemalan case, many of these groups emerged in agro-businesses in the second half of the twentieth century and have maintained their agricultural orientation, while simultaneously moving to other sectors of the economy. According to Segovia (2005), Guatemalan elite groups are amongst the most powerful in Central America after those in El Salvador.

These large business groups in the hands of a self-defined 'white' elite of European descent (Casaús Arzú 1995), together with transnational corporations (most of which have ladino managers) have generally benefited from the new economic model. They bought out most of the state-owned enterprises that were privatized during the 1990s, either directly or in joint venture with transnational corporations. Bull (2005, 2008) describes this process in detail in the case of the telecommunication sector, highlighting the role of traditional groups like Grupo Londrina and newcomers like the investment group Luca. As importers, they profited from the reduction of import duties and, as exporters, from trade liberalization and the introduction of various export incentives. Large business groups also succeeded in determining the pace of the reforms and in derailing those measures that they oppose (see the discussion of taxes below). According to Bull (2008: 213), 'several studies have pointed to how the unified private sector has prevented governments from implementing development policies and necessary tax adjustments'.

Policy-induced concentration at the top has had negative implications for the reduction of HIs for several reasons. First, it tends to increase the political power of the non-indigenous rich, who fund political campaigns, build business ties with politicians and former politicians and have preferential access to ministers (Segovia 2005). Second, the control of the media allows business groups to influence the political debate and, on many occasions, to promote racist stereotypes in order to consolidate the basic features of the political–economic model. High capital concentration limits access to credit for large segments of society and also reduces the probability of successful tax reforms.

The new economic model has not been able to generate high economic growth and has thus failed even to provide a 'trickle-down' effect with positive consequences for the poor. Guatemala's GDP per capita grew by just 1.4 per cent per year between 1996 and 2007, after the signing of the Peace Accords, and slightly more if one considers the

Table 7.5 Growth of GDP per capita in Central America (2000 US dollars) (1990–2007, %)

	GDP per captia growth 1990–2007	GDP per captia growth 1996–2007	GDP per capita 2007 (2000 US$)
Costa Rica	2.97	3.39	5,120
El Salvador	2.11	1.42	2,336
Guatemala	1.51	1.43	1,868
Honduras	1.78	2.24	1,419
Nicaragua	1.55	2.31	884
Latin America & Caribbean	1.82	1.86	4,580

Source: Own calculations with data from the World Development Indicators database.

first years of the 1990s. This was the lowest growth in Central America (together with that of El Salvador), and it was also well below that of Latin America as a whole (see Table 7.5).

The failure of the new economic model to promote economic growth has contributed to a lack of good jobs in the formal sector, particularly for indigenous peoples – a major policy objective of HI-correcting policies in a post-conflict environment (see Stewart's contribution to this volume). Table 7.6 reveals some of the structural weaknesses of the Guatemalan labour market and the permanence of HIs in the sector. Most indigenous workers do not have a formal contract, or access to social security, and their situation in these areas improved little over the 2000s. Between 2000 and 2006, the percentage of indigenous workers with formal employment decreased from 95 per cent to 92 per cent, while that of non-indigenous workers fell faster, from 84 per cent to 76 per cent. Both groups also suffered a dramatic increase in the number of workers paid below the minimum wage. Whilst the rate of increase was most dramatic for non-indigenous people (138 per cent, compared to 70 per cent for indigenous), pay below minimum standards still affected a disproportionate number of indigenous employees (70 per cent of indigenous against 41.9 per cent non-indigenous).

Remittances became a safety valve for many families and complemented labour market income. Guatemala has experienced a spectacular expansion of migration abroad since 1980: in 2001 there were at least 600,000 Guatemalans in the United States – a 125 per cent increase, compared to the situation in 1990 (PNUD 2008). As a result, remittances became a central component of Guatemalan economy, increasing from just US$ 375m in 1996 to an estimated US$ 4,315m in 2008. They also

Table 7.6 Some labour market indicators in Guatemala (2000–2006)

	2000	2006	Change
Workers without social security (% of active population)			
Non-indigenous	77.2	75.0	−2.85
Indigenous	92.6	92.2	−0.43
Workers without formal contract (% of active population)			
Non-indigenous	83.8	76.4	−8.83
Indigenous	95.1	92.3	−2.94
Workers with wage below the minimum wage (of the main occupation, % of active population)			
Non-indigenous	17.9	41.9	134.08
Indigenous	43.5	70.0	60.92

Source: PNUD (2008).

became the main generator of foreign exchange, well above traditional exports, tourism and other exports of goods (see Figure 7.1). Indigenous people, however, were slow to participate in migration and have thus benefited less from the arrival of remittances. According to data from PNUD (2005: 123), in 2004 just over 15 per cent of the Mayan population had some relative in a foreign country, compared to almost 40 per cent in the case of *ladinos*. As a result, 78.5 per cent of the more than 1 million Guatemalans who sent remittances in 2004 spoke Spanish, compared to just 21.5 per cent who spoke some indigenous language.

At the same time it is important to recognize that the combination of new economic model and transition to democracy created some opportunities for a small group of indigenous workers even before the signing of the Peace Accords. In his detailed analysis of the changes in the Guatemalan labour market, Perez Sainz (2007: 40) shows that there has been a growth in the indigenous middle class 'around public employment and the professional world [...] This last one is important [...] [because] it was a space historically prohibited for the indigenous and access to it has a high symbolic value.'

Table 7.7 shows some of these changes and compares the evolution of indigenous and non-indigenous workers. Three trends are particularly significant, although their future direction is not altogether clear. The percentage of day labourers – probably the group of indigenous people

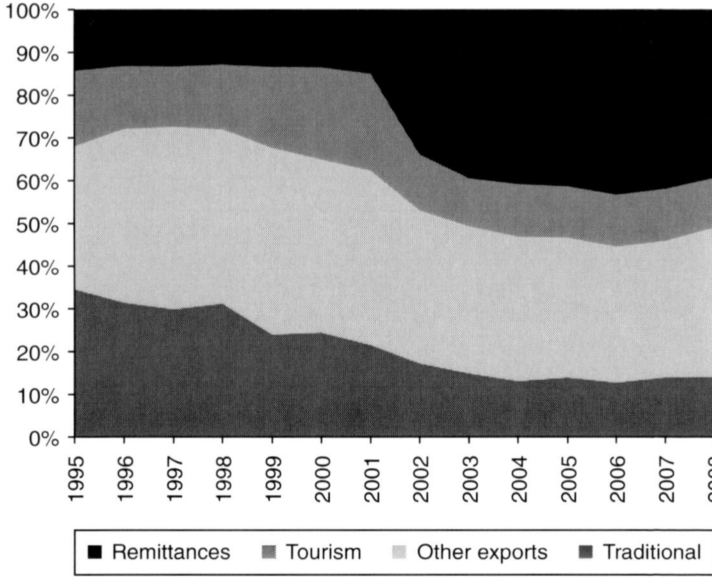

Figure 7.1 Sources of foreign exchange in Guatemala (1995–2008)
Source: Own calculations with data from the Central Bank of Guatemala.

with the worst labour conditions – decreased rapidly between 2000 and 2006. On the other hand, the share of public employment in the total has expanded steadily in the same period, going from 2.15 per cent to 3.26 – a 51 per cent growth, which is unmatched by non-indigenous workers. The last positive trend has to do with the long-term growth of indigenous employers, although the advance took place in the 1990s and not in the more recent period.

While Table 7.7 illustrates the growing complexity of Guatemalan society – partly made possible by the growth of indigenous civil servants such as teachers – it also demonstrates the persistence of HIs. Nearly 40 per cent of non-indigenous workers are private employers and, in many cases, they have access to some socials rights – compared to just 20 per cent in the case of indigenous peoples.

Summarizing, then, the new economic model may have created new structural obstacles for a sustained reduction of HIs by promoting capital concentration in a relatively small number of ladino-owned business groups and ladino-managed transnational corporations and by consolidating an economy dominated by informal jobs. This new economic model was supposed to accelerate economic growth, but it

Table 7.7 Comparative structure of the labour market, percentage of the total and total employed in thousands (1989, 2000 and 2006)

	1989	**2000**	**2006**	**% change, 2000–2006**
		Indigenous peoples		
Public employees	2.22	2.15	3.26	51.43
Private employees	26.01	16.89	19.61	16.12
Day laborer	n.a	16.64	11.83	−28.89
Domestic employee	n.a	2.69	2.30	−14.43
Self-employed	44.61	32.35	33.62	3.92
Employer	0.41	3.06	2.07	−32.59
Non-paid	26.74	26.22	27.31	4.18
Total number (thousands)	1036.6	1821.4	2111.1	15.91
		Non-indigenous		
Public employees	10.31	6.10	6.24	2.25
Private employees	50.00	35.95	39.94	11.12
Day labourer	0.00	9.13	6.94	−24.04
Domestic employee	0.00	3.97	3.80	−4.26
Self-employed	26.93	24.29	25.39	4.53
Employer	2.09	5.70	4.45	−21.90
Non-paid	10.67	14.85	13.23	−10.88
Total number (thousands)	1801.6	2584.1	3254.8	25.95

Source: Own calculations with data from PNUD (2008).

failed to do so and, even more importantly, never incorporated the active promotion of HIs as a primary goal.

The lack of the state capacity

A significant problem of many post-conflict societies in their pursuit of more successful and equitable economic policies is the weakness of state institutions. Years of civil war often result in severe weakness in the bureaucracy, the over-expansion of the military apparatus and the excessive influence of some private groups in decision-making. While the Guatemalan state was traditionally not as weak and ineffective as the state of many other countries discussed in this book (say, Congo or Burundi), it still had many shortcomings. According to Sieder

(1998: 246), the defining characteristics of Guatemalan regimes before 1996 were 'political exclusion, repression and extreme state violence'. The social state was practically absent from most of the country – with the partial exception of the capital – and the quality of institutions was low. In 1997–1998, Guatemala was ranked 128 out of 155 countries in the Kauffman et al. index of institutional quality (Agosin et al. 2004).

Any success in the reduction of HIs thus requires the strengthening of state institutions and the expansion of its autonomy *vis-à-vis* private interest groups. Unless these processes take place, progressive policies either will not be implemented due to outside pressures or will be ineffective due to insufficient resources and low human capital. These problems have been evident in Guatemala, where slow advance in the process of state-building has been one of the main hindrances to a rapid reduction of HIs.

The persistent weakness of the Guatemalan state has been evident in at least three related areas: its narrow tax base, the problems with the quality of public services and the excessive influence of legal and illegal interest groups. In the remainder of this chapter, we review these areas and discuss their responsibility for the slow reduction of HIs.

With less than 12 per cent of GDP, the tax burden in Guatemala is still one of the lowest in the world – and significantly below the level to be expected, given Guatemala's GDP per capita and Gini coefficient (Agosín et al. 2009). The Peace Accords tried to tackle this problem and aimed to increase the tax ratio from 8 per cent to 12 per cent by 2000 (see Table 7.3). There was an initial expansion of tax revenues due to the increase in the value added tax rate from 10 to 12 per cent and to the creation of a solidarity tax – the *impuesto de solidaridad, extraordinario y temporal* – which was supposed to last two years and of tax gross income of individuals and companies (at 1 per cent the first year and 1.5 per cent the second and last year). Successive governments managed to extend this tax but failed to create a more stable and ambitious tax system (ICEFI 2007). As a result, the tax burden remained stagnant around 10 per cent for a significant part of the post-conflict period (Figure 7.2). The tax regime still has a very regressive structure, with three fourths of total tax revenues in the period 2001–2007 coming from indirect taxes.

According to Agosin et al. (2009: 150), the lack of fiscal resources has negative consequences for Guatemala's development: 'the inadequacy of this model for long-term development is evidenced by the persistence of extreme poverty, weak infrastructure, and vulnerability to shocks

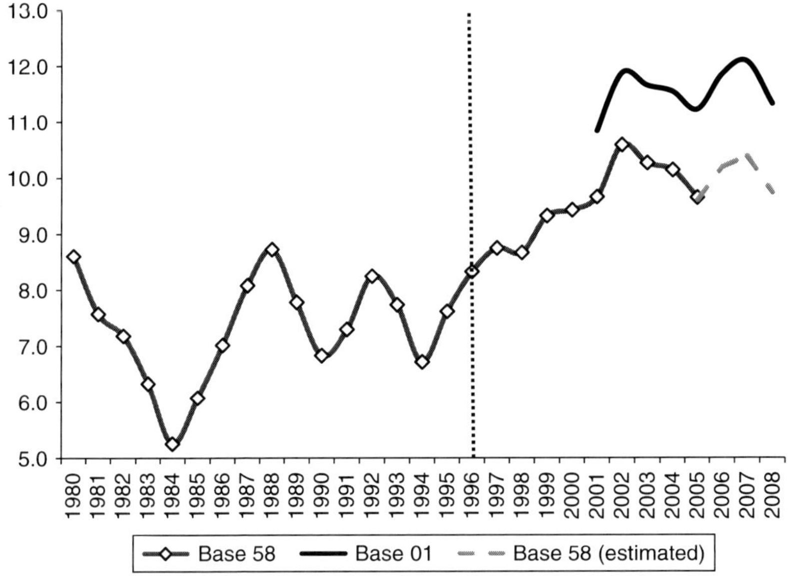

Figure 7.2 Tax receipts as percentage of GDP (1980–2008)

Notes: (1) The data for 2008 are preliminary. (2) Costa Rica changed in 2001 the base year in the calculation of the gross domestic product. The series 'Base 58 (estimated)' calculates the tax burden using a rule of three.

Source: Own calculations with data from the Central Bank of Guatemala.

such as those presented by natural disasters, like Hurricane Stan, during 2005. The tax system simply generates too few resources.' Insufficient public funds placed a strong limit on the expansion of social services, and thus constitute a major constraint on the reduction of HIs.

This is evident when one considers the evolution of public spending in health and education, which increased initially but remained stagnant after 2000 (Figure 7.3). In 2007 Guatemala spent just 1.6 per cent of GDP on health and 2.9 per cent on education – less than any other country in Latin America. Insufficient public spending in a context of expansion of the number of beneficiaries has affected the quality and effectiveness of the service. In education, for example, despite advances triggered by some decentralized programs (see previous section), the annual national tests organized by the government demonstrate the low quality of the educational system and the persistence of high HIs. In 2004 only 28 per cent of children in the first year of primary school knew how to do simple sums, and just 48 per cent could read simple

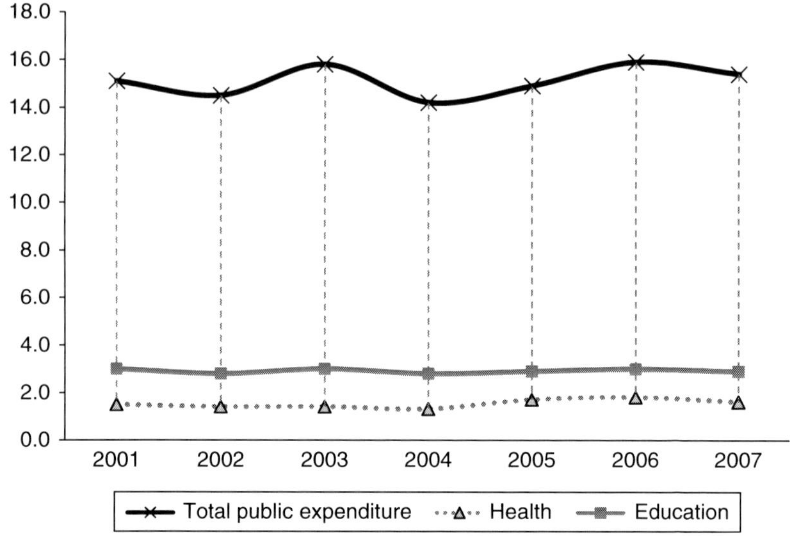

Figure 7.3 Public expenditure in Guatemala in total and in health and education (% GDP, 2001–2007)
Source: PNUD (2008).

sentences of five words – and the performance of indigenous children was particularly weak (PREAL 2008).

The inability of the state to raise the funds required in order to redistribute income and reduce HIs is the result of its weakness *vis-à-vis* other groups in society. For Schneider (2009: 180),

> Guatemala could be characterised by a powerful, concentrated, and well-connected opposition to reform [...]. Such sectors are protected oligopolies within industry, commerce, and finance, which are largely outside the formal tax net, and they act to prevent the formation of a reformist coalition. Their competitive advantage is the weakness of the state.

Two peak business associations – the Coordinating Committee of Agriculture, Commercial, Industrial and Financial Associations (CACIF in its Spanish acronym) and the Agricultural Chamber – have been particularly instrumental in slowing down all efforts to expand direct taxation and create a more efficient and modern tax system.

There are many examples of this dilatory approach (ICEFI 2007). In 1997, the objection of CACIF to a reform that would have increased the corporate and property taxes was one of the key factors behind the government's failure to introduce the measure. In 1998, the government together with the Commission in Support of the Peace Accords launched a social dialogue effort to reach a tax pact. Business associations, social movements and indigenous organizations participated in this unique initiative – it was the first time that Guatemala tried to increase taxes through broad negotiation. At the end, however, the process resulted in the approval of a small number of indirect taxes, but it did not significantly modify the tax regime. In 2001 CACIF appealed successfully to the Constitutional Court to stop an expansion of the corporate tax (PNUD 2008). In June 2004 the National Assembly approved a partial reform that included minor changes in the corporate income tax and a temporal tax on assets and sales, but it was less ambitious than initially planned and did not incorporate a proposed increase in the VAT due to the opposition of business groups.

The weakness of the state and the power of business groups have been evident in many other instances and have contributed to perpetuate high HIs. Business groups have been particularly successful in limiting the breadth of land redistribution programs and in fighting measures to protect trade unions and labour rights (PNUD 2008). When needed, they have used racist arguments to support their policy aims and to maintain the unequal economic structure. The best example of this approach was the involvement of many business groups in a referendum on key reforms agreed in the Peace Accords. In the 1999 referendum, the campaign for the 'Yes' vote was carried out primarily by indigenous popular organizations and trade union leaders, some sectors of the Catholic and evangelical churches. However, this was no match for the strong, vehement, ideologically coherent and well funded 'No' campaign (Jonas 2000: 200). Millions of Quetzales were disbursed to fund the media blitz of the 'No' campaigners in the few weeks that preceded the referendum. The 'No' campaign revelled in scare tactics and scaremongering, manipulating key fears of Guatemalan society: the threat of indigenous power and the threat of ethnic violence. Thus, whilst many of those who funded the 'No' campaign may have been concerned primarily with the notion of resisting tax increases – included in some parts of the new legislation – most of the campaigning focused on approval of the agreement on indigenous rights and identity. Leaflets screamed that the approval of the referendum would 'convert Guatemala into an indigenous state, marginalizing the non-indigenous, that citizens would be divided and that indigenous people would possess more rights than other citizens'. These arguments contributed to the failure of the referendum: only 18.5 per cent of the electorate went to the polls, and amongst those the 'No' vote prevailed by a margin of 55 per cent to 45 per cent (Jonas 2000: 199).

In the pursuit of their regressive objectives, business groups have benefited from the weakness of both the legislative and the executive power. The Guatemalan political system is characterized by a large number of political parties with a low life expectancy and a total inability to represent the interests of social movements (Schneider 2009). Politicians have few ties or loyalties to their parties, frequently changing political affiliation between and during electoral terms (43 per cent of the deputies changed their party affiliation during the Berger presidency, 2004–2008) (ASIES 2007: 7–8).

The weakness of the executive power has also contributed to the expansion of an 'economy of crime' and to the consolidation of violence in the country. According to PNUD (2008: 472), this parallel economy has influenced the economic and political system 'through money laundering, including financial transactions, acquisition of properties (goods and real state), various investments [...] in addition to financing of political parties and candidates to elected positions'. The economy of crime may contribute directly to consolidating HIs because it is generally controlled by non-indigenous peoples and because it leads to growing violence towards the poor. In 2006 alone, 5,500 were killed, a higher number than in most years during the civil war. Additionally, the development of a parallel economy led to the expansion of corruption and political scandals and debilitated those governments that aimed to undertake substantial reforms. The scandal that exploded in 2009, when the president was accused, without hard evidence, of organizing the assassination of a critic and the government became paralysed, constitutes the most recent example of the perverse links between a weak government, an economy of crime, and the failure to reduce HIs.

7.6 Conclusion

Guatemala's experience in reducing HIs in the post-conflict era has been contradictory. Some of the more progressive and sustained efforts at implementing change, such as new policies in education, have increased the enrolment of indigenous people and slowly modified their position in society – something that seems evident in some labour market indicators. New local and regional governance initiatives could increase the participation of indigenous peoples in decision-making and thus could result in direct and indirect policies towards the reduction of HIs.

Yet the main message of this chapter is that any evaluation of policies must be placed within a careful analysis of the structural constraints that post-conflict societies face in the current global era. We should not expect many improvements in education, health, trade policy and other policy arenas if the state remains in the hands of a minority or is characterized by an ineffective bureaucracy with no historical memory. Technocratic solutions to inequality may deliver some short-term gains and open new spaces for indigenous people, but they will not create radically new conditions unless they are accompanied by a new economic and political structure.

A second lesson from the Guatemalan case has to do with the interactions between ethnicity and class. Guatemala is not just characterized by high individual and group inequalities, but also by an extreme concentration of economic resources and political power at the top. A small group of non-indigenous business groups have profited from globalization as much as they did from previous economic models. Unless Guatemala and developing countries in similar situations are able to question the role of these groups, modify their behaviour and create some counter-balancing forces, the reduction of HIs and conflict will advance more slowly than we would like, or will not even take place at all.

Notes

1. Casaús Arzú's (1995) seminal work on the perception of identity by Guatemalan elite groups underlines that they reject the label of ladino because of its implication of a 'mixed' heritage, which they negate. Instead they affirm identities of white European descent, often articulated around lineage and 'pure blood lines'.
2. What 'indigenous' means and how to measure it are highly contested concepts. For a good summary of debates on ethnicity and measurement in Latin America, see Van Cott (2000), Assies et al. (2000) and Yashar (2005).
3. Some studies give a much larger number of victims. III (2005), for example, talks about 300,000.
4. All translations from Spanish sources are ours unless otherwise stated.
5. The World Health Organization data show a somewhat unexpected worsening of the maternal mortality rate to 290/100,000 but the Guatemalan 2005 UNDP report, which is based on national data, registers a more plausible improvement, to 138/100,000 (UNDP 2005: 192). The latter seems more in keeping with other health indicators (e.g. vaccination, infant mortality), pointing towards improvements taking place but still falling short of expected targets.
6. Stewart et al. (2008) identify three sets of policies for the reduction of HIs: direct policies, which involve affirmative action of different kinds;

indirect policies, which are general policies that we know to benefit specific groups (e.g. subsidies for informal workers or transfers to specific regions); and integrationist policies, which aim to eliminate the boundaries between groups.

7. The antecedents to decentralization processes (1985–2002) and a detailed description of the 1985 constitutional provisions are available in Puente and Linares (2004).
8. For a discussion of fiscal autonomy and municipal revenues, see Alcaraz and Linares (2004: 241–247).
9. Acuerdo Gubernativo 24-2002 set up the Presidential commission for state reform and citizen participation, and Acuerdo Gubernativo 312-2002 set up the Secretaria de Coordinacion Ejecutiva de la Presidencia de la Republica, which is the institution of government responsible for supervising the execution of the decentralization process. In 2004, Acuerdo Gubernativo No. 346-2004 set up a single institution to coordinate decentralization activities, the COPRE: Comisión Presidencial para la Reforma, Modernización y Fortalecimiento del Estado y de sus Entidades Descentralizadas: http://www.apc.org/apps/img_upload/f613737b233ddaa8d2567019944fabcb/G_ACUERDO_REFORMA_COPRE.rtf (Last accessed 8th April 2009).
10. Article 56 of the municipal code, which deals with issues of indigenous/formal authorities, is extremely ambiguous. On the one hand, the article stipulates that the town council must recognize local customs and community authorities and that both must be taken into account in local decision-making processes. However, the only community authorities recognized in the code are auxiliary mayors, and not traditional Mayan authorities (e.g. elders and the council of elders amongst others). In addition, local communities can express recommendations to the town council in choosing an auxiliary mayor or other representative; but the final word rests with the mayor of the municipality, a system blatantly open to abuse.
11. Noticias de Municipalidades de Guatemala, 18 Octubre 2008, http://noticias municipalesguatemala.blog.com, last accessed 8th April 2009.
12. Guatemalan law requires that 90 per cent of the funding MUST go to health, education, infrastructure and social services that improve standards of living and 10 per cent to general spending (III, 2005).
13. Article available online at http://www.elperiodico.com.gt/es/20071229/pais/47069, last accessed 8th April 2009.
14. There is often some confusion about the notion of a bilingual teacher. Many primary school teachers speak Spanish and a Mayan language, but, unless they are familiar with the written form of the language, their ability to teach will be severely circumscribed.
15. Interview with Demetrio Cojti, former vice education minister (2000–2004), 6th May 2005, Guatemala City.
16. This position came across very strongly in the course of interviews on the perception of identities in rural indigenous communities of Jalapa, Alta Verapaz and Quetzaltenango: CRISE perception survey, 2005 and 2006.
17. Data from other sources reveal a similar trend, but lower absolute numbers (see Figure 7.3 above).

18. Basic management decisions, such as teacher training and the management of human resources, are still made by the Ministry of Education, and the evolution of PRONADE has been at times contradictory – with a recent re-concentration of decision-making (PREAL 2008).
19. The following paragraphs draw partly from Guerra-Borges (2006) and PNUD (2005, 2008).

8

Post-Conflict Economic Policy and Group Inequalities in Peru

José Carlos Orihuela

8.1 Introduction

In the early eighties a violent armed conflict, precipitated by Shining Path, a Maoist insurgency group, arose and was dominant in Peru until the capture of the movement's leader Abimael Guzmán in September 1992.[1] The Truth Commission reported that the conflict cost approximately 70,000 – 75 per cent of them indigenous peoples. Development policy in post-conflict Peru, however, is said to look forward without considering the past. In early March, the government, enjoying a buoyant macroeconomy (Latin America's highest growth rate in 2008 at 9.8 per cent), rejected a US$2 million donation from Germany to install a memorial museum. The Truth Commission Final Report launched in 2003 has been criticized by dominant groups in the country for being 'biased'. Political and business elites maintain that Peru should look forward rather than backward.[2] Post-conflict economic policy seems to be designed without properly considering the socioeconomic sources and consequences of the internal struggle. Indeed, policy paradigms have limited state action to the large-scale provision of infrastructure designed to give priority to the rural poor. The Truth Commission recommendations, moreover, are being fulfilled in slow motion; they include a set of reparation measures ranging from the issuing of national identity cards to the provision of material and symbolic compensation. Reparations policies are mainly promoted by human-rights groups, while politicians and technocrats show little initiative and responsiveness. In more general terms, policy decisions that impact on living conditions in post-conflict areas – from free trade agreements to coca policies – are taken without adequately addressing causes of inequalities or potential development threats.

This chapter assesses the post-conflict evolution of group inequalities or horizontal inequalities (HIs) in Peru, with a focus on the regions most affected by political violence. HIs are differences in cultural, political and socioeconomic opportunities for development that are group-based rather than individual-based, groups being culturally formed ethnic, religious or regional collective identities (often of a fluid nature: Stewart 2001). CRISE research documents how HIs frequently constitute underlying motivations for contestation and violence and that they are also a consequence of struggle between societal groups (see Stewart 2008; and www.crise.ox.ac.uk). This chapter discusses how group inequalities have been affected by post-conflict economic policy in Peru. Following the conventions of the literature, by post-conflict I refer to post-Shining Path era politics; but this needs to be qualified, since conflict and the Shining Path have not disappeared. On the one hand, since 1992 new conflicts have developed in the country, but they are forms of contentious politics, not associated with civil war dynamics. On the other hand, the Shining Path is still an actor of potential relevance. It evolved into a set of groups of fairly minor national importance but with significant local reach in some coca-dominated river basins, where they operate in association with the drug economy. This needs to be borne in mind when one reads the post-conflict evolution of conflict in Peru.

The remaining of the chapter is organized as follows. Section 8.2 reviews the process of political violence and exclusion that occurred in Peru, discussing the Truth Commission's narrative of political violence. Section 8.3 analyses the post-conflict evolution of group inequalities. Section 8.4 explores major economic policy developments and their potential impact on HIs in post-conflict areas. Finally, Section 8.5 concludes by reflecting on the shortcomings of political and economic policy paradigms in post-conflict Peru.

8.2 Armed conflict and social exclusion

Peru's internal armed conflict started the day before the 1980 Presidential Elections, with the Maoist-inspired Shining Path sabotaging the voting process in Chuschi, a town in the Andes of Ayacucho.[3] Ballot boxes were set on fire, as a symbolic announcement that 'the times of peace were over' (CVR 2003, Annex 1).[4] The armed conflict has been the largest and bloodiest since the nation obtained its independence from Spain in the first quarter of the nineteenth century. Peru's Truth Commission (Comisión de la Verdad y Reconciliación, CVR) received reports of 23,969 deaths and missing people and estimated a total of 69,280

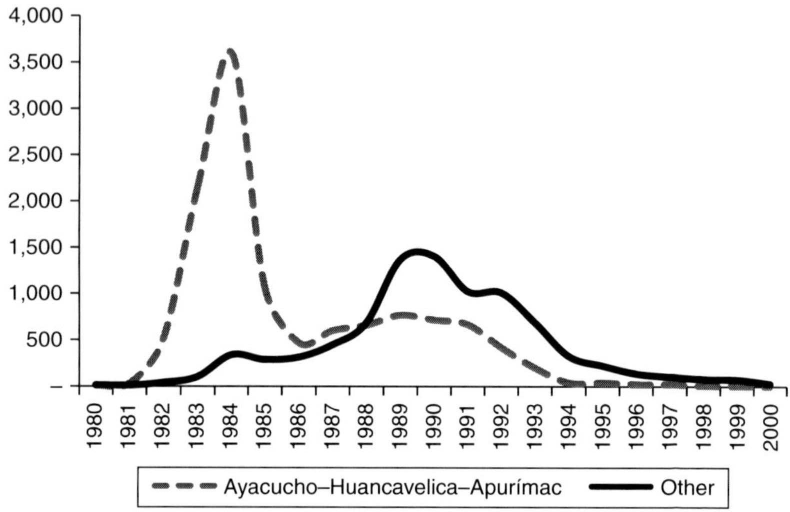

Figure 8.1 Peru: Victims of violence by region of conflict
Source: CVR (2003).

fatalities for the period 1980–2000. The region that bore the greatest burden was Ayacucho, registering 38 per cent of the total estimated number of deaths. Ayacucho's death toll represented 5 per cent of its 1981 total population of half a million people.[5]

The narrative of the CVR Final Report on the causes and consequences of the conflict is one of HIs. The commissioners concluded that social exclusion was fundamental in the genesis of political violence; yet 'poverty does not explain on its own the unprecedented violence [...] it was one of the factors that triggered conflict and the stage in which the drama developed' (CVR 2003, Vol. VIII: 28). Ayacucho, indeed, has been one of the poorest regions of the country throughout Peru's modern history. But the bloody revolution was not planned or carried out by the most excluded societal groups. The leadership of the Shining Path was mostly composed of middle-class professionals, many of them college professors such as Shining Path President Abimael Guzmán himself. Originally founded in the seventeenth century and reopened in 1959 after eight decades of closure, the Universidad Nacional San Cristóbal de Huamanga was, and continues to be, the only public university in the area. The CVR argues that the violent path advocated by Guzmán found fertile territory in the resentment of *cholo* and *mestizo* college students. According to the CVR, a significant portion of the militants were relatively educated young people who felt torn between two worlds – the traditional Andean one of their parents, which was not fully theirs any longer, and the urban-*criollo*, which rejected them because of ethnic prejudice (CVR 2003, Vol. II and VIII: 30). These radicalized young were used by the Shining Path as channels for reaching rural teachers and senior high school students.[6]

Peru's Truth Commission concludes that socioeconomic and political inequalities between periphery and metropolis, both between the Andes and Lima, and within the Andes, as illustrated in Tables 8.1 and 8.2 of Section 8.3 (on literacy), provided a rationale for political violence that interplayed with underlying emotions of historical exclusion:[7] the resentment of the educated Andean youth against the Creole 'system of domination'; and also the contempt and resentment of all the involved parties, particularly the military, towards indigenous peasants.[8] Soldiers and rebels frequently treated indigenous peoples as their inferior. Long-held ethnic prejudices about 'the stubborn, cruel, treacherous *indios*' had a strong comeback (CVR 2003, Vol. VIII: 38–39). The dehumanization of the 'others' contributed to the cruelty of war actions.

Periodization of Peru's internal armed conflict by critical events and regional setting
1. Armed struggle starts, May 1980–December 1982. From the Chuschi incident to the state decision of delegating to the Army Forces control over counter-insurgency actions in Ayacucho. 2. Militarization, January 1983–June 1986. Until the Massacre of the Prisons (*Matanza de los Penales*). Violence in Ayacucho reached its highest. 3. National escalation, June 1986–March 1989. Until drug barons backed a Shining Path attack on the Uchiza police station, in the north-central rainforest. Violence in the Huallaga front (north-central rainforest) developed. 4. The 'great crisis', March 1989–September 1992. Until the capture of Shining Path absolute chief Abimael Guzmán and other prominent leaders. Violence moved towards Lima. 5. Declination, September 1992–November 2000.

Source: CVR (2003).

The CVR thus maintains that the social exclusion of different groups is central to understanding the forms in which violence developed and the consequences it produced. Indeed, the insurgent movement and the state repression had the greatest impact on indigenous groups in *Sierra* and in *Selva Central* (Andes and Central Andean Amazon), taking some of its most cruel forms against women. The Shining Path ideology and strategy believed in selective assassinations, of those with local authority in particular, as a way of making exemplary punishment. Moreover, even though the peasantry rather than the proletariat were seen as the people chosen to achieve the revolution, their subordinate status as members of a 'peasant mass' did not entitle them to particular privileges. There were human rights violations against women, including rape, and compulsory sexual unions of female militants – both Andean peasants and rainforest natives – with militants and leadership, under the logic of guaranteeing the reproduction of the militias.

Among the most dramatically affected were the indigenous peoples of the central-eastern Andes rainforest (Ashánika, Yásesha and Nomatsiguenga are the most important ethnic groups). It is estimated that, from a population of 55,000 Ashánikas, about 10,000 were displaced by force, 6,000 died and 5,000 lived in captivity under the Shining Path (CVR 2003, Vol 5: 241), which makes the Ashánikas the population most affected by the internal war.

8.3 Post-conflict group inequalities

The narrative that group inequalities were behind political violence, as expounded by the Truth Commission Final Report, has factual foundations. The 1981 Census, for instance, found that, at the time when the Shining Path conflict started, Ayacucho and neighbouring regions, consisting of a majority of rural inhabitants, had the highest illiteracy rates across the country: Apurímac 50 per cent, Ayacucho 45 per cent and Huancavelica 43 per cent. In contrast, illiteracy rates reached only 8 per cent in Lima and 21 per cent in the country as a whole. Rural indigenous people and women in these regions were the most excluded groups in Peru at the time when conflict erupted. Hence we should differentiate inequalities between prosperous and poor regions (between Lima/the coast and Ayacucho/the Andes) from inequalities within the excluded regions (between the predominantly *mestizo* centre and the predominantly Quechua periphery, and between genders). Both types of inter-group inequalities are statistically significant and politically relevant (see Table 8.1).

In 1981, whereas Ayacucho residents had the second highest likelihood of being illiterate, living outside the capital (Huamanga) increased the chances of not having access to education, most significantly for Quechua speakers and women (see Table 8.2).

Table 8.1 HIs between regions: Illiteracy rates in Peru, Lima and Ayacucho (1981, %)

Political Region	Total	Men	Women
Lima	8	6	10
Urban	7	6	9
Rural	*19*	*13*	*26*
Ayacucho	45	33	57
Urban	27	17	37
Rural	*56*	*42*	*69*
Peru	21	15	27
Urban	11	8	14
Rural	*41*	*29*	*52*

Source: Peru National Census.

Table 8.2 HIs within the excluded: Illiteracy rates in Ayacucho provinces by mother tongue (1981, %)[9]

Province/Region	Total	Women
Huamanga province	35	45
Spanish	14	17
Quechua	*39*	*49*
Other provinces	48	60
Spanish	19	24
Quechua	*51*	*63*
Ayacucho region	45	56
Spanish	18	21
Quechua	*48*	*60*

Source: Peru National Census.

HIs persist in post-conflict Peru.[10] However, state action over the last two decades has reduced inter-group gaps in access to publicly provided goods and services. The reach of the state on the provision of infrastructure has grown significantly, particularly in those regions most affected by the Shining Path era of political violence. The improvements in education are much less prominent.

Behind these improvements lie both economic growth and public expenditure, targeted with the help of World Bank-sponsored Poverty Maps, to be discussed in the next section. Peru has experienced two

Figure 8.2 Peru: Map of regions most affected by Shining Path conflict
Source: CVR (2003).

decades of fairly positive growth, interrupted by the 1997–1998 financial crisis. The economy grew at an annual average rate of 5 per cent in the last decade and 8 per cent in the period 2004–2008, being bolstered by the soaring commodity prices. The sources of growth lie in mining and construction in the post-Shining Path economy, with markedly different labour requirements. While most metallurgical mining takes place in the *Sierra* and hydrocarbons in the *Selva*, construction – pushed by credit boom and subsidy schemes – flourishes in Lima and other less important urban centres.[11]

The export sector has been particularly dynamic. While GDP has almost doubled its 1994 level, exports had a seven-fold increase. Mining and hydrocarbons currently represent two-thirds of the total exports and have had the fastest sectoral growth rates in the last 15 years. Other products that have gained in importance for the national economy include coffee, non-traditional agriculture products and textiles. Except for coffee and coca, which grow in the high subtropical ecologies of the eastern Andes, the other industries are all located on the coast. Indeed, the other side of the coin of economic progress is that 46 per cent of the *Sierra* households have 40 per cent of their income coming from agriculture, compared to only 31 per cent in the *Selva* and 13 per cent in the *costa* (Zegarra 2008). Andean people, therefore, depend upon the economic activities with the least dynamism.

With such a panorama, there is no wonder that economic progress of the last two decades has had contradictory effects on group inequalities: on the one hand, it reduced the gaps in the access to basic infrastructure provided by the state, public and private goods previously absent or destroyed by the internal war or lack of maintenance (see Table 8.3); on

Table 8.3 Living conditions in the regions most affected by Shining Path conflict

Political regions	Percentage of population without water		Percentage of population without sanitation		Percentage of population without electricity		Illiteracy rates in adult population (%)	
	1993	2007	1993	2007	1993	2007	1993	2007
Central-Southern Andes								
Ayacucho	71	37	71	30	71	44	33	22
Apurímac	81	40	81	25	79	41	37	26
Huancavelica	86	60	86	58	78	42	34	24
Central Andes								
Junín	51	33	51	21	40	25	13	13
Central-Northern Andean rainforest								
Huánuco	70	53	70	26	64	56	23	20
San Martín	73	36	73	12	62	41	13	10
Lima	29	11	29	5	18	6	4	4
Peru	51	23	51	17	43	24	14	11

Source: Poverty Maps (1993, 2007).

Table 8.4 Poverty incidence in the regions most affected by Shining Path conflict (%)

Region	2004	2005	2006	2007
Central-Southern Andes				
Ayacucho	65.9	77.3	78.4	68.3
Apurímac	65.2	73.5	74.8	69.5
Huancavelica	84.8	90.3	88.7	85.7
Central Andes				
Junín	49.6	56.0	49.9	43.0
Central-Northern Andean rainforest				
Huánuco	78.3	75.8	74.6	64.9
San Martín	51.9	54.1	54.3	44.5
Lima	32.2	32.9	25.1	19.4
Peru	48.6	48.7	44.5	39.3

Source: National Household Surveys.

the other, the gaps on opportunities for economic growth and employment have widened. Growth has been the fundamental reason for the decrease of national poverty figures, improving public finance, internal markets and employment in aggregate; but the economic outcomes outside the urban coast and a small set of local markets in the interior are more contentious. Poverty rates have not decreased at the same rate as the growth in the macroeconomy. Indeed, they were increasing rapidly in 2004–2006 in Ayacucho, Apurímac and Huancavelica, before a strong improvement in 2007 (and probably one in 2008; see Table 8.4). In Peru, in 2007, the language of two-thirds of the poor is not Spanish; and half of the poor live in the rural *Sierra*. Economic progress, finally, has been faster and more consistent in Lima.[12]

From a long-term perspective, the observed phenomenon of growth that deepens group inequalities is not the exception, but the rule. Modern economic development not only failed to be consistent, as in the 1980s, but also failed to reduce inequalities among regions and ethnic groups. In 2007, still between a fifth and a fourth of the population in the Andes could not write or read, and the figures are worse for indigenous people and women. Lima had eliminated illiteracy before

Table 8.5 Geographical distribution of poor population (2007, %)

Domain	Poor	Extremely poor
Total Peru	100	100
Urban Costa	11	3
Rural Costa	5	4
Urban Sierra	12	8
Rural Sierra	42	68
Urban Selva	6	5
Rural Selva	10	12
Lima Metropolitana	14	1

Source: INEI.

Table 8.6 Illiteracy rates: Path-dependent exclusion (%)

Year	Lima	Costa Other	Selva	Sierra North and Centre	Sierra South	Ayacucho
1876	45	74	86	86	92	92
1940	10	40	51	66	80	85
1961	10	28	39	51	62	65
1972	10	23	34	44	50	61
1981	7	14	26	32	32	45
2007	6	11	17	22	17	23

Notes:
1. Lima = Lima and Callao provinces; Costa Other = Costa – Lima; Sierra North and Centre = Sierra of the departments of Lima, Junin and the north of them; Sierra South = Sierra – Sierra North and Centre. For 2007 we use the ENAHO district-level classification of domains.
2. Illiteracy rates:
I_{1876} = do not read or write/total population;
I_{1940} and I_{1961} = do not read or write and older than 6/population older than 6;
I_{1972}, I_{1981} and I_{2007} = do not read or write and older than 5/population older than 5.
Source: 1876–1981 National Censuses and 2007 National Household Survey.

the Second World War, when migration to the capital city was about to boom. Among the least favoured regions of the Southern Sierra, Ayacucho – like Apurímac and Huancavelica – have fallen behind throughout modern history (see Tables 8.5 and 8.6).

8.4 Post-conflict policy making

In order to understand Peru's post-conflict case, it is of fundamental importance to take into account the fact that the defeat of Shining Path and other smaller rebel groups by the government of Fujimori (1990–2000) occurred in conjunction with the adoption of structural economic reforms. Hence, economic policy making in Peru was fundamentally one of post-hyperinflation rather than one of post-conflict. The relevance of the post-conflict situation for the design and implementation of economic policies was minor in relation to the general logic of development policy after the first government of García (1985–1990), which consisted of stabilization, liberalization, privatization and safety nets. To achieve political stability and to improve living conditions for the poor, the Fujimori government carried out a 'pacification' strategy that combined intelligence-based counter-insurgency actions with the expansion of the reach of state services in rural areas, placing a particular focus on the areas most affected by violence. Roads, schools, clinics, sewerage systems, electrification schemes and small-scale irrigation works were built across the country. The impact has been significant, as is showed in Table 8.3 for conventional indicators of basic needs satisfaction. Escobal and Ponce (2002), moreover, found evidence that rehabilitated roads had increased non-agricultural income in rural households.

Administrations that followed have maintained the principles of development policy of Fujimori and deepened efforts in favour of improving the 'investment climate', trade integration and the provision of basic infrastructure. In conjunction with favourable international conditions, the strategy had had generally positive outcomes, but it also showed the persistence of regional gaps between Lima and booming coastal agriculture, on the one side, and the *Sierra* and *Selva* on the other. Among the highlands and the rainforest regions, the post-conflict areas are still the less favoured ones. According to official sources, poverty rates diminished from 44.5 per cent in 2006 to 39.3 per cent in 2007, a year in which the national economy grew by 8.9 per cent. Ten more years of high rates of growth, the conventional wisdom goes, and poverty should become history: trickle-down economics at work. Yet sceptical observers point to the exceptionally good performance of candidate Humala in the southern Andes in the run-off of the 2006 Presidential Elections, winning 70–85 per cent of the valid votes in each political region.[13] Most of the Andean and Amazonian population seems to be 'against the model' that brings a macroeconomic bonanza.

Resource-based development redistributive schemes

One of the reasons why trickle-down economics has not worked for Ayacucho as well as it did for the rest of the country in recent years is that, since mining is the generator of a quarter of fiscal revenue in 2007 and 2008, the redistributive *canon* scheme divides the fiscal contribution of mining 50–50 between the central state and the producing regions. Hence the non-producing regions do not participate in one of the largest sources available for public investments. Among the non-producers are precisely Ayacucho, Huancavelica and Apurímac (see Table 8.7).[14]

The canon is the result of a long-term history of unequal development between Lima and the interior and unfulfilled expectations of regional development. Its origin goes back to the 1970s and to the oil crisis, when the oil-producing region of Loreto, northern Amazon rainforest,

Table 8.7 Distribution of mining canon transfers to regions (2004–2008, %)

Regional government	Main domains	Canon share
Ancash	Northern Andes	27.1
Tacna	Southern Coast	15.9
Cajamarca	Northern Andes	12.2
Moquegua	Southern Coast	9.1
Pasco	Central Andes	6.5
Arequipa	Southern Andes and Coast	6.1
La Libertad	Northern Andes and Coast	5.1
Cusco	Southern Andes	4.8
Puno	Southern Andes	4.4
Lima	Central Coast	3.2
Junin	Central Andes	2.0
Ica	Southern Coast	1.4
Huancavelica	Central-Southern Andes	0.8
Ayacucho	Central-Southern Andes	0.5
Apurímac	Central-Southern Andes	0.5
Other regions		0.5

Source: Ministry of Economy and Finance.

demanded that it should receive a direct assignation of resource rents, to compensate for the rising living standards (the price of gasoline and all import goods rose in a region with no road access to the rest of the country); the assignation was finally approved in 1976 (Henriquez 1986; Rodriguez 1981). The paradox of plenty for this region was to have become an impoverished oil-producing region at a time of a resource boom. The 1979 Constitution gave the canon a stronger legal status, and future periods of political crisis brought new regional demands, such as for the oil-canon for Tumbes and Piura in the northern coast after the catastrophic consequences of the 1982 El Niño. A number of ear-marked redistributive schemes have been created since then, under the principle of benefitting producing regions.

Conflict – understood as contentious politics – triggered by socio-environmental factors represents about 45 per cent of the monthly cases registered by the Ombudsman Office (Defensoría del Pueblo). Conflicts have been on a positive trend since they first started being monitored in 2004, but cases have doubled since January 2008, when the figure was less than a hundred (see Figure 8.3). The Ombdusman Office defines conflict as manifestations of political contestation involving organized social groups – acts of violence associated with armed

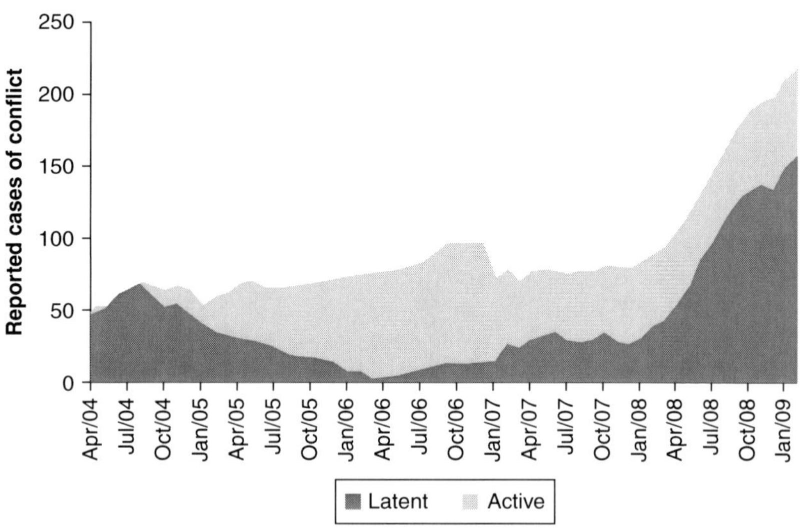

Figure 8.3 Monthly evolution of conflicts (2004–2009)
Source: Ombudsman Office. Conflictos Sociales Monthly Reports.

groups are accounted for separately. The conflicts so defined frequently entail acts of violence and, to a smaller extent, human-rights abuses. The death toll reaches dozens, but these are concentrated in a handful of violent events. Extractive industries (metals and hydrocarbons), which represented 65 per cent of exports and 25 per cent of fiscal revenues in 2008, offer the most important economic activity associated with the phenomena. Contestation in mining brings together different local agendas: commonly, they involve struggles of provincial and district capitals against Lima for a higher share of the resource-rent, on the one hand, and grievances against and fears of neighbouring communities concerning land and resources rights, access to water sources and environmental pollution, on the other.

Social funds and the predominance of infrastructure programs

In 1991–2004 FONCODES developed over 40,000 rural development projects amounting to a total of more than $2 billion (World Bank 2006). Created by the Fujimori administration (1990–2000), social funds and associated schemes for the reconstruction and upgrading of pre-existing productive and social infrastructure have been the most important policy novelty for the rural poor – the Andean people in particular. FONCODES was built on the logic that the transition towards a market economy required a safety net for the most vulnerable, a policy paradigm that was functional for the tactics of national politics. The top-down development strategy, mediated by executive communal assemblies, was to create a number of fairly autonomous agencies parallel to the conventional ministry lines, directed by competent engineers and supported by credit lines from the World Bank and the Inter-American Development Bank – since the country was still recovering from the public finance collapse in the late 1980s and the budget remained inadequate for investment projects throughout the decade. Ayacucho, indeed, was a privileged zone for infrastructural spending, and this was symbolized by the paving of the 500 km road that connected it with Lima. In the case of rural infrastructure, spending was targeted by using Poverty Maps, which is the reason why the poorest regions were favoured (see Table 8.3). No wonder, then, that the support for former president Fujimori, currently facing human-rights and corruption trials, remains significant in the rural *Sierra*.[15]

In addition to schemes for the provision of infrastructure, the Fujimori regime established the Program to Support the Repopulation (PAR), which offered a series of collective and individual incentives in conjunction with poverty-alleviation programs, for the repopulation of the most affected regions. The program failed to reverse the population trend, since Ayacucho, like neighbouring and poorer Huancavelica and Apurímac, has had the lowest annual rates of growth of adult population for the period 1981–2007: 1.4 per cent (compared to a national average of 2.8 per cent).

The enthusiasm for infrastructural development, however, was not properly matched with complementary initiatives to tackle the quality of education or the productivity of agriculture and economic activities in highlands and rainforest regions. Rural policy shortcomings show the limits of a development strategy restricted to cement. Without tackling structural conditions and dismantling what was left of the pre-existing institutional infrastructure for the promotion of agricultural development (Eguren 2004; Zegarra 2008), economic stability and trade liberalization further increased the income gaps between the Andes and the coast. Without a strategy for improving the quality of education in the highland and rainforest regions, and particularly in post-conflict areas (Ministerio de Educacion & Consejo Nacional de Education 2007), the mere creation of infrastructure and distribution of educational materials is not sufficient to reduce educational gaps. Thus, for the primary and secondary educational systems, disapproval and non-completion rates in *Sierra* and *Selva* are two to three times higher than in the residential districts of Lima (see Table 8.8).

Table 8.8 Reproduction of educational gaps

Domains	**Students that did not approve the year**			**Students that did not complete the year**		
	1998 (%)	**2001 (%)**	**2004 (%)**	**1998 (%)**	**2001 (%)**	**2004 (%)**
Lima core	4.2	4.7	4.6	2.9	3.1	2.7
Lima periphery	6.3	7.0	6.8	4.1	4.0	4.2
Others Costa	7.4	7.8	7.0	5.5	5.1	5.0
Southern Andes	10.3	10.2	8.6	8.8	8.7	7.6
Northern and Central Andes	10.8	11.6	10.4	9.5	9.6	8.5
Rainforest regions	10.9	11.9	11.0	8.8	9.0	8.0
Total	8.6	9.1	8.2	6.6	6.5	6.0

Source: Education Censuses.

Trade integration

In a recent conference with foreign bankers, President García proclaimed himself to be the 'guardian of the economic model against the anti-system'.[16] By the economic model García refers to maintaining macroeconomic stability, guaranteeing a favourable climate for foreign investment and promoting trade integration. The latter goal has been aggressively pursued by the last two administrations, following the example of Chile. The 2008 surge in food prices, for instance, opened the window of opportunity for a new decrease of tariffs, with the declared rationale of combating food inflation (see Table 8.9). Tariffs were not raised to previous levels after the food prices surge ended.

The most important steps reached in the race for trade integration have been the free trade agreements with the United States (2006) and China (2009). The agreement with China poses the greatest threat to the textile industry, located in Lima and the coast; while the agreement with the US was more controversial because of its impact on agriculture and the living conditions in the highlands and the rainforest, including post-conflict areas. The policy debate polarized public opinion between those who only saw opportunities and those who only saw the threats. Influential economist Hernando de Soto intervened in the heated debate to say that the country also needed a 'FTA [Free Trade Area] within'. A call for such an endeavour, also known as the 'complementary agenda', was announced; yet, once again, the policy slogans were not followed by sound diagnosis, brain-storming and responsible experimentation. Instead, a plain compensations scheme – arguably necessary, but insufficient – was set for producers at risk, without accompanying development policy machinery (technological transfer, assistance for vertical and horizontal association, marketing support and so on).

In their review of the literature on the expected impact of an FTA with the US, Escobal and Ponce (2007) point out that, even though forecasts by the state found significant expected gains, the impact on the rural

Table 8.9 Average of *ad valorem* duties (%)

Year	1998	1999	2000	2001	2002	2003	2004	2005	2006	2007	2008
Average duty	13.4	13.4	13.4	11.9	10.7	10.3	10.2	10.2	10.4	8.6	6.1

Source: WTO.

sector was not assessed. Moreover, the authors criticize these exercises for ignoring the time dimension and for making the implicit assumption of perfect mobility of the productive factors. Focussing the discussion on the short term, the authors find that most welfare losses are to be absorbed by the rural *Sierra* and *Selva*.[17] In their simulations, welfare gains by urban sectors represent between three and four times the welfare losses in rural sectors. Group inequalities are likely to be widened by trade integration.

After the return to democracy, the most prominent economic initiative for the Andes has been Sierra Exportadora, a high-profile scheme announced in 2006 by the government of President García – partly a political response to the Humala phenomenon. The slogan, however, lacked content, so that two and a half years later no analyst seems to have a clear idea of what it entails. The grandiloquent promise of large-scale investments in a domain of special structural conditions – difficult geography dominated by mountains and small valleys, small-scale holdings, peasant communities of all sizes and low human capital – is misplaced from the start. The sustainable improvement of economic development in the Andes would need much more than big-bang policy ideas.

Coca policies

Peru is the second largest producer of coca, most of it cultivated in three river basin systems of the eastern Andes rainforest: the Huallaga (Huánuco, centre-north Andean rainforest), the Apurímac-Ene valleys (Apurímac and Ayacucho, centre-south Andes) and the La Convencion-Lares valleys (Cusco, southern Andes). Indeed, the Huallaga and the Apurímac-Ene were very important in the second half of the armed conflict, so that strong links between drug barons and Shining Path and MRTA combatants developed (Soberon 2005). In the late 2000s, the remaining forces of the Shining Path – a rather different phenomenon from the earlier movements, according to observers – increased their activities in the Apurímac-Ene. Conflict is latent, but dozens of assassinations are reported each year.

The coca phenomenon has been addressed in the last two decades with a well-known carrot-and-stick strategy of promotion of alternative crops, on the one side, and with repression on the other, with heavy financial and advisory involvement from the US. After booming in the early nineties, at the time when Colombia production was under attack, cultivation was cut severely in the late 1990s, under forcible eradication policies (Cabieses 2005a), with Colombian production growing back

Table 8.10 Evolution of coca cultivation (Ha) by river basin

Basin	2001	2002	2003	2004	2005	2006	2007
Alto Huallaga (Huánuco)	14,481	15,286	13,646	16,900	16,039	17,080	17,217
Apurímac-Ene (Apurímac and Ayacucho)	12,600	14,170	14,300	14,700	15,530	15,813	16,019
La Convencion-Lares (Cusco)	13,980	12,170	12,340	12,700	12,503	12,747	12,894
Other	5,139	5,074	3,914	6,000	4,128	5,760	7,570
Total	46,200	46,700	44,200	50,300	48,200	51,400	53,700

Source: UNODC.

again. Since then, coca cultivation has been growing (see Table 8.10), although it has not reached previous peak levels (UNODC 2008).

The dangers for violent conflict and political instability are evident: neighbouring the central location of recent political violence (Ayacucho, Apurímac and Huánuco), an illegal economy flourishes providing jobs and opportunities to one of the most impoverished population groups in the country. A number of drug entrepreneurs – the business seems to have moved from a baron-era to a more competitive stage – operate by paying (former) Shining Path rebels for protection or buying such services from others. Associations of coca-leaf producers defy the state and fight for their freedom to grow the crop. For obvious reasons, the alternative-crops strategy is mostly a failure, since no agricultural product can compete with coca prices and no evident economic alternative exists. Returning to our previous discussion of rural development policies, the line of the argument, once again, is that Peru's technocratic state lacks the interest or vision to address this family of development challenges. The lack of economic opportunities creates waves of new *cocalero* migrants from the western to the eastern Andes. Since design and finance of coca policies have mostly belonged to the US, the reach of these policy initiatives is weak (Alvarez 2005).

The *cocalero* social movement – the political association of coca producers – has grown and evolved into different branches, triggered by the increase of eradication measures and animated by political developments in Bolivia. In open defiance of central-state policies of crop reduction, the regional governments of Ayacucho, Huánuco and Cusco passed decrees in favour of the cultivation, traditional use and industrialization of the coca leaf (Cabieses 2005b). The last presidential election represented an important political juncture. High-profile movement leaders joined Humala's Nationalist Party in the 2006 election and were elected to Parliament.[18] Hence the political weight of the coca producers has grown, which has allowed them to negotiate policies with state agencies. Yet political developments always return to an impasse: coca producers want to keep generating income, the state wants to reduce illicit crops. No easy economic and political compromise is apparent.

8.5 Policy-framing: Rights, order and progress

In summary, I have discussed the narrative of inter-group inequalities underlying the armed internal struggle, the post-conflict improvements of living conditions of the rural poor, the deepening of gaps in economic opportunities and the adverse effects of post-hyperinflation economic policy on highland and rainforest regions, with a focus on the areas most affected by political violence. I argue that the end of conflict has not meant much for the design of economic policy. In conjunction with the triumph of economic paradigms, moreover, conventional wisdom in the polity has led to a negative cultural environment for the design of more proactive inclusionary economic policies.

Political and economic chaos in the eighties favoured the triumph of a conservative view on what constitutes the best path towards national development. Policies were not carried out within a 'peace-process' framework; instead, order and reconstruction were the winning paradigms. The authoritarian and technocratic state of Fujimori cemented a development notion in which the rural poor were entitled to infrastructure and services, not to freedoms – in the sense expounded by Amartya Sen. The end of conflict meant the cultural victory of the 'strong-hand', and so the political consensus was that Peru had to sacrifice freedoms in order to achieve progress. Once Shining Path leader Guzmán was captured, the strategy for 'pacification' was to create and rehabilitate infrastructure and to 'finish the war against terrorism'. Since goals justified means, rights were not respected by the regime.

The return to democracy has done much good for bringing back the rule of human rights and political liberties; yet a failure to fully face the mistakes of the past persists among political and economic elites. The opposition to evaluating the past diminishes the political relevance of those groups of society that were the most affected by violence. Truth and compensation have been political goals for those who have not had consistent access to power – in particular, the agenda of associations of families of the victims, human-rights groups and a handful of left-wing and humanist/liberal personalities. It was the abrupt end of Fujimori, after his resignation because of a corruption scandal, that opened a window of opportunity for revisiting the causes and consequences of conflict. The vanguard that carried the torch of the Truth Commission was a minority within the transitional government of Paniagua (2001), a critical pressure group composed of a political adviser of the new president and two ministers. Neither Paniagua nor most of his ministers – from the centrist Accion Popular party, which ruled in 1980–1985 – were particularly keen on the idea of having a Truth Commission. The mandate of the transition was only to do house-cleaning and call for general elections, the internal opposition within government maintained. Nonetheless, Cabinet Chief Perez de Cuellar was a strong supporter of a Truth Commission, given his convictions and involvement in the peace process of El Salvador during his tenure as UN Secretary General.[19]

Hence, since its origin, Peru's Truth Commission had to face a path full of obstacles and indifference, in addition to the active opposition of those directly involved in human-rights abuses. In the logic of conservative pragmatism, in order to achieve national progress, concepts such as historical truth, justice, reconciliation and compensation have been of little value. Ratified months after its creation by the new administration of President Toledo (2001–2006), which renamed it as the Truth and Reconciliation Commission (CVR), the CVR produced a Final Report that was contested by almost all major political organizations. The program of reparations advocated there faced its own difficulties. It took a year to create a multi-ministerial commission to assess the CVR recommendations, and another year to pass a law for the Integral Program of Reparations. The latter is composed of symbolic and material reparations (individual and collective), support for psychological assistance, educational grants and restitution of citizen rights (ranging from legal advisory rights to the provision of national identity cards)[20] – measures that are carried out in a low-key manner.

The conservative political environment has interplayed with a Washington Consensus policy mindset, as we have seen. Since the process of stabilization and structural reforms of the early nineties, economic policy has been restricted to a few areas and a small repertoire. Policy lacks technocratic muscle beyond the safe borders of procuring a sound macro and 'investment climate'. Distrustful of the principle of policy exemptions – frequently with good reason – the Ministry of

Economy and Finance (MEF) leaves the formulation of development policy to sectoral ministries (Agriculture and Production), which are politically and technocratically weaker and do not generally have a collaborative relationship with the all-powerful MEF. Indeed, one may summarize policy goals as maintaining macroeconomic stability, building infrastructure and conducting 'damage control' upon the work done by the rest of the state administration. Thus, in spite of manifest discontent with the economy, the Andes have not been a policy priority, except for the large-scale provision of infrastructure.

The economic development strategy has proved to be effective for setting the macroeconomy back on a steady track – interrupted by the poorly managed 1997 financial crisis – and for providing infrastructure and services to rural Peru, two major historical achievements that have greatly benefited post-conflict areas. But the strategy does little more. As such, national economic progress does not embrace the *Sierra* and *Selva*, widens group inequalities and brings in new forms of conflict across the country, re-configuring a highly unpredictable, endemically contested political ecology.

Notes

1. For their very helpful comments, I would like to thank Corinne Caumartin, Maritza Paredes and Rosemary Thorp, as well as seminar participants at CRISE Post-Conflict Reconstruction Workshop, 16–17 April 2009, University of Makerere, Kampala.
2. Within weeks, the government announced that it had changed its mind and established a commission presided over by the influential writer Mario Vargas-Llosa, who had lobbied President García for a reconsideration of its decision.
3. The very complex geography of Peru can be reduced to three regions for the purpose of this chapter – used in official demographics: *Costa*, *Sierra* and *Selva*. The *Costa* (coast) is a thin desert between the Pacific Ocean and the *Sierra*. We will use *Sierra* (mountains) and Andes indifferently. The *Selva* is divided between eastern Andes, or Andean Amazon, (high altitude forest lands) and low Amazon rainforest.
4. The sub-national levels of government are regional governments, provincial municipalities and district municipalities, all of them currently elected by popular vote.
5. A second insurgent group, the Tupac Amaru Revolutionary Movement (MRTA), emerged in 1982. The rebel group resembled a more traditional case of Latin America guerillas, inspired by the then contemporary developments in Nicaragua, El Salvador, Guatemala and Colombia. The contribution of the MRTA to the death-toll and rights violations was significant, but minor when compared to those of the Shining Path and the armed forces of the Peruvian state.

6. For a discussion on the behavioural motivations of militants, see Portugal (2008), who argues that motivations of Shining Path militants varied according to their socioeconomic profile and position in the hierarchical party.
7. Political emotions, as defined by Elster (1999).
8. Referred ethnic categories have the following meaning in Peru: *criollo* is used for the inhabitants of the urban centres of the coast, who do not feel a strong cultural link to the Andes or the Selva; *mestizo* and *cholo* refer to intermediate categories, the latter having a much heavier weight 'from an Andean origin'; *indio* is used for the Andean inhabitants who do not live in the centres and, therefore, lack of education and class lineage. The bottom line is that these categories are not static and have different meanings among societal groups. For a discussion on the fluidity of ethnic identity in Peru and of the characteristics and consequences of ethnic prejudice, see CRISE research work by Canepa (2008) and Paredes (2007): the first discusses critically the literature, while the second analyses a CRISE perceptions survey and follow-up interviews.
9. Because of migration to the coast and to provincial centres, mother tongue is usually not a good criterion for group differentiation in Peru (see Figueroa and Barrón 2005). However, since the table illustrates group inequalities in Ayacucho, where the centre is mostly *mestizo* and the periphery is mostly Quechua, mother tongue is good enough here.
10. Figueroa and Barrón (2005) estimate HIs along the dimensions of human capital, labour market participation and income in 1993 and 2002, concluding that HIs were significant and persistent. Barrón (2008) compares gender and ethnic inequalities in Bolivia, Guatemala and Peru, the three countries with the largest shares of indigenous population in Latin America, finding that gender gaps in education, employment status and labour income are notably larger among the indigenous population. The multidimensional comparison also included health, housing quality and poverty indicators. Figueroa (2008) finds evidence that a reduction in inequality in years of schooling does not imply a fall in the degree of income inequality. Finally, Paredes (2008) discusses political representation across ethnic groups since the 1960s and the mechanisms that may have prevented indigenous people from finding channels of participation beyond voting rights. From educational, to economic, to political opportunities, inter-group differences are large in Peru.
11. A third of the 28 million Peruvian inhabitants live in Lima.
12. Indeed, the 2007 National Household Survey found that the regions with lower poverty incidence, in the range of 15 per cent and 25 per cent, were Lima and those located on the southern coast and enjoying the mining boom or modern agriculture developments. Arequipa, Tacna and Moquegua correspond to the mining group, Ica to the agricultural one. Low-density populated Madre de Dios in the southern rainforest – where agricultural colonizers, informal logging and gold mining flourish – also belongs to the low poverty cluster.
13. 76 per cent in Huancavelica, 83 per cent in Ayacucho, 74 per cent in Apurímac, 73 per cent in Cusco and 70 per cent in Puno; while APRA's (American Revolutionary Popular Alliance) candidate García obtained 53 per

cent of the national votes, 62 per cent in Lima, the capital city – concentrating 34 per cent of the electoral population. Ollanta Humala is a former military officer born in Ayacucho. In 2006, human-rights groups linked him to abuses during the armed struggle. In 2011, Humala won the presidential elections (over Fujimori's daughter).

14. Las Bambas, a major development run by Xstrata in Apurímac, is not yet in production.
15. Since 2001, after the fall of the Fujimori regime, FONCODES has had major processes of reengineering, progressively losing its technocratic aura. Using household surveys data, Schady (2000) found evidence that it was responsive to electoral imperatives. The administrations of Toledo and García have kept it operating, providing new missions and channeling new funds (World Bank and Inter-American Development Bank credit lines have decreased). Currently, FONCODES lives in a stage of permanent controversy, since its administration has been given to a high-profile party militant of disputed professional credentials, again interrupting a tradition of technocratic management.
16. 25 March 2009.
17. Assessing the overall trade integration strategy and its impact on rural poverty, Escobal and Ponce (2007: 68) observed that 'the Peruvian state aims to open and consolidate markets for agricultural exports and, at the same time, establishes a period of transition for the least developed sectors of agriculture [...] yet, the indispensable complementary agenda to use productively such time of transition has not almost been discussed'. The policy discussion and recommendations differ from others in the national debate in terms of the conceptualization of rural development, extending it beyond the promotion of agriculture, and their focus is on the economic opportunities of agents rather than on the promotion of particular crops – a view that draws on the discussion of the 'assets of the poor' and the role of state-provided services and infrastructure.
18. Nelson Palomino, a prominent leader of a different branch, was temporarily in prison, being accused of supporting terrorism. Once released, Palomino joined a member of the Humala clan to create a different political movement, Kuska Peru, with minor impact.
19. Interviews with the former Minister of Justice Diego García Sayán, Minister of Women and Human Development Susana Villarán and CVR Commissioner Sofía Macher.
20. A common action of the Shining Path was setting fire to local archives, with the consequent lost of birth certificates needed in order to access a national identity (ID) for exercising voting rights.

9

Inequality and Post-Conflict Fiscal Policies in Burundi

Janvier D. Nkurunziza

9.1 Introduction

Burundi is a war-torn country. Since its independence in 1962,[1] it has experienced five episodes of civil war, described by many analysts as ethnic fights between the country's two main groups, Hutus and Tutsis.[2] While ethnicity has been an important dimension of insecurity, a more serious analysis shows that civil wars in Burundi have been the result of deep rooted political and economic grievances. Politicians inherited the divisions instigated by the colonial power, taking advantage of the complexity of Burundi's ethnic identities to use ethnicity as an instrument for rallying the population to their political and economic causes.

Notwithstanding the ease with which conflicts in Burundi have been attributed to ethnic causes and despite the fact that crimes have been committed in the name of ethnic differences, Hutus, Tutsis, Ganwas and Twas are not four easily distinguishable 'ethnic groups' in the empirical sense of the concept. Horowitz (1985), for example, notes that ethnic groups are defined by ascriptive differences such as colour, language, grammar, religion or dress. None of this is applicable to Burundi, where the whole population shares one language, Kirundi, and one culture. Moreover, the different groups live together, being mixed in the same geographical spaces. This is not a denial of differences, imagined or real, among Burundians. As discussed in Section 9.2, what is considered to be hostile ethnic groups today is in a large part the result of a 'rigidification' and simplification, operated by colonial powers, of 'what used to be more fluid, complex and socially embedded categories' (Uvin 2002: 160). To some extent, the concept of ethnicity in Burundi remains malleable even today. These caveats should be kept in mind.

From the mid-1960s until 2003, with the exception of the period between July 1993 and July 1996, Burundi was led by three unelected presidents from Rutovu, a commune of the Southern province of Bururi. During this period the political elite and their associates enjoyed all the spoils of power while excluding the majority of the population from political and economic participation. Exclusion led to inequalities, humiliations, frustrations and discontent, which caused violent reactions from the excluded and, ultimately, civil wars.

The objective of this chapter is to assess the role of fiscal policies in addressing the country's deep-rooted socio-economic inequalities following the change in government in 2005, which transferred power to the traditionally excluded group. As explained above, it is impossible to carry out a comprehensive analysis of ethnic inequality because of the lack of ethnic data. However, in Section 9.3, we provide a glimpse of the phenomenon on the basis of some rare data we were able to obtain. Most of the analysis of inequality is based on some detailed statistics on the regional distribution of public goods. The central message is that, in the five-year period during which the new ruling elite has been in power, not much has been achieved in terms of addressing the inequalities inherited from the previous regimes. New measures, such as the provision of free primary education and health care, will probably have their intended effect in the medium to long term.

The chapter has five sections. The next section presents an overview of Burundi's conflict in order to lay the ground for further analyses. Section 9.3 discusses the nature of inequality in Burundi. Section 9.4 analyses some key fiscal measures taken by the new leaders in their first five-year term in power and their likely effect on the reduction of socio-economic inequalities. Section 9.5 concludes.

9.2 Overview of Burundi's conflict

Burundi has been torn by civil war since the mid-1960s.[3] The first outbreak of civil war was in 1965, being followed by four more episodes in 1972, 1988, 1991 and from 1993 to 2003. These conflicts have been characterized as opposing the country's two main groups, the 'Hutus' and the 'Tutsis'. Those advocating this thesis base their argument on the differences between the two groups and on the contentious thesis that they converged in Burundi from different parts of Africa several centuries ago (Chrétien 2000). Even if it were established that these two groups came from different parts of Africa, this should not be a reason to fight. Moreover, long coexistence must have created a common identity.

There is no historical evidence that Hutus and Tutsis fought each other in the pre-colonial period. Their peaceful coexistence within a hierarchical feudal society was regulated by a sophisticated social system. For example, whereas the Tutsis occupied relatively more administrative posts than the Hutus (though fewer than the Ganwas), the Hutus were by far the dominant members of 'Bashingantahe', the prestigious institution whose main role was to ensure that the justice system applied fairly to everyone. Through this institution, ordinary people could seek justice even against powerful leaders (Vansina 1972). The destruction of this system and the divisive policies instituted by the Belgian colonial powers are partly responsible for the devastating cycle of violence that has characterized Burundi (Table 9.1).

Table 9.1 Characteristics of Burundi Civil War

Characteristic	**1965**	**1972**	**1988**	**1991**	**1993–2003**
Duration (months)	2	4	2	1	120
Deaths (thousands)	5	200	15	1–3	300
Refugees (thousands)[a]	0	300	50	38	687
Ratio of deaths plus refugees over total population (%)[b]	0.2	14.0	1.3	0.7	17.1
Years from previous war	–	6	16	3	2
Provinces affected	Muramvya	Whole country	Ngozi, Kirundo	Cibitoke, Bubanza, Bujumbura	Whole country

Notes: [a]Number of Burundi refugees in DRC, Rwanda and Tanzania due to a specific conflict (UNHCR data). It is the difference between the total number of refugees and the number one year before the crisis (in 1965, there were displaced people within Burundi, but no refugees outside the country).
[b]Population at the beginning of war, except for the 1993 conflict, for which the population of reference is the mean of the 1993–2003 period.
Source: Ngaruko and Nkurunziza (2005).

Causes of civil war in Burundi

We propose three root causes of civil war in Burundi: the Belgian 'divide and rule' colonial policy sowed the seeds of divisions; Rwanda's 1959 Social Revolution had a demonstration effect in Burundi; and regionalism consolidated the divisions in the post-independence period.

The Belgian colonial authority 'racialized' the traditional differences between the Hutus and Tutsis. Tutsis were made to feel that they were superior to Hutus and entitled to dominate them. Tutsis were not considered as black Africans. In his description, Sandrart (1953: 2) refers to Hutus as 'backward black peasants', but the Tutsi is described in more flattering terms, as a giant herder, a free man, elegant and the like. The author writes that the Tutsi's 'elegant silhouette contrasts with the broken and crushed height of the black peasant' (meaning the Hutu).[4] The problem is that many Tutsis and Hutus internalized these descriptions and behaved accordingly.

However, the most influential divisive policy was the 'divide and rule' administrative reform introduced by Belgium starting from 1929. Its aim was to replace Hutu chiefs by Tutsis. From a relatively balanced distribution of posts between Hutus and Tutsis before the reforms, all chiefs were either Tutsis or Ganwas by 1945. As they trained future administrators who would work for them, the Belgians favoured the Tutsi group also in their educational policies. This reform humiliated the Hutu leaders, who saw their group marginalized from political representation. What was once a dynamic class system gradually became a rigid one, largely characterized by the Ganwa and Tutsi domination over Hutus and Twas (Chrétien 2000). This policy created resentment against the Tutsis, and it is arguably the single most important factor explaining the genesis of violent frictions between Hutus and Tutsis.

The second factor that played a key role in fuelling ethnic conflict in the early 1960s was the 1959 Social Revolution in Rwanda. Burundi's northern neighbour has the same population composition as Burundi. Until 1959, power was in the hands of a Tutsi dynasty that ruled over Tutsis as well as over Hutus. In 1959, with the help of the colonial authority, a bloody Hutu rebellion resulted in a power transfer from the traditional Tutsi monarchy to the Hutu group. Many Tutsis were killed and thousands were forced into exile, particularly to Burundi and other neighbouring countries. This power transfer had an important demonstration effect in Burundi. Some among Burundi's Hutu elite were keen to replicate this experience, feeling that their group's numerical majority should guarantee them *de facto* control of state institutions. Tutsi elites, on the other hand, were determined to prevent by all means a similar revolution in Burundi. Hence they tightened their grip on the state, especially on security institutions. This polarized view created suspicion and mistrust among politicians of both groups. Tension remained permanently so high that relatively simple incidents could trigger large-scale killings.

Regionalism is the third root factor of conflict in Burundi. Rather than attempting to find solutions to the problem created by the colonial power and amplified by the Rwandan social revolution, the post-colonial Burundian elite deepened the divisions. The group of Tutsis from Bururi who overthrew the monarchy in 1966 instituted a system of governance where most of the political and economic power was put in the hands of Tutsis from their province. Access to education, employment, economic and political opportunities was reserved for them. This led to severe inequalities (see Section 9.3) and to social polarization – not only between Tutsis and Hutus, but also between elites from the South and those from the rest of the country. The system instituted by the Bururi elite led to suffering and humiliations for those excluded. The politicization of the system of justice protected those responsible for the cycle of violence depicted in Table 9.1 because they were members of the ruling group.

In such a highly charged atmosphere, relatively manageable incidents sparked violence of untold proportions. For example, the assassination of the first non-Bururi and Hutu president by members of the Tutsi-dominated armed forces in October 1993 sparked a civil war. Hutu politicians used this as an excuse to settle old scores, calling for widespread killings of innocent Tutsi civilians (Ngaruko and Nkurunziza 2005). As usual, the Bururi-dominated army responded in a repressive way but failed to crush the rebellion. A number of Hutus started a bush war, with the ultimate objective of initiating political change. The precursor to the current governing party, CNDD-FDD (Conseil national pour la défense de la démocratie–Forces de défense de la démocratie), which later emerged as the main rebel group, was founded out of this rebellion. The war ended when the government and the rebels agreed on a political settlement. This was the first time in the country's history that genuine negotiations had been organized between the traditional political elite and the opposition. It was a remarkable achievement for all who had fought for equality.

Recent developments

In 2005, Burundian politics underwent a fundamental change. Leaders of CNDD-FDD, the Hutu-dominated party, won democratic elections following the conclusion of political negotiations to bring an end to the war. Burundians celebrated this victory as the beginning of a new era. Being among the prominent victims of the previous exclusionary policies and having campaigned on a promise of changing the political culture, the new leaders were expected to bring a higher sense of political responsibility and better governance.

The recent change does not seem to have significantly improved the country's political culture of predation, exclusion and injustice, the difference now being that the system is in favour of a group made of past victims. Many Southern Burundians and Tutsis have been sidelined from political and economic positions without any valid reason. But the most important criterion for exclusion has shifted to political affiliation. Members of CNDD-FDD are overly favoured in political, administrative and economic positions, even when they are not the most qualified. Corruption among the new governing elite is also rampant, as highlighted in a memorandum drafted by 32 civil society organizations (Mémorandum des Associations de la Société Civile du Burundi 2008).

9.3 Inequality in Burundi

What is the nature of inequality in Burundi?

As is the case in many societies, it is not easy to delineate inequality in Burundi empirically. The case of Burundi is further complicated by the fact that it fits loosely the definition of 'horizontal inequalities' (HIs), understood as 'inequalities in economic, social or political dimensions or cultural status between culturally defined groups' (Stewart 2008: 3). As discussed earlier, in many ways Burundi has a culturally homogeneous society. However, it is possible to identify some forms of political (in terms of representation and political power) and economic (access to economic assets) inequalities between the two main groups and across regions.

It is important to keep in mind that inequality is mostly felt by elites from both the Hutu and the Tutsi group. With the exception of the small elite of powerbrokers and their associates – they were mainly Tutsis until 2005, but are now predominantly Hutus – poverty and inequality have affected Hutus and Tutsis more or less equally. A Tutsi peasant in the countryside who does not have a relative associated with the country's urban-based political and economic elite is not necessarily better off than his Hutu neighbour, and vice versa. In rural areas, Tutsis do not necessarily have more land – the most important asset in a predominantly agrarian society – than Hutus. This is supported by the fact that the Gini coefficient of land distribution, irrespective of the ethnicity of landowners, varies between 0.15 and 0.30, depending on the regions considered (Ndimira 2000).

Inequality in Burundi results from the behaviour of political elites, who fight to capture the state and its associated 'rents to sovereignty' (Nkurunziza and Ngaruko 2008). These rents include the appropriation of foreign aid, the power to allocate public investment and public employment, the power to levy and allocate taxes and even the power to shape the economy in such a way that it disproportionately benefits members of a specific group. In a country where the state dominates economic and political activity, these rents represent the most important source of wealth.

Not all members of the ethnic group in power benefit from these rents. Apart from geographical spillover effects that can go beyond the targeted individuals, whether one benefits from these rents depends on an individual's closeness to those controlling power. Hence, inequality in Burundi can be analysed by differentiating between those who benefit from the rents from sovereignty and those who do not, whether Hutus or Tutsis. The conflict in Burundi is essentially distributional (Ndikumana 2005; Ngaruko and Nkurunziza 2000; Nkurunziza and Ngaruko 2008).

While generalizations about the identity of the elite can be made on the basis of the ethnic group controlling power, there is a complex process of shifting loyalties and other political changes that makes a precise identification of the members of the elite difficult. However, it is possible to identify some stable patterns if we focus the analysis on the pre-2005 period.[5] For most of the post-colonial period, elitism in Burundi has had a clear ethno-regional pattern. Table 9.2 proposes four main ethno-regional groups that help to explain Burundi's socio-political pecking order.

Generally speaking, Tutsis from Bururi had a better chance of political and economic success than any other group over these years. Assuming that Tutsis and Hutus are more or less homogeneously distributed across provinces, the fact that those who controlled the system are Tutsis

Table 9.2 Socio-political pecking order in Burundi (1966–2005)

	Bururi	**Rest of the country**
Tutsis	Bururi Tutsis	Non-Bururi Tutsis
Hutus	Bururi Hutus	Non-Bururi Hutus

from just one province suggests that, in all probability, they are the smallest of all four groups of Table 9.2. Therefore their predominance is not explained by their population size. Rather, it is the capture of political and military power in 1966 that explained their controlling economic and political institutions in order to enjoy their associated benefits exclusively.

The second undisputable fact is that non-Bururi Hutus have been the group with the least access to benefits, despite the fact that it is the largest population group. The group of non-Bururi Tutsis is probably larger than that of Bururi Hutus. What is not clear is which of the two enjoyed higher benefits. Both groups were at times associated with Bururi Tutsis on the basis of their 'ethnicity' (non-Bururi Tutsis) or of their regional attribute (Bururi Hutus). Clearly the latter benefited to some extent from positive spillovers from Bururi Tutsis, particularly in terms of access to education and employment.[6]

Obviously, Table 9.2 must be interpreted as a simplification of a complex reality. At times there were fights even within the Tutsi and Hutu groups (Ngaruko and Nkurunziza 2000, 2005). However, notwithstanding the limitations of this simplified model, it is widely known in Burundi that Bururi Tutsis' leadership is responsible for the regional inequalities observed in the country. Different methods were used to create and maintain these inequalities, including restricted access to education, employment and other forms of physical and human capital formation.

Discriminatory access to education and employment

Education is the channel through which employment is accessed and political aspirations are created (Fedderke and Luiz 2008). Therefore, controlling access of non-Bururi Tutsis and Hutus to primary, secondary and tertiary education was the best way to disqualify them from competing for positions in the country's institutional structures. The emphasis was on the civil service and the army, two sectors that account for up to 80 per cent of total formal employment (Ngaruko and Nkurunziza 2000). This discrimination led to strong inequalities.

Discriminatory access to education

Privileged access to education has a positive effect on school performance and long-term economic benefits.[7] In a cross-country analysis covering 41 countries, it was found that students enjoying privileges in terms of the amount of resources devoted to their education have better scores than other students. Inequality in income distribution favours privileged students because schools with more privileged students typically have more resources (Chiu and Khoo 2005). These privileges have long-term effects, because access to quality education leads to better jobs with higher pay, which in turn increases wealth (Pritchett and Filmer 1999). Additional discrimination in the job market in favour of the elite amplifies these effects. Continued discrimination in access to education can, therefore, perpetuate long-term inequalities in wealth.

Unequal distribution of education infrastructure was one of the tools used to implement the discriminatory education policy.[8] For example, a government reform undertaken in the 1980s made all high schools in the Southern province of Bururi institutions of excellence preparing the future elite for university education. The best teachers were sent there (Table 9.3) and external aid to the education sector was concentrated in this region. Elsewhere, previously good schools were downgraded to the status of primary teacher training schools, a profession associated with low social status and despised for its hardship. Many outside the Bururi circle who managed to access high-quality education went to seminaries and other schools controlled by the Catholic Church. Most Hutu leaders were educated in such schools.

Physical infrastructure was complemented by the deployment of human resources. This is confirmed by data in Table 9.3, which shows that Bururi has not only the highest number of teachers (two per classroom) but also the most qualified ones, with 94 qualified teachers for every 100 teachers. In contrast, Ngozi has 81 qualified teachers for every 100 teachers, the lowest ratio. Also, Bururi has the second highest number of pupils, the lowest ratio of pupils per teacher and the highest overall school enrolment ratio.

The privileged status of Bururi and, to some extent, of Southern provinces does not stop at the primary school level. The province has the highest number of secondary schools and by far the lowest ratio of population per secondary school. Muyinga, in comparison, has three times the ratio of the population per secondary school. The picture is amplified by the fact that Bururi natives are also found in secondary schools all over the country – which is not the case for non-Bururi natives, who tend to stay in their provinces. As a result of the situation in the primary and secondary schools, natives of Bururi also dominate tertiary education. For example, Jackson (2000) found that students from Mugamba commune of Bururi province, which currently represents 0.76 per cent of the country's population (République du Burundi 2009), accounted for 15 per cent of the 6,000 students of the University of Burundi in 1999, the only institution of higher learning in the country at that time.

Table 9.3 Provincial data on education in Burundi

Province	Number of pupils	Pupils per teacher	Ratio qualified teachers	Teachers per classroom	Number secondary schools	Population per secondary school
Bubanza	59,981	60	0.86	1.3	15	21,968
Buja rural	115,783	56	0.85	1.4	30	15,878
Bururi	141,069	38	0.94	2.0	59	7,983
Cankuzo	41,768	51	0.86	1.0	13	14,078
Cibitoke	84,576	52	0.92	0.9	20	22,488
Gitega	149,633	59	0.89	1.0	46	14,549
Karuzi	81,828	78	0.89	0.8	17	23,424
Kayanza	114,764	72	0.90	1.0	35	14,342
Kirundo	99,129	60	0.85	0.9	23	24,534
Makamba	87,546	50	0.94	1.0	25	17,536
Muramvya	69,274	57	0.86	1.0	20	13,320
Muyinga	85,416	74	0.87	0.9	22	25,176
Mwaro	62,100	40	0.90	–	29	8,320
Ngozi	123,181	68	0.81	1.0	29	23,263
Rutana	62,304	55	0.94	1.0	17	16,183
Ruyigi	70,381	59	0.86	0.8	17	20,296

Source: Data on the first three variables are for the year 2008 and are from ISTEEBU (2008). The data on teachers per classroom are from UNDP and MPDR (1999). Data on secondary school are based on UNDP and MPDR (2005).

Attempts to raise the genuine issue of inequality of treatment on the basis of regional origin were considered treason, leading to long jail terms. This is one of the main reasons why conflict in Burundi has often been presented as an ethnic problem between the Tutsis and Hutus. Without denying that the conflict in Burundi has had an ethnic dimension, overselling the ethnic factor served the interests of the ruling elites responsible for the catastrophic consequences of their discriminatory policies. Blaming an entire group for the ills inflicted by a relatively limited number of individuals protected the latter. As Jackson (2000) puts it, if Burundians did not fight ethnic wars, they would have fought wars based on regional origin.

Discriminatory access to employment

In order to control the system of rent collection and allocation, most of the strategic political posts were firmly in the hands of people from Bururi. Until the early 1990s, it was almost natural that the presidency, key ministries and other high-ranking political and non-political positions had to be in Bururi hands (see Table 9.4). This was not limited to the central government in Bujumbura. In the 1970s and 1980s, people from Bururi occupied most public positions, at all levels and throughout the whole country. In the army the dominance of Bururi was overwhelming; but the situation is changing.[9]

Empirical data in Table 9.4 confirm the thesis, developed in Table 9.2, that Tutsis from Bururi are most privileged in terms of accessing strategic posts in the civil service and the army. Despite the fact that they represent about 7 per cent of the total population (see Table 9.5), Bururi natives, both Hutus and Tutsis, represented the majority of state firm

Table 9.4 *Ethno*-regional background of Burundi leadership (%)

Period		By region		By ethnic group	
	Category	Bururi	ROC	Tutsis	Hutus
1967	Government composition	47	53	71	28
2000a	State firm managers	61	39	89	11
2000b	Army's high command	70	30	100	0
End-2001	Government composition	25	75	47	53

Notes: ROC = rest of the country. We cannot show these figures in proportions of the population due to the lack of ethnic data, as discussed earlier.
Source: Ngaruko and Nkurunziza (2005).

Table 9.5 Population weighted distribution of employment in the civil service

Province	Population (1)	Share of total population (2)	Number of civil servants (3)	Population per civil servant (4)	Share of total civil servants (%) (5)	Ratio of (5) and (2) (6)
Bubanza	348,188	4.03	2,243	155	3.96	0.98
Buja rural	565,070	7.00	3,887	145	6.86	0.98
Bururi	570,929	7.10	6,904	83	12.18	1.72
Cankuzo	221,391	2.80	1,549	143	2.73	0.98
Cibitoke	460,626	5.70	2,759	167	4.87	0.85
Gitega	715,080	8.90	4,898	146	8.64	0.97
Karuzi	433,061	5.40	1,974	219	3.48	0.64
Kayanza	586,096	7.30	2,977	197	5.25	0.72
Kirundo	636,298	7.90	2,737	232	4.83	0.61
Makamba	428,917	5.30	3,079	139	5.43	1.02
Muramvya	294,891	3.70	2,379	124	4.20	1.14
Muyinga	632,346	7.90	2,250	281	3.97	0.50
Mwaro	269,048	3.30	2,885	93	5.09	1.54
Ngozi	661,310	8.20	3,328	199	5.87	0.72
Rutana	336,394	4.20	2,206	152	3.89	0.93
Ruyigi	400,818	5.00	2,279	176	4.02	0.80

Source: Population data are from République du Burundi (2009). Data on the number of civil servants is from ISTEEBU (2008).

managers and the army's high command. State firms have always been an important source of rents. As for the army, rather than being a security institution protecting the country's integrity, it was used to protect the institutional structures supporting the country's predatory system. The representatives of the Bururi elite also accounted for almost half of the cabinet in 1966, after they overthrew the monarchy.

It is clear that this extraordinary concentration of power in the hands of natives from one province was not natural. The picture only changed at the end of 2001, when a new government of national unity was installed following the conclusion of political negotiations between the representatives of the two groups. These negotiations eroded Bururi Tutsis' stronghold on power, an indication of how other politicians despised them. Even if a proportion of 25 per cent is still too high for just one province, the decline was unprecedented in a country that had become accustomed to the political dominance of Bururi. Correcting these imbalances will take a long time.[10]

Information in Table 9.4 also clarifies the order in which the cells of Table 9.2 should be interpreted. Generally speaking, the empirical data show that Tutsis are more favoured than Hutus, even if the group of Tutsis is dominated by those from Bururi. At different times during their reign, Bururi Tutsis co-opted a number of Tutsis from the rest of the country, making them the next favoured group. Third is the group of Hutus from Bururi, and, lastly, Hutus from the rest of the country. These data suggest that inequality is both regional and ethnic; but the ethnic dimension cannot be further investigated due to data limitations.

Table 9.5 introduces population weights to show that the importance of Bururi cannot be justified on the basis of its population size. If the number of civil servants is a proxy for state support, and considering that the state in Burundi is almost the sole provider of education, health services, infrastructure, security and so on, a high number of civil servants means higher state support. Hence, the presence of more civil servants in a province implies higher benefits from the state. Following this logic, one civil servant in Bururi cares for only 83 persons, while a civil servant in Muyinga cares for 281 persons, which is more than three times larger. Another way of interpreting the statistics is that one in every 83 persons in Bururi is a civil servant from the province, assuming that all civil servants working in Bururi are originally from the province, which is normally the case. This is the highest probability of finding employment in the civil service. Adding the large number of Bururi natives working in other provinces, particularly Bujumbura, and the number of those within the army and other security institutions amplifies this dominance. In contrast, Gitega, Ngozi, Muyinga, Kirundo and Kayanza have the lowest probability of accessing employment in the civil service.

In the last column, an index of 1 represents a 'normal' number of civil servants if they are allocated according to the size of the population. Indices greater than 1 imply the presence of more civil servants than warranted by the size of the population, and vice versa.[11] On the basis of this index, Bururi stands out as being disproportionately covered by the civil service. The province has 72 per cent more civil servants than warranted by its population size. On the other hand, Muyinga province is undercovered. With an index of 0.50, Muyinga should have twice its current number of civil servants.

The next section attempts to identify the extent to which the new leaders, who gained power in 2005, have used fiscal policy to redress the wrongs created by the previous regimes. Even if they are not responsible for the problems of inequality they have inherited, the current leaders have a duty to find solutions for them. The choice to focus on the pre-2005 period is also motivated by the fact that the current regime has been in place for only 5 years, which is sufficient to detect policy directions, although not long enough to allow a comprehensive analysis of government policy. Data from the budgets covering 2007 and 2008 make up most of the fiscal data used.

9.4 Post-conflict fiscal policy

In Burundi, where conflict has been mainly due to distributional inequalities, fiscal policy is among the tools that could be used to reduce these inequalities. This could be achieved by using public resources to target less privileged segments of the society. Indeed, compared to other countries in Sub-Saharan Africa, Burundi does not seem to have an oversized public service (Ndikumana 2001; Ngaruko and Nkurunziza 2000), so the problem is mostly about the allocation rather than the size of public expenditures.

Burundi does not seem to have a coherent fiscal policy. Important decisions have been taken without proper planning to ensure their fiscal consistency. For example, in one of his National Day Speeches, the president announced a 34 per cent salary increase for all government workers, without ensuring that there were sufficient resources to finance this large salary hike. The failure to implement the president's decision led to strikes that paralysed the administration and the economy for several months, until the donors provided the funds to unlock the situation. In the absence of a clear fiscal policy, this section uses the country's 2007 and 2008 budgets to analyse the allocation of public expenditures and to determine whether or not this allocation helps to correct inequality.

Recurrent public expenditures

Considering the importance of education and employment in any strategy to combat inequality, these two aspects are given particular attention. In 2007 and 2008, recurrent expenditures represented 62 per cent and 59.5 per cent, respectively, of the total budget (République du Burundi 2006, 2008). Excluding the Ministry of Finance, the three most important sectors with the highest budgets are education (at all three levels), defence and security.[12] Alone, these three ministries account for 55 per cent of government expenditures. The concentration of resources on security and defence is understandable, given that the country is in a post-conflict period during which it has a number of security and military issues to address.

The size of the army and police increased substantially in the post-conflict period. This was the result of an important political agreement, reached in order to reduce the traditional imbalances in ethnic and regional representation within these security institutions. The quasi mono-ethnic and mono-regional composition of security institutions had become the symbol of Bururi Tutsi domination. Moreover, the army had been consistently used in the past to repress Hutu revolts, so the inclusion of a large number of Hutus was a major requirement of Hutu elites before they could contemplate ending their rebellions. Once in power, it was natural that Hutu leaders implemented this reform as a priority. The smoothness of the process of integration of former Hutu rebels and of the old Tutsi-dominated government army surprised many. As a result, HIs in security institutions are being properly addressed. It is expected that the size of these security institutions will slowly reach its optimal number as old members of the two forces retire.

The cost of education is understandably high because the number of civil servants working in the Ministry of Primary and Secondary Education represented 73 per cent of the total number of civil servants in 2008 (Sofos Consultants 2008). In order to understand whether the current education policy is reducing inequalities in education, one needs to look at the allocation of the budget to determine who benefits from these allocations.

The decision to offer free primary education was one of the first major measures taken by the new government in 2005. Despite its merit, the announcement was made in haste, without proper planning, which rendered implementation very difficult. The decision led to an 88 per cent increase in enrolments in the first year of primary school in 2005–2006. However, the country lacked the human, financial and logistical resources to cope with this sudden influx. The additional demand for education services increased class sizes from 76 to 87 pupils per classroom and from 49 to 55 pupils per teacher in the year the decision was made. In 2007, as a result of this policy, classrooms had, on average, one seat for 1.4 pupils (ISTEEBU 2008).[13]

As shown in Table 9.3, the picture in the education sector has not changed substantially from that identified ten years ago by Ngaruko and Nkurunziza (2000). The provinces that were the most neglected in terms of education access are still the same, and those privileged are still the same. So there is not much evidence to suggest that recent fiscal policy has succeeded in correcting the inequalities in access to quality education. However, it would be unrealistic to expect that the problems in the educational sector could be corrected in just a few years. What is important is to ensure that corrective policies are implemented over time. In this regard, the policy to provide free primary education for all goes in the right direction; but it will need to be refined and properly funded. Moreover, to be more effective, the policy will need to take into account the different needs of different regions. For example, more investments in educational infrastructure and a redeployment of human resources in favour of the previously neglected regions should be envisaged. A one-size-fits-all 'primary education for all' policy will not be good enough.

Wages alone represented 40 per cent of the total recurrent expenditures in 2008 (République du Burundi 2008). The concentration of so much recurrent expenditure on the wages of civil service and security personnel is the perpetuation of an old practice. The civil service absorbs most of the government budget, despite the fact that it represents only 0.67 per cent of the population (2006 data). In 1996, Burundi had one of Africa's smallest bureaucracies relative to the size of the population. The average civil servants wage was 15 times per capita GDP (gross domestic product) (Ngaruko and Nkurunziza 2000), the highest in Africa. In 2007, civil servants in Burundi were paid 12 times the country's GDP per capita.[14] Keeping the size of a highly paid bureaucracy small – not for efficiency reasons, but as a way of protecting the interests of a small part of the population – is a key characteristic of a predatory regime, which is interested in maximizing its rents. This has been done at the expense of the majority of the population in rural areas, which have access to very little government services.

Wages are not the only source of rents. Power-holders enjoy many other benefits, legal and illegal. The legal benefits include free transport, health insurance, travel abroad and pension, all funded by public resources. Illegal benefits include bribes, patronage and monetization of public service for personal gain. This use of public funds reduces the amount of resources used to address the genuine needs of the majority of the population. Moreover, the lopsided geographical distribution of employment implies that wages paid to civil servants and the other benefits associated with public office have benefited Bururi disproportionately. Again, correcting this imbalance will require a longer time horizon.

Capital public expenditures

Traditionally, Burundi's governing elites have tended to consider capital investment as a source of rents primarily used to advance their personal and group interests. For example, most of the resources used to implement the lopsided policies in favour of Bururi, such as the building of schools and health centres in the province, came from foreign aid. The last five-year development plan implemented in Burundi (1988–1992), which was mainly externally funded, allocated 66 per cent of gross fixed capital formation to Bujumbura, the capital city, to its surrounding areas and to the southern province of Bururi (Guichaoua 1991). Moreover, up to 60 per cent of foreign aid for the education sector in Burundi in the late 1980s was allocated to Bururi province (Jackson 2000). Data on the current geographical allocation of capital investments are not readily available, so it is not possible to make a comparison with these past trends.

The use of external aid to create these inequalities suggests that the international community did not help to prevent them. The donor community, which provides two-thirds of capital spending, has the capacity to influence Burundi's fiscal policy. For example, the donors could have been more forceful in conditioning aid on the implementation of more equitable policies. It is even more surprising that the International Monetary Fund (IMF), which is very influential in the implementation of fiscal measures in Burundi, could allow these skewed public investments to be made. The question of the international community's complicity in Burundi's policy failures is an important issue, which merits its own analysis.

Rebalancing the distribution of infrastructure in favour of the most neglected regions should be a priority. For example, massive investments in the education sector will be needed in order to implement successfully the 'Education for all' policy initiated by the government in 2005. Even if Burundi makes maximum efforts to mobilize domestic resources to finance the needed investments, foreign aid will continue to be a major source of funding for some time. Therefore, ensuring that resources address the genuine needs of the population rather than benefiting a small group should mobilize the attention of government and donors alike.

Other measures with important fiscal implications

In addition to the policies discussed above, a number of measures with important implications from the budget, both on the revenue and on the expenditure side, have been taken in the last five years. Some targeted the elite, but others were clearly directed at a large segment of the population. Among the former was the reduction of property taxes. Starting from the 2008 budget, taxes on property transactions were lowered from 13 per cent to 3 per cent of the sale value. The modernization of the tax system through the introduction of VAT and the creation of a revenue authority is imminent, but it is not clear to what extent these changes will generate more public revenue.

Another important measure was the decision to offer free health care to under five-year-old children and to pregnant women. As for providing free access to primary education, this measure could have had an important positive effect on the health of the most vulnerable segment of Burundi's society. It could have reduced inequalities between those with and those without access to health services. The problem is that the implementation of this new health policy required enormous financial, human and infrastructural resources, which were not available. Moreover, hospitals and health centres in rural areas ran out of basic medicines needed in order to offer this free health care. In the end, few children and pregnant women effectively benefited from the measure.

The two social measures (free education and free health care) were positive initiatives, but they have not delivered the expected results. These measures should have been well planned in order to put in place the appropriate infrastructure, prepare teachers and medical staff that would be needed and mobilize the required financial resources from both within and outside Burundi to cope with the increasing demand for social services.

There are some indications that this lacuna is being rectified. The budget of the Ministry of Health, for example, has doubled between 2007 and 2008, partly in order to increase the coverage of basic health services. Another sign of increased interest in the majority of the population is perceptible in the budget allocations to the rural sector, where 90 per cent of the population live. In 2007, the Ministry of Rural Development was among the least endowed ministries, with a lower budget than that of the Ministry of Information and Communication, for example. In 2008, this was rectified; the budget of the Ministry of Rural Development increased seven times in nominal terms. If these reallocations are generalized and maintained over the long term, they will help to bridge the gap between rural and urban standards of living.

9.5 Conclusion

Burundi's post-colonial history has been characterized by extreme insecurity. Conflicts have been described as ethnic contests between the two main ethnic groups, the Hutus and Tutsis. The animosity between elites from the two groups originates in Belgian colonial policies. Hutus and Tutsis, as distinct groups, predate the colonial period. These groups had been coexisting relatively peacefully, in a flexible environment, thanks to a sophisticated system of regulation, which protected each group's vital interests. The Belgian colonial power introduced measures that rigidified these groups as ethnic entities, favouring the Tutsis over the Hutus. After independence, rather than working towards the unification of Burundi's society, political elites, particularly the group of Tutsis from the Southern province of Bururi, consolidated their power by deepening the divisions inherited from the colonists. Privileged access to education and employment, as well as the control of security institutions, were the main channels they used to keep their grip on the country's rents.

With the recent coming to power of CNDD-FDD in August 2005, the situation has been reversed. The country is now in the hands of new elites, mainly composed of Hutus from different parts of the country, who suffered most from the discriminatory policies implemented under the previous regimes. It might be expected that, having endured the injustices of the past, the new leaders would be more sensitive to the problem of inequality inherited from their predecessors and that their experience would induce them to adopt fiscal policies that correct these inequalities.

It is too early to judge the policy successes or failures of the new regime. However, some measures that mark a departure from the past have been announced by the new leaders. The decision to provide free primary education and free health care for children below the age of 5 and for pregnant women could go a long way in reducing inequality in access to social services. However, the fact that the measures were taken without financial, human and infrastructural resources to implement them has drastically limited their effect. Also, the current leadership has neither acknowledged that tackling inequality should be among its policy priorities nor spelt out a strategy to address these problems inherited from its predecessors.

There are indications that budgetary allocations to social sectors and to the rural sector are increasing. If the trend is consolidated, it will be a clear indication that the new leaders are breaking with the past and intending to tackle inequality. Remarkable progress has already been achieved in terms of addressing HIs in security institutions, given the high importance accorded to this problem during the political negotiations that brought to power the current leaders. This example should be emulated in other sectors. While universal policies such as free primary education and health care are relevant ways of reducing social inequalities, differentiated measures will be needed in some situations to reflect regional differences. For example, public investment and the allocation of other resources should be targeted to the most under-privileged regions, while new transfers to well-served regions should be frozen.

Burundi's dependence on external aid makes it very responsive to its external partners' requirements. In this regard, the donors should ensure that their aid is not used to perpetuate inequality, as has been the case in the past. Instead, the aid community's approach to Burundi should be guided by the overarching objective of reducing the large inequalities inherited from the past. For example, the donors should require the government to develop a comprehensive strategy on how it intends to correct the current inequalities. This should be used as the basis for disbursing development assistance.

Notes

1. I wish to thank Frances Stewart and Arnim Langer for very useful comments on an earlier draft. My thanks also go to participants at the workshop on 'Post-conflict Reconstruction and Horizontal Inequalities', organized in Kampala, where the first draft of this chapter was presented. Responsibility for all remaining errors is my own.
2. Burundi's population is divided into four groups: the Hutu, the Tutsi, the Ganwa and the Twa. Estimates dating back to the 1930s have been widely used to show the relative importance of these groups. According to these estimates, 85 per cent of the population are Hutu, 14 per cent Tutsi and 1 per cent Twa. These statistics need to be taken with caution for several reasons. First, in addition to the fact that they do not give the proportion of the Ganwa group, the generation of these estimates was based on a

sloppy methodology. Second, the statistics do not take into account the large number of 'mixed' people born from inter-group marriages – a widespread practice. Third, the statistics do not take into account population dynamics. For example, in 1972 and 1993–2003, hundreds of thousands of people, largely Hutus, were either killed or forced to flee the country. This has surely increased the proportion of the Tutsi group (Lemarchand 1995). In the light of these caveats, it is safe to consider that the Hutus are the large majority group, while Tutsis are the largest minority group. Ganwas are a small group of the descendents of the country's traditional monarchs. The Twas are another small group, sometimes assimilated with pygmies; they are poorly integrated with the rest of the population.

3. This section draws from Ngaruko and Nkurunziza (2005).
4. Own translation from French.
5. The reason is that this is a long enough period to detect general trends.
6. Empirical data in Table 9.4 suggest that non-Bururi Tutsis were more privileged than Bururi-Hutus.
7. Until recently, data on education in Burundi were tightly controlled in order to hide the effect of the discriminatory policy on education (Guichaoua 1995). Owing to the recent political changes, data on education are being slowly released. However, it is still difficult to have a global picture of the question of education in Burundi, and this limitation on data will constrain our analysis.
8. Helping students in Bururi to cheat in major tests and exams was another method used to create the gap between Bururi and the rest of the country (see Jackson 2000).
9. For example, for the first time in recent history, a Hutu has been appointed as chief of staff of the army.
10. As recent data in Table 9.5 show, Bururi is still privileged in terms of the population weighted distribution of public service employment.
11. We thank Arnim Langer, who suggested that we construct this index.
12. The Ministry of Finance's budget represented about 19 per cent of the total budget in 2008. Eighty-six per cent of the ministry's budget in 2008 was used to reimburse the country's debts and to pay for interests (53 per cent and 33 per cent of the ministry's budget, respectively). These expenses are excluded, as they are not allocated to specific sectors within the country.
13. The overall picture hides geographical variations. As noted earlier, Bururi is still the region with the best primary school infrastructure, as a result of past policies. The ratio of pupils per teacher is lowest in Bururi (38 pupils) and highest in Karuzi (78 pupils).
14. The figure for 2007 is based on information from a study by Sofos Consultants (2008) and by République du Burundi (2006). The computation excludes the army and police personnel.

10
Structural Violence and Conflict: Vertical and Horizontal Inequality in Post-Genocide Rwanda

Sebastian Silva Leander

10.1 Introduction

While there is little or no empirical evidence of a systematic link between *vertical* (income) inequality and conflict (Collier 2000; Collier and Hoeffler 1996),[1] *horizontal* inequalities (HIs) in access to social advantages (such as social services, power, status, wealth) between geographic regions or ethnic groups have been found to be more likely to crystallize around group identities, and thus to degenerate into armed conflict (Auvinen and Nafziger 1999; Stewart 1998). Such violence may cluster around social, cultural or ethnic groups if there is a political capacity and social propensity to organize the discontent into a structured movement, or it may remain diffuse in the form of crime. In either case, such acts can be seen, if not as the consequence, at least as a continuation of a structural economic violence (on structural violence, see Galtung and Hoivik 1971; Köhler and Alcock 1976).

In the case of Rwanda, we have observed a sharp increase in inequality since the mid-1980s, which has been aggravated by the war and subsequent population displacements. Rwanda's increase in the Gini coefficient over this period, from 0.29 to 0.45 between 1984 and 2000 (WIDER 2007),[2] is one of the sharpest in the world – Rwanda is ahead of most countries from the former communist bloc (not including China). The recent publication of the Integrated Household Living Conditions Survey (EICV2) reveals a further increase of the Gini coefficient, from 0.47 to 0.51, between 2001 and 2006 (MINECOFIN 2007), which would place Rwanda among the 15 most unequal countries in the world, together with Latin American countries for the most part and a few high-inequality but much richer African countries, such as South Africa and Namibia. More worryingly, perhaps, we observe that Rwanda has experienced a surge in the gap between urban and rural poverty and now ranks second only to Zimbabwe on the African continent, and third in the world for its urban/rural divide. Because of the historical association of rural/urban identities with particular ethnic groups, this phenomenon could contribute to aggravating the structural tensions left by the war.

Importantly, we find that the ratio of top to bottom quintile incomes seems to have increased faster since the end of the transition than in the immediate post-war period.[3] This suggests that the observed changes are not exclusively linked to the massive social and demographic disruption caused by the war and genocide. Furthermore, we find that the observed changes in inequality are far larger than in other African countries with similar characteristics and policies. The difference, we suggest, may be accounted for in large part by the injection of additional resources to the Rwandan economy through the looting and re-export of mineral resources in neighbouring Democratic Republic of Congo, which accounted for at least 16 per cent of Rwandan gross domestic product (GDP) during the Second Congo War (1998–2002).

10.2 Trends in poverty and inequality

Pre-genocide trends in inequality in Rwanda

Although there has been a surge in income inequality after the war and the genocide, it is important to note that Rwandan society had been beset by deep and overlapping inequalities since the 1980s, which resulted in large part from the increasingly discriminatory and predatory policies of the Habyarimana regime (Braeckman 1994; DesForges 1999; Gordon 1993; Hanssen 1989; Reyntjens 1994; Sibomana 1999).

First, vertical inequalities (in income between households) started growing, from a very low level in the mid-1980s (Gini coefficient of 0.28 in 1982 in Deininger and Squire 1996), largely as a result of the steady deterioration of Rwandan agricultural productivity under the pressures of over-population and soil erosion (Verwimp 2000: 341). The rapid pauperization of rural areas, in turn, allowed powerful individuals with close links to the regime, the so-called Akazu, to accumulate large landholdings, notably to be exploited for the lucrative export coffee market (MacDermott 2001; Prunier 1995). By the late 1980s, it was estimated that 16 per cent of households owned 43 per cent of the cultivated lands, whereas the average land holding of Rwandan farmers was less than 1 ha (Gasana 1994). As a consequence of this, Uvin estimates, the income share of the richest decile of the population almost doubled from 22 per cent to 52 per cent between 1982 and 1994 (Uvin 2000). One study estimates that the Gini coefficient rose from 0.357 in 1982 to 0.505 in 1989 (Maton 1994). Even if the coverage and quality of these studies makes it difficult to generalize on the basis of this information, they point to a very sharp increase in inequality over this period, which is consistent with the findings of other available studies (see below).

Secondly, horizontal (ethnic) inequality between Hutus and Tutsis became more apparent at this time, as the government attempted to divert attention from the deteriorating economic situation by 'tapping into the cleavages which it had nurtured' for decades through its anti-Tutsi discourse (MacDermott 2001). Ethnic access quotas were, for instance, re-introduced (or enforced) in higher education and in the public sector employment, effectively restricting Tutsi access to just 10 per cent of available positions. The overt ethnic discrimination was used to divert attention from growing intra-ethnic inequalities – such as the growing regional divide between the north of the country, where President Habyarimana had his power base, and the south, which was seen as being loyal to the regime of his predecessor from 1961 to 1973, President Kayibanda – both of whome were Hutus (Ohlsson 2000). General Habyarimana's region of origin, Gisenyi, was grossly overrepresented in government jobs, in the security forces and in university education, as well as receiving a disproportionate amount of development aid (Cramer 2003).

In October 1990, Rwanda was invaded from the north by the Rwandan Patriotic Front (RPF), a rebel group largely composed of Tutsi refugees who had fled the 1959 pogroms in the wake of the decolonization process. The invasion marked the start of a protracted civil war that ended in July 1994, following the assassination of President Habyarimana; this assassination triggered one of the worst human rights catastrophes of the twentieth century, as over 800,000 Tutsis and moderate Hutus were killed in a genocide orchestrated by the Rwandan Armed Forces and extremist youth militias called Interhamwe. Although it would be inaccurate to claim that rising inequalities caused the genocide, it is clear that these were part of a broader pattern of rising structural violence, including increasing militarization and political repression, which undermined the social fabric of the country and enabled the ideology of hatred to flourish under the leadership of opportunistic politicians.

Vertical inequality and land distribution

On the basis of the internationally comparable data on income distribution that is provided in the WIDER dataset (WIDER 2007), we know that the income share of the poorest quintile in the total national income was halved between 1984 and 2000 from 10 per cent to 5 per cent of the total income. In absolute terms, this means a 30 per cent decrease in the real incomes of the poorest 20 per cent of the population over this period, based on Purchasing Power Parity (PPP) per capita gross domestic product (GDP) figures, or a halving of incomes (–52 per cent), based on gross national product (GDP) per capita figures (constant 1995 US$). In the same period, the real incomes of the top quintile of the population almost doubled (+90 per cent), based on PPP figures, and increased by close to one-third (+29 per cent) based on constant GNP figures. Importantly, using the same data sets to compare income trends in other African countries over the same period, we find that, even though inequalities have been increasing across Africa since 1980, Rwanda is the only country for which we have data where the incomes of the top and bottom income quintiles moved in *opposite* directions over this period, which means that there has effectively been a net transfer of income from the poor to the rich.

Crucially, however, the internationally comparable data do not tell us whether the observed changes occurred before or after the genocide, since the latest available quality data from this period are from 1984. On the basis of a combination of World Bank estimates of income distribution from the immediate post-genocide period and the 2001 and 2006 Household Living Conditions surveys (EICV: *Enquête intégrée sur la condition de vie des ménages*), the United Nations' Development Programme's (UNDP) National Human Development Report for Rwanda estimated that the average income of the top quintile of the population nearly tripled between 1995 and 2006, while the incomes of the poorest 20 per cent of the population remained virtually constant from 1996 onwards – increasing only from Rwf (Rwandan Francs) 17,400 in 1996 to 18,900 in 2006 (UNDP 2007). This would mean that the robust economic growth that the country has experienced since the war has benefited the rich disproportionately, while almost entirely bypassing the poorest segments of society (see Figure 10.1).[4] These estimates should, however, be treated carefully, in view of the lack of reliable data from the immediate post-genocide period.

The only reliable comparisons that can be made are for 2001 onwards, which use figures from the two EICVs. A comparison of these EICVs shows that the Gini coefficient increased from an already high level of

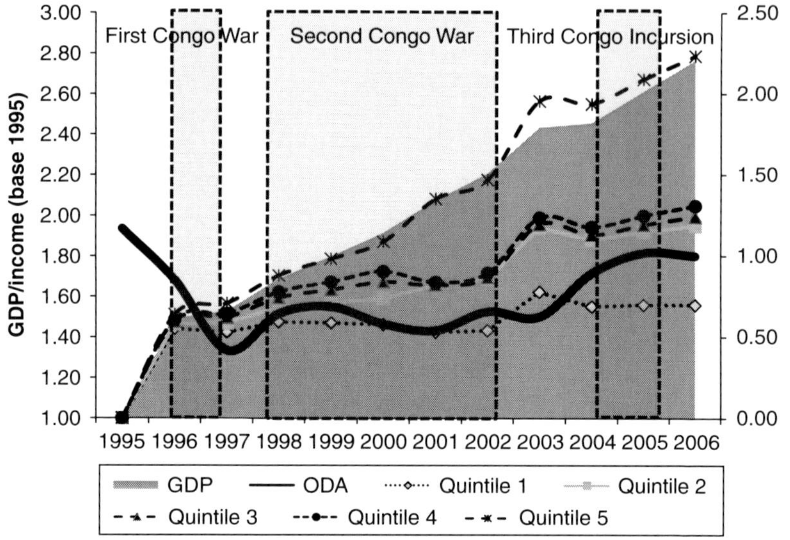

Figure 10.1 Trends: Average incomes (by quintile) and GDP/ODA (1995–2006)
Source: (UNDP 2007); GDP (Total, constant 2001 prices): World Bank; ODA: OECD.

0.47 in 2001 to 0.51 in 2006. In real terms, this means that the incomes (in constant Rwf) of the richest 20 per cent of the population rose more than three times faster than those of the poorest quintile over the five years from 2001 to 2006 (33 per cent increase vs. 9 per cent increase; see Figure 10.1 above). The finding is consistent with that of other studies covering the post-genocide period (see Ansoms 2005; Justino and Verwimp 2006; McKay and Loveridge 2005).

Importantly, the EICVs show that the most rapid increase in inequality in recent years has taken place in rural areas: in 2001 the Gini coefficient for rural areas was 0.37, which is only slightly higher than the latest available high-quality estimates from the pre-war period. By 2006, the rural Gini coefficient had jumped to 0.44. Importantly, the study carried out by Justino and Verwimp links this increase in rural inequality to growing land inequalities – the Gini coefficient on land inequality rose from 0.44 in 1990 to 0.59 in 2000 for their sample of households (Justino and Verwimp 2006). Other studies have also pointed to rising land inequalities after the genocide (see, for instance, Pottier 2006).

Given the role that land played in the Rwandan genocide, the issue of rising land inequalities is one of the most delicate and potentially explosive social issues facing Rwanda today.[5] A 2001 study by the National Unity and Reconciliation Commission, for instance, found ongoing land disputes to be 'the greatest factor hindering sustainable peace' (NURC 2001).

Horizontal inequality and rural/urban divide

The main source of HI[6] before the war was inequality between geographic regions, as President Habyarimana's northwestern region was favoured at the expense of the south. The policies of regional favouritism have been forcefully denounced by the post-genocide government, which has been keen to appear to distribute public resources exactly equally between provinces. The panel data study carried out by Justino and Verwimp appears to confirm very strongly the convergence of poverty levels across regions after the war, although the authors point out that this is due to a number of different factors, including the particularly severe impact of counter-insurgency operations in the regions that were loyal to the former president (Justino and Verwimp 2006). The EICVs, for instance, show that the northwestern province of Gisenyi saw the largest increase (+13 per cent) in poverty between 2001 and 2006, whereas the greatest decrease (–15 per cent) was observed in Umutara, where a large number of Tutsi refugees resettled after the war.[7]

Similarly, the post-genocide government has reversed the policies of explicit ethnic discrimination, such as the ethnically differentiated identity cards, and has made the fight against all forms of ethnicity into the centrepiece of its reconstruction strategy for Rwanda. This also means that it is difficult to analyse trends in HI at this level, since the official denial of the ethnic differentiation of Rwandans prevents collection of ethnically disaggregated data. Given Rwanda's recent history, however, it is clear that inequalities across ethnic groups – and, more importantly, the perception thereof – will play a key role in determining the country's long-term stability, since the historical resentment of the Hutu majority against the Tutsi 'upper class' has provided fertile ground for a political manipulation of the masses ever since independence.

While we cannot study ethnic inequalities directly, the rural/urban divide, which exists in most African (and third world) countries, is an important form of inequality, which also takes on an ethnic dimension in Rwanda. With a ratio of rural to urban poverty of 4.6 (65.7 per cent of the population below the national poverty line in rural areas vs. 14.3 per cent in urban areas), Rwanda has the largest rural/urban divide of any country in Africa, bar Zimbabwe, and the third largest in the world (the average ratio of rural to urban poverty is 1.98 in Africa[8]). In fact, it appears that the growing land inequality in rural areas has contributed to aggravating the rural/urban divide, since a number of those who own large swathes of land actually live in urban areas (Dorsey 2000).

Traditionally, Tutsis have been overrepresented in urban areas, as they were favoured to work in the colonial administration and engaged in commerce. As Verwimp has shown, the propaganda of the Habyarimana regime contributed to reinforcing this perception by constructing an idealized Hutu identity around the notion of rural 'purity' of the Hutu peasantry, which was opposed to the vice and corruption of the urban Tutsis (see Verwimp 2000).[9] It is important to point out, however, that the existence of a rural/urban divide precedes the war and that the Habyarimana regime, under the cover of a discourse of glorification of the Hutu peasantry, effectively protected the privileges of those already living in the cities (including the Hutu elite) – by, for instance, prohibiting migration to urban areas (Verwimp 2000).

The EICV has confirmed that the decreases in poverty in the 2000s failed to narrow the gap between urban and rural areas: the number of people under the poverty line dropped by 20 per cent in Kigali between the two EICVs, compared to a 5 per cent reduction in the number of rural poor. In recent years, however, the gap between rural and urban areas has tended to shrink in a number of living standard indicators, both as a result of largely foreign funded investments in areas such as education, and as a result of a transfer of poverty from rural to urban areas through the massive migration to urban areas that has taken place in recent years (see, e.g., access to improved water sources in Table 10.1 below and DHS, 2006).[10]

10.3 Behind the figures: Post-war policies

As Figure 10.1 illustrates, Rwanda's surge in inequality is composed of two separate and, we will argue, largely independent phenomena: on the one hand, incomes at the bottom of the income distribution have stagnated or worsened; on the other, there has been a massive surge in the incomes of the top income quintile. We will look at each of these phenomena in turn.

Decrease in bottom quintile incomes

The impoverishment of the Rwandan peasantry, which started in the early 1980s, was caused by a decline in agricultural productivity

Table 10.1 Trends in poverty and key social indicators, by location

	EICV1 (2000–2001)			EICV2 (2005–2006)			Change (%)	
		Other			Other			
	Kigali	Urban	Rural	Kigali	Urban	Rural	Kigali	Rural
Poverty headcounts by location (%)	16.1	46.5	66.1	13	41.5	62.5	−19.2	−5.44
Depth of poverty by location (% of poverty line)	34.4	36	42.1	29.3	37.3	40.4	−14.8	−4.0
Net enrolment rate at primary school	82.7	74.1	72.9	90.4	90.1	85.1	9.31	16.7
Access to improved water sources	88	68.8	61.7	81.6	73.7	61.6	−7.27	−0.16
Extreme poverty headcount (%)	8.4	28.5	45.7	6.3	25.3	40.9	−25	−10.5

resulting from the combined effects of overpopulation, land fragmentation and soil erosion. In this respect, the main failure of the post-genocide government has been its inability to reverse the long-term decline of Rwanda's agricultural sector, which still employs close to 80 per cent of the labour force. The government's development strategy – most clearly expressed in the Vision 2020 document (MINECOFIN 2002b) – has replaced the previous regime's violent anti-urban rhetoric with an equally forceful modernization discourse, which pins the country's hopes on sectors such as information technology and tourism, largely at the expense of the agricultural sector. In 2004, Rwanda had the lowest public expenditure on agriculture in Africa at just 0.6 per cent of total expenditures, against a continental average of 5.1 per cent (Fan et al. 2008). By 2007, however, investments in agriculture had increased to 3 per cent of total expenditures, although they were still largely concentrated in high-value added export crops, such as horticulture and tea.

It is important to point out that the above-mentioned agricultural stagnation started at a substantially lower level than before the war.

First, the war itself led to a considerable depletion of agricultural assets (Verpoorten 2007). Furthermore, the war was followed by a violent counter-insurgency campaign in 1997–1998, which killed significant number of civilians in the northwestern part of the country (AI 1997). Unlike the genocide, which targeted entire families, the counter-insurgency left many families without a head of household and, in many cases, headed by children, which made them even more vulnerable to poverty.

In addition to this direct destruction, the war generated massive population displacements, which contributed to changing the land ownership structure in Rwanda. After the victory of the Rwandan Patriotic Front (RPF) in 1994, over 3 million Rwandans (close to half of the surviving population) fled to refugee camps in neighbouring Congo, before being forcefully repatriated by the Rwandan army in 1995 and 1996. In the meantime, close to 1 million so-called 'old caseload' refugees (Tutsi refugees who had fled the 1959 pogroms) had returned, mostly from Uganda and Burundi, and in some cases relocated on land previously occupied by households that had fled to Congo after the victory of the RPF. The resulting land disputes between 'old' and 'new case' refugees had to be resolved through local level agreements and compromises, which often led to a further fragmentation of the land (McKay and Loveridge 2004).

In order to facilitate the resettlement process, the government adopted a controversial 'villagization' policy, called Imidugudu, which sought to regroup rural dwellers in planned settlement areas, so as to facilitate the provision of social services and to increase the availability of arable land. The policy, which had been foreseen by the 1993 Arusha accords, became a necessity for the government after the war, which was faced with a larger than expected resettlement problem, prompted by the double exodus of 'old' and 'new case' refugees. The policy also responded to a more ambitious aspiration, expressed in various public policy statements from the 1940s and shared by other African countries such as Tanzania, to break with the traditionally dispersed settlement patterns in order to promote the initiation of an urbanization dynamic, which was thought to be necessary to start the country's economic modernization (Obidegwu 2003).

The policy has received much criticism from human rights groups for the heavy-handed manner in which it was implemented, involving forced relocations and destruction of property (HRW 2001a). Others have pointed to biases in the implementation of the policy, with a particularly forceful implementation in the northwestern parts of the country – which suggests that the policy also responded to security and control imperatives on the part of the post-genocide government as it sought to impose its authority over restive areas (Jones 2000). Available evidence confirms that the policy has fuelled ethnic tensions in areas where it has been implemented, as many Hutu villagers perceived it as an instrument of control of the authorities (Crook 2006).

The forceful application of the policy had financial implications for settlers in certain areas, where farmers were forced to destroy their old homes without being given the means to reconstruct new ones in the designated locations (Marriage 2006). Furthermore, there is evidence suggesting that the policy may have had the effect of lowering yields due to land quality issues, as well as an increased risk of theft and shorter working days due to the increase in the distance from dwelling location to farm land and water points (Van Leeuwen 2001). While confirming that the Imidugudu policy has failed to achieve one of its stated objectives of improving agricultural productivity, existing studies do not, however, allow us to conclude that it has had a significant impact on rural poverty over and above the underlying trends of decreasing agricultural yields and overpopulation that have affected Rwandan agriculture since the mid-1980s (see, for instance, Napier 2007).

In 2006, an ambitious land law was adopted, after several years of internal consultation, targeting the structural causes of underperformance of Rwanda's agricultural sector (Diao et al. 2007). The stated objective of the policy is to overcome structural bottlenecks in Rwandan agriculture, so as to create an efficient high-value added agriculture, largely geared towards the export market (MINECOFIN 2002b). In so doing, the policy appears to give strong priority to issues of economic efficiency over equity (see Musahara and Huggins 2004: 288). The policy, for instance, bars the registration of land plots smaller than 1 ha and grants local authorities the power 'to approve the consolidation of small plots of land in order to improve land management and productivity' (Pottier 2006: 527; Republic of Rwanda 2005, Art.20).

Vagueness of definitions in the policy and the absence of dispute resolution mechanisms have raised concerns of abusive confiscation and reallocation of land by local authorities in the name of 'economic efficiency' (Wyss 2006). Such prospects are particularly grave in the Rwandan context due to the historical exploitation by Hutu politicians of popular fears that the RPF would seek to restore a pre-colonial feudal order over the Hutu peasantry if it came to power (Mamdani 2001).[11] Notwithstanding the idealized references to the pre-colonial order in earlier drafts of the policy (MINITERE 2004), the government appeared to be keenly aware of the sensitivity of these issues, and has made several very public attempts, over the years, to address perceptions of bias, notably by introducing a 25 ha ceiling on land ownership and by redistributing large plots of land that had been appropriated by powerful individuals in the regime in the wake of the RPF invasion (Ntagungira and Kimenyi 2008).

Surge in top quintile incomes

The effect of the war itself on top quintile incomes is ambiguous. On the one hand, the genocide largely targeted members of the upper class, and landowners in particular, thus dampening, and in some cases even reversing, the inequalities that existed before the war. Justino and Verwimp, for instance, found that households that were land-rich in 1990 were more likely to have fallen into poverty by 2002 than poorer households, which presumably were not targeted by the genocide (Justino and Verwimp 2006). The very rich, that is, those connected to the Habyarimana regime, would have fled the country after the victory of the RPF in 1994, but were quickly replaced by a new elite with close connections to the RPF.

In the immediate aftermath of the war, several cases of land-grabbing by the invading forces were recorded. In the Umutara region, for instance, it was reported that large chunks of land (about 25 ha for each 50 cows up to a maximum of 100 ha) were allocated to returning old case refugees for pastoralism. Despite subsequent subdivisions of the land, 'it seems that many large plots still remain in the hands of single households' (Bledsoe 2004). This is potentially a major source of inequality, if one thinks that the average plot size in Rwanda is less than 1 ha. The significance of such incidents should not be overstated, however, since, first, they were limited in time and benefited only a very small number of officials, and, secondly, they have been partly corrected since by a government that is keen to appear not to repeat the mistakes of the previous regime.

On the other hand, the genocide accentuated the ethnic divide between rural and urban areas. The number of Tutsis killed in the genocide was roughly equal to the number of old caseload refugees who returned after the RPF victory (between 800,000 and 1,000,000). But, while many of those killed in the genocide lived in rural areas, the Tutsi refugees who returned from camps in Uganda after the war were, for the most part, urbanized, usually fairly well educated, and they had little connection to the land (Prunier 1997). Many of them resettled in safer urban centres, particularly Kigali, which consequently doubled in size between 1991 and 1996 despite being severely affected by the genocide.[12] At the same time, a disproportionate number of Hutus who fled Rwanda after the RPF invasion came from urban areas, both because they had the economic means to escape and because many had been ringleaders in the genocide (or feared being mistaken for such). This resulted in a sort of ethnic segregation that effectively reinforces the traditional cleavage between urban and rural areas. The subsequent rural exodus and resettlement of new caseload refugees may alter the traditional ethnic balance and, in time, may help to break the association between ethnicity and rural/urban location.

After the war, the government pursued economic policies that can be characterized as being decidedly neoliberal with a clear urban and pro-growth (or pro-rich) bias. While most policies are in line with the prescriptions of international financial institutions, there have been cases of misspending and elite capture. In late 2003, for instance, the International Monetary Fund (IMF)'s Poverty Reduction and Growth Facility (PRGF) was suspended due to overspending by the government on the construction of two luxury hotels (Purcell et al. 2006). Subsequently, a public expenditure review in the health sector revealed significant departures from the sector's strategic plan and large overspending on the King Faycal Hospital in Kigali, which caters to expatriates and upper-class Rwandans (Corraille et al. 2006). The significance of these examples should not be overestated, however, since neither the overall size of the public envelope (roughly 15 per cent of GDP, excluding foreign contributions), nor its source (mainly import duties and state enterprises) make public spending a very effective tool for effecting income distribution patterns at a macro-level.

Secondly, the war was followed by a massive influx of donor aid, which could have contributed to aggravating economic disparities. In 2006, Rwanda received a total of US$548 million, which represented 22 per cent of GDP or $64 per capita and made it one of the most aid-dependent countries in Africa (after small island states). While there was a significant increase in Oversees Development Aid (ODA) to Rwanda over the post-conflict period, however, a historical perspective actually reveals a remarkable degree of constancy in the aid flows to Rwanda over the longer term. Apart from the years 1994–1995, in which there was a surge in humanitarian assistance (peaking at close to US$300 million), aid flows were almost constant, at around US$386 million dollars on average for the years 1997–2006, against US$334 on average for the period 1990–1993. In the preceding decade aid flows were only slightly lower, at US$283 million on average (in constant 2000 prices) for the period 1980–1989.[13] Furthermore, as shown in Figure 10.1, there does not appear to be any visible correlation between changes in aid flows and the distribution of incomes (correlation coefficient of 0.068).

In fact, in the case of Rwanda, the large inflows of aid may have helped to mitigate biases in public expenditure by bringing government policies back towards the mainstream of neoliberal policy prescriptions. One of the main changes in aid flows after the war was the introduction of direct budget support, which now represents over 50 per cent of Rwanda's total budget (close to 100 per cent of the investment budget). Donors used this instrument to influence resource allocation in key sectors, such as health and education. Public investments in education, for instance, saw a five-fold increase in the last decade (reaching close to USD200 million by 2007, largely financed by donors through direct budget support), with an ever larger proportion going to primary education.

As Table 10.2 shows, neither the fact that Rwanda experienced a violent conflict, nor the massive inflows of aid after the war is sufficient to explain the magnitude of the changes in income distribution observed since the 1980s. While both post-conflict countries and heavily aid-dependent countries experienced larger-than-average surges in the income shares of the top quintile, the change experienced by Rwanda is more than four times the average for these groups. Similarly, the decrease in the income share of the bottom quintile (–56 per cent) stands in sharp contrast with the large increases of bottom quintile income shares experienced across the continent since 1980 (more than doubling for post-conflict and aid-dependent countries).

Table 10.2 Changes in top/bottom quintile income shares since the 1980s in Sub-Saharan Africa

	Rwanda	**Sub-Saharan Africa**	**Post-conflict (SSA)**[14]	**Aid dependent (SSA)**[15]
1980s–2000s (top)	**+47%**	**+1%**	**+11%**	**+13%**
1990s (top)	–	+2.5%	+8.2%	+12%
1980s–2000s (bot.)	**–56%**	**+88%**	**+122%**	**+132%**
1990s (bottom)	–	+7%	+26%	+56%

Source: WIDER data set (2007).

10.4 The impact of the illicit war economy

Looting and re-export of Congolese resources

In order to understand the magnitude of the phenomenon, we need to look beyond conventional explanations relating to public policies and spending. As Figure 10.1 above clearly showed, the real decoupling of the top income quintile from the rest of the economy appears to have taken place after the turn of the millennium rather than in the immediate post-war period, when most of the large population displacements and resettlements took place. In fact, this phenomenon appears to have started during Rwanda's second war in Congo, and in particular after the year 2000, which saw a ten-fold increase in the price of coltan on the international commodities markets, due to the expansion of the mobile phone industry around this time – this is also the period for which we have higher quality and inter-temporally comparable data, allowing us to reach more robust conclusions (Romkema and Vlassenroot 2002).

The looting of Congo's natural resources by its neighbours has been extensively documented in official UN reports and elsewhere. Rwanda's official diamond exports surged from $0 to $720,000 during the first invasion of Congo in 1997, reaching close to $2 million during the Second Congo War (MINECOFIN 2001). Similar patterns can be found for most other minerals mined in eastern DRC (Democratic Republic of Congo), including gold, casserite and coltan (Renton et al. 2007). The UN Panel of Experts commissioned to investigate the looting of resources in Congo estimated that between 60 and 70 per cent of the coltan exported from DRC at this time was mined under the direct supervision of the Rwandan army – often by forced labour, including of women and children, and/or of prisoners imported from Rwanda – and immediately flown out of the country to be stored in government facilities in Kigali (UN Panel of Inquiry 2002).

In addition to mineral exploitation, it was estimated that about half of the production of papaya, tea and cinchona was fraudulently exported through Goma International Airport, and so was up to 60 per cent of the local coffee production (Romkema and Vlassenroot 2002). The Belgian Senatorial Commission of Inquiry on the Great Lakes estimated that products looted from the DRC accounted for about 8.4 per cent of Rwanda's exports in 1999 (Belgian Senatorial Commission of Inquiry on the Great Lakes 2001).

Finally, the UN Panel of Experts reported numerous cases of direct looting of physical assets, ranging from factories to cash in the central bank office in Bukavu, as well as more subtle forms of exploitation through the imposition of monopolies and control of commercial networks (UN Panel of Inquiry 2001).

It is difficult to estimate the real magnitude of the illicit re-export of Congolese resources, as most of this trade does not transit through registered channels. In 1999 and 2000, Rwanda reported coltan exports of 122 and 83 tonnes, respectively (Jackson 2002). However, during this period the UN Panel of Experts estimated the exports processed through Rwanda Metals, a screen company for the Rwandan army, to be 100MT per month, amounting to a total of $250 million in revenue over an 18 months period (UN Panel of Inquiry 2001). This suggests that actual exports may have been 10 to 12 times larger than officially reported. The steady decrease in reported exports from 2000 onwards, even though Rwanda was still present in Congo, could therefore indicate greater efforts on part of the authorities to disguise the re-export of Congolese resources, following the publication of the first report of the UN Panel of Experts on this issue.

In addition to under-reporting of exports from Rwanda, the estimates may be skewed due to the fact that part of the resources continued to be exported directly from Congo, under the Congolese flag, even though they were being sold by the occupying forces. Between 1998 and 1999, for instance, the United States reported 267 metric tonnes of imports of Tantalum ores from Congo, even though the Congolese Ministry of Mines registered no exports during this period (Montague 2002).

Finally, part of the discrepancy between the estimated production and the reported exports of minerals may be explained by the fact that some of the goods were exchanged through barter, without ever passing through the official commercial circuits. The UN Panel of Experts noted that the Russian Arms dealer, Victor Bout, for instance, used his personal aircrafts to evacuate part of the production of coltan from mines in Congo (UN Panel of Inquiry 2002), presumably in return for arms (Samset 2002).

In 1998, the IMF estimated that Rwanda's actual military expenditures were the double of the officially reported 4 per cent of GDP – excluding the costs incurred in Congo, which were largely financed locally, through looting and taxation (International Crisis Group 2000). The UN Panel of Experts puts the total military spending figure at 20 per cent of GDP for 1999 (i.e., 150 per cent of recurring budget expenditures for that year), 80 per cent of which ($320 million or 16 per cent of GDP) are thought to have been raised directly by the Congo Desk of the Rwandan Patriotic Army (UN Panel of Inquiry 2002). This only represents the 'public' side of the revenue generated in DRC through looting and taxation. It excludes revenues that may have been diverted for private benefit by officials within the Rwandan army, as well as the private profits generated by companies operating in the area of conflict, part of which would have reached the Congo Desk in the form of taxes. It would therefore not seem excessive to speak of an overwhelming dependency of the Rwandan State and economy on the illicit exploitation of Congolese resources at this time.

Institutionalization and re-investment

Even if the profits accruing from Congo are likely to have decreased significantly since its peak, the magnitude of this shock alone could be sufficient to explain not only the surge in inequality around this time, but also much of the continued rise in income gaps since then. It is important to bear in mind that these profits would have accrued in the first instance to members of the Tutsi minority – high-ranking Army officials or businessmen with close ties to the regime – thus potentially aggravating the ethnic dimension of economic inequality.

Given the magnitude of the surge in the stock of wealth, it is likely that there would also have been indirect economic benefits for a broader section of the population, as the capital was reinvested in the economy. This is visible, for instance, in real estate speculation, which has pushed the construction sector to double in size between 2002 and 2007, to become the largest industrial sector, representing close to 7 per cent of GDP.[16] Such externalities are largely limited to Kigali and may thus have contributed to widening the gap between rural and urban areas.

Finally, it should be noted that, over the years, Rwanda and Uganda have developed intricate business networks, relying on local traders and proxy rebel forces that allowed them to maintain control over the export of Congolese minerals without having to maintain a direct military presence in the country. To the date of writing, most of the mining concessions in Eastern Congo are being operated from Kigali and Kampala, even when they fall under Congolese ownership. Furthermore, the *comptoires* have long relied for credit and cash on Rwandan banks, which have used this power to extract additional profits by manipulating the exchange rate (Romkema and Vlassenroot 2002). Hence, even though the minerals are being exported from Congo, the profits still accrue largely to Rwanda and Uganda.

In 2007, mining still constituted the largest export sector for Rwanda, at $40 million per year, ahead of tourism, tea and coffee. Interestingly, this figure was still twice as high as the production value reported in the national accounts for the same year, while only 0.4 per cent of the labour force was reported as working in the mining sector in the EICV2.

10.5 Conclusion

In Rwanda, we have argued, the structural violence that underlay and permitted the emergence of an ideology of genocide has not disappeared, despite the end of open conflict. While geographic inequalities, which were the main source of HI before the war, have been reduced, there has been a massive increase in vertical (income) inequalities.

Due to the lack of data, it is very difficult to assess inequality between ethnic groups. However, we see that two trends give cause for concern. First, there has been a large increase in land inequality. Secondly, despite significant migratory flows towards the cities, the poverty gap between urban and rural areas has continued to grow and is now among the largest in the world. Since the rural/urban divide has tended to run along ethnic lines in Rwanda, there is a risk that such HIs could aggravate ethnic tensions in the long run.

Importantly, we found that the unparalleled increase in inequalities experienced by Rwanda in recent years could be linked to the war itself, as well as to Rwanda's military incursions into neighbouring Congo. Hence Rwanda has experienced a vicious circle in the past two decades, whereby rising inequalities contributed to creating the conditions that led to the war – which in turn aggravated inequalities, thus further straining the country's fragile social fabric. Achieving sustainable peace in Rwanda will thus depend, not only on the government's ability to maintain the current level of security, but also, more importantly, on its ability to break this cycle of structural violence at all levels – legal, political, economic and ethnic.

Notes

1. The evidence of a link between vertical inequality and conflict is inconclusive. For a long time the assumption of a link between inequality and conflict has been accepted almost as a matter of fact in the literature (see Gurr 1970; Moor 1966; Scott 1976; Wolf 1999). However, Grenier (1996) has argued that changes in inequality have little or no impact on conflict or on the end of conflict, whereas Collier and Hoeffler (1996) have found no link, or a negative link, between inequality and conflict.
2. In the WIID2 data set, the Gini coefficient for Rwanda in 1984 is described as covering only urban areas. However, in the Deininger and Squire (1996)

data set, the figure is reported as having national coverage. The same figure is used as a baseline for international comparisons in the EICV1 report (MINECOFIN 2002a).

3. The estimates represented in Figure 10.1, which is based on a combination of post-war surveys, show an increase in the top/bottom quintile ratio of 40 per cent between 2000 and 2006, compared to a 28 per cent increase between 1995 and 2000.
4. While the quality and quantity of data do not allow us to make significant statistical correlations, we have plotted GDP per capita trends, which shows the disconnection between GDP growth and income trends in all the quintiles except for the top one. This means that growth benefited almost exclusively the top 20 per cent of the population.
5. The importance of the land factor in the depletion of Rwanda's social capital in the years leading up to the genocide has been highlighted by the detailed study carried out by André and Platteau in the central region of Gitarama (André and Platteau 1998). The study showed that land-rich households had a higher probability of falling victim to murder compared to land-poor households and that, in the area studied, land ownership was a more important factor than ethnicity in determining who was targeted during the genocide.
6. On the concept of HI, see Stewart (1998, 2000).
7. According to the United Nations' Population Fund's (UNFPA) Socio-Demographic Survey (pp. 28–29), 42 per cent, in 1996, 42 per cent of Umutara's population was born abroad. As pointed out by Human Rights Watch, the actual percentage of returnees would have been even higher, since this figure does not account for returnees who were born in Rwanda (HRW 2001b).
8. Latest available internationally comparable poverty figures from the United Nations' Statistics Division MDG data set.
9. A passage from the infamous Kangura newspaper, which was used to spread the genocide ideology in the years leading up to the genocide, claimed that '85 per cent of the inhabitants of Kigali are Tutsi' (Kangura 1991 copied and translated from Chretien 1995: 145).
10. The EICV2 shows that 85 per cent of Kigali's population today is born outside of Kigali and that 40 per cent of the population has migrated there in the last 5 years.
11. Human Rights Watch (1999) 'has found evidence that certain extremist leaders circulated fake maps detailing which Hutu-owned lands would be expropriated' (quoted in Pottier 2006: 510).
12. In 1996, 17.4 per cent of Kigali's population was born outside of the country, compared to 5 per cent in the rest of the country, according to the 1996 Socio-Demographic Survey.
13. OECD-DAC, International Development Statistics.
14. The countries having experienced more than 1,000 combat deaths in any year since 1990 (Uppsala Conflict Data Program (UCDP) and International Peace Research Institute, Oslo (PRIO)'s Armed Conflict Dataset Version 4-2007). The countries included in this subset are Burundi, Central African Republic, Côte d'Ivoire, Djibouti, Guinea, Guinea-Bissau, Mozambique, Rwanda, Sierra Leone and Uganda.

15. The countries having received more than 20 per cent of GDP in aid since 1990 (World Development Indicators 2007, World Bank). The countries included in this category are Burundi, Guinea-Bissau, Malawi, Mozambique, Rwanda, Sierra Leone and Zambia.
16. Gross Domestic Product by Kind of Activity in 2001 prices (National Institute of Statistics of Rwanda).

11
A Dangerous Peace? Drugs, Post-Conflict State Building and Horizontal Inequalities in Afghanistan

Jonathan Goodhand, Christian Dennys and David Mansfield

11.1 Introduction

This chapter examines the complex interactions between protracted conflict, 'post-war' peacebuilding and horizontal inequalities (HIs). It focuses on the pathways and mechanisms through which the opium economy and internationally supported counter-narcotics (CN) policies have reconfigured HIs, particularly inter-group and spatial divisions. Our findings, perhaps counter-intuitively, suggest that the war years contributed to a rebalancing of power relationships by empowering borderland regions and minority groups. The illicit economy, whilst frequently seen as predatory and anti-developmental, played an important social protection role and had some developmental outcomes. Conversely, 'peace' – brought in in the wake of the US invasion – has been characterized by new regional power asymmetries and intensified inequalities. International development and CN policies may have inadvertently contributed to this state of affairs. Therefore there is a need to rethink the linkages between post-conflict peacebuilding, CN policies and HIs and to develop new policies accordingly.[1]

It should be noted that our conclusions require further testing and empirical research. Robust data that quantify inter- and intra-group inequalities in Afghanistan are not available. Perhaps more than in the other cases presented in this volume, there is a dearth of reliable micro- and macro-level data on Afghanistan – for example, even basic data on population size are contested. This can be attributed to several factors, including the historically limited capacity and outreach of the Afghan state, the lack of research during the war years and, more recently, the politicization of data in the post-conflict period. Often, where data do exist, they tend to aggregate data at the national, provincial or district level, on the basis of some notion of a 'representative sample' despite the absence of population data, rather than to explore the socio-economic diversity that exists within each of these administrative boundaries. As explored below, data are also frequently deployed and manipulated to support particular policy narratives and interventions, and nowhere is this more apparent than in the case of drugs and of the war on drugs.

11.2 Background: Horizontal inequalities in peace and war

The primary focus of this chapter is the post-2002 period, but some brief background on the pre-war period and the war years (1979–2001) is necessary in order to understand some of the defining features and changing dynamics of HIs in Afghanistan.

State formation and horizontal inequalities in pre-war Afghanistan

HIs in Afghanistan both are a product of, and helped shape, processes of state formation and development in the eighteenth and nineteenth centuries, and the faltering efforts of Afghan rulers in the twentieth century to build a modern state.

Arguably the primary and most enduring inequality in Afghanistan is the divide between countryside and bazaar, the rural and the urban. For most of the pre-state period, the territory of modern-day Afghanistan constituted a borderland or 'shatter zone' between competing empires. Conquerors passed over the mountainous regions occupied by autonomous tribes, since these could not easily be subdued or profitably administered (Barfield 2004). To this day, Pashtuns distinguish between the autonomous mountain tribes and the tax-paying tribes of the lowlands. Like many mountain societies, Afghanistan is characterized by extreme ethnic and linguistic diversity. This is not captured by the simplified demographic breakdown given in most government and aid donor documents: a Pashtun majority (40 per cent) and various minorities, including Tajiks (37 per cent), Hazaras (9 per cent), Uzbeks (9 per cent) and Turkmen (2 per cent) (Asia Foundation 2006).

These figures belie the contested, dynamic and porous boundaries between groups.[2] However, putting aside this caveat, the divide between Pashtuns and non-Pashtun minorities is a significant one that is recognized by most Afghans, as it maps onto a deep historic divide and an enduring power asymmetry. Ever since Ahmad Shah Durrani united the Pashtun tribes in 1748, the Afghan state has been dominated by Durrani Pashtuns and was never able to escape its tribal and Pashtun origins (Roy 1990). Pashtuns connected to the royal Muhammadzai family enjoyed particular privileges, and the power elite was primarily made up of individuals from this background.[3]

Afghan rulers largely relied upon external subsidies – first from the British and then from the US and Russia during the Cold War – in order to mobilize capital, coercion and legitimacy. This situation resulted in the emergence of an enclave or rentier state, with limited penetration of society. From 1930 until the 1970s, a conservative coalition composed of the Musahiban royal family, feudal landlords and the rural clergy (*ulema*) remained in power, effectively blocking processes of modernization and development. One indicator of this was the declining levels of taxation on land and agricultural production, in spite of their centrality to the Afghan economy (Rubin 1996). External subsidies provided a source of patronage, which enabled Afghan rulers to maintain a fragile political coalition. But in the face of growing contradictions within Afghan society, which were manifest in the growth of the Islamist and Communist movements, this coalition broke down. Both movements were largely elitist in make-up and orientation, and they were symptomatic of the growing frustration of a small urban middle class excluded from political power and economic opportunities. Therefore, group mobilization was ostensibly ideological rather than identity-based, but these ideological fault lines had strong class dimensions, and also masked a plethora of underlying social boundaries and conflicts (see Edwards 2002; Roy 1990; Rubin 1996).[4] The People's Democratic Party of Afghanistan (PDPA) regime's radical reform programme can be seen in some respects as an attempt to address vertical and HIs, which ultimately catalysed country-wide violent resistance.

The transformation of identities in wartime (1979–2001)

Localized resistance soon gave way to more organized political and military fronts, which mobilized around ethnic or regional identities. Some of these grew into more consolidated regional politico-military formations, described by Giustozzi (2009) as 'warlord polities'. Whilst few argue that the Afghan wars were ethnically driven, fighting became increasingly ethnically patterned, particularly after 1992, when the Soviet-supported Najibullah regime collapsed. Therefore, it is important to distinguish between identity as a *cause* and identity as a *result* of mobilization.[5]

Political entrepreneurs may have an acute understanding of ethnic and tribal boundaries. As Glatzer (1998: 180) notes, 'leaders of conflicts use ethnic and tribal emotions and the feelings of honour and shame connected with them as a tool or weapon as efficiently as a Stinger or Kalashnikov'. The combination of political mobilization, the refugee experience and the military prowess of the minorities meant that previously excluded groups such as the Hazaras, Uzbeks and Tajiks enjoyed new levels of power and autonomy and a heightened sense of group identity.

However, as already noted, ethnic boundaries are porous and compete with other forms of identity.[6] Whilst some political parties, such as Dawat-i-Islami or Hizb Wahdat (Khalili), were dominated by one ethnic group (Pashtun and Hazara, respectively), this was not always the case.[7] Furthermore, many of the conflicts generated as part of the resistance against the government had important class as well as ideological dimensions. This was perhaps most evident in the civil war in Hazarajat,[8] which re-calibrated power relations between the peasantry, clergy and landowners (Ibrahimi 2009a, 2009b), but more broadly the jihad marked a power shift in Afghan society with the ideologically driven *tanzims*, undermining the power base of the landed class represented by the traditionalist parties (cf Rubin 1996).

Therefore, what to outsiders often appeared to be a Manichean struggle between ideologically defined groups, in practice involved a welter of interconnected struggles with complex, cross-cutting and constantly mutating alliances (Barfield 2004). Hence there was no straightforward connection between identity groups, HIs and combatant mobilization, and intra-group and class-based boundaries were part of the complex story of boundary politics during the Afghan wars.

Conflict, spatial inequalities and the war economy

The emergence of regional politico-military formations after 1978, particularly after the collapse of the state in 1992, reversed the state building strategies of earlier rulers who had attempted to prevent regional power blocks from developing through administrative division.[9] The war years saw a re-calibration of centre–periphery relations in which borderlands were empowered politically and economically.

As Kabul declined as a political and economic centre in the 1990s, Afghanistan's borderlands became increasingly important. Regional power centres emerged, funded by neighbouring powers and tied into provincial and cross-border economies. Provincial cities, often linked to an urban centre across the border, played a catalytic role in stimulating trade and investment – examples include Jalalabad–Peshawar, Kandahar–Quetta and Herat–Mashhad. In many respects this reversed pre-war relationships and resource flows, the centre depending increasingly on the periphery. This mirrors the processes that Janet Roitman describes in the Chad Basin, where 'the urban economy is now in many ways dependent on commercial, financial and monetary activities taking place in the hinterland and especially along international borders' (Roitman 2003: 229).

As the peripheries became stronger, Afghanistan in many respects reverted to its pre-state status of a frontier zone with open borders crossed by trade routes and military–religious networks. Essentially the country became a marketing corridor for smuggling and contraband, and part of an extremely dynamic regional conflict system that linked conflicts in Kashmir, Baluchistan, FATA, Helmand, the Ferghana Valley and as far afield as Chechnya (Goodhand 2004). Therefore, HIs at a regional level became an increasingly important part of the dynamics driving the war economy. Spatial inequalities (especially between Pakistan and Afghanistan) and different regulatory regimes across borders provided the impetus for a thriving smuggling economy. Groups located on the border exploited their ability to straddle between, and connect, different regulatory authorities – for instance, the Pashtun smuggling mafia grew in importance both as an economic and as a political player and was instrumental in the emergence of the Taliban in the mid-1990s.

It is beyond the scope of this chapter to provide any in-depth analysis of the emergence of the opium economy,[10] but its growth was facilitated by Central Intelligence Agency/Inter-Services Intelligence (CIA/ISI) funding to the *mujihadeen*, which provided the start-up capital for commanders to invest in the opium trade. Its expansion and consolidation in the 1990s were related to several factors, including the decline of great power support for the war effort and the consequent need for commanders to generate funding locally; the success of CN policies in Pakistan, which led to cultivation and processing becoming increasingly centred on Afghanistan; the emergence of the Taliban, who brought increased security, which in combination with their treatment of opium as a licit commodity encouraged the consolidation and expansion of the industry.

Research in other contexts highlights the potential for war to provide an enabling environment for development by boosting surplus appropriation and capital accumulation (Cramer 2006). In Afghanistan, the growth of the opium economy has been an important factor in rural socio-economic change, as explored further below.

11.3 Political horizontal inequalities and Afghanistan's war to peace transition

The Bonn Agreement of December 2001 was supposed to lay out the provisions for the emergence of legitimate political authority in Afghanistan. However, rather than constituting a 'grand bargain' for peace, Bonn can best be understood as an elite pact involving those factions who fell on the 'right side' of the war on terror (Goodhand and Sedra 2007). It failed to address underlying power uncertainties and, most importantly, it did not provide sufficient political representation for Pashtuns, or address the security concerns of Pakistan.

A 'light footprint' was advocated by the UN Special Representative to the Secretary General (SRSG) Brahimi, local ownership being invoked as a defensive measure, which reflected concerns about neo-imperialism and the minimalist agenda of the US and its allies in pursuing the war on terror (Goodhand and Sedra 2009). The resulting strategy involved incorporating military strongmen into the new political settlement – a process described by Rubin (2006) as one of 'warlord democratisation'. Ministries were treated as positional goods by the factions, leading for instance to the wholesale incorporation of military groups into the police force. The key power ministries, including defence and the ministry of interior, were dominated by northern Tajiks.

The new political dispensation reflected power shifts that had occurred during the Afghan wars, as mentioned earlier, in which minorities, particularly northerners from the United Front, had become more organized and assertive. To a certain extent these gains were reflected in the new constitution, which protected minority rights, particularly with regard to language and religion. But at the same time, on paper, Afghanistan has one of the most centralized constitutions in the world, in a context in which *de facto* power relations are highly fragmented. This inevitably set up new tensions between centre and periphery.

It also increased inter-group tensions, since the minorities favoured a more decentralized parliamentary system whilst the Pashtuns favoured a centralized presidential system (Suhrke 2009).

Over time, the insurgency became more organized and spread geographically, knitting together diverse groups around an Islamic discourse that targeted foreign occupation and government corruption (Giustozzi 2007).

Transition from war economy to peace economy?

Protracted conflict and successive regimes in a context of poor infrastructure and porous borders have transformed the Afghan political economy. Economic institutions and markets have adapted, over the years, to a high risk and (for some) high opportunity environment. The bulk of economic activity (80–90 per cent) has been informal, decentralized and fragmented; even the drug economy, which is the nearest thing to a national sector, is in effect many drug *economies* with significant price differences between regions. The formal taxable sector remains less than 10 per cent of the gross domestic product (GDP) (World Bank 2005), and, as Table 11.1 shows, fiscal management has been a long-standing deficiency of the Afghan state. In a context where the state represents particularist interests, and in the absence of a fiscal contract that binds the population to the state, there may be a greater risk of HIs becoming more contentious and conflictual.

Real non drug-related growth averaged more than 15 per cent p.a. from 2002 to 2006 but dropped to 6.1 per cent in 2006–2007 and to 3 per cent in 2008/2009 because of increased petroleum and food prices and a renewed drought. This sheds doubt on the ability of the Afghan government to meet its annual economic growth target of 8 per cent. Structurally there are indicators of enduring fragility in the Afghan economy. Growth of output has been driven especially by construction projects linked to donor activities and by private consumption, rather than by a sustained expansion in sectors likely to support long-run growth (agriculture, mining and manufacturing).

The war economy exerted a strong centrifugal force on the Afghan political economy (Goodhand 2004; Rubin 2000), which presently works against the centripetal thrust of post-Bonn state building. There remains a strong constituency in the provinces hostile to the strengthening of the government (Byrd 2007). During the war years, local power holders in the borderlands were able to generate significant revenues by collecting import taxes at the border. Post-Bonn state building has involved repeated tussles between central state and peripheral elites over

Table 11.1 Fiscal limitations of the Afghan state

Year	Domestic revenue as share of GDP (%)	Government expenditure as share of GDP (%)
1935	6	6
1940	7	10
1945	3	3
1950	3	4
1955	5	5
1960	7	9
1965	6	7
1970	7	8
2002/03	3.2	...
2003/04	4.7	14.5
2004/05	5.0	15.3
2005/06	6.4	16.6
2006/07	6.0	21.5 (est.)
2007/08	6.6	8.0 (est. 6 months)

Sources: Giustozzi (2008, citing Fry 1974); World Bank (2005), IMF Statistical Appendix (February 2008).

the control of tax revenues from cross-border trade, which constitutes the largest source of state revenue, particularly the lucrative crossing points with Iran.[11]

The bulk of agriculture (which accounts for more than a quarter of total output, though some three-quarters of the population are employed in the sector) is rain fed and poorly supported by transport, irrigation and electricity infrastructure. Agricultural output remains weak and vulnerable to fluctuations. Nationwide poverty assessments indicate growing levels of poverty; in 2007, 42 per cent of the population were estimated to be below the poverty line, up from 33 per cent in 2005 (Azerbaijani et al. 2008).[12] Poverty is more prevalent in rural areas compared to urban areas, particularly in peripheral, mountainous regions (Azerbaijani et al. 2008).

Aid, development and horizontal inequalities

A series of donor conferences in Tokyo, Berlin, London and Paris were relatively successful in mobilizing international contributions to reconstruction in Afghanistan. Official overseas development assistance (ODA) by Organisation for Economic Cooperation and Development (OECD) members more than doubled between 2002–2006, going from $1.3 billion to just under $3 billion. This brings the total since 2002 to almost $11 billion. Aid flows amount to more than 50 per cent of Afghanistan's GDP.

The Afghan government's development vision was articulated in a succession of key policy documents, which have emphasized economic and public financial management reforms, private sector-led growth, infrastructural development and poverty reduction. However, an estimated 40 per cent of all aid to Afghanistan goes back to donor countries in corporate profits and consultancy salaries[13] – a total of some United States dollars (USD) 6 billion from 2001 to 2007 (Waldman 2008: 10). Furthermore, many donors give their aid off-budget, and in 2005 less than 30 per cent of all expenditures were channelled through the Afghan government's budget (Rubin 2006: 182). Off-budget funding has led to the emergence of a dual public sector – an internal public sector that the government manages and an external public sector that donors fund and manage. At the same time, the government lacks the capacity to absorb large inflows of aid, which run the danger of recreating an aid-dependent, rentier state, with the attendant problems of distorted accountability relations, corruption, Dutch disease and conflict over the control of aid resources. These problems are becoming increasingly visible, being accentuated by a Kabul-based bubble economy that has inflated land and commodity prices and rental markets, increased the basic cost of living and dollarized the economy. Therefore, aid is concentrated in and around the capital, or provincial capitals. As shown in Table 11.2, per capita aid spending in Kabul amounts to over $600 per person, falling to $50 per person in Wardak province; and within provinces there are extreme disparities, as explored below. The distribution of aid initially reflected prevailing post-Bonn power relations – over 70 per cent of higher government positions were held by non Pashtuns – assistance being largely channelled to the north through the politico-military networks of the United Front. The absence of a tangible peace dividend in rural areas, particularly in the south, intensified anti-government feelings, which fed into the insurgency. Increasingly, assistance was channelled to the south in the form of 'quick impact projects', in the belief that aid could win the 'hearts and minds' of the Pashtun population. However, there is no evidence that poorly conceived aid projects have had any positive effects on security, governance and faith in the government in the south (Fishstein 2010; Goodhand and Sedra 2010; Gordon 2007, 2011; Jackson and).

Table 11.2 Per capita spending per province of planned and committed aid (2007/2008, US $)

Province	**US$**
Kabul	606
Nimroz*	458
Helmand*	403
Zabul*	266
Farah*	250
Jawzjan	250
Kandahar*	227
Uruzgan*	207
Paktika	189
Parwan	174
Bamyan	158
Balkh	153
Paktiya	144
Badakhshan	142
Panjsher	136
Khost	132
Nuristan	122
Nangharhar	121
Laghman	120
Samangan	112

Table 11.2 (Continued)

Province	US$
Badghis	106
Herat	87
Kunar	83
Dai Kundi	79
Kapisa	78
Faryab	78
Baghlan	72
Takhar	63
Ghazni	62
Logar	55
Sari Pul	53
Ghor	51
Wardak	50

Note: * denotes southern provinces.
Source: Adapted from IWA (2008) and Waldman (2008).

11.4 An overview of the drugs economy and counter-narcotics instruments in Afghanistan

A resurgent opium economy

Afghanistan's emergence as the global leader in opium production was based upon a 'triple comparative advantage' of favourable physical, political and economic conditions: a cultivation environment that produces opium poppies with a high morphine content; chronic insecurity and institutional weakness, which have meant inadequate or non-existent forms of regulation; and poor infrastructure and rural poverty, which prevent the development of viable licit livelihoods. Over the years, Afghans have developed the know-how, expertise and market connections to build upon these comparative advantages in order to survive, accumulate or wage war (Goodhand 2008).

For a brief period, Afghanistan lost its position as the primary producer of opium after the Taliban ban for the growing season of

2000/2001. However, following US-led military intervention in October 2001 and the apparent collapse of the Taliban, there was a massive increase in the volume and geographic spread of poppy cultivation in Afghanistan. Several macro-level and micro-level factors contributed to this: first, the Taliban's edict against the production of opium led to a ten-fold increase in farm gate opium prices, whilst pushing rural households into further indebtedness. Second, with the fall of the Taliban and the absence of a strong authority in the countryside, farmers felt free once more to plant their fields – and there were even reports that the Taliban had sanctioned a return to cultivation prior to their collapse in November 2001. Third, international coalition forces initially did not prioritize suppression of the opium industry, possibly because of fears of compromising their relationships with allies in the war on terror, some of whom were deeply involved in the industry, but also due to concerns that a concerted attempt to reduce cultivation would alienate the rural population (Fellab-Brown 2005). Fourth, internationally supported state building had a range of paradoxical effects, which arguably sustained the opium rebound – for example, the criminalization of opium (to all intents and purposes it was a licit crop during the Taliban period) had the twin effects of keeping prices high, whilst those involved had to look for non-state or state protectors against CN programmes. Finally, CN policies often had perverse effects. For example, a buyout scheme in the 2001/2002 growing season, which provided compensation of $350 per jerib of poppy destroyed, paradoxically created incentives for farmers to grow poppy in the northeast, where the crop was planted in the agricultural year.

By 2005, poppy cultivation had spread to all 34 provinces, including regions with no previous tradition or expertise in poppy cultivation. According to the United Nations Office on Drugs and Crime (UNODC) (2007) figures, opium cultivation rose from 165,000 ha in 2006 to 193,000 ha in 2007 – this was after a 59 per cent increase between 2005 and 2006.[14] National production grew from 6,500 tons to 8,200 tons. In 2008, there was a 19 per cent decrease in the area of cultivation, but good yields meant that total production decreased by a modest 6 per cent, with total output an estimated 7,700 metric tonnes. The latest 2009 UNODC report shows a 22 per cent decrease in cultivation and a 10 per cent decrease in production.

However, national figures mask considerable fluctuations in cultivation over time and diversity amongst provinces (Mansfield 2006: 49).[15] Currently cultivation is concentrated in the south, 70 per cent of production being located in the five provinces bordering Pakistan. Helmand was responsible for 50 per cent of the entire opium crop in Afghanistan in 2007/2008 and produced more narcotics than any other country, but 2008/2009 cultivation declined by a third. In the north and centre poppy cultivation has diminished, and the number of poppy-free provinces more than doubled, from 6 to 13 in 2006, and by 2009 had further increased to 20.[16] The fact that some provinces are now poppy free and others have achieved sharp declines does not mean that these effects are sustainable, or that drug trafficking has ended in these areas. As Mansfield and Pain (2008) argue, these changes are more to do with shifts in political arrangements, security regimes and terms of trade than with effective CN policies, and they are vulnerable to sudden reversals when conditions change.

The vast bulk of value added in the drug industry is generated outside Afghanistan (Jonglez and Byrd 2006: 130). In 2006, the export value of drugs was $3.1 billion, compared to $2.7 billion in 2005. UNODC (2006) estimates that 76 per cent of the income from narcotics goes to traffickers and heroin refiners (most of which accrued to a limited number of bulk buyers and large-scale specialist traders) and 24 per cent goes to farmers. In order to reduce risks, a significant part of revenue is spent on payments to 'security providers' and government officials. As Giustozzi (2007: 79) argues, for political entrepreneurs the drug economy is a vehicle for accumulating power. Narcotic interests have permeated parliament and other central state organizations, while in some regions they also help to finance the strengthening insurgency (though opium is not the primary source of funding for insurgents).[17] The police force was described in one report as a 'shop for selling jobs', and it has been estimated by some Afghan officials that up to 80 per cent of the personnel in the Ministry of Interior benefit from the drugs trade (Wilder 2007). This assemblage of actors, networks and institutions, like the opium economy itself, is extremely footloose and flexible, and patterns of capture and corruption can shift across ministries and other institutions in order to evade regulatory mechanisms (Byrd and Buddenburg 2006: 6). Whilst there is little evidence to indicate the emergence of a hierarchically controlled, cartelized drug economy, a UNODC/World Bank study reports growing market integration, Helmand and Kandahar becoming centres of gravity that influence prices in other markets (Byrd and Jonglez 2006).

The Afghan opium economy has a number of important impacts on the broader economy. Opium provides a large amount of liquidity in many provinces, through money dealers called Hawaladar, who act as 'the linchpin at the intersection of "licit" and "illicit" transactions' (Thompson 2006). The Hawaladar have links with official banks, aid agencies, warlords and smugglers and, whilst they have facilitated money laundering, they have also been integral to processes of early development and are vital to the delivery of funds to the provinces (Maimbo 2003). Opium has been a driver of rural transformation, away from subsistence farming towards commercialized, export-oriented agriculture (Goodhand 2008; Rubin and Sherman 2008) and the expansion of labour force participation (including, to a limited extent, female employment). Further, commercialization has accelerated socio-economic differentiation, inequality and structural change in rural Afghanistan. Opium-related capital is therefore shaping economic opportunity, as well as strengthening networks – many of which are across national boundaries.

In October 2002, the Afghan government established the Counter-Narcotics Directorate (CND), which reported to the National Security Council. CND was responsible for CN strategy development and coordination. It was supported by the UK government, the lead nation for CN, which was one of five pillars in the Security Sector Reform (SSR) strategy. Two trends can be detected in CN efforts. First, there has been a broadening of the CN agenda, greater focus being placed on institution building and 'mainstreaming' CN, so that all areas of intervention are 'drug sensitive'. Therefore eradication – the physical elimination of the crop – is viewed as only one out of multiple CN instruments, including prohibition, building a CN infrastructure (such as a separate ministry of CN and special courts), developing alternative livelihoods programmes and the introduction of a CN trust fund, including good performance funds for provinces that achieve drops in production. Second, US involvement in CN policies, as a funder and instigator, has increased, largely due to concerns that narcotics have been a primary source of funding for the Taliban and to the belief that a rapid reduction of drugs production would bankrupt the insurgency. On this basis – as well as on a strong belief in crop destruction amongst some parts of the US administration – there was a push for a more coercive eradication-led strategy. Whilst under the Bush administration the focus had been on eradication, the Obama administration has shifted the emphasis to targeting so-called 'drugs kingpins' and trafficking networks. In order to combat corruption and improve intelligence gathering on opium networks, the United States assembled a new intelligence cell at Bagram air base, led by Drug Enforcement Administration operatives. Furthermore, the US compiled a 'kill or capture' target list of 367 named individuals, including 50 so-called 'nexus targets' with links both to drugs trafficking and to the insurgency.

11.5 The effects of drugs and counter-narcotics policies on state building, development and horizontal inequalities

Drugs, conflict and statebuilding

It has become received wisdom amongst policy makers that illegal drugs are both a symptom and a driver of state fragility. UNODC, for instance, has consistently argued that there are specific linkages between drugs and insecurity (see UNODC 2007, 2008a). Broadly, it is assumed that the existence of lootable resources such as drugs places critical limits on the state's ability to mobilize coercion, capital and legitimacy. First, they undermine the state's capacity to centralize the means of coercion; the drug economy, it is argued, provides the tax base for the insurgency, whilst also enabling other non-state military actors to maintain their autonomy and to fund their private militias. Second, drugs as a diffuse, illegal, high-value and easily transportable commodity are inherently difficult for state actors to control and tax – and, at around 40 per cent of GDP, drug revenues represent a significant revenue stream that is not officially taxed by the state. Third, the increased involvement of state actors and consequently the perceived corruption of the government have arguably played a role in delegitimizing the Karzai regime, particularly in the south, which in turn feeds the insurgency. As explored below, corrupt, unevenly implemented CN policies have tended to punish the poor and politically unconnected and have provided the Taliban with the opportunity to generate political capital by acting as the protectors of the peasantry. Further, it is agued that there is growing evidence of collusion and collaboration between corrupt government officials, drugs traffickers and elements within the Taliban, who all profit from the drugs–insecurity nexus.

However, this influential policy narrative, which associates lootable resources such as drugs with insurgency, warlordism and state collapse, simplifies a far more complex reality, particularly at the sub-national level. The debate about how much the drug economy supports the insurgency (or the other way round) is important, but tells us little about the specific linkages between violence and drugs. The current conflict, as with earlier phases of the Afghan wars, involves a complex welter of interconnected disputes, and drugs interact with the dynamics of violence in different ways in different parts of the country. For instance, Koehler and Zuercher (2007), in their research on drugs and conflict in the eastern provinces of Laghman and Nangahar, found that the opium economy has a conflict-*dampening* role, as 79 per cent of respondents stated that money, largely derived from drugs, was the most important factor in addressing disputes (followed by patronage and physical force). Furthermore, research in the north and north-east suggests that new forms of political order have emerged in the post-Taliban period, which is reflected in changing patterns of violence (Goodhand 2009).[18] Therefore, in some parts of the country – notably those that gained from the post-Bonn political dispensation – new interdependencies have emerged between centre and periphery, which are based upon joint control of the rents generated by drugs. As already noted, in many respects the drugs economy has played a role in ameliorating HIs. The drugs trade involves multi-sited and heterogeneous cross-border networks, which tend to be far more eclectic than politico-military structures – from an ethnic, religious, political party or socio-professional perspective. Although kinship is an important source of trust in a non-legal business environment, market principles require that crime networks reach beyond these narrow means of securing and enforcing trust. These networks are successful because they establish weak ties, which cross political and ethnic cleavages (Goodhand 2009). As argued below, state-led and internationally supported CN policies have the opposite effect; they inadvertently undermine emergent political orders and reinforce economic and political exclusion, generating antagonisms that follow geographic and identity-based fault lines.

International intervention, counter-narcotics and political exclusion

There is a growing realization that the international focus on CN has been ineffective not only on its own terms, but also in relation to broader state building and developmental goals. Programmes implemented to tackle drugs have not adequately taken into consideration other policy goals and measures, and they have largely been *ad hoc* and fragmented (Goodhand 2008; Rubin and Sherman 2008). CN policies are seen by many Afghans as part of a 'Western crusade' that disproportionately focuses on production, punishing poor farmers who have no alternative means of survival, whilst doing little to address the problem of demand in Western countries. Too close an association with CN policies may undermine the legitimacy of Afghan leaders. This dual legitimacy problem is a long-standing one for Afghan elites, who have found that too close an association with external backers in general has left them vulnerable to domestic legitimacy crises.

The CN infrastructure involves a complex assemblage of military and paramilitary organizations, and there has been an increased securitization of CN – with the setting up of paramilitary forces working at the sharp end of eradication and interdiction operations. Paradoxically, attempts to implement CN policies (including eradication) can also present new opportunities for corruption and for the consolidation of drug networks rather than their dispersal. Regular changes in police forces at the border present new threats, but also new opportunities to bring in compliant officials who effectively franchise out monopolies to agents on the border (Goodhand 2009).

Eradication efforts have undermined political support for the regime, particularly in the south, where CN measures are perceived as being implemented in a biased form against those outside and/or antithetical to the regime, and hence with the least political voice. Therefore, CN initiatives in the south have been seen as anti-Pashtun, in Helmand eradication is perceived to be targeted against less powerful tribes, such as the Naquil, and in Kandahar as being targeted against non-Barakzai and Popalzai. Therefore, eradication and poppy reduction efforts reflect and reinforce existing power relations and, as explored in the case study below, whether poppy is grown or whether it is eradicated is never the result of a simple economic cost–benefit analysis, but the product of complex *political* negotiations involving state and non-state actors. Those with access to capital, political networks and the means of coercion are able to buy immunity from eradication – whereas those lacking political, social or financial capital are the most vulnerable. Furthermore, the utilization of CN policies in order to undermine competitors is not just about inter-regional conflict and competition, but also about intra-regional and intra-ethnic or tribal group divisions.

Significant declines in poppy cultivation, rather than being a once-and-for-all measure, may be understood as part of an ongoing bargaining game between the central state and peripheral elites. In Nangarhar and Balkh, for instance, provincial governors have cleverly exploited their success in poppy elimination or reduction in order to extract resources and buy greater political autonomy from the centre. They in turn have negotiated with, bought off or coerced district-level elites to enforce opium bans. These negotiations are inevitably influenced by and, in turn, impact upon HIs – favoured groups or regions are better able to buy time, extract concessions in the form of alternative development projects and so on. CN institutions are themselves deeply embedded in tribal and ethnic networks, so it is unsurprising that their programmes reflect and reinforce existing power asymmetries between regions and groups.

CN policies may push low-income groups and the politically excluded into a closer relationship with the armed resistance. Indeed the way in which participants in the resistance see the potential for the Taliban and Hizb-i-Islami to contain the corruption of the government is a part of this story (Ladbury 2009). These core–periphery dynamics around CN policies are briefly explored below, by drawing on research conducted in Nangarhar.

Nangarhar case study

Nangahar province in Eastern Afghanistan has seen some of the biggest fluctuations in opium production since the fall of the Taliban, which can only be understood by looking at the complex negotiations over CN policies that occurred between international actors, central state elites, peripheral elites and the local population.[19] These negotiations were shaped by, and in turn had significant impacts upon, horizontal and vertical inequalities. They were also influenced by the wider regional environment, notably by shifts in regulatory and security regimes in Pakistan.

Prior to and during the Taliban regime, farmers in the province typically cultivated an estimated 15,000 to 20,000 hectares of opium poppy per year, making it one of the most significant opium producers after Helmand. This was briefly interrupted as a result of the Taliban ban of 2000/2001, but the following year poppy cultivation returned to an estimated 19,780 hectares and continued to rise until 2003/2004, reaching an unprecedented 28,213 hectares. However, in 2005, following an opium ban enforced by the then governor, Haji Din Mohammed, cultivation levels fell to 1,093 hectares – a 96 per cent reduction. As with the Taliban prohibition, a critical role was played by government recognized tribal elders, or Maliks, in key districts such as Achin and Khogiani. The Maliks are largely from influential land-owning families, as well as commanders who had acquired power and influence during the jihad. They act as intermediaries and gatekeepers between the state and the local population, mediating disputes, channelling patronage and providing privileged access to state resources such as development assistance.

In 2004, in November, the planting season for opium in the eastern region, the Maliks informed the population that cultivation was banned. By not cultivating opium poppy themselves, the Maliks signalled to others that the chances of eradication were high. To reinforce this message, strategic eradication efforts were conducted at an early stage in the cropping season – so timed as to deter the population in more accessible, low-lying areas from planting.

As with the pervious ban, peripheral elites drew upon the political capital and the threat of violence from authorities outside the province. In the case of the Taliban prohibition, it was the religious authority of Mullah Omar and the threat of violence that accompanied negotiations with key tribal groups, such as in the Shinwari. In the 2004/2005 growing season, Governor Haji Din Mohammed derived his authority not only from President Karzai's declaration of 'a jihad' against opium but also from the fact that many of the tribal elders in Nangarhar had solicited support for Karzai during the presidential election campaign, and to act against the president so soon after inauguration was regarded as unacceptable. Governor Haji Din Mohammed, district administrators and police commanders were all reportedly threatened with dismissal if they failed to enforce the ban.

Following the successful implementation of the ban in 2005, cultivation increased in 2005/2006 and then rebounded significantly in 2007, prompting further bans in the 2007/2008 and 2008/2009 growing seasons under the governorship of Gul Aga Shirzai. Reflecting changed political and military dynamics, the governor had to deploy different tactics from those of his predecessor in order to enforce the ban. Because of the growing legitimacy crisis of the Karzai regime, Gul Aga Shirzai depended more heavily on his relationship with the United States, combining the stick of threatened military reprisals with the carrot of promised development assistance. To some extent this worked in districts close to the provincial capital of Jalalabad, which received high levels of development assistance. But in outlying rural communities the absence of tangible support led to growing hostility towards Shirzai and the Afghan government.

By May 2009, two consecutive years of negligible levels of opium poppy cultivation had imposed a significant economic cost on much of the rural population, in all but the most accessible districts that are adjacent to Jalalabad. With few economic alternatives to opium poppy within the province and with growing insecurity and crime both in the southern provinces and in Peshawar in Pakistan – both, traditional sources of off farm and non-farm income – there was a significant rise in the number of households sending their sons to fight in the south for the Afghan National Army (ANA). Far from being a sign of support for the Karzai government in its efforts to quell the insurgency in the south, the increase in enrolment in the ANA was viewed by the population of these areas as a form of conscription by default.

Reactions to the deteriorating economic situation largely focused on the role of the Maliks, who were instrumental in the enforcement of the ban. The Maliks were accused of being 'the spies of the government', receiving payment for their role in the opium poppy ban and monopolizing the benefits of increased development aid. The governor himself was also accused of imposing a ban in order to win favour from the US government should he seek to run in the August presidential elections, something he eventually chose not to do. In October 2009, in the face of collective statements by the Khogiani tribe that they would return to opium poppy cultivation in the 2009/2010 growing season, the governor remained non-committal on the continuation of the ban into the 2009/2010 growing season and was seen to be buying time waiting for news of his anticipated promotion out of Nangarhar and appointment as minister in the forthcoming government. Furthermore, anti-government elements (AGEs) appeared to be residing in several districts of the province rather than engaging in cross-border incursions from Pakistan, as had been the case the previous year, whilst also offering protection against eradication to farmers in the outlying, upper parts of districts such as Achin, Deh Bala, Durbaba and Khogiani in the 2008/2009 growing season. There were also reports of AGEs taxing shopkeepers and traders in these areas.

Whilst reliable data on the drugs trade in Nangarhar are limited, it is clear that gaining a foothold in the trade is increasingly difficult for individuals without links to power holders in the provincial security and administrative system. During the Taliban period specific tribal groups, particularly the Shinwari, dominated the opium trade in Nangarhar, largely because of the concentration of both opium production and key opium bazaars in Loya Shinwar, and because of the tribe's presence on both sides of the Afghanistan–Pakistan border. By 2009, it was common practice for local residents to accuse their district administrator and head of district police of involvement in the drugs trade, in addition to members of parliament (MPs) from the province and former 'warlords' who had been given government appointments. Drugs traders reportedly pay large sums of money to individuals in the provincial and national authorities to facilitate the movement of drugs, or for the release of traffickers after they have been arrested.[20] The perception that state authorities are either directly or indirectly involved in the drugs trade in the province has further fuelled resentment towards counter-narcotics efforts that are aimed at farmers. In particular, eradication and the arrest of farmers cultivating poppy by the very same local officials who were believed to be the most heavily involved in trafficking were seen as evidence of an inequitable law enforcement campaign, which targeted the poor and pardoned the wealthy.

Drugs, counter-narcotics and development

Closely linked to the policy narrative of drugs and political disorder is the idea that the opium economy is anti-developmental – it constitutes a brake on taxation and investment, induces capital flight and undermines other productive, value adding activities. This, again, is an oversimplification, and one can identify a number of positive (though ambiguous) developmental impacts of the drugs economy.

Whilst much of the accumulated proceeds from the drug economy is invested outside the country, in drug-producing and trafficking areas there are visible signs of inward investment, and there has been a recycling of money into licit businesses. This includes the post-Bonn construction boom, which has been funded by a combination of drug money and development investments in infrastructure.

The opium economy has produced significant increases in rural wages and income and is an important source of credit for poor rural households; besides, the opium harvest in high producing areas attracts a significant number of labourers. Opium profits fuel consumption of domestic products and support imports of high-value goods (Thompson 2006). According to Buddenberg and Byrd (2006), the opium economy has had a stabilizing effect on the currency by having a significant net positive impact on Afghanistan's balance of payments. Further, the drug economy also provides a significant amount of finance and liquidity for the rest of the economy. This is particularly important in Badakhshan, where at certain times of the year up to 100 per cent of the liquidity in the financial transfer market governed by the hawaladars is believed to derive from payments for opium (Thompson 2006: 156).

CN policies may have perverse effects, both in terms of countering drugs production and on wider state building and developmental goals. As well as potentially pushing some groups into resistance, other state building processes such as the disarmament process can open up new opportunities in the drug economy. Disarmament Demobilization and Reintegration (DDR) programmes had the effect of pushing mid-level commanders, who lacked political or economic connections, into a closer relationship with the opium economy as a means of providing for their families and of restoring their social position, which was lost due to the formal disarmament process (Shaw 2006).[21] CN policies may inadvertently have the effect of intensifying vertical inequalities. For example, 'successful' eradication boosts farm gate prices, thus leading to a substantial shift in profits, from poor farmers to already wealthy traffickers. As detailed in the case study above, sharp drops in poppy cultivation lead to growing rural indebtedness, distressed sale of assets and urban migration within Afghanistan and the wider region. They also tend to intensify spatial inequalities, since communities living close to urban centres and markets are better able to adapt and find viable licit livelihoods than those living in marginal, remote environments.

It appears to be untenable for a weak, aid-dependent state, challenged by an intensifying insurgency, to transform the structure of the economy alongside the poor delivery of 'alternative livelihoods' projects, which offer little, in terms of sustainable market-based incomes, that might displace the illegal economy. In the absence of alternative sources of higher value added production, opium production has been a valued source of income for farmers and rural workers, as well as providing important access to land (through sharecropping arrangements) and to credit; and with processing capacities within the country allowing for a greater proportion of the value chain to be captured in country, it appears that the opium economy will continue as an important driver of economic and political relations for many years to come.

11.6 Conclusions

In conclusion, protracted conflict and the emergence of a war economy, of which opium was a significant part, have played a role in re-configuring horizontal and vertical inequalities. The war years have seen the growing assertiveness of minorities, the re-calibration of power relations between centre and periphery and the growing importance of the drug economy, which has dissolved or reconfigured inter-group boundaries, providing a means of social protection to vulnerable groups and bringing new wealth and investment to hitherto marginal regions.

The 'peace' which emerged following the Bonn Agreement appears to have had mixed effects on vertical and HIs. First, the Bonn agreement did not represent an inclusive 'grand bargain' for peace, but an exclusive elite pact. The new, externally imposed political coalition failed to reflect *de facto* power relations inside Afghanistan and the wider region – by marginalizing Pashtuns and the interests of Pakistan – and this led to growing inter- and intra-group tensions over time. The political settlement therefore reconstituted power relations between the historically dominant southern Pashtuns and the subordinate minorities from northern and central Afghanistan. The latter sought to lock in the new benefits of power by controlling key governmental positions and by monopolizing the rents accrued through the licit and illicit economies. This exclusive elite pact was highly unstable, as Pashtuns retained the capacity violently to contest the new political dispensation.

Furthermore, the perceived legitimacy of this minority-led coalition was weakened by its dependence upon foreign forces. Second, an overly centralized, top-down approach to state building exacerbated long-standing core–periphery and urban–rural conflicts. These were shown in several policy arenas, including DDR, public sector reform and reconstruction programmes in which central state and peripheral elites competed, often violently, over the control of valued resources. Third, the contradictory aims of international players – who attempted to simultaneously pursue the war on terror and war on drugs, reinvent the NATO alliance, stabilize and democratize the Afghan state and bring about broad-based development – led to fragmented policies, which exacerbated inter- and intra-group tensions and were easily co-opted and instrumentalized by domestic elites. Fourth, unbalanced international aid and government spending accentuated spatial inequalities, particularly north/south divisions, but also inter- and intra-provincial differences. Ultimately the war on terror trumped other policy goals. Increasingly, regional funding patterns were shaped by the logic of counter-insurgency operations, which were blind to HIs and undermined the goals of development programmes such as the National Solidarity Programme, which sought to build stable interdependencies across identity groups and integrate peripheral regions. Fifth, CN efforts accentuated these divisions and inequalities by focusing on those with the least political voice or economic leverage. An initial focus on eradication measures, particularly in the south, was perceived as anti-Pashtun, especially given the growing involvement of state actors in the drug economy. These policies contributed to growing horizontal (particularly spatial) inequalities and increased vertical inequalities, as CN efforts paradoxically increased the profits of the powerful and pushed those with the least assets further into destitution.

These conclusions lead to a number of broad policy implications:

- An inclusive political settlement, or broad-based coalition, which co-opts key politico-military elites, is a necessary precondition for peace consolidation. This may represent a rather limited, and indeed illiberal version of peace – involving pragmatic alliances and an elite division of the 'spoils of peace' – but the limitations of a narrow elite pact, combined with ambitious goals of liberal transformation, are amply illustrated in Afghanistan.
- Efforts to transform war economies into peace economies by criminalizing the former may impede the emergence of the latter. Illicit economic activities may provide an important source of protection

for the population and of accumulation for politico-military elites, out of which new political orders may emerge. CN policies and programmes, in the context of an escalating insurgency and of a weak state, have inadvertently undermined higher order policy goals, showing that peacebuilding and the war on drugs are by no means mutually reinforcing. This may mean de-prioritizing CN and addressing the issue indirectly, by tackling first order questions to do with security and governance.

– Policy makers need to be more sensitive to the ways in which their interventions may harden, accentuate or reconfigure HIs – peacebuilding efforts that fail to build broad-based growth, intensify inter-group and core–periphery conflicts and do not address inequalities within a wider regional context are based upon shaky foundations. Although HIs provide a useful conceptual lens for exploring the dynamics of drugs, war and post-conflict reconstruction, this also needs to be complemented with an appreciation of intra-group and class (vertical) divisions.

Notes

1. This chapter is based upon empirical research conducted over several years in Afghanistan by David Mansfield, Jonathan Goodhand and Christian Dennys. In addition, we draw upon (sometimes critically) relevant secondary material from the World Bank, United Nations Office on Drugs and Crime (UNODC), Afghan Research and Evaluation Unit (AREU) and various NGOs.
2. For instance, researchers have never been able to agree on the precise numbers of, or divisions between, ethnic, religious and linguistic groups in the country. Within the Pashtuns there are historic divisions and enmities, and there are many anomalies which blur inter-group boundaries – for example, there are urbanized, de-tribalized Pashtuns who only speak Dari, Tajiks who are mother-tongue Pashtu speakers, Shi'a Pashtuns and Sunni Hazaras.
3. See Rubin (1992) for a more in-depth analysis of the pre-war Afghan political elite.
4. Ghilzai Pashtuns, for example, who were historically excluded from political power by the Durrani elite, were particularly prominent in the leadership of the Parcham faction of the PDPA (Edwards 2002).
5. For instance, a study of Hezbi Islami and Taliban 'radicalization' found that fighters often joined because of material benefits, but became increasingly radicalized after mobilization (Ladbury 2009).
6. As Canfield writes: 'Contrary to what might be supposed, the actual operating units of socio-political coalition [...] are rarely genuinely "ethnic" in composition' (cited in Glatzer 1998: 179).
7. Some parties had significant minorities, such as Jamiat-i-Islami (86 per cent Tajik, 14 per cent other ethnic groups) or Hizb-i-Islami (Hekmetyar)

(66 per cent Pashtun, 44 per cent others), and some were highly mixed, such as Harakat-i-Islami (Mohseni) (Rubin 1996).

8. In Hazarajat, during the jihad, there were at least three primary conflict fault lines; first, between the Hazara political parties and the Soviet-backed government; second, between Hazaras and the Tajik and Pashtun resistance parties; third, intra-Hazara conflict often funded by different external backers and based upon social, political, religious and leadership divisions.
9. Abdur Rahman at the end of the nineteenth century, for example, increased the number of administrative divisions and married into powerful families, to prevent peripheral elites from building up regional power bases.
10. For more detail, see Rubin (2000); Goodhand (2004); MacDonald (2007).
11. The removal of Ismail Khan from the governorship of Herat in 2005, for example, was linked to concerns about his failure to provide tax revenues to the central government.
12. These figures are drawn from the Afghanistan national household survey, NRVA, which has allowed standard poverty analysis to be conducted.
13. Aid is funnelled through layers of contractors; for a large contract, there may be as many as five layers of international and national subcontractors, each of which takes a 10–20 per cent share of the resources as profit (Waldman 2008).
14. Both UNODC and the United States Government produce statistics on the amount of opium poppy cultivated and the level of opium production in Afghanistan. The estimates produced by these two parties do not always agree. For convenience, the estimates cited in this document are those of UNODC.
15. The post-Taliban period has seen the emergence of new areas of cultivation, including Bamyan, Nuristan, Khost and Wardak provinces. Many of these areas were not well suited to opium production, having neither the environmental conditions nor the skills required to make opium poppy cultivation a profitable endeavour once the price effects of the Taliban prohibition had dissipated.
16. The sustainability of these decreases can be questioned; opium trafficking also continues in the north, and the increase in marijuana production has been substantial.
17. The war economy for the insurgency is fragmented, especially because command and control of field units by the senior Taliban leadership continues to be weak. Individual Taliban groups will raise income from a range of sources, including informal taxation, bribery, kidnapping for ransom and the drug economy.
18. Politico-military actors who gained a strategic edge in the war years have been folded into new government structures, whilst consolidating their positions as principal actors within the drugs industry. Consequently, their primary concern is now to maintain market share and to secure contract compliance. Violence is bad for business and can be understood as a sign of market dysfunction.
19. This case study is based upon ongoing field work conducted by David Mansfield in Nangahar province, most recently in November, 2009.
20. The arrest and successful prosecution of a member of the former Governor Haji Din Mohammed's family in 2007 for transporting opium along with

four other men employed by Haji Zahir, the governor's nephew, offered a rare example of undisputed evidence of official involvement in the drugs trade These five men, including the former governor's nephew, were sentenced to jail for between 16 and 18 years. They were subsequently pardoned by President Karzai on 30 April 2009. At that time, Haji Din Mohammed was managing President Karzai's re-election campaign (Stockman 2009).

21. Zyck notes that the DDR programme, similarly to the argument made in this chapter, exacerbated inter-group tensions and social fragmentation, which could contribute to further escalations in conflict (Zyck 2009).

12
Nepal: First Steps Towards Redressing HIs?

Graham K. Brown

12.1 Introduction

Located high in the Himalayan mountain range and having avoided colonization as a classic 'buffer state' between (British) India and China, Nepal is marked in its political history by unique institutions and practices, including a hereditary prime ministership – the Rana dynasty between 1846 and 1953 (Whelpton 2005); a formally institutionalized caste hierarchy – the Muluki Ain, also abolished in 1953 (Höfer 1979); and, until 2006, a unique status as the world's only officially Hindu state. But its landlocked, mountainous terrain has provided less than fertile ground for development: with a gross domestic product (GDP) per capita of around US$200 in 1996, at the start of the conflict, and with poverty rates in excess of 40 per cent, Nepal ranks as one of the poorest countries outside of Sub-Saharan Africa. With such an unusual political history, it is perhaps less surprising that, in the mid-1990s, when post-Cold War liberal euphoria was at its peak and conflicts around the world were increasingly being seen as 'ethnic' instead of 'ideological', it was Nepal that saw the outbreak of an apparently 'old-fashioned' Maoist insurgency.

In this chapter we explore the dynamics of the conflict in Nepal and the ways in which post-conflict reconstruction efforts have attempted to address the root causes of the conflict. Despite the Maoist moniker of the insurgents, the conflict in Nepal was driven by political exclusions and economic horizontal inequalities (HIs). While the international community was slow to address the exclusionary nature of the Nepalese regime, even as the conflict escalated, post-conflict aid has taken up the challenge of addressing these inequalities across multiple dimensions. Moreover, aid agencies appear to be sharply aware that their efforts must not be seen to undermine the legitimacy of the new state. While a rosy future for Nepal is by no means certain, we suggest that the country's post-conflict trajectory appears to offer some positive experiences worthy of note, especially in relation to policies addressing HIs.

The structure of the chapter proceeds as follows. In the remainder of this introductory section, we first provide a brief overview of the political context of the conflict. The next section offers an overview of the nature of HIs in Nepal across multiple dimensions. Section 12.3 examines the internal dynamics of the conflict itself, and Section 12.4 discusses the role of international aid, both during and after the conflict.

The modern state of Nepal was founded in mid-eighteenth century, when the Gorkha King Prithvi Narayan Shah unified the three major kingdoms of the region. A century later, however, the Shah dynasty was effectively sidelined, although not displaced, by the powerful Rana family, which established a hereditary and autocratic prime ministership; the extensive (although factionally divided) Rana family controlled not only the premiership, but also all the major political posts in the country (Whelpton 2005). After the end of the Second World War, however, the shifting geo-politics of the region and internal pressures brought about the downfall of the Rana regime. Internally, local agitation for a more open regime achieved institutional form in the Nepali Congress, which was based in and largely controlled by India. In addition, the king, Tribhuvan Shah, was increasingly resentful of his marginalized position in the country; in 1950, he finally fled to India. With the Chinese invasion of Tibet, India moved to exert more influence over Nepal through its proxy in the Nepali Congress. The Nepali Congress quickly took control of large sections of the country, at which point India intervened to negotiate an agreement in which Tribhuvan returned to the country, and the Rana dynasty gave up its exclusive claims to power and entered into a coalition with the Nepali Congress. As Whelpton (2005: 73) notes, however, the revocation of the Rana's powers, together with the failure to institute a new constitution immediately, meant that 'it was the king who now held the ultimate authority in fact as well as in theory'. For Tribhuvan at least, though, this political victory was short-lived; he died in 1955.

Over the ensuing decade, attempts to move towards democracy stuttered. Elections were held in 1959 and won convincingly by the Nepali Congress, led by B. P. Koirala. Its failure to bring an immediate halt to ongoing factional disputes, however, gave the new king, Mahendra, the opportunity to complete the monarchy's re-ascendance, abolishing parliament and institutionalizing a 'partyless *panchayat*' system of government that left him in effective control. Disillusionment with the monarchy and the failure of development in the rural areas created the political space for a burgeoning underground communist movement. By the mid-1980s, however, this was matched by a growing urban discontent with the monarchist system, which led to agitations for democratization. The emergence of urban opposition to the monarchist regime, however, also led to a split in the Left, some advocating a tactical alliance with the Nepali Congress in order to achieve elections, others opposing electoral politics altogether. Once again, it was Indian intervention that provided the spark for regime change. Indian–Nepali relations had been worsening due to Nepal's improving relations with China, and in the late 1980s India imposed an effective trade blockade on Nepal by laying down stringent conditions for the renewal of trade agreements that expired in 1989; Kathmandu responded in a similarly aggressive manner (Garver 1991). Domestic blame for the subsequent economic collapse, however, was firmly directed towards the new king, Birendra Shah, and this galvanized what became known as the 'Jan Andolan' ('People's Movement'). Bowing to pressure, Birendra institutionalized multiparty democracy and the first elections were held in 1991.

The 1991 elections, the first since 1959, were won by the old Nepali Congress, and G. P. Koirala, the younger brother of B. P. Koirala, became prime minister. The Communist Party of Nepal (United Marxist–Leninist, UML), which was the main collaborator with the Nepali Congress in the democracy movement, emerged as the second largest party. The United People's Front (UPF), an alternative communist grouping that disavowed electoral politics and claimed only to take part to 'expose' the elections, won just under 5 per cent of the votes and seats. Although it did not win many votes, the UPF – from which the Communist Party of Nepal (Maoist) would emerge in the mid-1990s – was notable both for the strength of its regional voting around the district of Rolpa and Rukum, in the mid-west, and for its mobilization and recruitment among minority groups that had not assimilated into the Nepali–Hindu caste system (Whelpton 2005: 203).

Within two years, the Nepali Congress government was facing renewed Leftist agitation over the stalled economy and its perceived incompetence. At the same time, factional politics in the Congress forced Prime Minister Koirala to call for new elections in 1994. These elections resulted in a hung parliament, with the UML the largest party.

The UML formed a minority government, but it quickly collapsed and was replaced by a Nepali Congress-led coalition in 1995. At the same time, however, the UPF underwent its own internal schism and was all but wiped out in the 1994 elections. The two main factions within the party mounted legal challenges over control of the party, and the losing faction, led by Baburum Bhattarai and Pushpa Kamal Dahal (commonly known as Prachandra), broke away and formed the Communist Party of Nepal (Maoist), which submitted a list of demands to the government, including the abolition of the monarchy and the calling of a Constituent Assembly to draft a new constitution. Its demands not met, the party launched the 'People's War' in February 1996.

Parliamentary democracy continued to function throughout the early years of the conflict, but in 2002 King Gyanendra – recently crowned following the notorious palace massacre of 2001 – began to take a more active political role, first dismissing a series of prime ministers and finally, in 2005, reasserting an absolutist monarchy. Gyanendra's coup provoked a major popular backlash and another Jan Andolan movement. While the end of the monarchy had long been one of the Maoists' demands, with virtually all the political parties now unified against Gyanendra, a peace agreement was finally negotiated, with the expectation that the country would be transformed into a republic. A constituent assembly-cum-interim parliament was elected in April 2008, which returned the Maoists as the largest party; Prachandra took up the premiership, with Bhattarai as his finance minister. The assembly promptly moved to formally end the monarchy and, on 28 May 2008, Nepal was declared a Federal Democratic Republic; the status of Hinduism as the official religion was also abolished.

12.2 Overview of horizontal inequalities in Nepal

Nepal is a highly diverse country, with many interlocking identity groups – caste, ethnic, religious, regional and linguistic (Whelpton 2005). Nepali-speaking Hindus, the Parbatiyas, constitute around 40 per cent of the population, but this group is internally divided along caste lines, the politically dominant Brahmin and Chhetri castes each constituting around a third of the Parbatiya. The largest of the non-Nepali ethnic groups, the Newar, constitute around 5 per cent of the population and are concentrated in the Kathmandu valley. Two other ethnic groups, the Tarang and Magar, constitute around 5 per cent of the population, although they are also internally fragmented. The remainder of the population is even more highly fragmented: of the 103 caste and ethnic groups enumerated in the 2001 census, more than 80 constituted less than 1 per cent of the total population.

In 1854, an official Civil Code (*Muluki Ain*) formalized the Hindu caste hierarchy and, in a marked difference from the Indian experience, attributed each non-caste group – indigenous Janajati ethnic groups and others, such as Muslims – an explicit place within this hierarchy (Höfer 1979). Although the democratic constitution of 1990 expressly forbade discrimination on caste grounds, caste remains a significant barrier to social mobility, particularly for the 'untouchable' Dalit castes; a recent survey of caste discrimination found that almost half (46.4 per cent) of Dalit respondents encountered difficulty selling milk from their cattle due to their untouchable status (Johnsen 2002; quoted in Prandan and Shrestha 2005: 8). The UN Committee on the Elimination of Racial Discrimination has noted that, while 'the caste system in Nepal has been abolished by law [...] this system still functions and appears embedded in parts of the Nepalese culture' (CERD 1998: para. 10). In addition to caste differentials, ethno-linguistic minorities also suffer severe exclusion. Between 1996 and 2004, poverty dropped by 26 per cent across Nepal, but the non-caste hill Janajati groups and Muslims recorded, respectively, drops of only 10 per cent and 6 per cent. In contrast, poverty among the untouchable Dalit caste fell by 20 per cent, although they remain slightly poorer than the Janajati and the Muslims in absolute terms (Bennett 2005).[1]

Table 12.1 reports HIs by caste and ethnic group across four dimensions of socio-economic performance in 1996, collected shortly before the outbreak of the insurgency. Across all four dimensions, the Newar and Brahmin come out clearly and consistently as the top two groups, and the Chhetri third in three dimensions, although they have a poverty rate well above the national average – which suggests that within-group inequality among the Chhetri may be particularly marked. The position of the Newar requires some qualification, as more than half of the Newar live in the Kathmandu valley, which is their place of origin.

Using data from the two Nepal Living Standards Survey in 1996 and 2004, Salvi del Pero (2005) examines income inequality between what she terms the 'majority groups' – the Brahmin, the Chhetri, and the Newar – and the rest of the population. Using a Theil decomposition, she finds that the between-group component of overall income inequality has trebled over this period. Moreover, even holding for education, landownership, and other socio-economic variables, her

Table 12.1 Nepal: HIs by major caste and ethnic group across four dimension, ratio to national mean (1996)

	Per capita income		Poverty rate (inverted)		Adult literacy		Mean years of schooling	
Caste/Ethnic Group	Ratio	Rank	Ratio	Rank	Ratio	Rank	Ratio	Rank
Newar	1.558	1	1.818	1	1.492	2	1.939	2
Brahmin	1.293	2	1.311	2	1.580	1	2.062	1
Chhetri	1.009	3	0.909	6	1.144	3	1.236	3
Rajbansi, Yadav, Tharu, Ahir	0.901	4	0.998	4	0.749	5	0.754	5
Gurung, Magar, Sherpa, Rai, Limbu	0.861	5	0.790	7	0.959	4	0.897	4
Muslim	0.826	6	1.185	3	0.602	7	0.602	6
Occupational Castes (Dalit) (a)	0.644	7	0.957	5	0.648	6	0.545	7

Note: (a) figure for poverty rate among occupational castes includes other non-listed groups.
Source: Authors' calculations, based on NESAC (1998).

regression analysis shows that 70 per cent of the gap between the 'majority groups' – the Brahmin, the Chhetri, and the Newar – and the rest of the population is unexplained, which she attributes to discrimination.[2] It is important to note that the period between the two surveys coincides with the emergence and escalation of the Maoist rebellion, so it is difficult to know whether this increase in inequality was a cause of conflict escalation, an effect of the conflict, or both.

In addition to looking at summary figures, it is important to consider the entire distribution curve, in other words whether inequalities are predominantly located among the poorer sections of the population or among the richer sections. Table 12.2 shows the consumption ratios by ethnic group and national quintile. It is clear that the vast majority of the inequality is located in the top quintile – that is, the 'poor' of all ethnic/caste groups are roughly as poor as each other, but the major variations occur between the ethnic 'elites'.

In the political dimension, HIs along caste/ethnic lines are also evident and increasing. Figure 12.1 shows the relative representation of the three dominant groups caste groups – the Brahmin, the Chhetri, and the Newar – against all other groups in the national parliaments formed after the democratic 'experiment' in 1959 and the three elections

Table 12.2 Average consumption ratios to national average by national quintile

	1 (Poorest)	2	3	4	5 (Richest)
Hill Brahmin/Chhetri, etc.	1.03	1.01	1.01	1.00	1.05
Tarai Brahmin, etc.	1.00	1.02	1.03	1.01	1.07
Tarai middle caste	1.03	0.99	0.99	0.99	0.93
Newar/Thakali	0.97	1.01	1.02	1.04	1.68
Other Hill Janajati	0.95	1.00	1.01	0.99	0.96
Tarai Janajati	1.02	0.98	0.97	1.01	0.86
Hill Dalit	1.02	0.99	0.99	0.98	0.93
Tarai Dalit	0.98	0.99	0.99	0.99	0.72
Muslim	1.00	1.02	1.00	0.99	0.66
Other	1.00	0.94	0.90	1.11	1.46
HI	0.035	0.012	0.015	0.017	0.224

Source: Author's calculations from NIRS (2006).

between democratization in 1990 and the suspension of parliament in 2002. Also included is the national-level *panchayat* of 1981, which was not democratically elected. In the 1959 elected parliament, the Brahmin and the Chhetri dominated, but since the post-democratization period there has been increasing dominance of parliament by the Brahmin alone. In 1999, Brahmin accounted for almost half the seats in parliament, despite forming around 13 per cent of the population. Interestingly, the non-democratic national *panchayat* of 1981 was ethnically far more representative than any of the democratic parliaments, although it was still highly biased. In this respect, Dahal (2000a: 122) has noted that 'one of the positive elements of the Panchayat regime was that [...] they used to make selection from people of different social strata, including the occupational caste, ethnic/tribal groups, and the Madhesiya groups, as Members of the Rastriya Panchayat'.

In the bureaucracy, the recruitment of third class officers in government has reflected this political dominance (Figure 12.2). In 1984/1985, the three dominant groups accounted for more than two-thirds of new recruits. This situation worsened, despite democratization in 1990; in 2001/2002, more than 95 per cent of recruits came from these groups. The decline in the over-representation of the Newar parallels their relative decline in parliament since the 1981 *panchayat*. Unfortunately

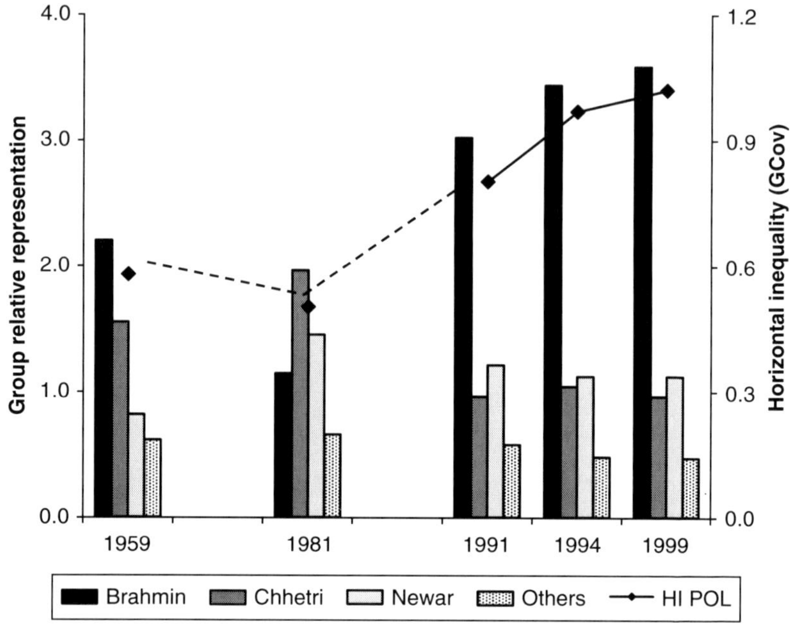

Figure 12.1 Nepal: Caste/ethnic representation in national parliament (1959–1999)

Notes: Relative representation defined as group proportion in parliament divided by group proportion in the population as a whole; population figures used for calculation of relative representation are those from the 1991 census.

Source: Authors' calculation, based on Baral (1983; 2005) and NESAC (1998).

these statistics are not disaggregated between Brahmin and Chhetri, so it is impossible to see whether the increased dominance of this group has been particularly in the hands of the Brahmin, as it has been in parliament.

In part, this bias is evidence of the problem of the *persistence* of HIs – lower caste and disadvantaged ethnic groups have poorer access to education and thus are less likely to possess the human capital necessary to fill high-ranking positions. Not least here is the requirement to speak Nepali, which is the national language, although it is the mother tongue of only around half the population. The post-democratization period has seen language and linguistic identity become increasingly politicized, largely for this reason. Thus far, however, a number of legal challenges to the official dominance of Nepali have come to naught (Dahal 2000b).

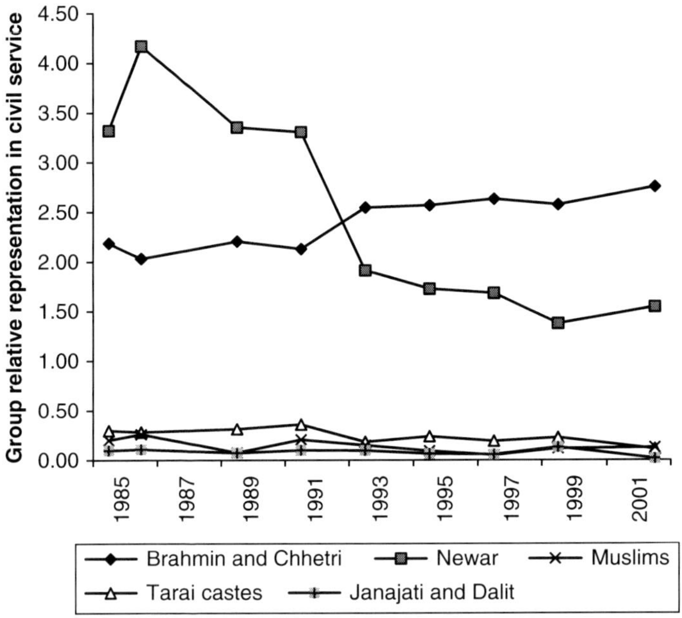

Figure 12.2 Nepal: Representation of caste/ethnic groups in the recruitment of gazetted third-class officers (1984/1985–2001/2002)
Source: Author's calculations, based on UNDP (2004: 178).

Whelpton (1997: 50) notes the 'overwhelming predominance of a Partabiya [hill caste]-Newar elite in Nepalese society', and the data presented here confirm this analysis. It is clear that, across the socio-economic and political dimensions, the Brahmin, the Chhetri, and the Newar enjoy considerable dominance, the Newar being particularly well-off in the economic dimension and the Brahmin increasingly dominant in the political dimension.

Regional inequalities have also attracted considerable attention in Nepal, particularly in the light of the Maoist insurgency. Separate statistical investigations have found that variations in the intensity of the insurgency at the district level are highly correlated with 'spatial HIs' in level of human development (Gates and Murshed 2005) and with increasing inequalities in land ownership in particular (Macours 2006; see below for further details).

Figure 12.3 shows the level of regional disparity in income and Human Development Index (HDI) according to different types of aggregation: by district (only the highest and lowest scoring districts

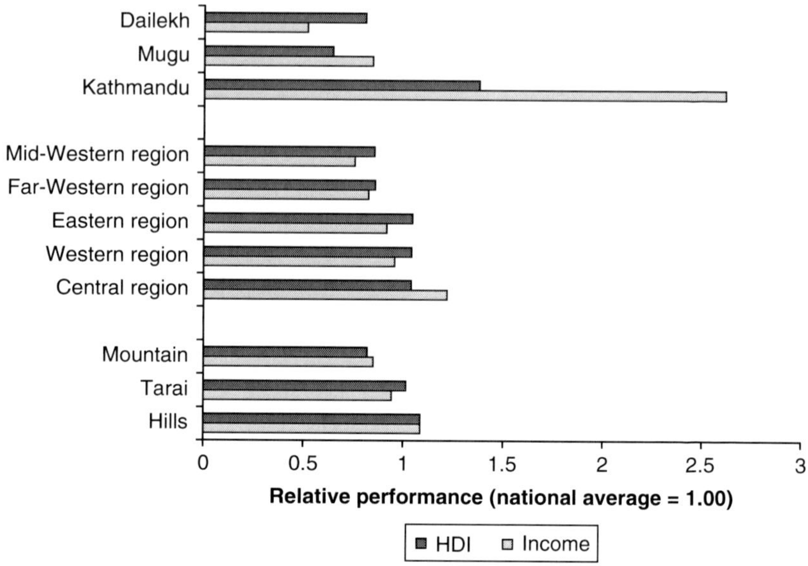

Figure 12.3 Nepal: Regional disparities in income and human development (2001)
Source: Authors' calculations, based on UNDP (2004).

are reported); by development region; and by ecological zone. Unsurprisingly, disparities are greatest at the lower district level of aggregation, with the national capital, Kathmandu, performing best and two mid-western districts performing worst in, respectively, HDI and mean income terms.

What is more surprising is that the disparity between the ecological zones, particularly in terms of income, is slightly lower than that between the development regions. Using the Group Coefficient of Variation (GCov) measure of regional inequality, income inequality between the development regions is almost twice that of the ecological zones (Table 12.3). This is important, because much of the regional

Table 12.3 Nepal: Regional inequality index, GCov (2001)

	Income	HDI
Development regions	0.171	0.078
Ecological zones	0.081	0.076

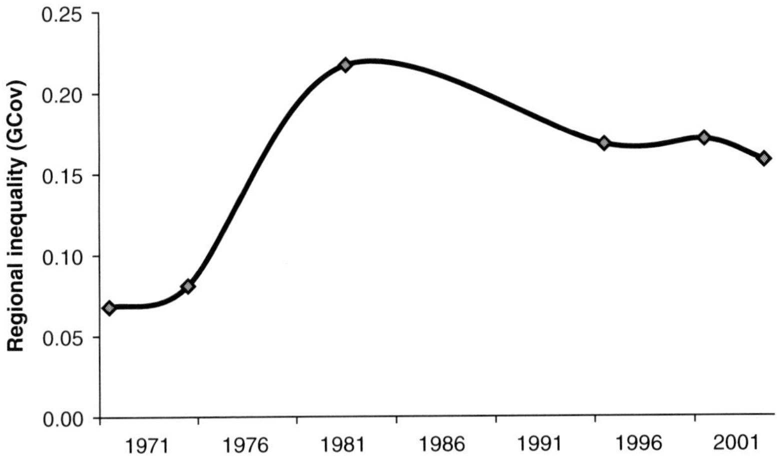

Figure 12.4 Regional income inequalities (1971–2005)
Note: As the Mid-Western region had not been created when the earlier data were compiled, it has been aggregated with the Far Western Region in the later period to ensure comparability.
Source: Author's calculations based on Amatya (1987); NESAC (1998) and Gurung (2005).

development strategy in Nepal has historically been focused on expanding development in the hill and mountain zones rather than across the development regions.

Figure 12.4 shows the evolution of income inequalities between the four development regions since 1971. Regional inequality rose significantly between 1971 and the early 1980s, then falling somewhat until the mid-1990s, after which it has remained essentially static. The drop in regional inequalities coincides with a period in which the Nepalese government started taking regional inequality more seriously. Although previous official publications had addressed the issue of regional inequality (see Gurung 1969), the plan documents had paid it scant attention until the Seventh Plan, which dedicated an entire chapter to redressing regional inequalities and to distributing development funds accordingly. Nonetheless, regional inequalities remain severe and, as already noted, empirical investigations show them to have been related to the intensity of the insurgency.

From a HIs perspective, it is also important to consider the dimension of 'cultural status' inequalities – the extent to which certain cultures and cultural practices are afforded a higher status formally and informally by the state (Langer and Brown 2008). While reduced to a purely ceremonial role under the 1990 constitution – at least until the royal takeover in 2002–2005 – the monarchy remained representative of the caste hierarchy (officially abolished, but still pervasive) and of the cultural dominance of Hinduism. Even in the 1990 Constitution, the symbolic dominance of caste Hinduism was maintained by provisions which stated that:

- His Majesty is a descendant of Great King Privithi Narayan Shah and an adherent of Aryan culture and the Hindu religion;
- Nepal is a Hindu monarchical kingdom; and,
- His Majesty is the symbol of Nepalese nationality and the unity of the Nepalese people.

(quoted in Hachhethu 2007)

Clearly, such symbolic dominance was particularly alienating for the non-Hindu Janajati groups. In this respect the democratic opening of 1990 provided the political space for the emergence and legitimization of ethnic claims and concomitant organizational mobilization (Bhattachan 1995). As Gellner (2007: 1825) notes, after democratization, 'ethnic difference began to acquire increasing political salience [...] Democracy, as all south Asians are aware, is a numbers game.' In this context it is perhaps unsurprising that the Maoist movement appealed particularly to, and recruited, particularly among non-Hindu groups.

12.3 The conflict: Old and new grievances

The insurgency by the Communist Party of Nepal (Maoist) – CPN(M) – was officially declared on 13 February 1996, and its public demands articulated through a 'Forty Point Plan'. The plan constituted a demand for Nepal to move towards a secular republic, but it was also deeply concerned with issues of discrimination and social exclusion, including greater inheritance rights for women, an end to caste discrimination and local autonomy (reproduced in Hutt 2004). Initially a relatively minor insurgency, the 'People's War', escalated after in 2001 and claimed over 10,000 lives between 2001 and the end of 2005, when moves towards a peaceful settlement gathered pace (see Figure 12.5).

There is significant econometric evidence that HIs are an important root insurgency. Their analysis does not consider ethnic and caste groups *per se*, but focuses on regional differences. Using a 'gap' measure of human development, Murshed and Gates find strong econometric support for a relationship between regional deprivation and the intensity of the rebellion, as measured by the number of conflict fatalities

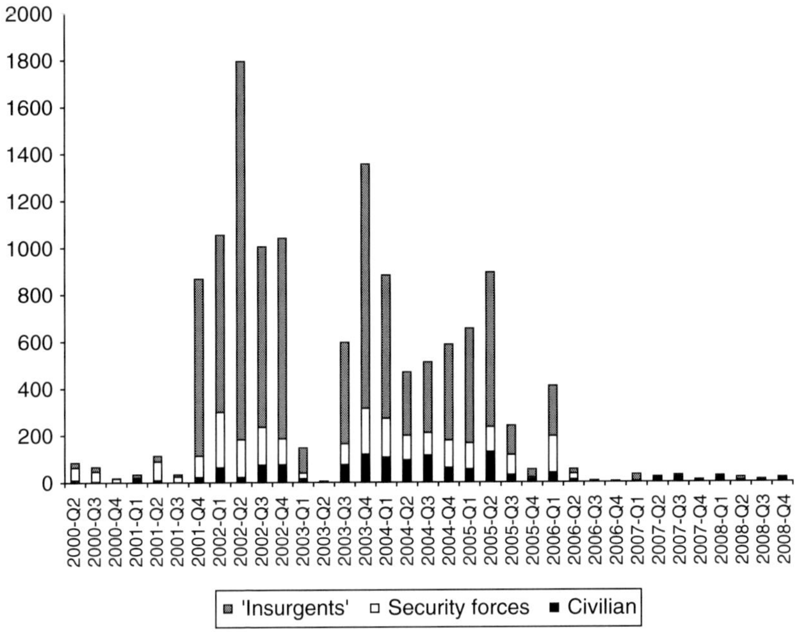

Figure 12.5 Fatalities in the insurgency by quarter (2000–2008)
Source: South Asia Terrorism Portal, data set online at http://www.satp.org/satporgtp/countries/nepal/database/fatalities.htm.

by district. A subsequent econometric analysis by Do and Iyer (2005) replicates this finding of regional deprivation – in this case, measured by the regional poverty rate and by the literacy rate – but adds additional variables relating to demographic characteristics. The authors find no significant correlation between intra-province caste diversity (as measured by the widely used fractionalization index) and conflict intensity, confirming cross-country analyses that find no such relationship (Collier and Hoeffler 2004). They do, however, find that caste polarization – the extent to which the provincial population is divided into two large caste groups – does correlate with conflict intensity, even when holding for level of *regional* deprivation. (Again, this conforms with cross-country analyses; see for instance Reynal-Querol 2002.)

These findings all relate to differences *between* provinces. Macours (2006) investigates the relationship between land inequality *within* provinces and the intensity of the Maoist rebellion. She finds only weakly significant evidence for a relationship between absolute levels of intra-province land inequality and the level of conflict, but a strong and consistent relationship between *increases* in the level of land *productivity* between 1995 and 2003 and the level of conflict. Measures for local caste dominance are also insignificant. Khatiwada's study replicates these findings, but discovers an additional positive relationship with the proportion of the population belonging to Janajati ethnic groups (Khatiwada 2006).

A final area of inequality and exclusion that is not addressed in the existing literature is the relationship between gender inequality and the intensity of the conflict. There is significant international evidence that gender inequality is positively related to conflict likelihood (Caprioli 2005). For this chapter, we have done a preliminary analysis on the basis of the gender empowerment measure of the UNDP (2004); see Table 12.4. The results are strong and surprising – conflict intensity as measured by the number of Maoist abductions per population is strongly and *positively* related to the level of gender *empowerment* in the district. A similar relationship holds with the level of fatalities, although not as strongly. This finding is potentially important, although very preliminary, and points to an interesting dimension of the conflict, worth further investigation.

How does this sit with qualitative and ethnographic accounts of the conflict and its mobilization? The evidence suggests that, despite its universalist anti-caste rhetoric, the Maoist movement appealed predominantly to, and gained most support in, regions and districts which *combined* relative socio-economic deprivation with particularly *ethnic* distinctiveness. The first major bedrock of support for the rebellion came from the ethnic Magar concentrated in the mid-west region, particularly in the Rolpa district (Center for Human Rights and Global Justice 2005;

Table 12.4 Poisson regression results for level of conflict (normalized number of abductions) by regional development and gender inequality

	Coeff.	t-stat
Human development	−6.355	−4.97***
Gender empowerment measure	17.862	3.23***
Caste fractionalization	−0.496	−2.02***
Constant	10.837	7.48***
Pseudo-R^2	0.3889	

Source: Author's calculations based on data from UNDP (2004).

Lecomte-Tilouine 2004). Rolpa ranks among the bottom ten districts in terms of human development. Similarly, its first establishment of a base in the east, in Dolakha district, 'emerged in the predominantly Thangmi and Tamang areas [...] indicating that the Maoists did indeed succeed in targeting and receiving support from these two ethnic populations' (Schneiderman and Turin 2004: 102). Moreover, there is some evidence that the broader Dalit caste population 'begun to feel extremely alienated and underserved by the very movement that purports to liberate them' (Center for Human Rights and Global Justice 2005: 38). In other words, while the Maoist movement was able to mobilize successfully around specific ethnic groups – many of which *were* low caste – it did not appeal successfully to a broader caste identity, or mobilize along these lines.

In addition to the socio-economic HIs that drove the conflict, as we have seen, the Maoists also demanded an end to the monarchy and the creation of a secular state.

In such a context, the decision taken by King Gyanendra to attempt to restore the absolutist monarchy heralded the beginning of the end of the conflict by undermining the legitimacy of the monarchy even in the eyes of many caste Hindus. From the outset, Gyanendra's popular legitimacy was suspect at best. He came to the throne after the notorious palace massacre of 2001, when the crown prince reportedly shot his parent and then himself, in a dispute over his choice of bride; and, although there was no evidence to support this, rumour quickly circulated that Gyanendra had in fact orchestrated the killings himself. It was a rumour of which the Maoists took ample advantage. After Gyanendra's final power-grab in 2005, virtually all the mainstream political parties in the country shifted towards a more republican stance (Hachhethu 2007). Together with trade unions and civil society organizations, a second Jan Andolan movement was organized, and Gyanendra was forced to restore parliament. With the legitimacy of the monarchy in tatters, the stage was set for negotiations between the Maoists and the government, which resulted in a peace agreement, an interim constitution in November 2007, and the election of a Constituent Assembly in April 2008.

12.4 Addressing root causes: International aid, domestic policy and the peace agreement

Political, socio-economic and cultural HIs have all been recognized in the peace process and its aftermath, and at least the first steps were taken to reduce them. The peace process itself addressed many of the political and cultural status inequalities that had driven the conflict, but eradication of socio-economic inequalities has, unsurprisingly, proved more difficult. The election to the constituent assembly that is drafting the new constitution was on a split system, with 240 members elected on a first-past-the-post constituency basis and 335 members elected on a national-level proportional representation party list system. The rules for the election encouraged parties to select ethnically and gender representative candidates for the constituencies, but they were much more explicit for the list system: 50 per cent of each party's list had to be women, 15.6 per cent from the Madhesi ethnic groups, 18.9 per cent from the Janajati ethnic groups, and 6.5 per cent form the Dalit castes. The elections were held in April 2008 and, as mentioned above, one of the first actions of the Maoist government formed after the election was the abolition of the monarchy and the declaration of Nepal as a secular state, removing one of the major sources of cultural status inequality in the country.

Addressing socio-economic inequalities is typically difficult; even in a middle-income country such as Malaysia, affirmative action policies have rarely met their targets within the specified time frame. Rectifying socio-economic inequalities between ethnic and caste groups in post-conflict Nepal, however, has been rendered particularly problematic by the extreme poverty in the country and the consequent reliance on external donors for revenues through which to implement such policies. Nonetheless, both the national government and the donors have taken a number of measures with the objective of reducing HIs.

Nepal has a long history of high dependence on foreign aid. The country's first development plan, the First Five-Year Plan (1956–1961), was entirely funded by financial assistance; the current Tenth Plan (2002–2007) is more than 60 per cent funded by aid (Shrestha et al. 2004: 8). Aid to Nepal as a proportion of GDP peaked in the mid-1980s, at around 7 per cent, falling to below 4 per cent in 2001. Outstanding foreign debt in the country has remained at around 50 per cent of GDP since 1990 (Figure 12.6).

From virtually nothing prior to 1970, multilateral aid to Nepal grew rapidly to constitute around 80 per cent of Official Development Assistance (ODA) in the mid-1970s, before falling off again after democratization in 1990. In 2003–2004, bilateral aid constituted 67 per cent of the total aid flows, of which around 20 per cent apiece (around 14 per cent of total aid) came from Japan, the UK and Germany. Most of the multilateral aid came from the International Development Association

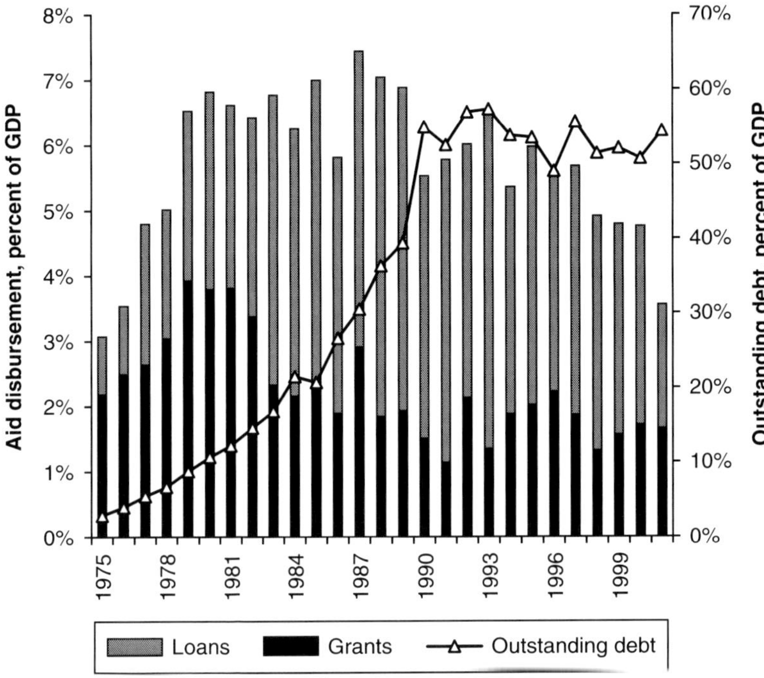

Figure 12.6 Nepal: Aid disbursement and debt as a proportion of GDP (1975–2001)
Source: Calculated from Shrestha et al. (2004: 9–10).

of the World Bank, which constituted 62 per cent of multilateral aid, or around 20 per cent of the total aid in 2004; the second significant multilateral aid donor was the Asian Development Bank (ADB), which gave 20 per cent of the total multilateral aid. After the king's dissolution of parliament, many donors withdrew support; aid flows resumed following the restoration of constitutional democracy in April 2006.

For most of the period up to, and including, the Maoist rebellion, HIs were ignored in aid distribution. Throughout much of the recent period, donor strategy and conditionality was mainly linked to macro-economic and governance reforms, with no reference to HIs. The World Bank's 1998 Country Assistance Strategy (CAS) proposed three different levels of lending: a 'low case' of up to $150 million; a 'base case' of $200–$350 million; and a 'high case' of $400 million or above. The factors triggering increased levels of lending were almost entirely related to macro-economic reforms aimed at increasing domestic revenue and at reducing domestic borrowing, including the 'satisfactory implementation of VAT'. None of the conditionalities related to inequality in any form (World Bank 1998: annex A1). However, the multilateral donors currently operating in Nepal *are* taking HIs and social exclusion seriously; but this is a very recent development.

The contrast between the World Bank's 1998 CAS and the 2003 CAS is marked. The 2003 CAS acknowledges in its opening paragraphs that 'there are significant ethnic and caste-based disparities' (World Bank 2003: 7). Consequently, the Bank included 'social inclusion and targeted programs' as one of the four 'pillars' of its new strategy, which includes three main aspects: 'equitable education', 'improved fiscal transfers to disadvantaged groups', and 'a civil service that better reflects the gender, caste and ethnic diversity of Nepal' (World Bank 2003: 32). Social inclusion was also included as a 'cross-cutting issue', which would be addressed in all programming. The new lending triggers in this document include 'strong measures implemented to improve access to basic education' among disadvantaged groups as a conditionality for the release of higher lending (World Bank 2003: 39).

An almost identical story can be told of the Asian Development Bank (ADB)'s country strategy documentation. The ADB Country Assistance Plan for the period 2000–2002 (ADB 1999) contained scant reference to inequality or social disparity of any sort, merely reporting gender and regional disparities in passing. In contrast, the current Country Strategy and Program for 2005–2009 (ADB 2004) pays considerable attention to HIs, identifying 'Inclusive Social Development' as one of the three 'pillars' of their country strategy. Similarly, the UK Department for International Development (DfID) states in its current Country Assistance Programme (CAP) that the 'overall purpose of UK development assistance to Nepal is to reduce poverty and social exclusion' (DfID 2004: 13).

This belated recognition of social inclusion as an important dimension of development by donor agencies working in Nepal related to evidence that socio-economic disparities on a regional and caste/ethnic basis were a fundamental cause of the Maoist insurgency and an important factor in accounting for variations in its intensity. The various assistance plans that mainstream social inclusion were all produced after the escalation of the conflict in 2000. The government also recognized the need to address socio-economic HIs. The Tenth Plan, which also served as the country's Poverty Reduction Strategy Paper (PRSP) (NPC 2003), formulated in consultation with donor agencies, and domestic stakeholders, recognized 'regional, gender, ethnic and caste-based inequalities' as an 'underlying cause' of the conflict and thus as an important area to be addressed. The peace agreement also reflected these issues, committing all parties to

> end the current centralized and unitary mode of state by means of an inclusive, democratic and far-reaching restructuring of the state to end discrimination based on class, caste, language, sex, culture, religion, and regionalism, and in order to address the problems of women, dalits, indigenous people, Madhesis, and oppressed, the ignored and minority groups, including the underdeveloped regions.[3]

In terms of specific projects, a major focus of the World Bank's new strategy in Nepal, have been education provision and the Poverty Alleviation Fund (PAF). The Education for All programme received $50 million in 2004–2007, and a further $60 million was committed in 2008. Geared primarily towards gender inclusion, the first phase of the project achieved a notable improvement in the Gender Parity Index in primary education from 0.87 in 2004 to 0.94 in 2006, although net enrolment rates have not increased as fast as expected.[4] The Poverty Alleviation Fund is more expressly geared towards ethnic exclusion and HIs. It was funded in its first phase by a $40 million grant; the Bank has committed to a further $100 million for the second phase covering 2008–2012. Modelled on the Kecamatan Development Programme in Indonesia (see Barron et al. 2003), the PAF is a community-driven initiative that facilitates the formation of Community Organizations (COs) at the village level, which then decide how to spend the funds allocated. The fund is also directed towards targeting excluded and vulnerable groups, such as women, Dalits, and non-Hindu minorities. Initially implemented in 25 districts (after a 6-district pilot phase), the fund now covers 55 of Nepal's 75 districts, with the expectation that it will be extended to the final 10 in the year 2009/2010. A comprehensive evaluation of the project's impact on poverty levels has yet to be undertaken, but data on the ethnic outreach of the project are available. Project impact evaluation of the PAF by the World Bank (2009) found that per capita consumption in PAF participant households grew more than 6 per cent faster than among control group households between 2006 and 2008, and more than 10 per cent faster in the poorer half of the population, targeted by the PAF. Table 12.5 reports the ethnic distribution of project beneficiaries and key position holders within the COs set up under the project,

Table 12.5 Composition of PAF community organizations by ethnicity (2007)

	Beneficiaries		Key Position Holders	
	Proportion	Ratio to Pop.	Proportion	Ratio to Pop.
Brahmin/Chhetri	22.3%	0.619	20.2%	0.561
Dalit	43.0%	2.722	49.4%	3.127
Janajati	27.5%	1.425	24.5%	1.269
Muslim	2.1%	0.333	2.0%	0.317
Others	5.1%	0.226	3.8%	0.168

Source: Authors' calculations from PAF Nepal (2007).

both as a raw percentage and as a ratio to the groups' share of the population in the districts in which the project has been implemented. As can be seen, the deprived groups, notably Dalits and Janajati, received more grants per head than other more privileged groups, involving some correction of HIs.

Yet many are left out. On the one hand, the programme is clearly reaching out considerably to the lower caste Dalit groups and, to a lesser extent, to the Janajati ethnic minorities, but other minority groups, including the Muslims and those classified as 'other', are significantly under-represented in the project. Moreover, while differences in ethnic classifications across samples make comparison difficult, the positive inclusion ratio for Janajati in particular may not be representative at the national level. While the proportion of project participants who are Janajati compares favourably to their share of the population in the districts where the project is active – 27.5 per cent of beneficiaries against 19.3 per cent of the districts population – the proportion of Janajati in the overall population is higher – 37.2 per cent according to the 2001 census classifications. In other words, while the PAF has been relatively inclusionary of Janajati in the districts in which it has been rolled out, those districts have relatively small Janajati populations compared to other districts.

The government also introduced a rural employment scheme similar to that in India, which received support from the World Bank and was targeted towards the conflict-affected and isolated districts. Possibly as many as 1.5 million households will be covered. This is discussed in Chapter 3 of this volume.

12.5 Conclusion

This review of the quantitative evidence and analytical accounts of the Maoist insurgency in Nepal point to a simple but important conclusion: while the rhetoric of the movement was largely ideological and caste-based, its mobilization was predominantly along ethnic and regional lines. Where regional deprivation coincided with ethnic discontents, particularly over representation in government, the movement was strongest. In the post-conflict era there has been increasing recognition, within and beyond Nepal, of the urgent need to address HIs and other forms of social exclusion, both through development projects and through a broader transformation of the institutions of government, although contemporary reports also suggest that implementation of these policies is faltering. While the government of Nepal and the international community have developed an explicit and apparently relatively effective inclusionary socio-economic development agenda, the country has still struggled to contain and control the political dimensions of ethnicity unleashed by the conflict, and the broader political process of reconstruction and state building has been beset with problems. As already mentioned, the post-ceasefire period has, however, seen an escalation of predominantly ethnic claims. In the early post-conflict years, the Maoist leadership was accused of 'playing the ethnic card' and, in doing so, of legitimizing emerging secessionist demands in the *tarai* regions bordering India (Regmi 2007; Thapa and Sharma 2009). Disputes over the incorporation of ex-combatants into the Nepalese army led to the resignation of the Maoist government in mid-2009; at the time of writing, it is too early to tell what impact this will have on development policy and economic management. While Nepal is thus a relatively successful case study of policy change in a post-conflict society, its experiences also caution that an enduring and inclusionary political settlement is a necessary companion for post-conflict socio-economic policies to address HIs and social exclusion.

Notes

1. Gender exclusion is also severe; women occupy a very low status in most Nepalese societies, irrespective of ethnicity or caste.
2. As with other such studies, the attribution of unexplained between-group variance to 'discrimination' is problematic, as this variance could equally be due to other unobserved variables, such as unequal social capital or quality of education; however, going in the other direction, some of the variables

included in such equations, such as education, incorporate elements of past discrimination.

3. Comprehensive Peace Agreement between the Government of Nepal and the Communist Party of Nepal (Maoist).
4. With 84.2 per cent enrolment in 2004, the project targeted 96 per cent enrolment by July 2009, but, while progress had been made, the target was not expected to be achieved according to a 2007 Report (World Bank 2007, 'Project paper on a proposed additional financing (grant) in the amount of SDR 38.7 million to Nepal for the Education for All project', *World Bank Report no. 41346-NP*, Washington, DC: World Bank).

Bibliography

Abadie, A., and Gardeazabal, J. (2001) *The Economic Cost of Conflict: A Case Control Study for the Basque Country*, NBER Working Papers No. 8478, National Bureau of Economic Research, Inc.

Adam, C., Cavendish, W., and Mistry, P. (1992) *Adjusting Privatisation: Case Studies from Developing Countries*, London: James Currey.

ADB (2004) *Country Strategy and Program (2005–2009): Nepal*, Manila: Asian Development Bank.

ADB (1999) *Country Assistance Plan (2000–2002): Nepal*, Manila: Asian Development Bank.

Agosin, M., Machado, R., and Nazal, P. (eds) (2004) *Pequeñas economías, grandes desafíos. Políticas económicas para el desarrollo en Centroamérica*, Washington, DC: Inter-American Development Bank.

Agosín, M. Machado, R., and Schneider, A. (2009) 'The Struggle for Tax Reform in Central America', in Sánchez-Ancochea, D., and Morgan, I. (eds) *The Political Economy of the Budget in the Americas*, London: Institute for the Study of the Americas.

Aguilera Peralta, Gabriel, Peace in Local Spaces: The Development Councils, http://www.irenees.net/fr/fiches/analyse/fiche-analyse-798.html.

Alcaraz, J., and Linares, L. F. (2004) 'A General of the Institutional State of Decentralization in Guatemala', in Tulchin, J., and Selee, A. (eds) *Decentralization and Democratic Governance in Latin America*, Woodrow Wilson International Centre for Scholars.

Alvarez, E. (2005) 'Reflexiones sobre Desarrollo Rural y Alternativo en los Andes', *Debate Agrario No. 38*. Lima: CEPES.

Amnesty International (2006) 'Bosnia and Herzogovina: Behind Closed Doors: Ethnic Discrimination in Employment', available at: http://www.amnestyusa.org/document.php?lang=e&id=ENGEUR630012006.

Amnesty International (1997) *Rwanda. Civilians Trapped in Armed Conflict: 'The Dead can no longer be Counted*, London: Amnesty International, 19 December 1997.

Amatya, D.B. (1987) *Perspectives in Regional Problems and Regional Development in Nepal*, New Delhi: Sterling Publishers.

Andeweg, R. (2000) 'Consociational Democracy', *Annual Review of Political Science, 3*, 509–536.

Andre, C., and Platteau, J.-P. (1998) 'Land Relations under Unbearable Stress: Rwanda Caught in the Malthusian Trap', *Journal of Economic Behaviour and Organisation, 34*, 1–47.

Ansoms, A. (2005) 'Resurrection after Civil War and Genocide: Growth, Poverty and Inequality in Post-conflict Rwanda', *European Journal of Development Research, 17* (3), 495–508.

Appleton, S. (2001) 'Changes in Poverty and Inequality', in Reinikka, R., and Collier, P. (eds) *Uganda's Recovery: The Role of Farms, Firms and Government*, Washington, DC: The World Bank.

Asia Foundation (2006) *A Survey of the Afghan People. Afghanistan in 2006*, Kabul, Afghanistan.

Assies, W., van der Haar, G., and Hoekema, A. J. (2000) *The Challenge of Diversity: Indigenous Peoples and Reform of the State in Latin America*, Amsterdam: Thela-Thesis.

Auvinen, J., and Nafziger, E. (1999) 'The Sources of Humanitarian Emergencies', *Journal of Conflict Resolution, 43*, 267–290.

Azam, J.-P., Morrisson, C., Chauvin, S., Rospabé, zam, J.-P., Morrisson, C., Chauvin, S., Rospabé, S., Klugman, J., Stewart, F., Goudie, A., Neyapti, B., and Organisation for Economic Co-operation and Development. Development Centre. (1999) *Conflict and Growth in Africa*, Paris: Development Centre of the Organisation for Economic Co-Operation and Development.

Klugman, J., Stewart, F., Goudie, A., Neyapti, B., and Organisation for Economic Co-Operation and Development. Development Centre. (1999) *Conflict and Growth in Africa*, Paris: Development Centre of the Organisation for Economic Co-Operation and Development.

Azerbaijani-Mogaddam, S., Pinney, A., Pain, A., and Masefield, A. (2008) 'DFID Understanding Afghanistan – Poverty, Gender and Social Exclusion Analysis', The Recovery and Development Forum.

Baral, L. R. (1983) *Nepal's Politics of Referendum: A Study of Groups, Personalities and Trends*, New Delhi: Vikas Publishing House.

Baral, L. R. (2005) 'Democracy and Elections: Trajectories of Political Development', in Baral, L. R. (ed.) *Election and Governance in Nepal*, New Delhi: Manohar.

Barfield, T. (2004) 'Problems in Establishing Legitimacy in Afghanistan', *Iranian Studies, 37* (2), 263–293.

Barrón, M. (2008) 'Gender and Ethnic Inequalities in Latin America: A Multidimensional Comparison of Bolivia, Guatemala and Peru', *CRISE Working Paper* No 32, Oxford: Centre for Research on Inequality, Human Security and Ethnicity, University of Oxford.

Barron, P., Diprose, R., Madden, D., Smith, C. Q., and Wollcock, M., (2003) 'Do Participatory Development Projects Help Villagers Manage Local Conflicts? A Mixed Methods Approach to Assessing the Kecamatan Development Project, Indonesia', *CPR Working Papers. Paper No. 9,* Social Development Department.

Bayliss, K. (2005), 'Post-Conflict Privatisation: A Review of Developments in Serbia and Bosnia-Herzegovina', ESAU Working Paper no. 12. London: Overseas Development Institute.

Bayliss, K., and Cramer, C. (2001), 'Privatisation and the Post-Washington Consensus: Between the Lab and the Real World?', in Fine, B. and Lapavitsas, C., and Pincus, J. (eds) *Development Policy in the 21st Century: Beyond the Post-Washington Consensus*, London: Routledge.

Belgian Senatorial Commission of Inquiry on the Great Lakes (2001) *Audition de M. Stefaan Marysse', professeur (UA), et 'de Mme Catherine André', chercheur (UA et UCL)*. www.senate.be.

Bennett, L. (2006) *Unequal Citizens: Gender, Caste and Ethnic Exclusion in Nepal*, World Bank, Document prepared for the Arusha Conference, 'New

Frontiers of Social Policy', available at: http://siteresources.worldbank.org/INTRANETSOCIALDEVELOPMENT/Resources/Bennett.rev.pdf.

Bennett, L. (2005) 'Gender, Caste, and Ethnic Exclusion in Nepal: Following the Policy Process from Analysis to Action', *Paper presented at the World Bank Conference on New Frontiers of Social Policy: Development in a Globalised World*, Arusha 12–15 December.

Berdal, M., and Mousavizadeh, N. (2010) 'Investing for Peace: The Private Sector and the Challenges of Peacebuilding', *Survival, 52* (2), 37–58.

Bhattachan, K. (1995) 'Ethnopolitics and Ethnodevelopment: An Emerging Paradigm in Nepal', in Kumar, D. (ed.) *State, Leadership and Politics in Nepal*, Kathmandu: Centre for Nepal and Asian Studies, Tribhuvan University.

Bigsten, A., and Kayizzi-Mugerwa, S. (1999) *Crisis, Adjustment and Growth in Uganda: A Study of Adaptation in an African Economy*, Basingstoke: Macmillan Press.

Birdsall, N., and Nellis, J. (2003), 'Winners and Losers: Assessing the Distributional Impact of Privatization', *World Development, 31* (10), 1617–1633.

Bledsoe, D. (2004) *Republic of Rwanda Land Policy and Law, Trip Report: Findings and Recommendations*, RDI/USAID/MINITERE.

Bosna i Hercegovina (2008) *Socijalna Zastita (Social Welfare) 2002–2007*, Tematski Bilten 07, Sarajevo: Agencija za statistiku Bosne I Hercegovine.

Bowen, M. (2000) *The State against the Peasantry: Rural Struggles in Colonial and Postcolonial Mozambique*, Charlottesville, VA: University of Virginia Press.

Boyce, J. (2007) 'Public Finance, Aid, and Post-Conflict Recovery', *UNDP Working Papers*. Available at: http://www.undp.org/cpr/content/economic_recovery/Background_1.pdf.

Braeckman, C. (1994) *Rwanda: Histoire d'un génocide*, Bruxelles: Fayard.

Bray, J. (2009) 'The Role of Private Sector Actors in Post-Conflict Recovery', *Conflict, Security & Development, 9* (1), 1–26.

Brown, G. (2008) 'Horizontal Inequalities and Separatism in Southeast Asia: A Comparative Perspective', in Stewart, F. (ed.) *Horizontal Inequalities and Conflict: Understanding Group Violence in Multiethnic Societies*, London: Palgrave Macmillan.

Brown, G. (2007) 'Social Exclusion, Horizontal Inequalities and Conflict in Nepal: Issues and Evidence', mimeo, Note for the Office of High Commissioner for Human Rights.

Brown, G., Langer, A., and Stewart, F. (2008) 'A Typology of Post-conflict Environments : An Overview', *CRISE Working Paper No. 53*, Oxford: Centre for Research on Inequality, Human Security and Ethnicity, University of Oxford.

Brown, G., and Stewart, F. (2006) 'The Implications of Horizontal Inequality for Aid', *UNU-WIDER Conference on Aid: Principles, Policies and Performance, June 17–18*, Helsinki: UNU-WIDER.

Brown, I. (1997) *Economic Change in South-East Asia, c.1830–1980*, Kuala Lumpur: Oxford University Press.

Brune, N., Garrett, G, and Kogut, B. (2004) 'The International Monetary Fund and the Global Spread of Privatization', *IMF Staff Papers*, Vol. 51.

Bull, B. (2008) 'Transnational Groups and Business Associations in the Privatisation of Central America's Telecommunications', in Fernandez, J., and Hogenboom, B. (eds) *Big Business and Economic Development. Conglomerates and Economic Groups in Developing Countries and Transition Economies under Globalisation*, London: Routledge.

Bull, B. (2005) *Aid, Power and Privatization: The Politics of Telecommunication Reform in Central America*, Cheltenham and Northampton, MA: Edward Elgar.

Bulmer-Thomas, V. (1987) *The Political Economy of Central America since Independence*, Cambridge: Cambridge University Press.

Byrd, W. (2008) 'Responding to Afghanistan's Opium Economy Challenge: Lessons and Policy Implications from a Development Perspective', *Policy Research Working Paper* No. 4545, World Bank.

Byrd, W., and Buddenberg, D. (2006) 'Introduction and Overview', in Buddenberg, D., and Byrd, W. (eds) *Afghanistan's Drug Industry: Structure, Functioning, Dynamics and Implications for Counter-Narcotics Policy*, UNODC and The World Bank.

Cabieses, H. (2005a) 'Coca Compleja, Drogas y Cocaleros en los Andes', in Cabieses, H., Cáceres, B., Rumrrill, R., and Soberón, R. (eds) *Hablan los Diablos*, Quito: ABYA-YALA, TNI and MLAL.

Cabieses, H. (2005b) 'Sobre Coca, Cocaleros y Drogas: Fallos Satanicos y Debates de Fondo', *Debate Agarario No.* 39, Lima: CEPES.

Campell-White, O., and Bhatia, A. (1998) *Privatisation in Africa*, Washington, DC: World Bank.

Canepa, G. (2008) 'The Fluidity of Ethnic Identities in Peru', CRISE Working Paper No. 46. Centre for Research on Inequality, Human Security and Ethnicity, University of Oxford.

Caprioli, M., (2005) 'Primed for Violence: The Role of Gender Inequality in Predicting Internal Conflict', *International Studies Quarterly, 49* (2), 161–178.

Casaús Arzú, M. (1995) *Guatemala : linaje y racismo*, 2nd edn, San José, Costa Rica: Flacso.

Castel-Branco, C., Cramer, C., and Hailu, D. (2001) 'Privatization and Economic Strategy in Mozambique', WIDER Discussion Paper 2001/64.

CDP, Centro Pluricultural para la Democracia (2003) 'La experiencia de la conformación de los consejos comunitarios de Desarrollo como proceso de cultura democrática', Paper presented at III Conferencia Centroamericana y el Desarrollo Local de Centroamerica, Managua, 20–22 de octubre de 2003, www.monografias.com.

Caumartin, C. (2006) 'Indigenous People and Politics? Issues in the Measurement, and Interpretation of Political Horizontal Inequalities in Guatemala', Paper read at CRISE Annual workshop, 25 September, at Santa Cruz de la Sierra, Bolivia.

Caumartin, C. (2005) 'Racism, Violence, and Inequality: An Overview of the Guatemalan Case', CRISE Working Paper No 11, Centre for Research on Inequality, Human Security and Ethnicity, University of Oxford.

Cederman, L.-E., Gleditsch, K. S., and Weidmann, N. B. (2010) *Horizontal Inequalities and Ethno-nationalist Civil War: A Global Comparison*, Zurich: Center for Comparative and International Studies.

CEH, Comisión de Esclarecimiento Histórico. (1999) *Guatemala: Memoria del Silencio. Tomo I: Mandato y Procedimiento de trabajo; Causas y Origineses del enfrentamiento armado Interno*, Oficina de Servicios para Proyectosde las Naciones Unidas (UNOPS). Available at: http://shr.aaas.org/guatemala/ceh/.

Centre for Human Rights and Global Justice. (2005) *The Missing Piece of the Puzzle: Caste Discrimination and the Conflict in Nepal*, New York: New York University, Centre for Human Rights and Global Justice.

CERD (1998) 'Concluding Observations in Nepal', *Committee on the Elimination of Racial Discrimination Fifty third Session*, Geneva.

Chen, D., Matovu, J., and Reinikka, R. (2001) 'A Quest for Revenue and Tax Incidence', in Reinikka, R., and Collier, P. (eds) *Uganda's Recovery: The Role of Farms, Firms and Government*, Washington, DC: The World Bank.

Chiu, M., and Khoo, L. (2005) 'Effects of Resources, Inequality, and Privilege Bias on Achievement: Country, School, and Student Level Analyses', *American Educational Research Journal, 42*, 575–603.

Chrétien, J. P. (2000). *L'Afrique des Grands-Lacs. Deux Mille Ans d'Histoire*, Paris: Aubier.

Chrétien, J. P.(1995) *Rwanda: Les medias du génocide*, Paris: Karthala.

Chu, K.-y., Davoodi, H. R., and Gupta, S. (2000) *Income Distribution and Tax, and Government Social Spending Policies in Developing Countries*, World Institute for Development Economics Research.

Cobham, A. (2005) 'Causes of Conflict in Sudan: Testing *The Black Book*', *European Journal of Development Research, 17* (3), 462–480.

Colletta, N. J., Kostner, M., and Wiederhofer, I. (1996) *Case Studies in War-to-Peace Transition: The Demobilization of Ex-Combatants in Ethiopia, Namibia, and Uganda*, Washington, DC: World Bank.

Collier, P. (2009) 'Post-conflict Recovery: How Should Strategies Be Distinctive?, *Journal of African Economies, 18* (1), 99–131 (forthcoming).

Collier, P. (2004) 'Aid, Policy and Growth in Post-Conflict Societies', *European Economic Review, 48* (5), 1125–1145.

Collier, P. (2000) 'Doing Well Out of War: An Economic Perspective', in Berdal, D., and Malone, D.(eds) *Greed and Grievance: Economic Agendas in Civil Wars*, Boulder and London: IDRC/Lynne Rienner.

Collier, P., and Reinikka, R. (2001) 'Reconstruction and Liberalization: An Overview', in Reinikka, R., and Collier, P. (eds) *Uganda's Recovery: The Role of Farms, Firms and Government*, Washington, DC: The World Bank.

Collier, P., and Hoeffler, A., (2004) 'Greed and Grievance in Civil War', *Oxford Economic Papers, 56*, 563–595.

Collier, P., and Hoeffler, A. (1999) *Justice Seeking and Loot-Seeking in Civil War,* Draft Paper. Available at: http://74.125.155.132/scholar?q=cache:KbqjBLDhQw0J:scholar.google.com/+Justice-Seeking+and+Loot-Seeking+in+Civil+War&hl=en&as_sdt=2000.

Collier, P., and Hoeffler, A. (1998) 'On Economic Causes of Civil War', *Oxford Economic Papers, 50* (4), 563–573.

Collier, P., and Hoeffler, A. (1996) *On Economic Causes of Civil War*, Oxford: Mimeo. Centre for the Study of African Economies.

Commander, S., and Killick, T. (1988), 'Privatisation in Developing Countries: A Survey of the Issues', in Cook, P., and Kirkpatrick, C. (eds) *Privatisation in Less Developed Countries*, Hemel Hempstead: Harvester Wheatsheaf.

Commission of the European Communities. (2008) *Commission Staff Working Document: Bosnia and Herzegovina 2008 Progress Report*, SEC 2693 final (Brussels, 05.11.2008).

Commission of the European Communities. (2006) *Commission Staff Working Document: Bosnia and Herzegovina 2006 Progress Report*, SEC 1384 (Brussels, 08.11.2008).

Contreras, C. (2004) *El aprendizaje del capitalismo: Estudios de historia económica y social del Perú republicano*, Lima: IEP.

Cook, P., and Kirkpatrick, C. (1995) 'The Distributional Impact of Privatisation in Developing Countries: Who Gets What and Why?', in Ramanadham, V. V. (ed.) *Privatisation and Equity*, London: Routledge.

Cormack, R. J., and Osborne, R. D. (1983) *Religion, Education and Employment: Aspects of Equal Opportunity in Northern Ireland*, Belfast: Appletree.

Cornia, G. A. (2004) *Inequality, Growth, and Poverty in an Era of Liberalization and Globalization*, Oxford: Oxford University Press.

Corraille, G. D., Quie Nechtigal, J., and Munyenpenda, J. (2006) *Health Sector Public Expenditure Review*, Kigali: MINISANTE, Government of Rwanda.

Cramer, C. (2006) *Civil War Is Not a Stupid Thing*, London: Hurst and Company.

Cramer, C. (2003) 'Does Inequality Cause Conflict?', *Journal of International Development, 15*, 397–412.

Cramer, C. (2001) 'Privatisation and Adjustment in Mozambique: A "Hospital Pass"?', *Journal of Southern African Studies, 27* (1), 79–103.

Crispin, S. (2007) 'The Rise and Rise of a Cambodian Capitalist', *Asia Times online*, 1 September.

Crook, J. (2006) 'Promoting Peace and Economic Security in Rwanda Through Fair and Equitable Land Rights', *California Law Review, 94*, 1487, 1487–1536.

CVR, Comision de la Verdad y Reconciliacion (2003) *Informe Final*, Lima: CVR.

Dahal, D. R. (2000a) 'Nepal's Governing Elite; Their Composition and Role in Constituting the State', in Kumar, D. (ed.) *Domestic Conflict and Crisis of Governability in Nepal*, Kathmandu: Centre for Nepal and Asian Studies. Tribhuvan University.

Dahal, D. R. (2000b) 'Language Politics in Nepal', *Contributions to Nepalese Studies, 27* (2), 155–190.

Date-Bah, E. (2003) *Jobs after War: A Critical Challenge in the Peace and Reconstruction Puzzle*, Geneva: International Labour Office.

Davies, V. (2007) 'Capital Flight and War', *Post-Conflict Transitions Working Paper* No. PC13, Washington, DC: World Bank.

Davies, Victor A.B. (2007) 'Capital Flight and War', World Bank Policy Research Working Paper No. 4210.

Davies, V. (2000b) 'Language Politics in Nepal', *Contributions to Nepalese Studies*, 27 (2), 155–190.

Degregori, C. I. (2000) *La Década de la Antipolítica: Auge y Huida de Alberto Fujimori y Vladimiro Montesinos*, Lima: IEP.

Deininger, K., and Squire, L. (1996) 'Measuring Income Inequality: A New Data-Base', *World Bank Economic, 10* (3), 565–591.

DesForges, A. (1999), *Leave None to Tell the Story: Genocide in Rwanda*, New York, Washington, London, Brussels: Human Rights Watch.

DfiD (2007) *Development Dilemmas: Challenges of Working in Conflict and Post Conflict Situations in South Asia*, DFID, UK.

DfiD (2004) *Nepal Country Assistance Plan 2004–2008*, London: Department of International development, UK Government.

DfiD (2004a) *Regional Assistance Plan for the Western Balkans 2004/05–2008/09*, London: Department for Internaitonal Development.

DHS, Demographic and Health Survey. (2006) *Rwanda Demographic and Health Survey 2005*, Maryland, USA: Calverton.

Diao, X., Fan, S., Kanyarukiga, S., and Yu, B. (2007) *Agricultural Growth and Investment Options for Poverty Reduction in Rwanda*, IFPRI Discussion Paper, Development Strategy and Governance Division, Washington DC.

Didik, N., and Gligorov, V. (2007) *Current Account Deficit Sustainability in Bosnia and Herzegovina*, Unpublished Research Paper (March).

Dijkstra, A. G., and Van Donge, J. K. (2001) 'What Does the "Show Case" Show? Evidence of and Lessons from Adjustment in Uganda', *World Development, 29* (5), 841–863.

Divjac, B. and Pugh, M. (2008), 'The Political Economy of Corruption in Bosnia and Herzegovina', *International Peacekeeping, 15* (3), 373–386.

Do, Q-T., and Iyer, L. (2005) *An Empirical Analysis of Civil Conflict in Nepal*, Unpublished manuscript, Boston, MA: Harvard Business School.

Donais, T. (2005) *The Political Economy of Peacebuilding in Post-Dayton*, Bosnia: Routledge.

Dorsey, M. (2000) 'Violence and Power-building in Post-genocide Rwanda', in Doom, D., and Gorus, J. (eds) *Politics of Identity and Economics of Conflict in the Great Lakes Region*, Brussels: VUB University Press.

Duffield, M. R. (1994) 'The Political Economy of Internal War: Asset Transfer, Complex Emergencies and International Aid', in Macrae, J., and Zwi, A. (eds) *War and Hunger: Rethinking International Responses to Complex Emergencies*, London: Zed Books.

Edwards, P. (1996) 'Ethnic Chinese in Cambodia', *Interdisciplinary Research on Ethnic Groups in Cambodia*, Centre for Advanced Study, Pnomh Penn.

Edwards, D. (2002) *Before Taliban. Genealogies of the Afghan Jihad*, Berkeley, CA: University of California Press.

Eguren, F. (2004) *Las Políticas Agrarias en la Ultima Década: Una Evaluación*, SEPIA X, available at: http://www.piuraonline.org/webot/semregagro14nov/fernandoegurensepia2003.pdf.

Elster, J. (1999) *Alchemies of the Mind: Rationality and the Emotions*, New York: Cambridge University Press.

Escobal, J., and Ponce, C. (2002) 'The Benefits of Rural Roads: Enhancing Income Opportunities for the Rural Poor', Grade Working Paper 40. Grupo de Analisis para el Desarrollo, Lima.

Escobal, J., and Ponce, C. (2007) 'Liberalizacion Comercial, Tratados de Libre Comercio y Pobreza Rural', in Grade (ed) *Investigación, Políticas y Desarrollo en el Peru*, Lima: Grade.

Evans, A., and Piron, L. H. (2004) *Politics and the PRSP Approach*, ODI Working Paper No. 237.

Evans, P. (1989), 'Predatory, Developmental, and Other Apparatuses: A Comparative Political Economy Perspective on the Third World State', *Sociological Forum, 4* (4), 561–587.

Faaland, J., Parkinson, J., and Saniman, R. (2003) *Growth and Ethnic Inequality – Malaysia's New Economic Policy*, Kuala Lumpur: Utusan Publications & Distributors Sdn Bhd.

Fagernas , S., and Roberts, J. (2004) 'Fiscal Impact of Aid: A Survey of Issues and Synthesis of Country Studies of Malawi, Uganda and Zambia', *ESAU Working Paper* No. 11. Overseas Development Institute.

Fan, S., Zhang, X., and Rao, N. (2004) 'Public Expenditure, Growth and Poverty Reduction in Rural Uganda', DSGD Discussion Paper No. 4, Washington, DC: International Food Policy Research Institute (IFPRI).

Fan, S., Johnson, M., Saurkar, A., and Makombe, T. (2008) *Investing in African Agriculture to Halve Poverty by 2015*, Washington, DC: IFPRI, Development Strategy and Governance Division.

Fedderke, J. W. and Luiz, J. M. (2008) 'Does Human Capital Generate Social and Institutional Capital? Exploring Evidence from South African Time Series Data', *Oxford Economic Papers, 60* (4), pp. 649–682.

Feibengaum, H., and Henig, J (1994), 'The Political Underpinnings of Privatization: A Typology', *World Politics*, 46, 185–208.

Felbab-Brown, V. (2005) 'Drugs and State Building in Afghanistan', *Précis,* 15 (1), 4–19.

Festic, A., and Rausche, A. (2004) 'War by Other Means: How Bosnia's Clandestine Political Economies Obstruct Peace and State Building', *Problems of Post-Communism, 51* (3), 27–34.

Figueroa, A. (2008) 'Education, Labour Markets and Inequality in Peru', CRISE Working Paper 48, Centre for Research on Inequality, Human Security and Ethnicity, University of Oxford.

Figueroa, A., and Barron, M. (2005) 'Inequality, Ethnicity and Social Disorder in Peru', CRISE Working Paper 8, Centre for Research on Inequality, Human Security and Ethnicity, University of Oxford.

Figueroa, A., Altamariano, T. and Sulmont, D. (1996) 'Social Exclusion and Inequality in Peru', Geneva: International Labour Institute.

Fishstein, P. (2010) Winning Hearts and Minds? Examining the Relationship between Aid and Security in Afghanistan's Balkh Province Paul Fishstein November 2010 Feinstein International Centre, Tufts University, Medford, USA.

Frerks, G., and Klem, B. (2006) *Creating Peace among Protagonists: A Study into the Use of Peace Conditionalities in the Sri Lankan Peace Process*, Clingendael: Netherlands Institute of International Relations.

Fukuda-Parr, S., Fuentes, J. A., Parakrama, A., Ruane, B., and Tran V. T. (2007) 'Integrating Human Rights into National Poverty Reduction Strategies: The Challenge of Development with Equity and the Liberia iPRS', Report for the UN Office of High Commissioner for Human Rights.

Fukuda-Parr, S., and McCandless, E. (2009) 'An Integrated Framework for Peacebuilding, Human Rights and Development: Reflections on Liberia's Poverty Reduction Strategy', in Omeje, K. (ed.) *War to Peace Transition: Conflict Intervention and Peacebuilding in Liberia*, Lanham, Maryland: University Press of America.

Fulbook, D. (2004), 'Chinese Migrants and the Power of Guanxi', *Asia Times online*, 30 July 2004.

Galtung, J., and Hoivik, T. (1971) 'Structural and Direct Violence. A Note on Operationalization', *Journal of Peace Research, 8* (1), 73–76.

Garver, J. W., (1991) 'China-India Rivalry in Nepal: The Clash over Chinese Arms Sales', *Asian Survey, 31* (10), 956–975.

Gasana, L. (1994) *L'homme, l'arbre et la forêt au Rwanda. Problèmes d'un pays enclavé et très peuplé*, Zurich: ETR.

Gates, S., and Murched, M. S., (2005) 'Spatial Horizontal Inequality and the Maoist Insurgency in Nepal', *Review of Development Economics, 9* (1), 121–134.

Gelb, A. (1989) 'Financial Policies, Growth, and Efficiency', *Policy Research Working Paper Series No. 202*, Word Bank.

Gellner, D. N., (2007) 'Caste, Ethnicity and Inequality in Nepal', *Economic and Political Weekly*, 19 May.

Gershberg, A., Meade, B., and Andersson, S. (2009) 'Providing Better Education Services to the Poor: Accountability and Context in the Case of Guatemalan Decentralization', *International Journal of Educational Development, 29*, 187–200.

Ghai, D., and Court, D. (1974) *Education, Society and Development: New Perspectives from Kenya*, Nairobi: Oxford University Press.

Ghose, A. K., Majid, N., and Ernst, C. (2008) *The Global Employment Challenge*, Geneva: International Labour Office.

Giustozzi, A. (2009) *Empires of Mud: Wars and Warlords in Afghanistan*, London: Hurst.

Giustozzi, A. (2007) *Koran, Kalashnikov and Laptop, The Neo Talban Insurgency in Afghanistan*, London: Hurst & Company.

Glatzer, B. (1998) 'Is Afghanistan on the Brink of Ethnic and Tribal Disintegration?', in Maley, W. (ed.) *Fundamentalism Reborn? Afghanistan and the Taliban*, London: Hurst & Co.

Global Witness (2007) *Cambodia's Family Trees: Illegal Logging and the Stripping of Public Assets by Cambodia's Elite*, Washington, DC: Global Witness.

Goldstone, J. A. (1991) *Revolution and Rebellion in the Early Modern World*, Berkeley: University of California Press.

Golooba-Mutebi, F. (2008) *Economic Liberalization and Politics in Uganda*, Paper prepared for the 'Economic Liberalisation and War' project.

Gomez, T. (2005) 'The Perils of Pro-Malay Policies', *Far Eastern Economic Review, 168* (8), 36–40.

Goodhand, J. (2009) *Bandits, Borderlands and Opium Wars. Afghan Statebuilding Viewed from the Margins*, DIIS Working Paper.

Goodhand, J. (2008) 'Corrupting or Consolidating the Peace? The Drugs Economy and Post Conflict Peacebuilding in Afghanistan', *International Peacekeeping, 15* (3), 405–423.

Goodhand, J. (2005) 'Frontiers and Wars: The Opium Economy in Afghanistan', *Journal of Agrarian Change, 5* (2), 191–216.

Goodhand, J. (2004) 'Afghanistan in Central Asia', in Pugh, M., Coper, N., and Goodhand, J. (eds) *War Economies in a Regional Context: Challenges for Transformation*, London: International Peace Academy/Lynne Rienner, pp. 45–89.

Goodhand, J. (2001) *Aid, Conflict and Peacebuilding in Sri Lanka*, London: Centre for Defence Studies, King's College.

Goodhand, J., and Sedra, M. (2009) 'Who Owns the Peace? Aid, Reconstruction and Peacebuilding in Afghanistan', *Disasters 10* (4), 78–102.

Goodhand, J., and Sedra, M. (2007) 'Bribes or Bargains? Peace Conditionalities and "Post Conflict" Reconstruction in Afghanistan', *International Peacekeeping, 14* (1), 41–61.

Gordon, N. (1993) *Murders in the Mist*, London: Hodder and Stoughton.

Gordon, S. (2011) Winning Hearts and Minds? Examining the Relationship between Aid and Security in Afghanistan's Helmand Province Stuart Gordon April 2011 Feinstein International Centre, Tufts University, Medford, USA.

Government of Liberia. (2008) *National Budget for the Fiscal Year July 1, 2008 to June 30, 2009*, Bureau of the Budget.

Government of Nepal. (2007) *Three Year Interim Plan 2008–2010*, National Planning Commission, available at: http://www.npc.gov.np/en/plans-programs/detail.php?titleid=19.

Government of Nepal. (2006) *Comprehensive Peace Agreement*, available at: http://www.unmin.org.np/downloads/keydocs/2006-11-29-peace_accord-MOFA.pdf.

Government of Nepal. (2003) *The Tenth Plan (Poverty Reduction Strategy Paper 2002–2007)*, Nepal: National Planning Commission.

Government of the Islamic Republic of Afghanistan. (2007) 'Afghan National Development Strategy', *Provincial Development Plan* (in Pashto), Kabul.

Government of the Islamic Republic of Afghanistan. (2003) *Securing Afghanistan's Future*, Kabul.

Grenier, Y. (1996) 'From Causes to Causers: The Etiology of Salvadoran Internal War Revisited', *Journal of Conflict Studies* (Fall), 26–43.

Guannu, J. S. (2009) 'The Political History of Liberia and the Civil War', in Omeje, K. (ed.) *War to Peace Transition: Conflict Intervention and Peacebuilding in Liberia*, Lanham, Maryland: University Press of America.

Guerra-Borges, A. (2006) *Guatemala: 60 años de historia económica (1944–2004)*, Guatemala City: United Nations Development Program.

Guichaoua, A. (1995) 'Scolarisation des élites et renforcement de la conscience ethnique,' in Guichaoua, A. (ed.) *Les crises politiques au Burundi et au Rwanda (1993–1994)*, Paris: Karthala.

Guichaoua, A. (1991) 'Les Travaux Communautaires en Afrique Centrale', *Revue Tiers Monde, 32* (127), 551–573.

Gupta, K. L. (1987) 'Savings, Financial Intermediation, and Interest Rate', *The Review of Economics and Statistics, 69* (2), 303–311.

Gurr, T. (1970) *Why Men Rebel?* Princeton: Princeton University Press.

Gurung, H. (1969) *Regional Development Planning for Nepal*, Kathmandu: National Planning Commision.

Gurung, H. (2005) 'Nepal Regional Strategy for Development' *ADB Nepal Resident Mission. Working Paper No.3.* Kathmandu: Asian Development Bank.

Hachhethu, K. (2007) 'Legitimacy Crisis in the Nepali Monarchy', Paper presented at the Wilton Park Conference on Democracy, Politics, and Development (WP874), Steyning: Wilton Park.

Hallward, P. (2007) *Damming the Flood: Haiti, Aristide, and the Politics of Containment,* London and New York: Verso Press.

Hanlon, J. (2002) 'Bank Corruption Becomes Site of Struggle in Mozambique', *Review of African Political Economy, 29* (91), 53–72.

Hansen, A., Julie, N., and Joy, W. *Final report*, Washington, DC.: USAID (2002) *Creative Associates International. Final Evaluation of the Office of Transition Initiatives' Program in Sierra Leone.*

Hanssen, A. (1989). *Le Désenchantement de la Coopération: Enquêteau Pays des Mille Coopérants*, Paris: L'Harmattan.

Hartzell, C., and Hoddie, M. (2003) 'Institutionalising Peace: Power Sharing and Post-Civil War Conflict Management', *American Journal of Political Science, 47* (2), 318–332.

Hayden, W. (1999) 'The Kosovo Conflict: The Strategic Use of Displacement and the Obstacles to International Protection', *Civil Wars, 2* (1), 35–68.

Henriquez, N. (1986) 'Notas y tesis sobre los movimientos regionales en el Peru', in Ballon, E. (ed.) *Movimientos Sociales y Crisis: El Caso Peruano*, Lima: Desco.

Hodges, T., and Tibana R.(2004) *'The Political Economy of the Budget in Mozambique'*, Mimeo.

Höfer, A. (1979) *The Caste Hierarchy and the State in Nepal: A Study of the Muluki Ain of 1854*, Innsbruck: Universitätsverlag Wagner.

Horowitz, D. L. (1985) *Ethnic Groups in Conflict*, Berkeley, C.A.: University of California Press.

HRW, Human Rights Watch. (2001a) *Uprooting the Rural Poor in Rwanda: Women, Children and the Elderly*, New York: Human Rights Watch Report.

HRW, Human Rights Watch. (2001b) *Uprooting the Rural Poor in Rwanda*, New York: Human Rights Watch.

Hughes, C. (2003) *The Political Economy of Cambodia's Transition, 1991–2001*, London: Routledge. Humphreys, M., and Richards, P. (2005) 'Prospects and Opportunities for Achieving the MDGs in Post-conflict Countries: A Case Study of Sierra Leone and Liberia', CGSD Working paper No. 27, Center of Globalization and Sustainable Development, The Earth Institute, Columbia University. Available at: http://www.earthinstitute.columbia.edu/cgsd/documents/HumphreysRichards.pdf.

Hutt, M. (ed.) (2004) *Himalayan "People's War": Nepal's Maoist Rebellion*, London: Hurst and Co.

Ibrahimi, N. (2009a) *At the Source of Factionalism and Civil War in the Hazarajat*, Crisis States Research Centre, LSE, London. Available at: http://www.crisisstates.com/download/wp/wpSeries2/WP41.2.pdf.

Ibrahimi, N. (2009b) *Divide and Rule: State Penetration in Hazarajat (Afghanistan) from the Monarchy to the Taliban*, Crisis States Programme, Crisis States Research Centre, LSE, London.

ICEFI (2007) *Historia de la tributación en Guatemala (desde los Mayas hasta la actualidad)*, Guatemala City: Instituto Centroamericano de Estudios Fiscales (ICEFI).

ICG (2008) Sierra *Leone: A New Era of Reform? Executive Summary and Recommendations*, London: International Crisis Group.

IDA (2007) *Interim Strategy Note for Nepal*, Washington, DC: International Development Association, World Bank.

III, Instituto Interuniversitario de Iberoamérica(2005) *Perfil de Gobernabilidad de Guatemala*, Salamanca: Ediciones Universidad de Salamanca.

IMF (2008) *Liberia: Joint Staff Advisory Note of the Poverty Reduction Strategy Paper, IMF* Country Report No.8/289.

IMF (2004), *Bosnia and Herzegovina: Poverty Reduction Strategy Paper – Mid-Term Development Strategy*, Washington, DC: IMF Country Report No. 04/114.

International Crisis Group (2000) *Scramble for the Congo: Anatomy of an Ugly War*, Brussels: Africa Report.

Irvin, G. (1993) *Rebuilding Cambodia's Economy: UNCTAC and Beyond*, ISS working paper No. 149.

ISTEEBU-Institut de statistiques et études économiques du Burundi (2008) *Enquête sur le suivi des dépenses publiques et le niveau de satisfaction des bénéficiaires dans les secteurs de l'éducation, de la santé et de justice en République du Burundi. Volet éducation*, Bujumbura: Rapport principal des résultats.

Jackson, S. (2002) 'Making a Killing: Criminality and Coping in the Kivu War Economy', *Review of African Political Economy, 29* (93), 517–536.

Jackson, S. (2001) 'The Challenges and Contradictions of Development and Conflict', *A Background Paper for the INCORE Summer School*, 10–14 June.

Jackson, T. (2000) 'L'Egalite d'accès à l'éducation: Un impératif pour la paix au Burundi', *International Alert*, London. Unpublished manuscript.

Jackson, M., and Gordon S. (2007) 'Rewiring Interventions? UK Provincial Reconstruction Teams and "Stabilization" ', *International Peacekeeping, 14* (5), 647–661.

Johnsen, U. H. (2002) *Caste-Based Prejudices and Discrimination in Nepal: A Survey Report*, Report Submitted to DANIDA/HUGO.

Jonas, S. (2000) *Of Centaurs and Doves : Guatemala's Peace Process*, Oxford: Westview Press.

Jones, L. (2000) 'The Evolution of Property Use in Rwanda', *Refugee Survey Quarterly, 19* (3), 130–150.

Jonglez, O., and Byrd, W. (2006) 'Prices and Market Interactions in the Opium Economy', in Buddenberg, D., and Byrd, W. (eds) *Afghanistan's Drug Industry: Structure, Functioning, Dynamics and Implications for Counter-Narcotics Policy*, UNODC and The World Bank.

Justino, P., and Verwimp, P. (2006) *Poverty Dynamics, Violent Conflict and Convergence in Rwanda*, HiCN Working Paper, Households in Conflict Network.

Kasozi, A. B. K. (1999) *The Social Origins of Violence in Uganda, 1964–1985*, Montreal & Kingston: McGill-Queen's University Press.

Kayizzi-Mugerwa, S. (2002) *Fiscal Policy, Growth and Poverty Reduction in Uganda*, WIDER Discussion Paper No. 2002/33, WIDER United Nations University.

Kayizzi-Mugerwa, S. (1999) *Uganda at the End of the 1990s: A Medium-Term Assessment*, Country Economic Report, Stockholm: Swedish International Development Cooperation Agency (SIDA).

Keen, D. (2005) *Conflict & Collusion in Sierra Leone*, Oxford: James Currey.

Keen, D. (1998) *The Economic Functions of Violence in Civil War*, Oxford: Oxford University Press for the International Institute of Strategic Studies.

Khatiwada, L. K. (2006) *Inequality and Conflict: A Case of Western Hill of Nepal*, Paper presented at the 2006 Rural Sociology Society Annual Meeting, Louisville, KY.

Klugman, J., Neyapti, B., and Stewart, F. (1999a) *Conflict and Growth in Africa, Vol. 2: Kenya, Tanzania and Uganda*, Paris: OECD.

Klugman, J. (2000) 'Kenya: Economic Decline and Ethnic Politics', in Nafiziger, E. W., Vayrynen, R., and Stewart, F. (eds) *War, Hunger and Displacement: Weak States and Vulnerable Economies: Humanitarian Emergencies in Developing Countries*, Oxford: OUP.

Klugman, J., Neyapti, B., and Stewart, F. (1999b) *Conflict and Growth in Africa. Vol. 2: Kenya, Tanzania and Uganda*, Paris: Organisation for Economic Cooperation and Development.

Kluve, J. (2007) *Active Labor Market Policies in Europe: Performance and Perspectives*, Berlin, New York: Springer.

Koehler, J., and Zuercher, C. (2007) 'Statebuilding, Conflict and Narcotics, in Afghanistan', *Journal of International Peacekeeping, 14* (1), 62–74.

Kohler, G, and Alcock, N. (1976) 'An Empirical Table of Structural Violence', *Journal of Peace Research, 13* (4), 343–356.

Kostic, R. (2002) *Bosnia and Herzegovina Conflict Analysis: A Report for the Swedish International Development Co-Operation Agency*, Uppsala: Centre for Multiethnic Research.

Kostic, R. (2007), *Ambivalent Peace: External Peacebuilding, Threatened Identity and Reconciliation in Bosnia and Herzegovina*, Doctoral dissertation, Department of Peace and Conflict Research, Uppsala University, Sweden.

Kraay, A., and Van Rijckeghem, C. (1995) *Employment and Wages in the Public Sector: A Cross-Country Study*, SSRN, IMF Working Paper No. 95/70, Washington, DC: IMF.

Kreimer, A., Collier, P., Scott, C. S., and Arnold, M. (2000) *Uganda Post-Conflict Reconstruction*, Washington, DC: World Bank.

Krishnamurty, J. (2003) 'The Labour Market and Conflict', in Date-Bah, E. (ed.) *Jobs After War*, Geneva: ILO.

Kymlicka, W. (2003)' Multicultural States and Intercultural Citizens', *Theory and Research in Education, 1* (2), 147–169.

Ladbury, S. (2009) *Testing Hypotheses on Radicalisation in Afghanistan. Why Do Men Join the Taliban and Hizb-i Islami? How Much Do Local Communities Support Them?*, Kabul: Cooperation for Peace and Unity (CPAU).

Langer, A. (2009) 'Living with Diversity: The Peaceful Management of Horizontal Inequalities in Ghana', *Journal of International Development, 21* (4), 534–546.

Langer, A. (2008) 'When Do Horizontal Inequalities Lead to Conflict? Lessons from a Comparative Study of Ghana and Cote d'Ivoire', in Stewart, F. (ed.) *Horizontal Inequalities and Conflict: Understanding Group Violence in Multiethnic Societies*, Basingstoke: Palgrave Macmillan.

Langer, A. (2005) 'Horizontal Inequalities and Violent Group Mobilization in Cote d'Ivore, *Oxford Development Studies, 33* (1), 25–45.

Langer, A., and Brown, G. (2008) 'Cultural Status Inequalities: An Important Dimension of Group Mobilization', in Stewart, F. (ed.) *Horizontal Inequalities and Conflict: Understanding Group Violence in Multiethnic Societies*, Basingstoke: Palgrave Macmillan.

Le Billon, P. (2002) 'Logging in Muddy Waters: The Politics of Forest Exploitation in Cambodia', *Critical Asian Studies, 34* (4), 563–586.

Lecomte-Tilouine, M. (2004) 'Ethnic Demands within Maoism: Questions of Magar Territorial Autonomy, Nationality, and Class', in Hutt, M. (ed.) *Himalayan "People's War": Nepal's Maoist Rebellion*, London: Hurst & Co.

Lemarchand, R. (1995) 'Rwanda: The Rationality of Genocide', *African Studies Association, 23* (2), 8–11.

Lijphardt, A. (2008) *Thinking about Democracy: Power-Sharing and Majority Rule in Theory and Practice*, Abingdon: Routledge.

MacDermott, J. (2001). *The Livelihood Conflicts Approach on Trial: Towards a Political Critique*, DESTIN Working Paper Series No. 01-21, London School of Economics and Political Science, Development Studies Institute.

MacDonald, D. (2007) *Drugs in Afghanistan. Opium, Outlaws and Scorpion Tales*, London: Pluto.

Macours, K. (2006) *Relative Deprivation and Civil Conflict in Nepal*, Unpublished manuscript, Washington, DC: John Hopkins University, School of Advanced International Studies.

Maimbo, S. M. (2003) *The Money Exchange Dealers of Kabul: A Study of the Hawala System in Afghanistan*, Washington, DC: Finance and Private Sector Unit, South Asia Region, World Bank.

Mamdani, M. (2001) *When Victims Become Killers: Colonialism, Nativism, and the Genocide in Rwanda*, Oxford: James Currey.

Mancini, L. (2005) *Horizontal Inequality and Communal Violence: Evidence from Indonesian Districts*, CRISE Working Paper No. 22, Oxford: Centre for Research on Inequality, Human Security and Ethnicity, University of Oxford.

Mancini, L., Stewart, F., and Brown, G. (2008) 'Approaches to the Measurement of Horizontal Inequalities', in Stewart, F. (ed.) *Horizontal Inequalities and Conflict: Understanding Group Violence in Multiethnic Societies*, London: Palgrave Macmillan.

Manning, C. (2002) *The Politics of Peace in Mozambique: Post-Conflict Democratization, 1992–2000*, Santa Barbara, CA: Greenwood.

Mansfield, D. (2006) 'Responding to the Challenge of Diversity in Opium Poppy Cultivation', in Buddenberg, D., and Byrd, W. (eds) *Afghanistan's Opium Industry: Structure, Functioning Dynamics and Implications for Counter Narcotics Policy*, UNODC and World Bank.

Mansfield, D., and Pain, A. (2005) *Alternative Livelihoods: Substance or Slogan?*, Kabul: Afghanistan Research and Evaluation Unit.

Mansfield, D., and Pain, A. (2008) *Counter-Narcotics in Afghanistan: The Failure of Success?*, Kabul: Afghanistan Research and Evaluation Unit (AREU).

Marques, J., and Bannon, I. (2003) *Central America: Education Reform in a Post-Conflict Setting, Opportunities and Challenges*, CPR Working Papers No 4.

Marriage, Z. (2006) 'Defining Morality: DFID and the Great Lakes', *Third World Quarterly, 27* (3), 477–490.

Masseyy, G., Hodson, R., and Sekulic, D. (1999) 'Ethnic Enclaves and Intolerance: The Case of Yugoslavia', *Social Forces, 78* (2), 669–693.

Maton, J. (1994) *Developpement economique et social au Rwanda entre 1980 et 1993: le deixieme decile en face de l'apocalypse*, Université de Gand, Faculté des Sciences Economiques.

Matovu, J.-M. and Stewart, F. (2001) 'The Social and Economic Consequences of Conflict: A Case Study of Uganda', in Stewart, F. and Fitzgerald, V. (eds) *War and Underdevelopment: Country Experience*, Oxford: Oxford University Press.

McCrudden, C., Ford, R., and Heath, A. (2004) 'Legal Regulation of Affirmative Action in Northern Ireland: An Empirical Assessment', *Oxford Journal of Legal Studies, 24* (3), 363–415.

McEwan, P., and Trowbridge, M. (2007) 'The Achievement of Indigenous Students in Guatemalan Primary Schools', *International Journal of Educational Development, 27*, 61–76.

McKay, A., and Loveridge, S. (2005) *Exploring the Paradox of Rwandan Agricultural Household Income and Nutritional Outcomes in 1990 and 2000*, Michigan State University, Department of Agricultural Economics, Staff Paper.

McKay, A., and Loveridge, S. (2004) *Agricultural Household Income Strategies in the Context of Political Instability and Decreasing Land Availability: Comparing Rwanda in 1990 with 2000*, University of Bath and Michigan State University.

Mémorandum des Associations de la Société Civile du Burundi (2008) Bujumbura.

MINECOFIN (2007) *Integrated Household Living Conditions Survey 2*, Kigali: Ministry of Finance and Economic Planning.
MINECOFIN (2002a) *Integrated Household Living Conditions Survey in Rwanda*, Final Report. Kigali: Ministry of Finance and Economic Planning, Statistics Department, Republic of Rwanda.
MINECOFIN (2002b) *Vision 2020*, Kigali: Ministry of Finance and Economic Planning, Republic of Rwanda.
MINECOFIN (2001) *Rwandan Official Statistics*, Ministry of Finance and Economic Planning, Statistics Department. Kigali: Republic of Rwanda.
Ministerio de Educacion (2006) *Construyendo sobre lo construido. A diez años de los Acuerdos De Paz*, Guatemala City: Ministry of Education (evaluation report).
Ministerio de Educación and Consejo Nacional de Educación (2007) *Proyecto Educativo Nacional al 2021*, available at http://pen.cne.gob.pe/ documentos.php.
MINITERE (2004) *National Land Policy*, Kigali: Ministry of Lands, Environment, Forestry, Water and Natural Resources.
Montague, D. (2002) 'Stolen Goods: Coltan and Conflict in the Democratic Republic of Congo', *SAIS Review, XXII* (1), 103–118.
Morgan, G. (1990) 'Violence in Mozambique: Towards an Understanding of Renamo', *The Journal of Modern African Studies*, 28 (4), 603–619.
Moor, B. (1966) *Social Origins of Dictatorship and Democracy: Lord and Peasant in the Making of the Modern World*, London: Penguin.
Mudoola, D. M. (1991) 'Institution-Building: The Case of the NRM and the Military in Uganda 1986–9', in Hansen, H. B. and Twaddle, M. (eds) *Changing Uganda*, London: James Currey.
Muller, E., and Seligson, M. (1987) 'Inequality and Insurgency', *American Political Science Review, 81* (2), 425–451.
Murshed, S. M. (2007) *The Conflict-Growth Nexus and the Poverty of Nations*, DESA Working Paper No. 43 ST/ESA/2007/DWP/43.
Murshed, S. M., and Gates, S. (2005) 'Spacial Horizontal Inequality and the Maoist Insurgency in Nepal', *Review of Development Economics, 9* (1), 121–134.
Musahara, H., and Huggins, C. (2004) 'Land Reform, Land Scarcity and Post-Conflict Reconstruction: A Case Study of Rwanda', *Eco-Conflicts, 3* (3), 269–346.
Nachega, J. C. (2001) *Financial Liberalization, Money Demand and Inflation in Uganda*, IMF Working Paper 118, Washington, DC: IMF.
Napier, M. J. (2007) *Land Reform in Post-Conflict Rwanda: An Evaluation of the Villagisation Policy and Its Effects on Poverty Reduction*, The Florida State University, Department of Urban and Regional Planning.
Ndikumana, L. (2005) 'Distributional Conflict, the State and Peace Building in Burundi', *The Round Table, 94* (http://www.informaworld.com/smpp/title~content=t713448095~db=all~tab=issueslist~branches=94-v94381), 413–427.
Ndikumana, L. (2001) *Fiscal Policy, Conflict and Reconstruction in Burundi and Rwanda*, WIDER Discussion Paper No. 2001/62.
Ndimira, P.-F. (2000) 'Dimension économique de la résolution du conflit burundais', *Paper presented at the Forum sur la dimension économique de la résolution du conflit burundais*, Burundi: Bujumbura.
NESAC (1998) *Nepal Human Development Report 1998*, Kathmandu: Nepal South Asia Centre.

Netter, J., and Megginson, W. (2001) 'From State to Market: An Empirical Survey of Privatization', *Journal of Economic Literature, 39* (2), 321–389.

Ngaruko, F., and Nkurunziza, J. D. (2005) 'War and Its Duration in Burundi', in Collier, P., and Sambanis, N. (eds) *Understanding Civil War: Evidence and Analysis*, Volume 1: Africa, Washington, D.C.: World Bank Publications, pp. 35–62.

Ngaruko F., and Nkurunziza, J. D. (2000) 'An Economic Interpretation of Conflict in Burundi', *Journal of African Economies, 9* (3), 370–409.

Nicholls, D. (1985) *From Dessalines to Duvalier, Race, Colour and National Independence in Haiti*, New Brunswick: Rutgers University Press.

NIRS (2006) *Socio-Economic Status of Indigenous Peoples*, Kathmandu: Nepal Integrated research Team.

Nkurunziza, J., and Ngaruko, F. (2008) 'Why Has Burundi Grown So Slowly? The Political Economy of Redistribution', in Ndulu, B. J., O'Connell, S. A., Azam, J. P., Bates, R. H., Fosu, A. K., Gunning, J. W., and Njinkeu, D (eds) *The Political Economy of Economic Growth in Africa 1960–2000*, Cambridge: Cambridge University Press.

Nordstrom, C. (1997) *A Different Kind of War Story*, Philadelphia: University of Pennsylvania Presss.

NPC, (2003) *The Tenth Plan (Poverty Reduction Strategy Paper) 2002–2007*, Kathmandu: National Planning Commission, Hi's Majesty's Government Nepal.

Ntagungira, F., and Kimenyi, G. (2008) *Rwanda: Use Land Properly – Kagame*, Kigali: The New Times.

NURC (2001) *Brookings Initiative in Rwanda*, Kigali: National Unity and Reconciliation Commission, Republic of Rwanda.

Obidegwu, C. (2003) *Rwanda: The Search for Post-Conflict Socio-Economic Change 1995–2001*, World Bank.

OECD/DAC (2009) *Reporting System*, Online Statistics at: www.oecd.org/dac/stats.

Ohlsson, L. (2000) *Livelihood Conflicts: Linking Poverty and Environment as Causes of Conflict*, Stockholm: SIDA.

Okidi, J. A., Okwi, P., and Ddumba-Ssentamu, J. (2003) *Welfare Distribution and Poverty in Uganda, 1992 to 2000*, Occasional Paper No. 22, Kampala: Economic Policy Research Centre (EPRC).

Okidi, J. A., Ssewanyana, S., Battegeka, L., and Muhunmuza, F. (2005) *Distributional and Poverty Impacts of Uganda's Growth: 1992 to 2003*, Research Series, Kampala: Economic Policy Research Centre (ECPR).

Omeje, K. (2009) 'Introduction: Discourses of the Liberian Civil War and the Imperatives of Peacebuilding', in Omeje, K. (ed.) *War to Peace Transition: Conflict Intervention and Peacebuilding in Liberia*, Lanham, Maryland: University Press of America.

Østby, G. (2006) *Horizontal Inequalities, Political Environment and Civil Conflict: Evidence from 55 Developing Countries*, CRISE Working Paper No. 28, Oxford: Centre for Research on Inequality, Human Security and Ethnicity, University of Oxford.

PAC (2000) *The Heart of the Matter: Sierra Leone, Diamonds and Human Security*, Ottawa: Partnership Africa Canada.

PAF Nepal (2007) *Annual Report 2006/07m*, Kathmandu: Poverty Alleviation Fund Nepal.

Pain, A. (2006) 'Opium Trading Systems in Helmand and Ghor Provinces', in Buddenberg, D., and Byrd, W. (eds) *Afghanistan's Drug Industry: Structure,*

Functioning, Dynamics and Implications for Counter-Narcotics Policy, UNODC and The World Bank.

Paredes, M. (2008) *Weak Indigenous Politics in Peru*, CRISE Working Paper 33, Centre for Research on Inequality, Human Security and Ethnicity, University of Oxford.

Paredes, M. (2007) *Fluid Identities: Exploring Ethnicity in Peru*, CRISE Working Paper 40, Centre for Research on Inequality, Human Security and Ethnicity, University of Oxford.

Paris, R. (2004) *At War's End*, Cambridge: Cambridge University Press.

Patrinos, H., and Velez, E. (2009) 'Costs and Benefits of Bilingual Education in Guatemala: A Partial Analysis', *International Journal of Educational Development, 29* (6), 594–598.

Peeters, P., Cunningham, W., Acharya, G., and Van Adams, A. (2009) *Sustainable Livelihood Opportunities in a Post-Conflict Setting. Youth Employment in Sierra Leone*, Washington, DC: World Bank.

Perez Sainz, J. P. (2007) *Desigualdad, mercado de trabajo y etnicidad en Guatemala*, Unpublished CRISE Background Paper available on request (corinne.caumartin@qeh.ox.ac.uk).

PNUD (2008) *Guatemala, ¿una economía al servicio del desarrollo humano? Informe Nacional del Desarrollo Humano, 2007–2008*, Guatemala: United Nations Development Program.

PNUD (2005) *Informe Nacional de Desarollo Humano: Diversidad Etnico-Cultural: La Ciudadania en un Estado Plural*, Guatemala: PNUD.

Piñol, G. (2008) "Derrota de un dogma", *Revista Eslabón*, No 40, December [downloaded from http://www.ms.dk/sw10077.asp].

Pitcher, A. (2002) *Transforming Mozambique: The Politics of Privatization, 1975–2000*, Cambridge University Press.

Portugal, A. (2008) *Voices from the War: Exploring the Motivation of Sendero Luminoso Militants*, CRISE Working Paper 57, Centre for Research on Inequality, Human Security and Ethnicity, University of Oxford.

Pottier, J. (2006) 'Land Reform for Peace? Rwanda's 2005 Land Law in Context', *Journal of Agrarian Change, 6* (4), 509–527.

Prandan, R., and Shrestha, A. (2005) 'Ethnic and Caste Diversity: Implications for Development', *Asian Development Bank, Nepal Resident Mission*, Working Paper No. 4.

PREAL (2008) *Educación: un desafío de urgencia nacional. Informe de progreso educativo de Guatemala*, Guatemala: CIEN y Preal.

Pritchett, L., and Filmer, D (1999) 'What Educational Production Functions Really Show: A Positive Theory of Education Spending', *Economics of Education Review, 18* (2), 223–239.

Puente, J., and Linares L. F. (2004) 'General View of the Institutional State of Decentralization in Guatemala', in Tulchin J., and Selee, A. (eds) *Decentralization and Democratic Governance in Latin America*, Woodrow Wilson Center Report on the Americas #12, available at: http://www.wilsoncenter.org/topics/pubs/ACF18E5.pdf.

Pugh, M. (2006), 'Post-war Economies and the New York Dissensus', *Conflict, Security & Development, 6* (3), 269–289.

Pugh, M. (2002) 'Postwar Political Economy in Bosnia and Herzegovina: The Spoils of Peace', *Global Governance, 8*, 467–482.

Purcell, R., Dom, C., and Ahobamuteze, G. (2006) *Joint Evaluation of General Budget Support 1994–2004: Rwanda Country Report*, University of Birmingham, International Development Department, School of Public Policy.
Prunier, G. (1997) *Rwanda: the Social, Political and Economic Situation*, WRITENET, UK.
Prunier, G. (1995) *The Rwanda Crisis: History of a Genocide*, London: C. Hurst & Company.
Ramachandran, V., and Shah, M. K. (1999) 'Minority Entrepreneurs and Firm Performance in Sub-Saharan Africa', *Journal of Development Studies, 36* (2), 71–87.
Regmi, A. (2007) 'The New Nepal: Enter Ethnic Politics?' *Nepal Monitor*, January http://www.nepalmonitor.com/2007/01/the_new_nepal_enter.html.
Reinikka, R. and Collier, P. (2001) *Uganda's Recovery: The Role of Farms, Firms and Government*, Washington, DC: The World Bank.
Renton, D., Seddon, D., and Zeilig, L. (2007) *The Congo: Plunder and Resistance*, London: Zed.
Reno, W. (2000) 'Liberia and Sierra Leone: The Competition for Patronage in Resource-Rich Economies', in Nafziger, E. W., Stewart. F., and Vayrynen, R. (eds) *War, Hunger and Displacement: The Origin of Humanitarian Emergencies*, Oxford: Oxford University Press.
République du Burundi (2009) *Décret No. 100/11 du 16 janvier 2009 portant publication des résultats préliminaires du troisième recensement général de la population et de l'habitation du Burundi de 2008*, Bujumbura: Cabinet du Président.
République du Burundi (2008) *Loi No. 1/19 du 22 août 2008 portant fixation du budget général révisé de la République du Burundi pour l'exercice 2008*, Bujumbura: Cabinet du Président.
République du Burundi (2006) *Loi No. 1/38 du 30 décembre 2006 portant fixation du budget général de la République du Burundi pour l'exercice 2007*, Bujumbura Cabinet du Président.
République d'Haiti (2007), *Pour réussir le saut qualitatif, document de stratégie nationale pour la croissance et la réduction de la pauvreté*, Ministère de la Planification et de la Coopération Externe, DSNCRP (2008–2010).
Republic of Liberia (2008a) *Poverty Reduction Strategy*, Executive Mansion, Monrovia, Liberia. Available at: http://www.emansion.gov.lr/doc/Final%20PRS.pdf.
Republic of Liberia (2008b) *National Budget for the Fiscal Year 2008–2009*, Liberia: Executive Mansion, Monrovia.
Republic of Rwanda (2005) *Organic Law No. 08/2005 of 14/7/2005 Determining the Use and Management of Land in Rwanda*, Kigali: Republic of Rwanda.
Republic of Uganda (2003) *Post-Conflict Reconstruction: The Case of Northern Uganda*, Kampala: Ministry of Finance, Planning and Economic Development, Government of Uganda.
Reynal-Querol, M. (2002) 'Ethnicity, Political Systems and Civil Wars', *Journal of Conflict Resolution, 46* (1), 29–54.
Reyntjens, F. (1994) *L'Afrique des Grands Lacs en crise: Rwanda, Burundi: 1988–1994*, Paris: Karthala.
Riddell, B. (2005) 'Sierra Leone: Urban-Elite Bias, Atrocity and Debt', *Review of African Political Economy, 103*, 115–133.
Rivera, R. (2005) 'La descentralización en Centroamérica: entre el discurso de la modernización institucional y las resistencias del centralismo', in

Gobernabilidad en América Latina: Balance reciente y tendencias al Futuro, available at: http://bibliotecavirtual.clacso.org.ar/ar/libros/costar/flacso/roy.pdf.

Rodríguez, M. (1981) 'El Frente de Defensa del Pueblo de Loreto: Ensayo de Interpretación de un movimiento social'. Lima: Taller de Estudios Urbano Industriales, PUCP.

Robinson, M. (2005) *The Political Economy of Turnaround in Uganda*, Paper prepared for the Low Income Countries under Stress (LICUS) Initiative, The World Bank.

Robinson, W. (2003) *Transnational Conflicts. Central America, Social Change, and Globalization*, London: Verso.

Roitman, J. (2003) Unsanctioned Wealth; or the Productivity of Debt in Northern Cameroon', *Public Culture, 15* (2), 211–237.

Romkema, K., and Vlassenroot, H. (2002) *The Emergence of a New Order? Resources and War in Eastern Congo*, available at: http://jha.ac/articles/a111.htm.

Rosenthal, G (2005) *Haiti: Short and Long-Term Development Issues*, ECLAC, LC/MEX/L.683 18.

Roy, O. (1990) *Islam and Resistance in Afghanistan*, Cambridge: Cambridge University Press.

Rubin, B. (2006) 'Peace Building and State-Building in Afghanistan: Constructing Sovereignty for Whose Security?', *Third World Quarterly, 27* (1), 175–185.

Rubin, B. (2000) 'The Political Economy of War and Peace in Afghanistan', *World Development, 28* (2), 789–1803.

Rubin, B (1996) *The Fragmentation of Afghanistan. State Formation and Collapse in the International System*, Lahore: Vanguard Books.

Rubin, B. (1992) 'Political Elites in Afghanistan: Rentier State Building, Rentier State Wrecking', *International Journal of Middle East Studies, 24* (1), 77–99.

Rubin, B., and Sherman, J. (2008) *Counter-Narcotics to Stabilize Afghanistan: The False Promise of Crop Eradication*, New York: CIC.

Salvi del Pero, A. (2005) *Ethnic Inequality in Nepal: A Regression-Based Analysis*, Unpublished Manuscript, Milan: Dipartimento di Economic Politica e Aziendale.

Samset, I. (2002) 'Conflict of Interests or Interests in Conflict? Diamonds & War in the DRC', *Review of African Political Economy, 93/97*, 463–480.

Sánchez-Ancochea, D. (2005) 'Domestic capital, Civil Servants and the State: Costa Rica and the Dominican Republic under Globalization', *Journal for Latin American Studies, 37*, 693–726.

Sandrart, G. (1953) 'Le Ruanda-Urundi: Terre des rois-pasteurs', in Dessart, C (ed.) *Ruanda-Urundi*, Brussels: Plus Oultre.

Schady, N. (2000) 'The Political Economy of Expenditures by the Peruvian Social Fund (FONCODES), 1991–95', *The American Political Science Review, 94* (2), 289–304.

Schetter, C., Glassner, R., and Karokhail, M. (2007) 'Beyond Warlordism: The Local Security Architecture in Afghanistan', *Journal for International Relations and Global Trends, 2*, 137–152.

Schneider, A. (2009) 'Socio-economic Change and Fiscal Challenges in Central America: Globalisation, Democratisation and the Politics of Reform', in Sánchez-Ancochea, D. and Morgan, I. (eds) *The Political Economy of the Public*

Budgets in the Americas, Institute of the Studies of the Americas, University of London.
Schneiderman, S., and Turin, M. (2004) 'The Path to Jan Sarkar in Dolakha District: Towards an Ethnography of the Maoist Movement', in Hutt, M. (ed.) *Himalayan "People's War": Nepal's Maoist Rebellion*, London: Hurst & Co.
Scott, J. (1976) *The Moral Economy of the Peasant: Rebellion and Subsistence in Southeast Asia*, New Haven: Yale University Press.
Segovia, A. (2005) *Integración real y grupos de poder económico en América Central: implicaciones para el desarrollo y la democracia de la región*, San José, Costa Rica: Friedrich Ebert Foundation.
Segovia, A. (2004) 'Centroamérica después del café: el fin del modelo agroexportador tradicional y el surgimiento de un nuevo modelo económico', *Revista Centroamericana de Ciencias Sociales*, 1 (2), 5–38.
Sen, A. K. (1975) *Employment, Technology and Development*, New Delhi: Oxford University Press.
Sharer, R. L., De Zoysa, H. R., and McDonald, C. A. (1995) *Uganda: Adjustment with Growth, 1987–94*, Occassional Paper No. 121, Washington, DC: IMF.
Shaw, M. (2006) 'Drug Trafficking and the Development of Organized Crime in Post-Taliban Afghanistan', in Buddenberg, D., and Byrd, W. (eds) *Afghanistan's Drug Industry: Structure, Functioning, Dynamics and Implications for Counter-Narcotics Policy*, UNODC and The World Bank.
Shone, M. (2003) 'Labour-Based Infrastructure Rebuilding', in Date-Bah, E. (ed.) *Jobs After war*, Geneva: ILO.
Shrestha, B., Shrestha H. S., and Bhatt, S. (2004) *Foreign Aid Utilization at the Grassroots Level: A Case Study of Local Development Fund*, Report Submitted to the South Asia Network of Economic Research Institute, Kathmandu: Institute for Integrated Development.
Sibomana, A. (1999) *Hope for Rwanda: Conversations with Laure Guilbert and Hervé Deguine*, London and Sterling, V.A.: Pluto Press.
Sieder, R. (ed.) (1998) *Guatemala after the Peace Accords*, London: Institute of Latin American Studies.
Simon, A. (2003) *Ex-Combatants' Re-integration: Key Issues for Policy Makers and Practitioners, Based on Lessons from Sierra Leone*, London: DFID.
Sisk, T. (1996) *Power Sharing and International Mediation in Ethnic Conflicts*, Washington, D.C.: United States Institute of Peace.
Soberon, R. (2005) 'Narcotrafico y Derechos Humanos', in Cabieses, H., Caceres, B., Rumrrill, R., and Soberon, R. (eds) *Hablan los Diablos*, Quito: ABYA-YALA, TNI and MLAL.
SOFOS Consultants (2008) *Mission de recensement des fonctionnaires civils de l'Etat du Burundi. Document d'évaluation du recensement*. PAGE/C/009/07. Bujumbura.
Songsore, J. (2003) *Regional Development in Ghana: The Theory and the Reality*, Accra: Woeli Publishing Services.
Stewart, F. (ed.) (2008) *Horizontal Inequalities and Conflict: Understanding Group Violence in Multiethnic Societies*, Basingstoke: Palgrave Macmillan.
Stewart, F. (2005) *Policies towards Horizontal Inequalities in Post-Conflict Reconstruction*, CRISE Working Paper 7, Centre for Research on Inequalities, Security and Ethnicity, University of Oxford.

Stewart, F. (2001) *Horizontal Inequalities: A Neglected Dimension of Development*, WIDER Annual Lectures 5, Helsinki: WIDER.

Stewart, F. (2000) 'Crisis Prevention: Tackling Horizontal Inequalities', *Oxford Development Studies, 28* (3), 245–263.

Stewart, F. (1998) *The Root Causes of Conflict: Evidence and Policy Implications*, Conference on War, Hunger and Displacement: The Economics and Politics of the Prevention of Complex Humanitarian Emergencies, 15–16 June, Stockholm: UNU/WIDER.

Stewart, F., Brown, G., and Cobham, A. (2009) *The Implications of Horizontal and Vertical Inequalities for Tax and Expenditure Policies*, Working Paper No. 65, Centre for Research on Inequality, Human Security and Ethnicity, University of Oxford.

Stewart, F., Brown, G., and Cobham, A. (2007) *Promoting Group Justice: Fiscal Policies in Post-Conflict Countries*, University of Massachusetts, Amherst: Center on International Cooperation. Political Economy Research Institute.

Stewart, F., Brown, G., and Langer, A. (2008) 'Policies towards Horizontal Inequalities', in Stewart, F (ed.) *Horizontal Inequalities and Conflict: Understanding Group Violence in Multiethnic Societies*, Basingstoke: Palgrave Macmillan.

Stewart, F., Fitzgerald, V., and Associates (2001) *War and Underdevelopment: The Economic and Social Consequences of Conflict*, Vol. 1, Oxford: Oxford University Press.

Stockman, F. (2009) 'Presidential Pardons Nullify Drug Court Gains. Well Known Drug Traffickers Set Free Ahead of Elections', *Boston Globe*, 4 July 2009.

Stubbs, P. (2001), ' "Social Sector" or the Diminution of Social Policy? Regulating Welfare Regimes in Contemporary Bosnia-Herzegovina', in Zarko, P. et al. (eds) *International Support Policies to SEE Countries – Lessons (Not) Learned in Bosnia-Herzegovina*, Sarajevo: Fond Otvoreno Drustvo Bosne I Hercegovine, Open Society Fund/Soros Foundation.

Stuckler, D., King, L., and McKee, M. (2009) 'Mass Privatisation and the Post-communist Mortality Crisis: A Cross-National Analysis', *The Lancet, 373* (9661), 399–407.

Surkhe, A. (2009) 'The Dangers of a Tight Embrace: Externally Assisted Statebuilding in Afghanistan', in Paris, R., and Sisk, T. (eds) *The Dilemmas of Statebuilding: Confronting the Contradictions of Postwar Peace Operations*, London and New York: Routledge.

Thapa, G. B., and Sharma, J. (2009) 'From Insurgency to Democracy: The Challenges of Peace and Democracy-building in Nepal', *International Political Science Review, 30* (2), 205–219.

Thompson, E. (2006) 'The Nexus of Drug Trafficking and Hawala in Afghanistan', in Buddenberg, D., and Byrd, W. (eds) *Afghanistan's Drug Industry: Structure, Functioning, Dynamics, and Implications for Counter-Narcotics Policy*, UNODC and the World Bank.

Thorp, R., and Bertram, G. (1978) *Peru, 1890–1977: Growth and Policy in an Open Economy*, London : Macmillan.

Torres-Rivas, E. (2005) *Guatemala: Estado, heterogeneidad estructural y ciudadanía*, Paper presented in the Workshop Pueblos indígenas de América Latina, Barcelona, 27 and 28 April.

Tzifakis, N., and Tsardanidis, C. (2006), 'Economic Reconstruction of Bosnia and Herzegovina: The Lost Decade', *Ethnopolitics, 5* (1), 67–84.

Uganda Ministry of Finance Planning and Economic Development. (2000) *Poverty Reduction Strategy Paper. Uganda's Poverty Eradication Action Plan. Summary and Main Objectives*, Kampala: Government of Uganda.

Ukiwo, U. (2008) 'Horizontal Inequalities and Ethnic Violence: Evidence from Calabar and Warri, Nigeria', in Stewart, F. (ed.) *Horizontal Inequalities and Conflict: Understanding Group Violence in Multiethnic Societies*, Basingstoke: Palgrave Macmillan.

UNDP (2008) *Post-Conflict Economic Recovery: Enabling Local Ingenuity*, New York: UNDP.

UNDP (2007) *Turning Vision 2020 into Reality: From Recovery to Sustainable Human Development*, Kigali: UNDP.

UNDP (2007b) *National Human Development Report 2007: Social Inclusion in Bosnia and Herzegovina*, Sarajevo: UNDP.

UNDP (2007c) *Human Development Report 2007–2008: Fighting Climate Change: Human Solidarity in a Divided World*, New York: UNDP.

UNDP (2006), *Early Warning System Research (EWSR) 2000–2006*, Special edition, Bosnia and Herzegovina: UNDP.

UNDP (2006b) *Early Warning System (EWSR): 2006 First Quarterly Report*, Bosnia and Herzegovina: UNDP.

UNDP (2005), *National Human Development Report 2005: Better Local Governance in Bosnia and Herzegovina*. Bosnia and Herzegovina: UNDP.

UNDP (2004) *Nepal Human Development Report 2004: Empowerment and Poverty Reduction*, Kathmandu – Nepal: UNDP.

UNDP (2004a) *Human Development Report 2004: Cultural Liberty in Today's Diverse World*, New York: UNDP.

UNDP (2002), *Human Development Report 2002: Bosnia and Herzegovina*, Bosnia and Herzegovina: UNDP, available at: http://hdr.undp.org/fr/rapports/national/europecei/bosniaherzegovina/Bosnia_and_Herzegovina_2002_en.pdf.

UNDP and MPDR (2005) *Rapport national sur le développement humain*, Bujumbura.

UNDP and MPDR (1999) *Rapport sur le développement humain au Burundi. La pauvreté au Burundi*, Bujumbura.

UN Panel of Inquiry (2002) *Final Report of the Panel of Experts on the Illegal Exploitation of Natural Resources and Other Forms of Wealth of the Democratic Republic of the Congo.*,New York: UN Security Council Document (S/2002/1146).

UN Panel of Inquiry (2001) *Report of the Panel of Experts on the Illegal Exploitation of Natural Resources and Other Forms of Wealth of the Democratic Republic of the Congo*, New York: UN Security Council Document (S/2001/357).

UNODC (2008) *Coca Cultivation in the Andean Region. A Survey of Bolivia, Colombia and Peru*, available at www.unodc.org.

UNODC (2008a) *Afghanistan Opium Survey 2008*, New York: United Nations Office on Drugs and Crime. Available at: http://www.unodc.org/documents/publications/Afghanistan_Opium_Survey_2008.pdf.

UNODC (2007) *Afghanistan Opium Survey 2007*, New York: United Nations Office on Drugs and Crime.

UNODC (2006) *Afghanistan Opium Survey 2006*, New York: United Nations Office on Drugs and Crime.

UNODC (2005) *Afghanistan Opium Survey 2005*, New York: United Nations Office on Drugs and Crime.

UNOWA (2007) 'Youth Unemployment and Regional Insecurity in West Africa': United Nations Office for West Africa.

Urdal, H. (2006) 'A Clash of Generations? Youth Bulges and Political Violence', *International Studies Quarterly, 50* (3), 607–630.

USAID (2007) *Meeting EFA: Guatemala PRONADE*, Case Study Educational Quality Improvement Program.

USAID (2006a) *Cross-border Cooperation and Reconciliation (CBCR)*, Washington, DC: USAID.

USAID (2006b) *Project to Enhance Stability and Security: Democracy, Conflict and Humanitarian Assistance : Nepal*, Washington, DC: USAID.

USAID (2005) *Youth and Conflict*, Washington, DC: USAID.

USAID (1994) *Uganda Demobilization and Reintegration Project*, Washington, DC: USAID.

Uvin, P. (2002) 'On Counting, Categorizing and Violence in Burundi and Rwanda', in Kertzer, D., and Arel, D. (eds) *Census and Identity: The Politics of Race, Ethnicity and Language in National Censuses*, Cambridge: Cambridge University Press.

Uvin, P. (2000) 'Rwanda: The Social Roots of Genocide', in Nafziger, D. (ed.) *War, Hunger, and Displacement: The Origins of Humanitarian Emergencies* (Vol. 2, pp. 159–185). Oxford: Oxford University Press.

Uvin, P. (1998) *Aiding Violence: The Development Enterprise in Rwanda*, West Hartford, CO.: Kumarian Press.

Uvin, P. (1997) 'Prejudice, Crisis, and Genocide in Rwanda', *African Studies Review, 40* (2), 91–115.

Van Cott, D. L. (2000) *The Friendly Liquidation of the Past: The Politics of Diversity in Latin America, Pitt Latin American Series*, Pittsburgh: University of Pittsburgh Press.

Vandenberg, P. (2006) *The African–Asian Divide: Analyzing Institutions and Accumulation in Kenya*, Routledge: London.

Vandenberg, P. (2003), 'Ethnic-Sectoral Cleavages and Economic Development: Reflections on the Second Kenya Debate', *The Journal of Modern African Studies, 41* (3), 437–455.

Van de Walle, D., and Nead, K. (1995) *Public Spending and the Poor: Theory and Evidence*, Baltimore and London: Published for the World Bank by Johns Hopkins University Press.

Van Leeuwen, M. (2001) 'Rwanda's Imidugudu Programme and Earlier Experiences with Villagisation and Resettlement in East Africa', *Journal of Modern African Studies, 39* (4), 623–644.

Vansina, J. (1972) *La légende du passé: Traditions orales du Burundi*, Archive d'Anthropologie No. 16. Tervuren: Musée royal de l'Afrique centrale.

Venugopal, R. (2009) 'The Making of Sri Lanka's Post-Conflict Economic Package and the Failure of the 2001–2004 Peace Process', in Newman, E., Paris, R., and Richmond, O. (eds) *New Perspectives on Liberal Peacebuilding*, Tokyo: UNU Press.

Verner, D. (2008) *Making Poor Haitians Count*, World Bank Policy Research Working Paper 4571.

Verwimp, P. (2000) 'Development Ideology, the Peasantry and Genocide: Rwanda Represented in Habyarimana's Speeches', *Journal of Genocide Research, 2* (3), 325–361.

Verpoorten, M. (2007) *Household Coping in War- and Peacetime: Cattle Sales in Rwanda, 1991–2001*, Center for Economic Studies, Development Economics. http://www.econ.kuleuven.be/ces/discussionpapers/default.htm.
Waldman, M. (2008) *Falling Short: Aid Effectiveness in Afghanistan*, Kabul: ACBAR.
Warnock, F., and Conway, P. (1999) *Post-Conflict Recovery in Uganda*, Washington, DC: World Bank.
Whelpton, J. (2005) *A History of Nepal*, Cambridge: Cambridge University Press.
Whelpton, J. (1997) 'Political Identity in Nepal: State, Nation, and Community', in Gellner, D. N., Pfaff-Czarnecka, J., and Whelpton, J. (eds) *Nationalism and Ethnicity in a Hindu Kingdom: The Politics of Culture in Contemporary Nepal*, Amsterdam: Harwood Academic Publishers.
WIDER (2007) *World International Inequality Database (WIID2)*, Helsinki, Finland: World Insitute for Development Economics Research.
Wilder, A. (2007) *Cops or Robbers? The Struggle to Reform the Afghan National Police*, Kabul: AREU.
Willmott, W. E. (1967), *The Chinese in Cambodia*. Vancouver, BC: University of British Columbia.
Wolf, E. (1999) *Peasant Wars of the Twentieth Century*, Norman: University of Oklahoma Press.
Wood, A., and Ridao-Cano, C. (1996) *Skills, Trade and International Inequality*, IDS Working Paper No. 47, Sussex: IDS.
Woodward, S. (1995) *Socialist Unemployment: The Political Economy of Yugoslavia, 1945–1990*, Princeton: Princeton University Press.
World Bank (1996a) *Bosnia and Herzegovina: The priority reconstruction and recovery program – The challenges ahead*. Washington, DC: World Bank.
World Bank, (2009) *Implementation Completion and Results Report (IDA H91-NEP and IDA H258-NEP) on Grants in the Amount of SDR 10.1 Million and SDR 16.9 Million (US$ 15 Million and US$25 Million Equivalent) to the Republic of Nepal for a Poverty Alleviation Fund*, World Bank Report No. ICR00001197, Kathmandu: Sustainable Development Sector Unit, World Bank South Asia Region.
World Bank (2008) *Republic of Haiti: Public Expenditure Management and Financial Accountability Review* (PEMFAR), Washington, DC: World Bank.
World Bank (2008a) *'Kosovo, Youth in Jeopardy. Being Young, Unemployed, and Poor in Kosovo'*. A Report on Youth Employment in Kosov, Washington, DC: World Bank.
World Bank, (2007) *Project paper on a proposed additional financing (grant) in the amount of SDR 38.7 million to Nepal for the Education for All Project*, World Bank Report No. 41346-NP, Washington, DC: World Bank.
World Bank (2007a) *Project Appraisal Document on a Proposed Grant in the Amount of Sdr65.24 Million (Us$100 Million Equivalent) to Nepal for a Poverty Alleviation Fund Project November 6, 2007*, Washnington, DC: World Bank.
World Bank (2007b) *Project Information Document (Pid), Concept Stage. Project Name Nepal: Post-Conflict Emergency Employment Program*, Washington, DC: World Bank.
World Bank (2007c), *Sharing Growth: Equity and Development in Cambodia*, Washington, DC: World Bank.
World Bank (2006) *DR-CAFTA: Challenges and Opportunities for Central America*, Washington, DC: Central American Department and Office of the Chief Economist, Latin America and Caribbean Regions.

World Bank (2005) *Toward a Conflict-Sensitive Poverty Reduction Strategy: Lessons from a Retrospective Analysis*, SDV/ESSD Report No. 32587, Washington DC: World Bank.

World Bank (2005a) *Policy Paper: Young People in Kosovo*, Washington, DC: World Bank.

World Bank (2005b) *Descentralizing Education in Guatemala: School Management by Local Communities*, Washington, DC: Education Notes, February.

World Bank, (2004) *Rwanda: Country Assistance Evaluation*, Washington, DC: World Bank Operations Evaluation Department.

World Bank (2004a) *Transitional Support Strategy of the World Bank Group for Kosovo*, Washington, DC: World Bank.

World Bank (2003) *Nepal Country Assistance Strategy 2004–2007*, Washington, DC: World Bank.

World Bank (2003a) *Conflict-Affected Countries: A Comprehensive Development Framework Approach. Lessons from a Roundtable Discussion*, Washington, DC: World Bank.

World Bank, (1998) *Memorandum of the President of the International Development Association to the Executive Director on a Country Assistance Strategy of the World Bank Nepal*, Report No. 18578-NEP, Washington, DC: World Bank.

World Bank (1993) *Uganda: Growing Out of Poverty*, Washington, DC: The World Bank.

World Bank (1992) *Cambodia: Agenda for Rehabilitation and Reconstruction*, Washington, DC: World Bank.

World Bank (1991) *Structural Adjustment Credit Agreement between Republic of Uganda and International Development Association*, Washington, DC: World Bank.

World Bank (1990) *Economic Recovery Credit II*, Washington, DC: World Bank.

World Bank (1987) *Economic Recovery Program between The Republic of Uganda and International Development Association*, Washington, DC: World Bank.

World Bank/OED (2004) *The Poverty Reduction Strategy Initiative: An Independent Evaluation of the World Bank's Support through 2003*, available at: http://lnweb18.worldbank.org/oed/oeddoclib.nsf/DocUNIDViewForJavaSearch/6B5669F816A60AAF85256EC1006346AC/$file/PRSP_Evaluation.pdf.

Wyss, K. (2006) *A Thousand Hills for 9 Million People: Land Reform in Rwanda: Restoration of Feudal Order or Genuine Transformation?* Swiss: Peace Foundation.

Yashar, D. (2005) *Contesting Citizenship in Latin America: The Rise of Indigenous Movements and the Postliberal Challenge* (Cambridge Studies in Contentious Politics), Cambridge: Cambridge University Press.

Zegarra, E. (2008) *Una agenda agraria para el desarrollo de la sierra peruana*, Working paper available with the author.

Zyck, S. A. (2009) 'Former Combatant Reintegration and Fragmentation in Contemporary Afghanistan', *Conflict, Security & Development, 9* (1), 111–131.

Author Index

Subject Index